I0890197

Lines in Water

Gender and Globalization
Susan S. Wadley, *Series Editor*

Other titles in the Gender and Globalization series

Bodies That Remember: Women's Indigenous Knowledge and Cosmopolitanism in South Asian Poetry
Anita Anantharam

Family, Gender, and Law in a Globalizing Middle East and South Asia
Kenneth M. Cuno and Manisha Desai, eds.

From Patriarchy to Empowerment: Women's Participation, Movements, and Rights in the Middle East, North Africa, and South Asia
Valentine M. Moghadam, ed.

Hijab and the Republic: Uncovering the French Headscarf Debate
Bronwyn Winter

Imperial Citizen: Marriage and Citizenship in the Ottoman Frontier Provinces of Iraq
Karen M. Kern

La Chulla Vida: Gender, Migration, and the Family in Andean Ecuador and New York City
Jason Pribilsky

Making Miss India Miss World: Constructing Gender, Power, and the Nation in Postliberalization India
Susan Dewey

Policing Egyptian Women: Sex, Law, and Medicine in Khedival Egypt
Liat Kozma

Super Girls, Gangstas, Freeters, and Xenomaniacs: Gender and Modernity in Global Youth Cultures
Susan Dewey and Karen J. Brison, eds.

Transforming Faith: The Story of Al-Huda and Islamic Revivalism among Urban Pakistani Women
Sadaf Ahmad

Lines in Water

≈

Religious Boundaries in South Asia

≈

Edited by Eliza F. Kent
and Tazim R. Kassam

SYRACUSE UNIVERSITY PRESS

Copyright © 2013 by Syracuse University Press
Syracuse, New York 13244-5290

All Rights Reserved

First Edition 2013
13 14 15 16 17 18 6 5 4 3 2 1

∞ The paper used in this publication meets the minimum requirements of the American National Standard for Information Sciences—Permanence of Paper for Printed Library Materials, ANSI Z39.48-1992.

For a listing of books published and distributed by Syracuse University Press, visit our website at SyracuseUniversityPress.syr.edu.

ISBN: 978-0-8156-3319-8

Library of Congress Cataloging-in-Publication Data

Lines in water : religious boundaries in South Asia / edited by
Eliza F. Kent and Tazim R. Kassam.
pages cm. — (Gender and globalization)
Includes bibliographical references and index.
ISBN 978-0-8156-3319-8 (cloth : alk. paper) 1. India—Religion—Congresses.
2. South Asia—Religion—Congresses. I. Kent, Eliza F., 1966–
II. Kassam, Tazim R.
BL2001.3.L56 2013
200.954—dc23 2013009667

Manufactured in the United States of America

To our parents:

Clarence C. Kent and Margaret Neal Kent

and

Rahim Count Kassam Jivraj and Laila Kassam Jivraj

≈

Contents

≈

Illustrations

Preface

THIS VOLUME emerges from a conference held at Syracuse University in April 2004, "Drawing a Line in Water: Religious Boundaries in South Asia." Dara Shikoh (1616–59 CE), son of Mughal emperor Shah Jahan, purportedly said that distinguishing between different religions was like drawing a line in water. Koanlike, the image stops us short. How implausible, intriguing, illusory, and irresistible.

Whether Shikoh said this or not, the image of drawing lines in water offers a different paradigm through which one might approach the question of religious identities in South Asia. Accounts of Hinduism, Islam, Jainism, and other religions on the Indian subcontinent tend to present them as uniform, historically given entities and as discrete, well-marked, separable units with distinct boundaries. The lived realities of religious practice and social exchange, however, so richly elaborated in the conference and in this volume, would appear to refute this view.

Interdisciplinary in scope, the conference was funded by the Ray Smith Symposium in the Humanities and cosponsored by the Department of Religion, the South Asian Studies Program, and the Religion and Society Program at Syracuse University. Its objective was to bring together scholars with a common interest in the many ways that religious boundaries and identities, like Shikoh's lines in water, appear, disappear, and reappear in specific contexts. In contrast to Samuel Huntington's infamous clash of civilization thesis, the various articles in this volume underscore that religious identities are not rooted solely in difference. More likely, they frustrate any attempt to capture and freeze them like a snapshot and hence to deny their relational, constantly shifting, merging selves.

South Asia is home to one of the most religiously plural societies in the world and has been for centuries. The realities of religious identities in South Asia reflect a disorderly pluralism. By seeking to narrate this history from below through life histories, oral traditions, devotional music, and funerary rituals, we challenge the normative view that "difference," supposedly the cornerstone of identity, is inherently divisive.

Indeed, as the studies in this volume show, difference is not necessarily divisive, and insights on the formation of religious identity might equally be gained by approaching difference as diversity, a constructive and integrating category, a social practice constituted by exchanges that occur at multiple levels. This reframing calls for a more complex vocabulary, as it were, to grasp the meanings of identities that are in the process of constant negotiation, adaptation, and reinvention.

How does one go about appreciating and deconstructing the decidedly confounding complexity at play when Christian priests perform funerary rites for a Hindu Brahman, Rajasthani women wear amulets with Qur'anic verses, *qawwali* singers give recitals at Hindu weddings? What happens at liminal and unpredictable spaces that exist between religious groups and religious encounters—that is, at those sites of contact and exchange that result in complex mixtures intimated by terms such as *syncretism, hybridity, bricolage, creolization,* and so on? Distinguishing between different kinds of boundaries as a heuristic device might take us closer toward appreciating these realities.

The conference organizers (Ann Grodzins Gold, Sudipta Sen, Susan Wadley, Joanne Waghorne, James Watts, and myself) ventured a typology—a conceptual framework, as it were—that might illuminate and critically appreciate what happens in the liminal spaces that exist between religious groups and what emerges from these transactions. The categories proposed are meant to be neither exhaustive nor definitive but are an attempt to understand relationships by parsing and refining the concept of boundaries. Some are *attractive* and centripetal and draw together different groups; others are *porous* and *permeable,* allowing only particular ideas to travel back and forth; and yet others are so blurred that they are easily *transcended* and *erased* like lines in water.

Each of the following examples engages the notion of boundaries in one way or another. Why would Hindu women feel more at ease to speak of their woes to a Sufi *pir* (spiritual teacher)? What motivates an American anthropologist to perform a unique *yatra* (pilgrimage) whose stops include holy places of different faiths? Why did Ismaili *pir*s settle on the concept of avatar to reveal their Imams? Why would middle-class Hindus scrupulously maintain a household shrine to the spirit of a Muslim *baba*? All these category-defying instances run counter to the presumption of irreducible religious identities. Each of the richly textured essays in this volume reaches for a language and conceptual framework that would most skillfully navigate the fluid and watery mixtures of religions in South Asia.

Eliza Kent and I thank the authors for taking up the challenge to resist drawing confining lines in the land of five rivers. I thank my coeditor, Eliza, to whom I owe a profound debt of gratitude for surely and securely ferrying us through these uncharted waters.

Tazim R. Kassam
January 2013

Lines in Water

≈

Introduction

ELIZA F. KENT

SINCE INDEPENDENCE, communal violence in South Asia has attracted considerable attention. The spectacle of medieval mosques demolished by mobs and luxury hotels besieged by heavily armed gunmen makes for riveting broadcast news, but these tragic events have come to stand for India in a way that distorts the on-the-ground reality. Many factors have contributed to the upsurge of communalism in Indian society since the 1980s, where communalism can be defined as "collective antagonism organized around religious, linguistic, and/or ethnic identities" (Ludden 1996, 12).[1] They include the liberalization of the economy, a widening gap between rich and poor, the allocation of state benefits in public higher education and state employment according to caste and religious identity, and the breakdown in the 1980s of the Congress Party's vast network of patronage and alliance

I would like to acknowledge that although I wrote this introductory essay, it is the result of the work of many minds. First of all, it arises out of extended conversations with my coeditor, Tazim Kassam, to whom I owe profound thanks for enriching the process of assembling this "salad" of essays. Many of the ideas and several long stretches of words are hers. I also gratefully acknowledge valuable feedback from Meika Loe, Ann Grodzins Gold, Corinne Dempsey, and an anonymous reviewer for Syracuse University Press. I alone am responsible, however, for any errors it may yet contain.

1. In its Indian English usage, *communalism* refers not so much to the loyalty and cohesion of groups who share significant traits, but to the darker side of this same coin—namely, the hostility to others outside whatever group is considered one's own.

followed by the rise of Hindu nationalist parties such as the Bharatiya Janata Party (Indian People's Party) and the Shiv Sena. In addition, one can point to the reframing of local antagonisms in communal terms by aspiring religious leaders and politicians, as in the case of the Hindu–Muslim violence in Gujarat in 2002 and the Hindu–Christian violence in Orissa in 2007–2008 (Bauman 2010; see also Brass 1987). However, although these conflicts are a key part of the immediate backdrop to the contributions in this volume, they do not portray the overriding social reality of religious tolerance and pluralism in India.[2] The authors in this volume focus their lens on the latter and offer an alternative portrait that counters the tendency of mass media to amplify interreligious and communal conflict in India.

With all the attention on interreligious conflict, the study of how Indians and South Asians more generally have managed to live in pluralistic communities has been comparatively neglected. Relatively few previous studies have traversed this ground. For example, Yoginder Sikand's impassioned journalistic account *Sacred Spaces: Exploring Traditions of Shared Faith in India* (2003) documents his odyssey across India to visit several multireligious sites. Several monographs, including some written by the contributors to this volume, have examined the history and dynamics of religious pluralism in India through careful, in-depth examinations of particular communities (see, for example, Bellamy 2011; Bigelow 2010; Dempsey 2001; Flueckiger 2006; Gottschalk 2000; Kassam 1995; Khan 2004; Raj 2002; Ramey 2008). But with this collection of essays, we seek to examine the subject of interreligious and inclusive community formations more broadly, from a variety of different angles and through a diverse

2. Statistical evidence supports the claim that, tragic episodes of extreme violence notwithstanding, the on-the-ground reality in India is one of relatively peaceful coexistence. Political scientist Ashutosh Varshney writes that the large majority of ethnic violence in India takes place in just a handful of cities: "Between 1950 [and 1995], rural India, where more than two-thirds of Indians live, accounted for a mere 4 percent of all deaths in Hindu–Muslim riots. Such rioting is primarily an urban phenomenon. Moreover, within urban India itself, eight cities accounted for about 46 per cent of all deaths. These riot-prone cities have less than a fifth of India's urban population and a mere 6 per cent of the country's total population, urban as well as rural" (2004).

sample of case studies—from independent churches in colonial South India to cremation-ground ascetics on the banks of the Ganges, from Sindhi Hindus who revere the Sikh religious text the Guru Granth Sahib to an East African Ismaili Muslim singer of devotional hymns called *ginans*.

In particular, we focus here on the trope of boundaries, drawing inspiration from the Mughal prince Dara Shikoh (1615–59), who is said to have replied when asked to demarcate the differences between religions: "How can you draw a line in water?" The favorite son of Emperor Shah Jahan, Dara Shikoh was deeply influenced by Sufi thought, a more mystical and devotional orientation to Islam. His exploration of spiritual truths led him to converse with religious scholars and seekers of all kinds. An accomplished author, he produced a Persian translation of the Upanishads and supposedly of the Bhagavad Gita. His most creative and provocative work, however, was the *Majmah ul-bahrain*, "The Meeting Place of the Two Seas," which catalogs a host of similarities between Islamic and Upanishadic thought. The title, *Majmah ul-bahrain*, is taken from the Qur'an, Sura 18:60–61, in which Moses and an unnamed companion search for a mysterious confluence of rivers. Interpreters over time have identified this spot as the meeting place where salt water meets fresh or where exoteric religion meets the esoteric mystical essence or, as Dara Shikoh did, where "the truth and wisdom of two Truth-knowing groups" run indistinguishably into each other (Shikoh 2006, 66). Shikoh's attempt to transcend boundaries drawn by religious authorities proved too daring for the orthodoxy of the time, and he was ultimately executed for apostasy.

The essays in this volume suggest other possible meanings for Dara Shikoh's metaphoric commingling of waters. Perhaps it refers to the vast body of shared human qualities that invites and yet resists division—our vulnerability to affliction, our solidarity in the face of injustice and poverty, and our celebration of love, as when devotees see themselves as an assembly of lovers. One can also view the watery confluence as that ocean of experience in which scholars and poets as well as ordinary religious adherents of all kinds ceaselessly endeavor to establish clear divisions between religious communities in South Asia's irreducibly pluralistic religious worlds. In short, the essays investigate the projections and fantasies, conflict and cooperation, borrowing and purifying that take place around religious boundaries in South Asia and in the South Asian diaspora. In doing so, they illuminate how multifaceted, diverse, and dynamic religious boundaries actually are and in so doing advance a view of boundaries as flexible and permeable rather than permanently fixed and inviolable. Before I discuss the typology of religious boundaries that organizes the chapters in this volume, it would be helpful to know something about when and how religious differences became so salient in India.

Scholarship on the History of Religious Boundaries: Narratives of Conflict and Division

Scholars debate the historical origins of the social divisions between different faiths in India. Some argue that it is wrong to project into the past the modern world's vision of religions as mutually exclusive and often antagonistic (Stewart 2000, 2001), but others make the case that clear differences between religious communities were recognized in premodern India (Lorenzen 1999), although more so in some settings (such as mosques and temples) than in others (tombs and shrines of Sufi saints) (van der Veer 1994).

Romila Thapar, the notable historian of India, argues for a very early dating of the perception of difference and divisions. In "Imagined Religious Communities: Ancient History and the Modern Search for a Hindu Identity" (1989), Thapar locates the origins of communal antagonism as far back as the eighth century BCE. She argues that one of the most salient social boundaries in ancient India was between Brahmanas and Shramanas, where the former regarded the orally transmitted heritage of the Vedas as authoritative, and the latter (encompassing a spectrum of Jain, Buddhist, and Ajivika sects) did not. The well-documented persecution of Shramanas by Shaiva rulers suggests that tensions surrounding these theological differences (which may have overlapped with other conflicts, such as rivalry over patronage or control over trade routes) did at times erupt into violence (Thapar 1989, 219–20).

With the rise of what Thapar calls "Puranic religion" (referring to the Puranas, the mythological digests organized around particular deities such as Vishnu, Shiva, and Skandha), Indian religion grew as a mosaic of sects. This history gave rise to a very different understanding of religion and of "sect" than that which arose in the Semitic religions (Islam, Christianity, and Judaism), in which a branching complex of sects descended from an apical founder or text and split into diverse forms owing to schisms (Thapar 1989, 216). In medieval India, where identity was organized in a segmentary fashion, "the notion of community was not absent, but there were multiple communities identified by locality, language, caste, occupation and sect" (222). In other words, religious boundaries in premodern India were clearly established among those indigenous to the Indian subcontinent, but they existed alongside other important markers of social difference: linguistic, regional, occupational, and so on. Medieval Indians did not think of themselves as a unified group, nor did they regard in a unified way the various sorts of Muslim merchants, scholars, and rulers entering the subcontinent beginning in the eighth century CE.

For many scholars of religion in South Asia, the question of the origins of religious boundaries is bound up with another vexing issue—whether and when "Hinduism" was invented. In the 1999 article "Who Invented Hinduism?" David Lorenzen argues against those scholars who assert that Hinduism—if by that we mean an internally coherent, discrete religious tradition—was constituted as such by the British during the colonial period. According to a historical narrative assumed by many scholars, the British took a geographical term, *al-Hind*, that had been used by Persian-speaking peoples to refer to lands beyond the Indus River (and by extension to the people who lived there) and loaded it with new meaning. Where it had been a purely geographical designation, the narrative goes, the British used it to denote a religion, as they understood it, such that "Hindooism" became a single entity that encompassed an array of texts, sects, doctrines, and customs that "Hindoos" themselves had not previously recognized as sharing anything essential in common (632).

Lorenzen asserts that the historical evidence does not support this narrative but rather shows that Hindus had a clear sense of religious self-identity well before the British era. Although he acknowledges that Sanskrit texts composed during centuries of extensive Hindu–Muslim contact *are* remarkably silent on the question of the manners, customs, and theology of the *turuska*s (Turks) and *mlecchas* (foreigners) in their midst, he disputes the conclusion drawn from this silence that the authors of these texts lacked a "clear contrastive awareness of their own religious identity" (1999, 648). To counter this conclusion, Lorenzen points to polemical discourses found in the vernacular poetry of devotional saints from as early as the fifteenth century (especially of the *nirguna sant* tradition, such as Kabir, Eknath, Anantadas, and Vidyapati). Here poets use the names "Turka" and "Hindu" not to refer to people only in an ethnic-geographical sense (as some argue), but to distinguish sharply between different groups with varying religious customs and rituals. One striking example is the fifteenth-century poet Vidyapati's description of the Muslim quarters of his city in the historical romance *Kirtilata*:

> The Hindus and the Turks live close together.
> Each makes fun of the other's religion (*dhamme*).
> One calls the faithful to prayer. The other recites the Vedas.
> One butchers animals by bleeding,
> The other cuts (off their heads). . . .
> Some (read) astrological signs, others fast in Ramadan.
> Some eat from copper plates, others from pottery.
> Some practice *namāz*, others do *pūjā*.
>
> (quoted in Lorenzen 1999, 651)[3]

In the face of such evidence, why have many scholars insisted that firm religious boundaries and antagonism between communities on the basis of religion arose only with the modernist constructs of religion introduced by the British in the 1800s? Lorenzen's answer is that such a "blame the British" narrative may be more palatable to anticommunalist historians than the one he proposes. He asserts that the emergence of a clear sense of belonging to a discrete and somehow unified Hindu community and thus ensuing tensions between Hindus and members of other religious communities should be traced to the era of extensive Hindu–Muslim contact beginning with the Delhi sultanates (1206–1526 CE).

3. Copyright 1999 Society for Comparative Study of Society and History. Reprinted with the permission of Cambridge University Press.

Just as scholars of Hinduism have problematized the uncritical use of the label *Hinduism* as a simplistic reification of a vast and internally varied mosaic of traditions, so have scholars of Islam sought to unpack the use of the label *Islam*. The essays in the notable collected volume *Beyond Turk and Hindu: Rethinking Religious Identities in Islamicate South Asia* (Gilmartin and Lawrence 2000a) take a somewhat different stand on the origins of religious boundaries through their investigation into a wide range of premodern literary texts and architecture. In their introduction, editors David Gilmartin and Bruce Lawrence (2000b) suggest that people in Islamicate India (that is, in those kingdoms where Persian and Turkish modes of governance and civilizational styles prevailed) shared broad frames of reference that functioned like genres, shaping norms but not dictating their exact particularistic expression in local forms.[4] Drawing on both Indic and Islamicate cultural frames of reference, Indians of diverse ethnic and religious backgrounds could share sacred sites, figures, texts, rituals, literary motifs and genres, clothing, and architectural styles within more encompassing frameworks of meaning and normativity.

A good example of this analytical framework is found in Richard Eaton's widely cited contribution to this volume, "Temple Desecration in Indo-Muslim States" (2000). In it, Eaton explores premodern religious differences by analyzing the history of the destruction of temples (and some mosques) between 1192 and 1729 CE by rulers who were religiously Muslim but often referred to by ethnonyms such as *yavana*, *Turk*, and *Mongol*. He

4. In this view, Gilmartin and Lawrence follow Marshall Hodgson's signature distinctions between Islam, Islamic, and Islamicate in *Venture of Islam: Conscience and History in a World Civilization*, vol. 1 (1974). In this seminal and magisterial work, Hodgson offered the first systematic critique of the usage of Islam as a monolithic entity and proposed a different vocabulary to distinguish between "Islam"—a body of ritual, texts, and laws related primarily to religious matters existing in different forms according to historical and geographic contexts—and "Islamicate," a name meant to capture the expansion of Muslim rule from North Africa to Central Asia as a civilizational force that stimulated a surge of economic, cultural, and intellectual activity within a common ethos. Whereas "Islam" pertains to Muslims' faith as such, "Islamicate" can apply to a person or group belonging to any faith or race. Many thanks to Tazim Kassam for drawing my attention to this text.

makes the case that Indo-Muslim rulers' attitudes toward and treatment of Hindu temples depended largely on whether they were expanding into new territory or seeking to consolidate power. In the consolidating mode, they were more likely to sponsor and patronize religious centers of diverse kinds, including Brahmanical temples and pandits (priests), whereas they were more likely to destroy them when they arrived as conquerors. The most notorious among the warrior-conquerors was Mahmud of Ghazni (r. 998–1030 CE), whose plunder of temples in the name of defending Islam seems to have been motivated by the relatively simple desire to appropriate the wealth and power concentrated in these sites.[5] But the alternation one sees in later centuries between sponsoring and destroying sacred sites suggests that Indo-Muslim rulers understood the importance of temples not merely as sites of worship, but also as potent symbols of and even surrogates for royal sovereignty, just as Indo-Hindu and Indo-Buddhist rulers did. Indeed, the shared understanding that temples were loci of power—religious, economic, and political—is precisely why sacred images of gods (*murtis*) were seized as booty by rulers advancing into new territory—not just Muslim rulers, but Hindu and Buddhist kings as well (Eaton 2000, 254–56, 259).

In their consolidating mode, however, Indo-Muslim rulers were more sensitive to the symbolic and social significance of temple-based religion than is granted by the textbook stereotype of fanatically iconoclastic Muslims bent on eliminating idol worship. Mughal rulers such as Akbar (r. 1556–1605) actively sponsored temple construction, provided for the maintenance of existing temples, and patronized arts that brought together artists and aesthetics drawn from both Islamicate and Indic contexts. Moreover, he did so in the role of sovereign patron as an expression of a widely shared understanding of the intimate relationship between sacred, social, and sovereign power (Eaton 2000, 261–63).

5. One might also add that on top of looting Hindu temples in India, Mahmud of Ghazni also fomented a virulent and violent intramural campaign of persecution against Indian Muslims regarded as "heretics"—such as Shi'a Muslims and Sufis.

In sum, Muslim rule in India spanned several centuries and came from different regions and cultures. Some rulers were more warrior dynasties, some more interested in establishing a peaceful basis for commerce and exchange over the long term. In the course of centuries of coexistence on the Indian subcontinent, however, Indians that were religiously Muslim and Hindu (and we might add Christian, Sikh, Jain, and so on) developed what Gilmartin and Lawrence (2000b) refer to as shared "genres" that, in the realm of religion, gave shape to ritual, textual, and architectural expressions that had much in common while allowing for both sectarian individuation and the exchange of motifs, figures, texts, ideas, and ritual gestures. However, the stereotype of the violent, marauding Muslim has been exaggerated and exploited by politicians and scholars alike.

These negative stereotypes proved very useful for British rulers seeking to represent themselves as a more benign form of sovereign than the Mughals, whom they regarded as "foreign" like themselves, despite the fact that Muslim rulers had reigned in different areas on the subcontinent for more than four centuries. Even as scholars disagree about how stark and rigid the boundaries distinguishing communities along religious lines were in previous eras, about how much the differences between them were understood as religious rather than ethnic, and about whether these differences gave rise to violent antagonism, most agree that a pronounced intensification of socially constructed boundaries based on religion occurred during the period of British rule. Extensive research has been done on the decennial Indian census, which, starting in 1872, sought to quantify the Indian population and classify it neatly into categories based on language, religion, caste, occupation, age, and so forth (Appadurai 1993; Cohn 1987; Dirks 2001, 198–227; Frykenberg 1987). Other scholars have focused on the divisive effects of the reification of separate bodies of personal law for Hindus, Christians, and Muslims governing marriage, inheritance, and other aspects of personal life (Kent 2004; Mani 1987; Nair 1996).

Though the overt purpose of the census was to provide an accurate representation of Indian society and that of religious personal law was to adjudicate conflict effectively, these policies had the effect of forcing Indians to choose and inhabit ascribed identities in order to attain recognition by the state. As religious identities became shaped more by written scripture than by community customary law (which varied considerably from region to region), practices specific to a region or a particular subcommunity came to be seen as deviant and in need of reform in order to conform to scripturally defined orthodoxy. In turn, these definitions precipitated changes within communities such that members of diverse reform movements vied with each other to establish who among them were *truly* Hindu or Muslim, Christian or Sikh, and so on. The overall effect was a significant fracturing of Indian society along many lines. Reformers critiqued traditions of sharing sacred texts, motifs, practices, and sites as suspect and sought to make their religious tradition, broadly conceived, more standardized and homogenous. Consider, for example, the pamphlet wars engaged in by Punjabi preachers from the Arya Samaj in competition with Protestant missionaries that codified what it meant to be a Hindu and what distinguished Hindus from Sikhs, Muslims, and others (Jones 1976, 94–114). At the same time, particular sects resisted the reformists' strategies of encompassment, often turning to the British courts for official recognition of their distinctiveness—as when the leader of the Satpanth Ismaili Muslims, Aga Khan III, fought and won a court case by submitting to the British court a long treatise called the *Dasa avatar* (Ten Avatars) to establish the fact that they were neither Hindu nor Sunni, but bona fide Shi'a Muslims (see Kassam, chapter 5 in this volume).

The divisive policies of British colonial rule, combined with the energetic mobilization of Indians around boundaries constructed on the basis of religion, led to the tragic partition of British India in 1947, when Indians won their political independence, but at the cost of dividing the country into the majority Muslim Pakistan (encompassing both modern-day Pakistan and Bangladesh) and the ostensibly secular but majority Hindu India. Prompting one of the largest movements of population across a political border in human history, Partition further solidified religious boundaries between communities, especially between Hindu and Muslim, and left both physical and psychological scars that endure to this day.

In the first decades of the twenty-first century, one finds in South Asia and in the South Asian diaspora a complex situation in which suspicion and antagonism across religious divides coexist with efforts to resist the pigeonholing of groups and individuals by religion. The essays in this volume illustrate how ordinary people negotiate these divisions—describing, changing, reinventing, dissolving, and maintaining religious boundaries in diverse ways. Some essays explore how these differences got formed historically. Some discuss how people live together or worship alongside each other in spite of sociopolitical contexts shifting rapidly under their feet as deeper divisions are forced upon them. Still others explore how religious boundaries are transcended as the depth of a shared religious culture or the urgency of pragmatic needs becomes more important than interreligious differences. In sum, the authors bring to the foreground manifestations of religious diversity that challenge the view that difference is inherently antagonistic, polemical, and invariable—be it in terms of faith, ethnicity, race, locality, or something else. Rather, the boundaries that typically delineate these differences—like lines drawn in water—exhibit highly dynamic characteristics and interactions.

Theorizing Religious Boundaries in a Context of Pluralism

Boundaries are commonly understood to be fixed lines of demarcation that clearly set the parameters of entities, including nations, peoples, selves, and so forth. A key challenge, therefore, is how to theorize on the nature of the multiplicity of interactions that take place at "boundaries," that is, how to describe their characteristics and what kind of boundaries they might be. This volume attempts to draw attention to these questions by suggesting a general typology under which the various chapters have been placed. As indicated by the headings of each section, these boundaries may be *attractive* or *porous*; *firmly drawn*; or somehow *transcended*. Cross-cultural contact, whether because of historical encounter or owing to side-by-side living in a context of pluralism, provides the impetus for many of these dynamics. Whereas *attractive* boundaries invite confluence while affirming the differences between self and other, *permeable* boundaries facilitate movement and exchange back and forth, leading to the creation of new combinations as the self selectively adopts features of the other. *Firmly drawn* boundaries that separate and distinguish sometimes foment hostility and ignorance, but not always. Whether the result of schism or internal reform or sectarian differentiation, drawing boundaries that highlight distinctions between self and other can facilitate coexistence by recognizing and respecting real differences, without necessarily arousing antagonism. Finally, even though people recognize the significance of religious boundaries, they may choose to *transcend* them temporarily or permanently so that their importance fades in the wake of more encompassing, inclusive concerns. It is important to point out that boundaries, whatever the type, not only separate but also bind and bring together what is on each side so that something new arises or something old is reshaped, whether fleetingly or more permanently—a new community, a new text or ritual, or a new aesthetic style.

Although this volume as a whole endeavors to develop a hermeneutic framework that helps to make sense of the complex dynamics surrounding religious boundaries, the section headings are an attempt to indicate generally where each essay's content and analysis fall. There is considerable overlap between them, and their placement in one section does not preclude their equally plausible placement in another. As Tazim Kassam discusses in the preface, the intention in bringing these essays together was to provide a different perspective from that offered by a "world religions" approach to the study of religion in South Asia, where examples of each broad tradition are brought on board like animals entering Noah's ark. The contributors to this volume, in contrast, draw on intimate, on-the-ground experience to show the subtle dynamics at work as people negotiate a context of enormous diversity. Rather than constituting the "last word" on boundary dynamics in a context of religious pluralism, our four-part typology is meant to prompt further discussion and refinement.

Attractive Boundaries

Boundaries establish a point of demarcation, and yet the differences highlighted across that line may become a source of attraction for those who see themselves on the other side. In such cases, the differences between the two groups are not so much elided and blurred by borrowing (as in different kinds of syncretism or "sharing") as they are maintained and even heightened so as to generate tension. The opportunity to pass over temporarily into the other's world, to imaginatively identify or experience intimacy with the other, offers relief, shelter, or an exciting alternative to one's own worldview or community. The attraction is sometimes strong and harmonious enough to create a permanent bond and union forming a synthesis. The dynamics of attractive boundaries are an underappreciated dimension of living in pluralistic societies such as one finds in South Asia, as the first three essays in the volume illustrate with special clarity.

At an historical moment in which Hindu chauvinism has become respectable and normal in some quarters, it is perhaps surprising to find a powerful fascination with Muslim figures among middle-class Hindus. In his essay "Sufis and Movie Stars: Charismatic Muslims for Middle-Class Hindus," Daniel Gold probes many middle-class Hindus' infatuation with tantalizingly vital and virile Muslim actors. Gold's essay demonstrates that although the construction of religious boundaries can exaggerate differences and create a kind of distorted caricature of the other, that very exoticized other is often quite appealing and attractive. The fantasized images of Muslims that Gold examines draw from two types of tropes, both of which seem grounded to some extent in historical realities. The first type comes from the North Indian courtly past, in which a kind of secular cosmopolitanism fostered a refined, romantic cultural style. The second is drawn from the contemporary Muslim working class, which is considered, in stark contrast, to be coarse, earthy, and distinctly unrefined.

Gold draws on years of experience teaching and researching South Asian religion and culture to discuss a range of contexts in which one sees these fantasized images in action: in the allure of Urdu for Hindi-speaking Indians studying in the United States, in the scrupulous care given to resident *baba*s enshrined in middle-class Hindu homes, in the exciting rhythms of *qawwali* (Sufi devotional music), and in the sex appeal of Bollywood's many Muslim male leading stars. A common pattern, he argues, is that the appeal of charismatic Muslim figures, almost always male, may "begin with something especially gritty and other, become refined by its association with an elite cosmopolitan culture . . . and is finally . . . made safe by existing in a predominately Hindu . . . world" (53).

We may discern a similar dynamic at work in Carla Bellamy's research on non-Muslim devotees at Muslim saints' shrines. In her essay "An Other's World: Healing at Husain Tekri Sharif," Bellamy acknowledges that Muslim saints' shrines have become more communal—that is, more explicitly and exclusively Muslim—in the past ten years. Among the clearest examples of this process are changes in the labels affixed to the shrines or placards directing pilgrims to them. At the Tekri Husain Sharif *dargah* (Sufi saint's tomb) in the state of Madhya Pradesh, for example, an archway adorned with Urdu and Arabic letters now hangs over the road leading to the shrine. The arch, combined with a massive new mosque adjacent to the shrine, whose minarets are visible from a long distance, signals unambiguously that the religious site is Islamic.

And yet, argues Bellamy, Hindu pilgrims put to good use the shrine's exaggerated Muslim identity; in other words, its very otherness is among its most appealing qualities. It principally provides anonymity to visitors (often women afflicted by spirit possession) so that sensitive personal and familial problems can be worked out quietly in a relatively noncoercive environment away from the prying eyes of neighbors and kin. The shrine's otherness also offers treatments for maladies that elude the explanatory framework of the pilgrim's own religious healing tradition, providing alternative diagnoses when, for example, a Hindu visitor's horoscope does not indicate any underlying astrological misalignment.

Ironically, the very forces of globalization and modernization that have exacerbated communal tension may also be enhancing the appeal of these shrines. Bellamy notes that improved transregional transportation and media networks have spread the shrines' fame as destinations for devotees as well as for those seeking relief from affliction. In this way, pilgrims can claim to be going to the shrine not to resolve potentially embarrassing financial or familial problems, but simply to visit the Muslim saint for a holy man's blessings, or *barakah*.

Dominique-Sila Khan's study "Vavar Swami: A Hindu–Muslim Saint of Kerala" takes up the subject of religious boundaries that attract in a different way, by focusing on a celebrated example of what she calls interreligious "conviviality." The pilgrimage to Lord Ayyappa's hilltop shrine in Sabarimala, Kerala, is one of the largest and fastest-growing pilgrimages in South Asia. It is widely lauded for its universalist ethos, according to which devotees from all castes and creeds are warmly welcomed into the virtually all-male brotherhood of pilgrims. Among the sites at which pilgrims pay homage before the last arduous leg of the journey is a grand Indo-Persian mosque and shrine dedicated to the Muslim saint Vavar Swami, said by some to have been a marauding pirate before he was pacified by Lord Ayyappa. In some ways, the inclusion of Vavar in Ayyappa's entourage is reminiscent of the pattern Daniel Gold identifies where the gritty power of the Muslim other is made safe for Hindus by being incorporated in *their* world. And yet Khan draws on detailed ethnographic knowledge of the shrines to show how Vavar Swami is understood very differently by people with diverse religious orientations. For example, not all regional Ayyappa temples have a shrine to Vavar Swami; indeed, some local Brahmins whom Khan interviewed found the very idea of a Muslim figure within the precincts of such a temple unthinkable. Moreover, Muslim attendants at the grand mosque-shrine to Vavar at Erumeli do not see Vavar as a ferocious sea bandit but regard him as Ayyappa's equal and friend, who joined him in efforts to bring peace to their region. In their eyes, Vavar was a powerful Sufi endowed with special powers through the practice of yoga and meditation. They are less interested in locating him in Ayyappa's story than in the story of the spread of Islam in the South by other Sufi saints. The variant stories surrounding Vavar illustrate the ways that individuals accommodate difference by narrating multiple histories of local religious heroes, thereby connecting diverse communities in practice. In other words, participants in the multireligious rituals at Erumeli (like the blessing of pilgrims' bundles by Vavar's Muslim shrine attendants) experience the "conviviality" of the shrine without tension by ascribing different meanings to key figures and elements of worship, while not insisting that others subscribe to those meanings themselves. In contrast to these pluralistic models of coexistence, Khan describes how Hindutva (Hindu nationalist) reformers with the Vishwa Hindu Parishad (World Hindu Committee) and similar organizations have gone to great lengths to retell the narratives in such a way as to minimize the significance of Vavar Swami in the popular Ayyappa cult.

Porous Boundaries

One theme that arises when one considers how Indians live with religious pluralism has to do with the many ways in which people blur the boundaries between communities or cosmologies, incorporating into their own religious worldviews, rituals, or ways of life certain elements drawn from a different religious tradition. We have entitled the second section "Porous Boundaries" in part to draw on the metaphor of semipermeable cellular membranes, which highlights the highly selective nature of processes of cross-cultural exchange. Whereas some features of the other's religious practices or cosmology might be congruent or complementary to one's own, some are not. Which elements are incorporated (or dropped), when, and by whom vary considerably depending on the social and historical context. Discerning the logic behind this process of selective appropriation is thus a crucial element of analyzing the religious and cultural mixtures that arise out of cross-cultural encounter.

The dynamics surrounding porous boundaries also vary depending on the degree of deliberateness involved. Cross-cultural mixtures may arise as a result of deliberate and strategic interventions, as when Christian and Muslim preachers seek to translate the theologies and cosmologies of their tradition into words, motifs, themes, or rituals familiar to their audiences in order to make them accessible and intelligible. As historian of religion Selva J. Raj (2002, 2004) has shown, such strategic inculturation happens both "from above" (through the agency of official religious leaders) and "from below" (through the more spontaneous but still conscious maneuvers of people living in multireligious contexts). Exchanges across porous or permeable boundaries may also arise in a less deliberate fashion; or, perhaps more accurately, the assertion by scholars outside these religious contexts that some kind of "mixing" or "blurring" of boundaries has taken place is premised on the notion that the participants recognize those boundaries in the first place. Perhaps what outsiders view as "syncretisms," "hybrids," or "mixtures" are not seen as such at all by participants, who regard themselves as operating within a single cultural or religious framework. Finally, the history of the transmission of Christianity and Islam to South Asia suggests that people's comfort with more porous boundaries has allowed for engagement in forms of multiple belonging without relinquishing loyalties to either side—a dynamic that has often frustrated the efforts of evangelists and reformers to promote a "purer" instantiation of their faith in the region.

Intimately related to the dynamics of porous boundaries is the question of how to represent whatever emerges from the points of contact, as, for instance, in the case of Dara Shikoh's *Majmah ul-bahrain*, which draws on two textual traditions from vastly different origins, such as the Upanishads and Sufi thought. Noting that the mixtures that arise as a result of such cultural exchange across porous boundaries may be more or less enduring, some scholars distinguish between syntheses, in which the elements brought together at one moment in time merge into a single new whole, and syncretisms, in which the aggregates brought together under certain conditions can eventually be disaggregated. Others reject the language of "syncretism" altogether, arguing that whatever metaphors are used to describe its operations—whether botanical (hybrid), chemical (solution, mixture), or physical (amalgam, bricolage)—they all implicitly disparage the phenomena in question as artificial, inauthentic, and ultimately impermanent (Stewart 2000, 22).

In my essay "Syncretism and Sin: An Independent Christian Church in Colonial South India," I argue for the continued usefulness of the term *syncretism* in spite of its history of usage as a term of contempt. Plutarch first used it in the first century CE to describe the strategic banding together of rivals against a common enemy, but it has frequently been used as a term of derision by missionaries, religious reformers, and even some scholars to describe what they view as informal, partial, or graceless combinations of belief and practice. If we keep Plutarch's early usage in mind, the concept of syncretism helps us direct a spotlight at an important facet of the process of identity formation. I argue that syncretism is fueled in part by people's desire to distinguish or ally themselves with others by rejecting or absorbing elements of those others' cosmologies and practices. In the creativity of independent Protestant churches that broke free from missionary patronage to instantiate their own understandings of Christianity, we can see the usefulness of syncretism as Indian Christians selectively appropriated elements of other cultures in order to fashion new identities and social connections.

The history of one such independent Christian church in 1875, known variously as the Kanneet Revival Church, the Six Year's Party, and the Yuomayan sect, thus offers rich material for exploring the sociopolitical dynamics of syncretism. This church was a schismatic millennialist sect that broke off from the Anglican Church Missionary Society in the wake of a religious revival among Indian Christians in a southern district of the Madras Presidency (in what is now Kerala). Consistent with its frequent changes in name, this community transformed its religious life numerous times. During the heat of the evangelical revival, it absorbed local shamanistic practices; when the founder was trying to negotiate with missionary mentors and remain within the Protestant fold, the members took on features of Protestant church life; and later, after the failure of the founder's prediction of Jesus's Second Coming, it integrated Brahmanical customs such as vegetarianism. As I demonstrate, each syncretistic innovation brought them closer to or farther away from potential allied communities within the local landscape.

Tazim Kassam's essay "The Living Tradition of Ismaili *Ginans*: Negotiating Cultures in Poetry and Performance" offers additional tools for thinking through the varieties of mixtures that arise out of cross-cultural contact by analyzing the meaning and use of *ginan*s by contemporary Ismaili Muslims in diaspora. The term *ginan*, probably a multilinguistic word derived from both the Sanskrit noun *jñana* (wisdom) and the Arabic verb *ganna* (to sing), refers to a religious song composed in South Asia between the twelfth and eighteenth centuries by the *pir*s ("saints" or spiritual teachers) who disseminated Ismaili teachings throughout North India. Composed in Hindi and Gujarati and set to local folk and bhakti (devotional) tunes, these songs convey essential Ismaili teachings in terms embedded in and derived from the local religious ethos of north India. For example, many *ginan*s convey the special status granted to the living Imam in Shiʿism as the enlightened guide of the faithful by identifying him with Kalki, the tenth and final avatar of Vishnu in Vaishnava theology. Today, however, some regard the use of Indian myths and symbols in *ginan*s as belonging to a superceded past that can now be discarded to create a "purer" expression of Islam.

The first half of Kassam's essay relates *ginan*s' history and ironic fate in the contemporary moment: the very texts that were used in British India by Aga Khan III, the Ismailis' spiritual leader, to authenticate the distinct identity of Indian Ismaili Shiʿa Muslims have been radically displaced from the canon in the twentieth and twenty-first centuries. Once regarded as sacred texts with authority comparable to the Qur'an and the Vedas, they are performed and memorized less nowadays as Aga Khan IV seeks to downplay the Indic style of Ismaili ritual life in order to foster a more inclusive global Ismaili identity. In the second half of the essay, in order to consider *ginans*' enduring ability to negotiate religious boundaries in the pluralistic contexts in which Ismailis find themselves in diaspora, Kassam focuses on an accomplished Canadian *ginan* singer of Gujarati descent who lived for twenty-five years in Kenya. The theme of migration surfaces not only here, but also in Steven Ramey and Lindsey Harlan's essays, as I discuss shortly. These essays raise the question of whether the experience of dislocation heightens people's desires for clearer boundaries between self and other or, as in the case Kassam describes, can also generate a powerful attraction to precisely those kinds of hybrid cultural forms that tend to distinguish subgroups within large and rather abstract formations such as "Islam" or "Hinduism."

Steven Ramey's essay "Liminal Hindus: Disputed Boundaries and Their Impacts on Sindhi Hindus" focuses on a religious community profoundly affected by the Partition of 1947. As he shows, the echoes of Partition continue to resound in a host of policies enacted by postcolonial governments in both Pakistan and India to "protect" religious communities from state interference and from each other, exacerbating tendencies to see religions as discrete, utterly distinct, and internally coherent entities. And yet even in this context, Sindhi Hindus persist in maintaining a complex religious identity whose instantiation of Hinduism is inclusive enough to incorporate veneration for texts, sites, and figures that others consider to be exclusively Muslim and Sikh.

The Sindhi homeland in northwestern India in the region of Sindh is located at the cultural crossroads of western Asia and the Punjab, where Muslims, Hindus, and Sikhs have been in constant contact for centuries. After Partition, however, the Hindus of the Sindh region found themselves on the "Muslim" side of the new border—that is, in Pakistan. Although some Sindhi Hindus chose to stay, most migrated over time to India. Focusing on the latter group, Ramey explores the rhetorical strategies that Sindhi Hindus enlist to negotiate a political and social environment that typically insists on much more precisely demarcated boundaries than those historically recognized by residents of Sindh.

What Ramey calls the "liminal" elements of Sindhi Hindu religiosity are particularly evident in their veneration of the Guru Granth Sahib, which to Indian Hindus seems to complicate the Sindhi Hindus' claims to be Hindu. In response to charges that the Granth is an exclusively Sikh text, Sindhi Hindus point out how many songs in it were composed by lovers of God now regarded as "Hindu" and "Muslim." To them, it is a perfectly Hindu text, where "Hinduism" is more than just the archive of texts and commentary descended from the Vedas. However, the Sindhi Hindus' expansive understanding of what falls within the category of "Hindu" violates the narrower understanding of Sikhism advanced by advocates of twentieth-century Sikh movements to assert a clear and unified Sikh identity. This understanding has led to conflict over control of shrines where the supposedly exclusively Sikh Guru Granth Sahib is installed and revered by Sindhi Hindus.

Besides offering fascinating material about a group that complicates easy classification of people into the categories of Sikh, Muslim, and Hindu, Ramey's essay makes a contribution to our understanding of *who* draws boundaries between communities and why—the focus of part three. The political boundary created at Partition has obviously had an enormous effect on Sindhi Hindus. They continue to be vexed by the boundaries that governments reinforce between religious communities through policies such as the assignment of sacred sites to different official administrative bodies (Hindu, Sikh, and Muslim). And yet, as Ramey argues, Sindhi Hindus are not just passive victims of these moves. They, too, are invested in drawing lines to distinguish their community from others.

Firmly Drawn Boundaries

What motivates individuals and communities to draw boundaries distinguishing groups of people from each other and themselves from others? As suggested by the historical investigation into the origins of religious boundaries in South Asia, political and religious leaders for centuries have found it expedient to categorize people on the basis of differences that today we would identify as "religious." This history demonstrates how the drawing of firm boundaries can have grim consequences, leading to hostility and ignorance, persecution, and even violence. Such observations have led many scholars to critique the modernist construction of religions as consisting of internally coherent, discrete entities, which are theologically incommensurable (and, as a silent logic often dictates, therefore inevitably antagonistic). But as the essays in part three illustrate, the drawing of boundaries is not the exclusive prerogative of elites. The drawing of firm boundaries is sometimes a self-defensive reaction, instigated by minorities fearful of being engulfed by an overwhelming majority, as when orthodox Sikhs insist on the community's strict adherence to the five Ks (maintaining unshorn hair, *kesh*; wearing a *karpan* or symbolic sword and metal bangle; and so on) to resist being lumped together with Hindus (as they are legally, along with Jains and Buddhists, in Article 25 of the Indian Constitution).

Beginning with Bernard S. Cohn's pathbreaking work, a great deal of scholarship has clarified how British efforts to understand India helped to foster divisions that led to the partition of India at independence and that persist within Indian, Pakistani, and Bangladeshi society to this day (see, e.g., Cohn 1987; Dirks 2001; Frykenberg 1987). Peter Gottschalk's essay "Mapping Boundaries: The Science of Knowing Communal Identity in British Cartography" deepens our understanding of the effects of British epistemic projects on Indian society by analyzing British cartography at three different moments from the late eighteenth century to the early twentieth century. Gottschalk demonstrates how British aspirations to understand India in a strictly scientific way were combined with a fixation on religion as *the* central defining aspect of Indian identity, leading to the calcification of boundaries—especially between Muslims and Hindus—that had once been more flexible. Maps not only offer an illuminating metaphor for British knowledge production in colonial India but were in themselves highly effective tools of governance, reducing complexity and bringing clarity (or at least appearing to do so) in order to facilitate British objectives such as generating revenue and reducing conflict between groups of Indians and between Indians and themselves.

British cartography provides a vivid example of how thoroughly colonial epistemic projects were suffused with an ambition to quantify all aspects of Indian society and analyze its dynamic complexity into a fixed set of discrete and mutually exclusive categories. For example, maps helped reify the differences between religious communities that British administrators assumed, as when revenue mapmakers generated unique icons for religious structures and insisted that all structures be categorized as either mosque or temple or Sufi shrine. With a stroke of a pen, they made invisible, perhaps even illegitimate, the many kinds of sharing and collaboration that took place at powerful holy sites (and continue to take place, as described in several essays in this volume). These representational and epistemic moves had tragic consequences when census data regarding religious affiliation were projected onto the cartographic image of India that had by 1947 become iconic. The new map's familiar form was by then firmly fixed in the imagination of both colonists and colonized and had become the object of nationalist aspirations. At that time, as is well known, the dark red (Hindu) areas of the map were forcibly separated from the dark green (Muslim) areas of the map, and on the ground thousands of lives were lost and millions more were disrupted irrevocably in the bloody partition of British India into two independent states—Pakistan and India.

In the face of such evidence of the power of governmental boundary drawing, one does not want to exaggerate the potency of individual agency. But it is important to acknowledge, as the next essays in this section demonstrate, that individuals and small groups are also invested in drawing boundaries between religious communities. In his essay "In a Single House: Fluid Boundaries in Performed Urdu Poetry," Christopher Lee explores the performative nature of social boundary production through an examination of all-night poetry festivals in North India called *mushaira*s. At these often massively popular affairs, poets from all over India employ the built-in ambiguities of Urdu poetics to conjure a range of imagined communities for the predominately male, working-class, and very enthusiastic Muslim audience. These imagined circles of belonging can be as expansive as those embodied in the devotional lives of the Sindhi Hindus whom Ramey examines, such that Hindus and Muslims are figured as quarrelling but ultimately loving relatives residing "in a single house" (that is, India). At times, though, Muslim poets configure the audience and themselves in all-Muslim imagined communities, bound to a distant, cruel, dangerous, but also beloved Hindu other.

Lee argues that the creative work of the *mushaira* is not only in the poets' hands; the audience, too, with its vigorous applause or loud hooting conveys its approval or disapproval. Adept poets know how to improvise in response to audience feedback—rearranging the order of couplets in a composition or editing them on the fly in order to develop a theme that resonates with a particular audience. Although the poets' performance skills are reminiscent of the fiery yet at times delicately responsive speechifying of populist politicians, which has fanned the flames of communal rage, it is striking to see how the crowd at *mushaira*s pushes back against communal rhetoric. Lee's work deepens our understanding of the power of literature to create a space for counterhegemonic visions of community that resist the easy binarisms of communalist ideology.

Nancy Martin's essay "Fluid Boundaries and the Assertion of Difference in Low-Caste Religious Identity" also explores the imaginative potential of literature in the face of communalism. It is set in the context of the communal violence that swept through the eastern state of Gujarat in the wake of one of the worst riots in contemporary India. Accounts of the events precipitating these riots vary, but all basically agree that on the morning of February 27, 2002, a train pulled into the Godhra station carrying *kar sevak*s ("volunteers" active in Hindu nationalist organizations) who were returning from a rally in Ayodhya, the site ten years earlier of the demolition of a medieval mosque by Hindu mobs. As the train pulled out of the station and began moving through this predominately Muslim area, a fire broke out in one of the compartments and killed fifty-seven people. Rumors immediately swirled about who was responsible, goading angry mobs into a rampage of violence that left at least one thousand individuals dead and displaced tens of thousands (most of them Muslim).

Based on fieldwork conducted just two years after the riots, Martin documents the efforts of activists in the region to restore trust among the largely working-class, low-caste Hindus and Muslims who are often provoked by fundamentalist agitators to see each other as enemies. Making use of Sathianathan Clarke's metaphor of religious communities as tents (which simultaneously are open to the world and embrace their own internal differences), Martin draws our attention to how frequently antagonism and a sense of superiority to those outside a tradition are accompanied by intolerance to internal diversity as well. The fortresses built by religious extremists to defend against incursions from outside often conceal fierce rivalries that lead to purges within as well as pogroms without.

"The solution lies," argues Martin, not in finding facile commonalities, but in "recogni[zing] and maint[aining] complex identities and affiliations" (254). As important as it is to realize that Muslims and Hindus have a great deal in common, it is equally important to recognize the existence of multiple Hinduisms and Islams. Martin's essay explores the question of how low-caste people avoid being conscripted into hegemonic forms of Islam and Hinduism. Her focus is on low-caste communities of performers, singers, and drummers from Rajasthan to Tamil Nadu. In the songs they sing for themselves in their own religious gatherings, one finds the clearest expression of a distinctive style of religiosity that Martin argues is shared by subaltern groups across sectarian and religious boundaries. This style is characterized by the uninhibited selection and rejection of elements of the dominant religious tradition as well as affirmation of the dignity and equality of all people in alternative value systems not based on birth, wealth, or power. These qualities resonate easily, argues Martin, across the boundaries of religious traditions in part because they emerge out of something broadly shared—the lived experience of oppression transformed by profound religious faith and practice. In this way, low-caste performers model through their art what it means to affirm difference in a way that is not antagonistic, oppositional, or exclusive.

Transcending Boundaries

The essays in part four draw our attention to another dynamic related to the fluidity of boundaries among religious communities and traditions in India—that is, the ways in which boundaries may be transcended in the name of something grander and more encompassing or by virtue of sharing something more fundamental. It is perhaps not a coincidence that so many religious teachers and sects arising out of the intensely diverse milieu of South Asia proclaim that abolishment of all socially constructed boundaries is the telos toward which spiritual practice aspires. As the iconoclastic bhakti saint Kabir sings,

> This union with the guru, O Kabir,
> Sets me free; like salt mingled
> With flour, I am no more I!
>
> Now I have no caste, no creed,
> I am no more what I am!
>
> O dear brother!
> By what name would you call me?
>
> I do not quote from the scriptures;
> I simply see what I see.
>
> When the bride is one
> with her lover,
> who cares about
> the wedding party?
> (translated by Azfar Hussain in Hussain 1999, 56)[6]

And yet, in examining this dynamic closely, one finds that in practice boundaries are rarely transcended without also having been inscribed. This is more than just a matter of semantics, but a logical necessity: as soon as a group affirms a boundary between itself and others, it emphasizes the commonality of those encompassed within itself. The examples here also suggest that the alternation between affirming and transcending boundaries stems from the difficulty of transcending boundaries indefinitely. People typically suspend for a limited time the differences that ordinarily structure social life, passing temporarily into a different,

6. Thanks to Azfar Hussain for his translation from Kabir's *Bijak*, initially published in *Reading about the World*, vol. 2, edited by Paul Brians, Mary Gallwey, Azfar Hussain, Richard Law, and Michael Meyers (New York: Harcourt Brace College, 1999).

more encompassing social formation. Just as lines in water are drawn only to be eventually blurred or effaced, so are bodies of water rarely so still that no lines appear on their surfaces.

Where Daniel Gold, Carla Bellamy, and Dominique-Sila Khan's essays in part one examined people's attraction to multireligious religious sites or religious others on the basis of their perceived difference, the first two essays in part four, "Transcending Boundaries," demonstrate that people may also be attracted to multi- or interreligious sites by the opportunity to let those differences subside in the embrace of a new community of belonging. In her essay "Religious Healing and Ritual Relationships at a Religious Crossroads in South India," Joyce Flueckiger's insights into the flexible nature of religious boundaries stem from her observations of the healing room presided over by a husband–wife team of Sufi healers and teachers in Hyderabad, an urban center in Andhra Pradesh. In this charmed space, social and religious borders that elsewhere have starkly real strength weaken and fade, and others come into sharper focus. Amma (literally, "mother") matter-of-factly declares, "There are only two castes/*jati* . . . men and women" (274), emphatically dismissing the relevance of Hindu, Muslim, and Christian identities, but affirming the reality of social divisions based on gender. Flueckiger offers the image of the *caurasta,* or crossroads, to illuminate the distinctive characteristics of this space: "In Indian cities and towns, *caurasta* are meeting places where roads and people come together. . . . When someone asks for directions in a traditional Indian town or city, he or she is often given a response beginning with: 'Well, go to X *caurasta* [X being marked by some identifiable building such as a hospital, theater, government building, and so on].' Although *caurastas* serve as important identity markers of social space, very few people who pass through them actually live there or even stay there very long" (274–75). Amma's clients may suspend their religious differences for a time in pursuit of healing, but when they return "home" to contract marriages or to perform formal prayers, they may operate within very different frameworks of meaning.

In Amma's discourse on religious history, categories such as *"nabi"* (prophet) and "avatar" (embodied earthly form of a divine being) expand to encompass a wide range of divine and holy beings, irrespective of religious community. But not everything is up for grabs. Vaishnava avatars are equated with the 124,000 prophets whom the Prophet Muhammad said had been sent by God to all the people of the world. Even the Prophet himself is compared to Hindu *shakti*s (powerful Hindu goddesses). But in their discourses, Abba and Amma are consistent in their elevation of Allah as single and unique, the one creator who created all other beings. As we see in Tazim Kassam's essay, a similar dynamic is found in Ismaili devotional songs, wherein the living Imam is identified as the final tenth avatar who will rescue believers from the darkness of end times (the Kali Yuga). The presence of Hindu mythology and cosmic drama does not alter, in either case, the overall theological framework, which is identifiably Muslim. Moreover, as the quote from Amma suggests (and as Khan and Lee's essays also indicate), gender differences may become more salient when religious differences fade into the background.

Ann Grodzins Gold's essay "'Ainn-Bai's Sarvadharm Yatra': A Mix of Experiences" offers reflections on an "all-religions pilgrimage" undertaken in part to gather materials for a new course on Indian pluralism. Over two weeks in the summer of 2006, Gold hit the road in the company of her frequent collaborator and coauthor, Bhoju Ram Gujar; his wife, Bali; and his friend, Shiv Lal Mina. In the process of visiting dozens of Sikh, Jain, Hindu, and Muslim sacred sites, they encountered a "common South Asian religiosity encompassing sensual and aesthetic as well as emotional elements." For example, remarkable similarities in the expectations placed on visitors allowed Gold's Hindu companions to adjust with relative ease to the requirements of Sikh *gurdwara*s, Jain temples, and Muslim saints' shrines. These expectations typically involve some sort of washing or bathing, circumambulation, prostration, and the use of food, flowers, incense, and music. Interestingly, the very similarity in these gestures invites comparison—whereas one offers rose petals at the shrines of Muslim saints, marigolds are the flower of choice at Hindu shrines.

Gold's journey reminds us that even as there are reasons to draw boundaries, there are reasons for and conditions under which these boundaries are suspended or transcended. Here, the work of comparing religions provides an occasion to transcend these boundaries in the role of (semi)detached observer. It seems that insofar as taking such a transreligious pilgrimage involves collecting, comparing, and contrasting examples of something that is the same and yet intriguingly different in each manifestation, it easily gives rise to comparative thinking. Gold's Indian companions themselves jumped into the game of ordering difference through categorization and classification. As Gold notes, before they even left on the journey, Bhoju Ram and Shiv Lal offered a classificatory scheme for making sense of differences: Jain and Sikh sites, they hypothesized, would be more like Hindu ones because those religions are *apna*, "our own," by virtue of having originated in India. At Muslim shrines, however, things are *ulta*, "upside down," from how things are done at Hindu sites. And yet by the end of the journey everyone's assumptions were challenged. For one thing, rural/urban and regional (Rajasthani versus Punjabi) distinctions seemed to be more salient in shaping the religious style and atmosphere of the shrines than broad sectarian differences such as Hindu/Muslim, Jain/Hindu, Muslim/Sikh, and so on.

The regional pilgrimage sites that Gold examines (along with Bellamy, Khan, and to some extent Flueckiger) are an ideal setting for the kind of pragmatic religiosity that can ignore the social boundaries drawn firmly at places such as mosques and temples. In this way, they create fleeting communities of people driven by needs that transcend social differences (for example, for the boon of children, success in business, healing from disease or spirit possession). And yet gratitude for boons granted can forge long-lasting connections, as illustrated by the case of the Hindu couple Gold encountered on the stairs to a hilltop Muslim shrine. They had been climbing those stairs every day for forty years in fulfillment of a vow taken in thanks for the birth of a son.

Jishnu Shankar's essay introduces us to another way that boundaries are transcended in South Asia—namely, through the radically nondualist vision of reality espoused by tantric schools, which aspire to a point of view that encompasses and subsumes the divisions and differences that mean so much to people "on the ground." In "From Liminal to Social in the Modern Age: Transcendent Sacrality and Social Service in the Aghor Tradition," Shankar examines the history of a lineage of cremation-ground ascetics (Aghors) led by a pioneering guru, Baba Bhagwan Ram. Beginning in 1953 with his establishment of an ashram on the banks of the Ganges, Baba Bhagwan Ram transformed his followers from a group of wandering *sadhus* (religious mendicants) who lived on the margins of society into a monastic order of ascetics working in collaboration with lay disciples. Their shared goal, as Shankar describes, was to realize through social service the radically egalitarian ethos that flows from their nondualist vision of reality. In particular, Shankar analyzes the subtle moves made by the guru as he discouraged or banned some of the most transgressive forms of *aghor* asceticism among his disciples in order to align them anew with conventional society. Instead of seeking their own individual liberation through the practice of extreme, socially shocking forms of asceticism, Baba Bhagwan Ram's disciples were taught to redirect the energy created by spiritual practice into social work. Among his lineage's greatest achievements is a leprosy hospital that serves more patients than any other in the world.

Baba Bhagwan Ram's reform efforts represent in some ways a risky departure from tradition because the expectations surrounding extreme forms of cremation-ground ascetics are that their spiritual powers (*siddhis*) derive precisely from their courageous flaunting of normal social conventions, especially those having to do with purity and pollution. When they wear garments made from the shrouds used to wrap corpses in the cremation ground or drink copious amounts of alcohol, they demonstrate their heroic freedom from all attachments—indeed, from all the social conventions that delimit what is possible or not in ordinary reality. As with many forms of tantra, the aura of awesome power surrounding Aghors derives from the existence of clear social boundaries delineating what is pure from what is polluting and forbidden. That is, the magical powers and feelings of absolute freedom that are said to come from transgressive practices depend on there being lines of propriety and order to violate in the first place. When Baba Bhagwan Ram banned alcohol use and the display of *siddhis*, he drew lines to distinguish himself and his ashram from that of his more typically *aghori* guru. However, it is worth noting that in establishing that boundary, he blurred another line between his own practice and that of other twentieth-century gurus who encourage social work (for example, Mata Amritanandamayi and the Ramakrishna Order). As Shankar argues, the drawing of lines happens not only between religious communities, but also within them as different subgroups distinguish themselves from others in response to new insights, revelations, and historical forces.

Lindsey Harlan's essay "Indian Arrival Day: Shifting Boundaries in the Celebration of a National Holiday in Trinidad" takes us beyond the subcontinent to Trinidad. Like India, Trinidad is a former British colony and a religiously and ethnically diverse nation that seeks to foster a cohesive sense of national belonging through strategies of integration that allow for differences to exist in "suspension" rather than in "solution." As some might say, Trinidad is an ethnic salad bowl rather than a melting pot (or a cake). The Indo-Trinidadian community comprises about half the population; most members of this community are descendents of indentured servants brought to work on sugar cane plantations after the emancipation of African slaves in 1834. Though sharing a distinctive ethnic identity as Indians, they are religiously diverse. The rhetorical work that the community has done in order to affirm both membership within the Trinidadian-Tobagan nation and its ethnic unity allows for a fresh consideration of how social boundaries are created and blurred along religious lines in the context of the South Asian diaspora.

Harlan's essay provides a multifaceted examination of Indian Arrival Day, a national holiday declared officially in 1995. In it, she argues that though the debates about the holiday were characterized by interethnic tension between Afro-Trinidadians and Indo-Trinidadians, performances celebrating the occasion and pamphlets educating citizens about its meaning portray the holiday as a model of "felicitous solidarity" (383) not only among Indo-Trinidadians, but for the ethnically diverse nation as a whole. Indo-Trinidadians' ability to cohere as a community despite religious differences is held up as an example for the whole nation as to how national unity might be fostered.

Harlan's work in Trinidad reveals an intriguing possibility—namely, that the assertion of social boundaries can be important in an interreligious, interethnic society precisely in order to facilitate integration, such that all parties feel like members of the whole. So long as the Afro-Trinidadians had "their" national holiday, Emancipation Day, commemorating the abolition of slavery in Trinidad, Indian nationals felt left out, invisible, unimportant. The establishment of Indian Arrival Day, though contentious, secured Indo-Trinidadians in their sense of national belonging.

Conclusion

All these essays raise several issues that deserve further investigation within the study of religious boundary formation in a pluralistic context. First, they highlight the inherent limitation, now widely recognized in academic scholarship on any religious tradition, of labels such as *Islam* and *Hinduism* insofar as they make invisible the pluralism and multiplicity that exist under their larger rubrics. As Tazim Kassam shows, Satpanth Ismailism, for example, represents the development of a Shiʿa Muslim minority that created a vernacular song tradition that drew on bhakti and Vaishnavism to deepen understanding of Muslim and, specifically, Shiʿa concepts. The Sindhi Hindus examined by Steve Ramey also illustrate the difficulty of ascribing a simple "Hindu" or "Sikh" or "Muslim" label to groups with a rich history of interaction with others on the subcontinent and the violence that is done conceptually and perhaps even actually when one does so.

Second, the diverse terms used by the authors to capture the complexity of identities and of interreligious interaction at sacred sites (Khan's *conviviality,* Ramey and Shankar's *liminal,* Flueckiger's *caurasta* [crossroads], and so on) reflect the need for theoretical apparati that would enable scholars to come to terms with those religious traditions that seem to fall *between* two or more normative religions. Scholars have used a variety of terms to describe these "in-between" places of religious life and expression, whether they are institutionalized or informal, personal or political, spatial or visual, oral or textual, national or transnational: *religious pluralism, synergy, syncretism, sharing, polytropy, synthesis, hybridity,* and so on. It is important to recall that all of these terms are scholarly categories used by scholars to make sense of histories, identities, texts, communities, and rituals that people engage for their own reasons in their own ways. Each has its uses so long as we do not confuse the scholarly label with people's lived reality, whose complexity inevitably exceeds the concepts that scholars devise to understand it. Perhaps instead of looking for the one term that will once and for all capture what we mean by this "phenomenon" (which is actually not one phenomenon, but many), we should employ a wider range of terms to describe the many different dimensions of boundary formation in the context of pluralism.

In recent decades, scholars have attempted to represent the phenomenon of religious exchange and interface in a positive light, often with the intention to validate these movements (see, e.g., Raj 2002; Sikand 2003). This is especially evident in studies of informal contexts and shared spaces. Indeed, the third feature illustrated by a number of essays in this volume is the suspension of religious or caste differences in the context of sacred sites such as tombs of saints (Bellamy, A. Gold, D. Gold), Hindu temples during pilgrimage (Khan), and the "healing room" of a female Muslim spiritual healer (Flueckiger). Here diverse participants are often united in their common need for healing, their differences transcended by faith in the therapeutic, beneficent powers to be received at a sacred site or from a holy person.

At the same time, it is important to note that these interactions are also often temporary or transitional; they do not necessarily create enduring new boundaries that encircle those that come together at a shrine or healing center. In her book *Crossing the Threshold* (2004), Dominique-Sila Khan invokes Victor Turner's concept of liminality, usually applied to rites of passage, to explain this phenomenon. Pushing the etymological meaning of Turner's key concept, Khan applies the idea of two communities being together at a threshold for a short period of time and retreating but also taking something back. A similar notion is evoked by Joyce Flueckiger's concept of the *caurasta*, or crossroads—here people's paths are conjoined, though the ends of the roads they follow may be quite far apart indeed. This exchange or coming together and its counterpoint of retreat and reintegration into "one's own" community are also illustrated in the context of the poetry contest described by Lee and the idealized romance in Bollywood's film industry described by Daniel Gold.

Finally, scholars need to explore more systematically how gender differences factor into the negotiation of religious boundaries. We know that sexual violence has played a significant role in conflicts in India organized around religious differences, whether in the abductions of women by all sides during Partition or in the mass rapes and mutilations that took place during the communal riots in Gujarat in 2002. And yet what role does gender play in contexts where religious boundaries are not so firmly drawn and defended? The papers by Lee and Khan suggest that religious divisions subside more easily in all-male gatherings (such as the all-night poetry festivals and the days-long pilgrimages to Sabarimala), where men can bond as members of a single community—perhaps because they do not have to worry about protecting "their women" from an other feared as rapacious and aggressive.

Conversely, in multireligious sites, such as Amma's healing room where Muslim, Christian, and Hindu patients together seek divine relief from their troubles, Flueckiger finds that the only *jati*, caste, that matters is gender. And yet it is somewhat surprising to find unaccompanied Hindu women seeking (and finding) shelter and healing at the Sufi shrines that Bellamy examines. Further comparative work on this aspect of religious boundary formation would yield important insight.

As evidenced by the chapters in this book, the boundaries that people draw between religious communities are caught up in a host of complex social dynamics. People may sometimes find something attractive in the other on the far side of a boundary distinguishing self and other. The maintenance of more porous boundaries may lead to the creation of what appear to be hybrid forms by merging and blending features of traditions regarded as distinct (though it is important to bear in mind that the appearance of such hybrids may result more from *our* perception of clear-cut, coherent traditions). In addition, in the complex encounters between and among communities, people variously located find reasons to draw, blur, or transcend boundaries in attempts to secure advantage, create order, craft alliances, or defend against threatening others. When one looks at these dynamics carefully in their historically and regionally specific context, as these essays allow us to do, one discovers that although religious diversity in South Asia is rarely found without conflict, resentment, and concessions to hierarchy, an imperfect harmony nonetheless endures.

Works Cited

Appadurai, Arjun. 1993. "Number in the Colonial Imagination." In *Orientalism and the Postcolonial Predicament,* edited by Carole A. Breckenridge and Peter van der Veer, 314–40. Philadelphia: Univ. of Pennsylvania Press.

Bauman, Chad. 2010. "Identity, Conversion, and Violence: Dalits, Adivasis, and the 2007–08 Riots in Orissa." In *Margins of Faith: Dalit and Tribal Christianity in India,* edited by Rowena Robinson and Joseph Marianus Kujur, 263–90. Los Angeles: Sage.

Bellamy, Carla. 2011. *The Powerful Ephemeral: Everyday Healing in an Ambiguously Islamic Place.* Berkeley: Univ. of California Press.

Bigelow, Anna. 2010. *Sharing the Sacred: Practicing Pluralism in Muslim North India.* New York: Oxford Univ. Press.

Brass, Paul. 1987. *Theft of an Idol: Text and Context in the Representation of Collective Violence.* Princeton, NJ: Princeton Univ. Press.

Cohn, Bernard S. 1987. "The Census, Social Structure, and Objectification in South Asia." In *An Anthropologist among the Historians and Other Essays,* 224–54. Delhi: Oxford Univ. Press.

Dempsey, Corinne. 2001. *Kerala Christian Sainthood: Collisions of Culture and Worldview in South Indian Christianity.* New York: Oxford Univ. Press.

Dirks, Nicholas B. 2001. *Castes of Mind: Colonialism and the Making of Modern India.* Princeton, NJ: Princeton Univ. Press.

Eaton, Richard M. 2000. "Temple Desecration in Indo-Muslim States." In *Beyond Turk and Hindu: Rethinking Religious Boundaries in Islamicate South Asia,* edited by David Gilmartin and Bruce B. Lawrence, 246–81. Gainesville: Univ. Press of Florida.

Flueckiger, Joyce B. 2006. *In Amma's Healing Room: Gender and Vernacular Islam in South India.* Bloomington: Indiana Univ. Press.

Frykenberg, Robert E. 1987. "The Concept of 'Majority' as a Devilish Force in the Politics of Modern India." *Journal of Commonwealth History and Comparative Politics* 25, no. 3: 267–74.

Gilmartin, David, and Bruce B. Lawrence, eds. 2000a. *Beyond Turk and Hindu: Rethinking Religious Identities in Islamicate South Asia.* Gainesville: Univ. Press of Florida.

———. 2000b. "Introduction." In *Beyond Turk and Hindu: Rethinking Religious Identities in Islamicate South Asia,* edited by David Gilmartin and Bruce B. Lawrence, 1–20. Gainesville: Univ. Press of Florida.

Gottschalk, Peter. 2000. *Beyond Hindu and Muslim: Multiple Identity in Narratives from Village India.* New York: Oxford Univ. Press.

Hodgson, Marshall. 1974. *Venture of Islam: Conscience and History in a World Civilization.* Vol. 1. Chicago: Univ. of Chicago Press.

Hussain, Azfar, trans. 1999. "Selected Poems" by Kabir. In *Reading about the World,* vol. 2, edited by Paul Brians, Mary Gallwey, Azfar Hussain, Richard Law, and Michael Meyers, 56–57. New York: Harcourt Brace.

Jones, Kenneth W. 1976. *Arya Dharm: Hindu Consciousness in Nineteenth-Century Punjab.* Berkeley: Univ. of California Press.

Kassam, Tazim. 1995. *Songs of Wisdom and Circles of Dance: Hymns of the Satpanth Isma'ili Muslim Saint, Pir Shams.* Albany: State Univ. of New York Press.

Kent, Eliza F. 2004. *Converting Women: Gender and Protestant Christianity in Colonial South India.* New York: Oxford Univ. Press.

Khan, Dominique-Sila. 2004. *Crossing the Threshold: Understanding Religious Identities in South Asia.* London: I. B. Tauris and Institute of Ismaili Studies.

Lorenzen, David N. 1999. "Who Invented Hinduism?" *Comparative Studies in Society and Society* 41, no. 4: 630–59.

Ludden, David, ed. 1996. *Contesting the Nation: Religion, Community, and the Politics of Democracy in India.* Philadelphia: Univ. of Pennsylvania Press.

Mani, Lata. 1987. "Contentious Traditions: The Debate on *Sati* in Colonial India." *Cultural Critique* 7: 119–56.

Nair, Janaki. 1996. *Women and Law in Colonial India: A Social History.* Delhi: Kali for Women.

Raj, Selva J. 2002. "The Ganges, the Jordan, and the Mountain: Three Strands of Santal Popular Catholicism." In *Popular Christianity in India: Riting Between the Lines,* edited by Selva J. Raj and Corinne Dempsey, 39–60. Albany: State Univ. of New York Press.

———. 2004. "Dialogue 'On the Ground': The Complicated Identities and the Complex Negotiations of Catholics and Hindus in South India." *Journal of Hindu-Christian Studies* 17: 33–44.

Ramey, Steven W. 2008. *Hindu, Sufi, or Sikh: Contested Practices and Identifications of Sindhi Hindus in India and Beyond.* New York: Palgrave-Macmillan.

Shikoh, Dara. [1929] 2006. *Commingling of Two Oceans: Majma-'Ul-Bahrain.* Translated by M. Mahfuz ul-Haq. New Delhi: Hope.

Sikand, Yoginder. 2003. *Sacred Spaces: Exploring Traditions of Shared Faith in India.* New Delhi: Penguin Books.

Stewart, Tony K. 2000. "Alternate Structures of Authority: Satya Pir on the Frontiers." In *Beyond Turk and Hindu: Rethinking Religious Identities in Islamicate South Asia*, edited by David Gilmartin and Bruce B. Lawrence, 21–54. Gainesville: Univ. Press of Florida.

———. 2001. "In Search of Equivalence: Conceiving Muslim–Hindu Encounter Through Translation Theory." *History of Religions* 40, no. 3: 260–87.

Thapar, Romila. 1989. "Imagined Religious Communities? Ancient History and the Modern Search for a Hindu Identity." *Modern Asian Studies* 23, no. 2: 209–31.

Van der Veer, Peter. 1994. *Religious Nationalism: Hindus and Muslims in India*. Berkeley: Univ. of California Press.

Varshney, Ashutosh. 2004. "Understanding Gujarat Violence." On the Contemporary Conflicts website, hosted by the Social Science Research Council, Mar. 24. At http://conconflicts.ssrc.org/archives/gujarat/varshney/index.html#e10. Accessed July 20, 2011.

PART ONE

≈

Attractive Boundaries

1

≈

Sufis and Movie Stars

Charismatic Muslims for Middle-Class Hindus

DANIEL GOLD

WHEN WE DRAW a boundary line in a fluid ethnic mix such as we find in South Asia, the other that we find is usually one that we create. Standing in opposition to us, that other sometimes appears inimical as well, but—enemy or not—it can also exert its own appeal. Instances of this attractive dynamic regularly occur in contemporary India. Even with the current cultural respectability of Hindu nationalism, which tends to view Islamic traditions in a less than favorable light, middle-class Hindus may harbor images of Muslims that are attractive in different ways. Because these images are largely fantasy, they are not conveniently applied to Muslims met everyday as individuals with their usual quirks. Instead, they are more important for understanding perceptions of larger-than-life Muslim personalities—Urdu poets of the past, contemporary movie stars, and old Sufi saints whose power lingers on.

Although these fantasized images can become complex, they draw, I think, on two contradictory components that seem grounded in historical realities. One is the North Indian courtly culture of the still-remembered past, a culture seen as refined, elite, and romantic. The other is a contemporary Muslim working class that is, by contrast, seen as distinctly *un*refined—both socially and religiously. With its power from below, this component is able to provide some tantalizing excitement and, through its holy persons, some earthy, effective magic. I have come to these formulations over several years through interactions with Hindus in the United States and—more significantly—in India. In order to flesh out some ways in which these contrasting images of Muslims come together, then, it seems natural to work from a personal narrative.

A Fascination for Urdu Style

The first component of the attractive Muslim image to impress itself on me was the romantic, historical one embodied in the Indo-Muslim poetic tradition. In the mid-1990s, I was regularly teaching Hindi and Urdu literature. The literary texts that we read were beyond the linguistic ken of most American-bred South Asians, so the students in the class, mostly undergraduates, had typically received their secondary education, albeit in English, in India or Pakistan. These undergraduates were generally good students from elite cosmopolitan backgrounds whose families had the desire and wherewithal to send them to an Ivy League institution. Although all the students were enrolled in one course, after the first year I started meeting the Hindi and Urdu students separately. A few observations on the two sections are worth noting.

First, the tone in the Urdu section was consistently more serious than that in the Hindi one. I do not want to discount the students' personalities here or the dynamics in the different groups, but I think that some cultural factors also came into play. The students in the Urdu section seemed to have more respect for the literature. They approached it with a sense that there was more to get out of it. The students in the Hindi section, by contrast, needed to be persuaded of the value of reading the Hindi texts—medieval devotional poets and works of modern fiction—and my attempts were not always successful. Everybody in the Urdu class, though, knew about Ghalib and Mir and wanted to read them. These poets represented a tradition of classical secular literature commonly recognized as great and also reasonably accessible—one with no real cultural counterpart on the Hindi side.

This lack of a comparable Hindi tradition meant, second, that the Hindi students (who mixed with the Urdu-*walla*s outside of class) often expressed a desire to read classical Urdu *ghazal*s. We began by looking at them in Devanagari, but, to my surprise, the Hindi students were also usually eager to learn Urdu script. This eagerness to learn the other writing system was not shared, I am afraid, by students in the Urdu section, who were mostly from Pakistan, but the cosmopolitan students from India were open to Urdu—curious about and attracted to it. They had seen Urdu script on signboards in India and recognized it as part of their extended culture.

What might be the cultural significance of these students' fascination with Urdu literature and script? As mentioned earlier, the *ghazal* tradition represents a rewarding genre of classical secular literature of a sort that has no Hindi equivalent with the same degree of prestige. It is seen as something worth knowing. This is certainly an important factor. But I think there may have been a little more at work as well. The world of the *ghazal*s was accessible to the Hindi students, but it was also a little alien. It was an Indian world, but it was not quite *their* world. It carried something of the fascination of the other, yet an other that was both culturally understandable and linguistically penetrable. I think their excitement about learning Urdu script derived in good part from their taking a real plunge into an aspect of Indian culture with which they had some familiarity, but which they had not known in such a concrete way before. For most of them, Urdu script would have little practical value. Their excitement instead derived in part from taking a definitive step in assimilating something from Indo-Islamic worlds that fascinated them.

My foray into teaching Urdu literature then led to an invitation to a conference on Urdu in India. In researching a paper for that conference, I found that my students' enthusiasms, whatever their depth, seemed to have some parallels in North Indian literary culture. In an article published in the Indian journal *Shabkhoon* in 1998, the Pakistani writer Intizar Husain tells of a recent visit to the "new India."[1] In it, he gives some ironic glimpses of Hindi speakers' appreciation of and fascination with an Urdu style. There is a gathering of poets from different parts of India, he writes,

1. *Shabkhoon* was an Urdu literary journal edited by Shamsurrhaman Faruqi and published monthly from Allahabad, India. It ceased publication in 2005. Thanks to Mehr Farooqi for referring me to the article.

giving readings in their own languages. At the end of each one's reading, everyone applauds politely. But when Ahmad Faraz begins reciting his *ghazal*s, the reaction is totally different, the magic begins, and Husain, too, is won over. The audience is imbued with the spirit of Hindi and English, he tells us, but it is for *ghazal*s that they express their appreciation. About some people he is less generous: of Hindi writers, for example, who do not know much Urdu but attempt an Urdu literary manner, he says, "They're writing Hindi stories but make efforts to be writing in Urdu" (27). He tells of another who in his personal manner tries to *act* like an Urdu writer: "It was very confusing. Hindi writers have their own fashions. How come this guy tried to steal Urdu ones?" (28). Taken together, Husain's observations finally led him to see a continuing, if diminished, role for Urdu in India. It certainly isn't as vital now as it was before Partition, he notes, but it is now no longer "a cause for anger or retaliation" (28). And it is in part because the Urdu style is no longer seen as a threat by the majority community, I think, that it is possible for it to be adopted as a fashion.

What does this enthusiasm for Urdu style on the part of a few Hindi writers and a larger Hindi-speaking public imply? As with my students, I think, it demonstrates an appreciation of an engaging secular literature as well as a fascination with a prestigious, somewhat exotic, but also accessible other. The sense of the other here as primarily elite, however, does not mean that *all* its connotations are high class and refined. For most Hindus, I think the idea of a fashionable Urdu style elicits the world of the *ghazal*—a high-class world of romance, longing, and literary allusion, but one that also offers an elegant sensuality. Images abound of wine cups and parties long into the night. In exquisite diction and images, there are hints of sensual excitement with practical implications that are neither very elegant nor very respectable. In a different register, my students' excitement about learning Urdu script may have derived in part from gazing at signboards during exciting forays to less than prestigious neighborhoods. Although my Hindu students mixed easily with their upper-class Muslim friends, they also had ideas about a more plebeian, tougher Muslim world (suggested in part, perhaps, by Bollywood gangster movies) from which they were largely sheltered. For contemporary Hindus, even when the image of the attractive Muslim is built mostly from the elite courtly culture, it may also carry an earthier, working-class thrill.

Muslim Spirits in a Hindu World

This less-refined component of an attractive Muslim image was one that I first seriously encountered in its own right when I began doing fieldwork on urban religion in Gwalior, Madhya Pradesh, in 1997. The next major stop on the rail line south from Agra, Gwalior has a population of about one million, which includes a Muslim population estimated at only about 6 or 7 percent.[2] It also has a decidedly Hindu cultural tenor. Understanding this, I was—rightly or not—taken aback by the considerable activity surrounding Gwalior's Sufi shrines. Although most of the shrines were by no means grand or constantly busy, most attracted at least some visitors on Thursdays, and all really came to life during their annual festivals, which almost always featured *qawwali* singing. In part, I was impressed by the sheer number of active shrines. Yusuf Niyazi, a popular local *qawwal,* enumerated sixteen shrines to whose annual festivals he might be invited—and these were just the ones with well-funded celebrations. Of course, I expected there would be at least some Hindu participation at these shrines, but Yusuf impressed on me that the Hindu participation was *extremely* high: according to him, Hindus were 99 percent of the attendees *and organizers.* I later confirmed that Yusuf's figure for attendees was only a moderate exaggeration, and there were plenty of Hindu names on most of the shrines' organizing committees. Although the numbers made sense given the popularity of the shrines and the demographics of the town, it was still surprising considering my sense of Gwalior's general communal ambience.

2. This rough estimate of Gwalior's population represents a consensus of some knowledgeable Gwalior businesspeople circa 2005 and tallies with current figures on the Web; the latest available official estimate at the time of this writing is 720,068 (Guru and Bhatnagar 1992, "Provisional Figures of Census 1991"). The percentage of Muslims is an informed estimate by Rashid Khanuni, the hereditary spiritual head of Khwaja Khanun shrine (interview, Gwalior, June 11, 1997).

Gwalior is a predominantly Hindu city in more than population alone. Although the city with its fort was incorporated into the Mughal Empire for a while—which accounts for some of its old Sufi shrines—at the end of the eighteenth century it became the headquarters of the Maratha ruler Mahadji Scindia, thus standing as the northernmost continuing outpost of Maratha power. Since then, Hindus have ruled politically and economically, with Gwalior in British times the capital of an important princely state ruled by Mahadji's descendents. Located in the cowbelt, moreover, it is a city where Hindu nationalism thrives. It is the birthplace of A. B. Vajpayee, a longtime prime minister as leader of the Hindu nationalist Bharatiya Janata Party—the "Indian People's Party," usually just called the BJP—and was also the hometown of another BJP founder, the late Gwalior Rajmata Vijaye Raje Scindia. The city has remained quiet during the communal disturbances of the recent past in good part because the Muslim community is not assertive, and the Hindus don't see it as a threat. Although that community contains a few prominent individuals and some middle-class tradespeople and professionals, its majority is lower class. And so, from certain Hindu points of view, *are many Muslim spirits and saints.* It took me a while, though, to figure this out.

My initial understanding of the disproportionately large Hindu participation at Sufi shrines began from my experience with my students' enthusiasm for Urdu: the Hindu devotees at the shrines, I thought, were attracted by a somewhat exotic other. And I think this element is indeed an important part of most attractive images of Muslims. But as I probed deeper, other factors came to light that gave that other a decidedly different coloring than the high-class courtly one that came to my attention earlier. In general, people gave two sorts of very believable reasons for going to Sufi shrines: first, the shrines were particularly effective for getting some practical work done; and, second, they liked the *qawwali.* Both these reasons suggest that—from middle-class Hindu perspectives—the powers associated with the shrines can be seen as considerably less than high and refined.

Let us first turn to the quality of the shrines' powers. For many Indians, especially those from lower urban classes and rural areas, the idea of a somewhat shady—and for that reason particularly powerful—being is a familiar one. Such beings are worshipped at small local shrines in many parts of India. They include guardian spirits attached to particular places and good members of bad supernatural hordes—beings that Alf Hiltebeitel (1989) calls "demon devotees." Most important for us, they also include the deified dead. Among the latter, Muslim spirits have frequently figured alongside those of deceased Hindu ascetics as well as those of heroes and Brahmins who suffered a violent or untimely demise; all may be readily resorted to by Hindus and Muslims alike (see Gottschalk 2000). The effective power of all these entities, moreover, derives in good part from their being seen to reside close to the human world, certainly closer than supreme deities. Willing to intervene readily in human affairs, they may remain less than completely pure. The boundaries between these effective, close-to-the-ground beings are very often blurred (Coccari 1989, 251–56), and there can easily be a practical convergence among them all as providers of practical help. Certainly, the powers at a small Sufi shrine—a localized memorial to a deceased Muslim holy person—explicitly suggest those of a Muslim spirit, a spirit of a place, and a deceased hero. For some Hindus, a shade of the "demon devotee" may linger in the background as well.

Small Muslim shrines in Gwalior include not only minor tombs of saints where *qawwalis* are sometimes sung, but also many small public shrines to more generic Muslim personages—often known as "Kamaal Khan" or "Balli Badshah." Their relative abundance may be due in part simply to the fact that small shrines identified as Muslim tend to find a wider scope as seats of powerful local helpers in predominantly Hindu cities than in predominantly Hindu villages: although villages often boast a number of down-to-earth local deities, Hindu shrines and temples in urban areas are largely dedicated to high transregional divinities, who offer devotees salvation along with boons and may not always be so attentive to the latter. Although some, in particular the Goddess and Hanuman, are usually understood to be more attentive than others, none is taken as a specialist exclusively devoted to practical help. And Gwalior Hindus, even while recognizing the usefulness of powerful local spirits dedicated to effective work, identify few of their own. Instead, they may turn to Muslim ones when available.

These Muslim shrines' practical effectiveness derives in good part from their status as sources of vital otherworldly powers found also at seats of, say, demon deities; but for Hindus, their Muslim provenance, I think, can make them seem all the more effective. Like Western pharmaceuticals (known as "English" medicines), their powers can seem alien and perhaps even a little unnatural—not to be taken every day, but handy in an emergency. Coarse and strong, in some circumstances they are seen as dangerous. Nevertheless, in the general Gwalior ambience, middle-class Hindus readily approach small Muslim shrines. Why are they not more hesitant? Embedded as the shrines are in resolutely Hindu worlds, their less-than-pure energies, I think, are taken as safely contained.

Indeed, the power of a Muslim shrine can be so safely contained that—and this came as another surprise—middle-class Hindu families may maintain them in their own houses. Interviews about temple-going practices with several Gwalior Aggarwals—a large and respectable North Indian Hindu mercantile community—revealed two families who had thus adopted Muslim spirits. One of the spirits, known in the family simply as "*baba*," was initially described to me as "Balli Badshah," a name it was presumed I would know; the other was called by another common honorific, "Sayyad Baba." The shrine in each house was a small niche built into a wall—an empty space for a spirit to dwell, but itself properly aniconic. In both cases, the families performed simple weekly rituals, forms of generic popular worship that managed to recognize the spirits' Muslim provenance. On Thursdays, the usual day for Sufi celebrations, the shrines were adorned with a *sahra*, the five short strings of flowers that Hindus sometimes use as a sort of bridegroom's veil; a lamp was lit, and incense was burned. The lamp and incense were also used in serving images of Hindu deities, around the necks of whom a flower garland might be put, but the *sahra*—regularly offered at Sufi shrines—was reserved for the spirit installed at the niche shrine.

The service was also short—just a few minutes—but, as all affirmed, was performed regularly. Maintaining the service was important because it obliged the resident spirit to pay attention to the family members' requests—and who knows what might happen if the regular service, once started, were stopped? Once, I was told, there was a near disaster involving a child's fall when the service was inadvertently forgotten during the bustle of a family festival—no doubt a warning! At the same time, together with their fear, several members of that family also displayed feelings of heartfelt reverence for their *baba*. Even brothers who had moved out of the family home, I was told, came to see the *baba* of the niche shrine when they had special problems. And although all family members visited gods at different temples, *baba* was the one some trusted most.

Further questioning on this apparently curious phenomenon revealed that in neither case did the Aggarwal families themselves originate the shrines. Rather, the shrines were there first, in their houses before the families took up residence in them. Over the decades, the families and the shrines adapted to one another: as old houses were renovated and expanded, room was always made *somewhere* for the *baba*'s niche.

The Aggarwals' continuing reverence to and accommodation with the Muslim spirits in their houses say something significant about the endurance of important forms of Indian secularity. This sense of secularity is different than the one seen in the courtly world of the classical Urdu poet. The latter sense suggests a notion of the secular familiar from Western discourse: the idea of a sphere of life distinct from the religious, one that in urban India as elsewhere can foster cosmopolitanism and its fascinating others. The Aggarwals' attitude, by contrast, plays on a more characteristically Indian understanding of secularity: a respect of some sort for all religions and, more important, a learning to live with them, a willingness to let them have their due. The Aggarwals did not start out loving the *baba*s they found in their homes, but they gave them a place, worked out arrangements with them that they understood as mutually beneficial, and eventually recognized them as their own.

Like the nonreligious secular of Indo-Muslim courts and cosmopolitan Indian cities, here, too, this tolerantly religious secular entails a sense of a common culture that includes an other that is also one's own. And like the nonreligious secular, the tolerantly secular extends through that common culture's higher and humbler realms, giving attractive images of Muslims a potentially very wide valence. Thus, just as the courtly, nonreligious world of the *ghazal* contains coarser sensuous innuendos, a Hindu's tolerantly religious attitude toward a humble Muslim shrine may attempt to transform it into the shrine of a grand old Sufi. For me, understanding this latter dynamic came less as a surprise than as a solution to a puzzle.

Mir Badshah and Urduization

In Gwalior, a few Sufi shrines are in fact legacies of specific noteworthy saints from a more Muslim past. These shrines have attested lineages and sometimes significant endowments; one, moreover—that to Khwaja Khanun—has had erudite hereditary spiritual heads knowledgeable in traditional lore. But the shrine in Gwalior that was avowedly the most popular at the turn of the twenty-first century—and certainly the one with the best-known annual festival—is not among these old attested shrines. That shrine, called "Mir Badshah," started from a neglected tomb in the main bazaar that was reclaimed in 1958 by one B. B. Bhonsle, a Gwalior Maharashtrian, and popularized in part by a Brahmin named Ramjilal Sharma. In their economic status, both gentlemen were from the modest end of the middle class: Bhonsle worked in the fire brigade near the shrine; Ramjilal had sporadic income from journalism work that was supplemented by a share in some village landholdings. In 1997, both remained on the shrine's five-person arrangements' committee, which then consisted of three Hindus and two Muslims. The big annual festival staged by the committee in the middle of the main bazaar appeared as a model of communal cooperation in celebration of a Sufi saint (see Gold 2005). Mir Badshah thus became the shrine that particularly piqued my interest during my 1997 visit. I focused some research on it, later did some writing, and circulated drafts. A frequent response to the early drafts was that the article would have broader interest if it were framed in terms of Indian Sufi shrines generally, and I was pointed to works by respected colleagues on aspects of historical Indian Sufism. None of those works, however, seemed to provide a relevant parallel. It took another visit, when I was working with Aggarwals, to find a lead that seemed to work.

At one Aggarwal house, the daughter of the family, who had been married in the city, was at home taking care of her new baby girl. She recounted an oft-told story: she and her husband had been trying to conceive for years and were successful only after a visit to a shrine. In their case, the effective shrine was that of a Muslim spirit Sabir Baba—a shrine that had been inherited by a Hindu potter named Pyarelal. It was a Thursday—the weekly festival day for Sufi shrines—and so a good time to go to Pyarelal's place, which was in a very modest neighborhood on the southern edge of the city. The shrine was busy, with a number of scooters and motorcycles parked outside and devotees waiting in the courtyard of Pyarelal's house to get into the shrine room. There, familiar ritual transactions involving small amounts of money on one side and sweets and ash on the other were sometimes supplemented by Pyarelal's brushing the suppliant with a small broom—again nothing particularly extraordinary under the circumstances. What did seem noteworthy were the several obviously middle-class members of the crowd assembled at a humble home shrine in an out-of-the-way district. A few days later we returned to talk to Pyarelal and get a better look at the place.

Pyarelal, it turned out, was eclectic in his religious beliefs, and his association with Sabir Baba had its limits. He had never been possessed by the saint, he said, but administered his blessings only by brushing devotees with his broom. He was also a disciple of one of the popular North Indian gurus of the day, a holy man called Jai Guru Dev, based in Mathura. Jai Guru Dev had a very broad, largely lower-class following and offered initiation into specific meditation practices that were said to lead to salvation. When I asked Pyarelal about the differences between the two main spiritual personages in his life, his immediate response was startling: he looked at me as though wondering how I could ask such a stupid question and said, "Well, Sabir Baba is a Muslim." I took the main import of his statement to mean that the kind of Muslim spiritual presences he knew were good for getting work done, but that for his own salvation, at least, a Hindu guru was appropriate. Whatever Pyarelal's response meant, however, it showed that even for him, who served Sabir Baba regularly, the saint's Muslim difference was something very essential to his nature.

At the same time, that difference seemed obscured somewhat through the communally relaxed presentation that Pyarelal gave to Sabir Baba. The shrine room was adorned with lithographs of both Hindu deities and famous Sufi shrines. The yearly festival, though called, in the Sufi style, an *'urs,* is timed to coincide with Vasanta Navaratri, a nine-day spring celebration of Durga and other Hindu goddesses. Although an *'urs* is typically a multiday affair, most don't run longer than three days, so nine is unusually long. The last day of Vasanta Navaratri, moreover, is the festival celebrating the birth of Lord Ram, a paragon of moral virtue, and also the day that Pyarelal singled out as the most important in his own celebration. The commemoration of Baba Sabir's *'urs,* then, seemed to enhance his persona with the powers of the Goddess and the righteousness of Ram. Not only were the festivities grand for their locale, but they also seemed unusually syncretic.

The *'urs* of Sabir Baba, though, was not attended by the Aggarwal couple seeking a child, despite their successful petition to him. In fact, the wife never came again after their initial visit, and the husband visited just a few times more. ("If they had come more often, they would have gotten a boy," said Pyarelal. The couple seemed happy with their baby girl.) Although the couple respected Sabir Baba's power and were ready to honor Pyarelal by inviting him to their home for a meal, their middle-class upbringing did not really let them feel comfortable spending more time than necessary at Pyarelal's establishment; the larger portion of his clientele, were, after all, lower class and lower caste. For the couple, the shrine was a powerful place whose resources they wanted to be able to tap when necessary, but it was not a place with which they wanted to be particularly associated.

Sabir Baba's low-class, highly syncretic shrine gave me a broader context for looking at the more elaborate and more Muslim-style shrine of Mir Badshah—a sort of reverse parallel, for Sabir Baba's shrine suggests an alternative way in which the shrine to Mir Badshah might have developed. Mir Badshah was in its origins just an unknown tomb, and Bhonsle, its discoverer, seemed in fact to have a closer personal relationship to his saint—whom he called "Baba"—than Pyarelal did to his. Mir Badshah spoke to Bhonsle and gave him advice. Circumstances of social class, however, seem to have helped orient the Mir Badshah shrine in a different direction. Although some of the shrine's early enthusiasts were from *economic* classes likely to visit establishments such as Pyarelal's, all the first main Hindu organizers were, like the Aggarwal couple, from respectable communities: a Brahmin and a Gwalior Maharashtrian. Familiar with saints' shrines developed in Hindu styles among the humbler strata of society, they did not want to identify with them. What evolved, then, was *not* an attempt to incorporate Mir Badshah into a sort of popular Hinduism—the first step of a process that South Asia scholars have long called "Sanskritization." Instead, what seemed to occur was a process we might in this context call "Urduization"—an attempt to present a humble local shrine in the style of higher, prestigious Indo-Islamic culture.[3] For the members of Mir Badshah's arrangements committee, glorifying the saint thus conceived has meant making him look like a proper Muslim Sufi, not like the sort of local Muslim spirit whose powers he can also manifest. Nevertheless, even as a great Sufi, Mir Badshah should still be a Sufi readily accessible to local Hindus. One easy way of access would eventually be through exuberant *qawwali* performance, but before I get to *qawwali* singing, I want to go the movies.

The Khans' Charisma

After thinking about Urdu and Hindi literature in the 1990s, in the early 2000s I, like many others, turned my attention to Bollywood films. One of the things likely to impress anyone encountering Bollywood at the turn of the twenty-first century is the drawing power of the three Khans—Salman, Aamir, and Shah Rukh—arguably the top male leads of the 1990s and still going strong in the new millennium's second decade. Certainly there is much contributing to these Muslim stars' success, including their own talent and the openness of the industry to people from *any* community who can add to a film's artistic and commercial value. But is there anything about these stars' unabashed Muslim identity that has contributed to their appeal? As I thought about it, I began to see in the nonreligious world of movieland a parallel to the elevated, somewhat glamorized packaging of the powerful Muslim other that I had seen at Mir Badshah.

3. Classic works on Sanskritization include Singer 1972 and Srinivas 1952. Hindi scholars occasionally use the term *Urduized* informally to refer to the language of a Hindi speaker who uses Urdu forms, sometimes in an artificial way and not always correctly. (Terms such as *Persianized* and *Islamicized*, more commonly used by scholars, don't seem quite right to talk about the romantic evocation of a particular Indo-Islamic cultural style.)

In its elite glamour, the world of the Bombay film industry may be the closest counterpart to the glittering, slightly decadent court life of the recent past that the contemporary Indian world has to offer. It is a place where people are not like the rest of us: they are not only rich and worldly, but also free and very cosmopolitan. Hindus and Muslims working in films mix without restraints and even marry each other now and then—not too often, to be sure, but certainly much more than most of their fans. Like court life, the lives led by Bombay film stars can be the stuff of people's dreams.

The worlds portrayed in Hindi films themselves are also the stuff of people's dreams, but most are cosmopolitan in only limited ways. True, Urdu poets working in the film industry have sometimes written song lyrics in *ghazal* style; dialogues use everyday Urdu vocabulary freely and avoid stuffy Sanskritisms; and caste is hardly mentioned. But the worlds depicted in Hindi films have always been largely Hindu and seem to be getting more so. In earlier decades, some movies were made in the genre known as the "Muslim social,"[4] which usually evoked old Lucknow or Hyderabad, but by the 1990s that genre had fallen into disfavor, and the Muslim supporting characters that one now sometimes sees do not often have developed personalities. Muslim actors, however, are found in a disproportionately high number—especially among the leading men. What, if anything, do the cosmopolitan Muslim elements in the personas of important male stars bring to the sympathetic Hindu characters they almost always portray on screen?

Let us reflect on the unrefined, earthy power seen in vital Muslim spirits. Does not a related energy in a different aspect come into the worst Hindu stereotypes of Muslim lust?[5] In the Muslim stars, however, you do not see the worst stereotypes. The stars are elegant and glamorous and, whatever their origins, inhabit a world filled with other sexy, glamorous,

4. See, for example, the film *Chaudhvin ka Chand* (1960), produced by and starring Guru Dutt.

5. "Muslim lust" (John 1996, 139) has been a common stereotype in Hindu nationalist circles (Gupta 2002, 243–59). Both Mary John (1996) and Kalyani Menon (2002, 178) cite references to it in the discourse of Hindu nationalist women.

and not-so-inhibited people. What some of them may offer to their Hindu fans, though, is an added dose of sexual charisma—one that is, moreover, especially forbidden. At the same time, though, their Muslim identities are safely contained within the Hindu world on the screen, so any vestige of the sensuously exotic other latent in those identities is liable only to enhance the star's appeal: As long as he is also seen as a kind of regular guy, wouldn't most any male film personality like to be able to project a bit of lusty spirit? Thus, like the magical powers at Mir Badshah, the sensual auras of the contemporary Muslim stars may begin with something especially gritty and other, become refined by its association with an elite cosmopolitan culture (here, the real-life Bollywood social world), and is finally (through its embodiment in screen characters) made safe by existing in a predominantly Hindu film world.

The situation was different during the so-called golden age of Hindi film, the late 1940s and 1950s, years when the pain of communal rivalry accompanying the 1947 partition of the subcontinent was still raw. There were great Muslim stars then, too, but in those days they often found it expedient to adopt Hindu-sounding stage names. In the buttoned-up 1950s, Yusuf Khan became a wildly popular matinee idol as Dilip Kumar, "the tragedy king"; today, Salman Khan is a romantic lead who has been regularly given scripts that require him to doff his shirt and show off his muscle-bound torso. This represents a change in the mores of Hindi film, to be sure, but one that can give a special appeal to the image of the identifiably Muslim male—one that is not threatening, but sensually exciting in an unsubtle way.

Qawwali, Rhythms, and Transcendence

Qawwali, found in films as well as in shrines,[6] can be sensually exciting, too. At Sufi shrines, however, *qawwali* rhythms play out against a tolerantly religious chord, not a nonreligious one. The excitement of *qawwali* in that context is thus normally oriented toward higher, more transcendent goals.

6. Perhaps most famously in the film *Amar, Akbar, Anthony* (1977), in which Rishi Kapoor plays a professional *qawwal*.

As a musical genre, artful *qawwali* differs from both classical and popular Hindu devotional song in several ways—the most noticeable, perhaps, being the viscerality of its rhythms. No arithmetically intricate classical Indian *talas* here, but a driving one-two, often maintained by steady hand clapping among members of a *qawwali* troupe. In contrast to popular Hindu devotional styles—which also often have strong, simple rhythms—the clapping in *qawwali,* done by the musicians themselves, is (musicologically speaking) *ahead* of the beat: that is, the clapping comes just at the beat's onset.[7] It thus helps contribute to the audience's sense that the rhythm is driving the performance along, that it is especially important. The strong rhythmic framework of *qawwali* is called *zarb,* "pulse"—"often compared with the heartbeat (also called *zarb*) by *qawwal*s and Sufis alike." It is "considered essential if the soul is to be moved" (Qureshi 1995, 60). The corresponding Hindi term, even when used in an expression meaning "to beat time" (*tāl bajānā*), lacks the connotations of both the centrality to performance and the very physicality implicit in *zarb* as "pulse."

Distinctive also is the typical vocal production of professional *qawwals*, who tend to cultivate a roughness in the voice (some readers may recall the singing of the late great Nusrat Fateh Ali Khan). This roughness, reminiscent of village singers, helps keep the audience aware of *qawwali* as something connected to the body. Even as trained professionals, *qawwals* sound down to earth. And singing as they do at high volume to a loud rhythmic accompaniment, they may also offer a performance that seems to push the limits of conventional restraint. They thus usually present a whole-body experience that feels more instinctually rooted than that of their Hindu devotional counterparts—who, as they become more professional, are more likely to be able to demonstrate restrained art and elicit increasingly refined ecstasies.

The pulsating rhythm of *qawwali* is complemented by a repetitive tune—usually fairly simple—framed around particular devotional verses. The driving beat is exciting, potentially arousing listeners to a physically

7. Thanks to Carol Babiracki of Syracuse University for the musicological observations on *qawwali* in this and the following paragraph.

grounded ecstasy. At the same time, the songs' tunes can capture listeners' attention, while their words direct that attention toward the transcendent. Their regular repetition in a lengthy performance, like the repetition of sacred utterances in Sufi (and Hindu) religious practice, are likely to draw listeners inward. With their spirits aroused and attention turned within, both Hindus and Muslims may then find themselves in an emotionally heightened, mildly ecstatic state—not articulately theologized or even particularly religious in any sectarian sense. When *qawwali* succeeds in producing in its listeners a sense of rapture in the music—the goal of most Indian devotional song—it can do so very forcefully, producing even in the less spiritually refined some ecstatic loss of self.

Exceptional Sufi saints are understood to have experienced a similar loss of self, but in states more complete and more intense. Even a figure usually called on for mundane help, when contemplated during *qawwali* at his shrine, may well be perceived as someone who has known such states—someone who even while able to manifest effective powers on earth can climb to the heights, too. As a spiritual being, he spans the very high and very low. It is the extremes in this range, I think, that may be what is especially characteristic of the attractiveness Hindus may find in their images of larger-than-life Muslim personages. Those images fascinate not just because they present an exotic other that is one's own too, but also because they can contain both a low, earthy vitality and a high, cosmopolitan elevation that can sometimes approach the transcendent.

Works Cited

Coccari, Diane. 1989. "The Bir Babas of Banaras and the Deified Dead." In *Criminal Gods and Demon Devotees: Essays on the Guardians of Popular Hinduism,* edited by Alf Hiltebeitel, 251–69. Albany: State Univ. of New York Press.

Gold, Daniel. 2005. "The Sufi Shrines of Gwalior City: Communal Sensibilities and the Accessible Exotic under Hindu Rule." *Journal of Asian Studies* 64, no. 1: 127–50.

Gottschalk, Peter. 2000. *Beyond Hindu and Muslim: Multiple Identity in Narratives from Village India.* New York: Oxford Univ. Press.

Gupta, Charu. 2002. *Sexuality, Obscenity, Community: Women, Muslims, and the Hindu Public in Colonial India.* New York: Palgrave.

Guru, S. D., and P. K. Bhatnagar. 1992. *Gwalior (Supplement).* Madhya Pradesh District Gazetteers. Bhopal, India: Directorate of Gazetteers, Department of Culture, Madhya Pradesh.

Hiltebeitel, Alf, ed. 1989. *Criminal Gods and Demon Devotees: Essays on the Guardians of Popular Hinduism.* Albany: State Univ. of New York Press.

Husain, Intizar. 1998. "Diyaar-e-Hind main Urdu." *Shabkhoon* 213: 25–28.

John, Mary E. 1996. *Discrepant Dislocations: Feminism, Theory, and Postcolonial Histories.* Berkeley: Univ. of California Press.

Menon, Kalyani Devaki. 2002. "Dissonant Subjects: Women in the Hindu Nationalist Movement in India." PhD diss., Syracuse Univ.

Qureshi, Regula. 1995. *Sufi Music of India and Pakistan: Sound, Context, and Meaning in Qawwali.* Chicago: Univ. of Chicago Press.

Singer, Milton. 1972. *When a Great Tradition Modernizes.* New York: Praeger.

Srinivas, Mysore N. 1952. *Religion and Society among the Coorgs of South India.* London: Oxford Univ.

2

≈

An Other's World

Healing at Husain Tekri Sharif

CARLA BELLAMY

IN CONTEMPORARY INDIA, Hindus, Muslims, Christians, and Sikhs commonly seek healing and intercession at the thousands of structures built in memory of notable Muslim individuals, chiefly Sufis and, to a lesser extent, martyrs. The most common Hindi/Urdu term for these structures is *dargah,* a word derived from the Persian noun meaning both "portal" and "court," and Indian *dargah*s are indeed recognized by pilgrims as conduits of a divine power that can be accessed through rituals steeped in the language and symbolism of royal and legal courts. Non-Muslim patronage of *dargah*s begs the question of why Hindus in particular visit and venerate these *dargah*s in such high numbers, given that there exist Hindu shrines and temples—in particular those built to honor Hanuman and certain forms of the Goddess—that are widely recognized to offer relief from the same sorts of afflictions commonly treated at *dargah*s (Dwyer 2003; Kakar 1982; Nabokov 2000). In short, if Hindu venues exist for the treatment of illness, financial ruin, and familial problems, why do Hindus seek healing in Islamic venues?

Peter Gottschalk (2000) has shown that some Hindus patronize *dargah*s because Hindus possessed by a malevolent Muslim spirit believe that the Muslim spirit will recognize only Muslim authority; Peter van der Veer (1992) has similarly speculated that Hindus in particular find *dargah*s effective places of healing because they see the shrines as polluted and therefore (dangerously) powerful. In contrast to this view, the mainstream media and some scholars have suggested that a shared ritual vocabulary encourages cross-tradition patronage of these shrines (Bigelow 2004; Burman 2002); devotional religion in particular is often cited in this context (Jackson 1989). Alternatively, as the work of Tony Stewart (2004) has demonstrated, narratives about powerful religious figures such as Satya Pir, a Bengali saintly personage with both Hindu and Muslim aspects, reflect a worldview in which the malleable nature of narrative and the realities of everyday life have rendered exclusive, doctrine-based religious identities largely irrelevant; in such a world, the very question of why Hindus would patronize a Muslim institution does not take the local meaning of these categories into account. Along these lines, Joyce Flueckiger's (2006) study of a female Muslim healer in the southern Indian city of Hyderabad has shown that in the context of religious healing gender divisions are often more meaningful and operative than the distinction between Hindu and Muslim. Several ethnographic studies of *dargah*s have supported the idea that mutually exclusive categories of Hindu and Muslim are not operative in *dargah* culture. Defending the idea of a sense of *communitas* in which pilgrims are united by the desire to challenge socially sanctioned collective identities, Shail Mayaram (1999) has suggested that *dargah*s are "microcosmic public spaces" in which individuals negotiate new identities (see also Lambek 1981). Jackie Assayag's (2004) study of Hindu and Muslim participation in the ritual and everyday life of a Karnataka-based *dargah* makes a similar point, arguing in particular against the use of the term *syncretism* to explain Hindu–Muslim patronage of *dargah*s and proposing instead that adherents of both traditions have such extended histories of mutual influence and cooperation that the impermeable categories of "Hindu" and "Muslim" cannot reflect the reality of the practice of these two traditions. In this way, the argument implies, it is not accurate to categorize *dargah*s as Islamic institutions.

The list of explanations for non-Muslim use of Muslim shrines as places of healing is, it seems, both extensive and varied, with scholars arguing that non-Muslims patronize *dargah*s because only Muslim saints can deal with Muslim spirits; because a ritually polluted place is the most effective place to combat a ritually impure invasive spirit; because shared ritual grammars and beliefs encourage non-Muslim participation in *dargah* life; and, finally, because the rigid, impermeable categories of Hindu and Muslim are not operative on the level of local, lived religion in India. *Dargah* culture is highly complex owing to the diversity of its pilgrims and its participation in both local culture and subcontinental and global Islamic networks, and it is therefore not surprising that reasons for Hindus' relationships with *dargah*s reflect a wide range of beliefs, practices, and worldviews. My ethnographic research at the northern Indian pilgrimage center of Husain Tekri does not disprove any of these arguments regarding Hindu patronage of *dargah*s, all of which offer a partial picture of the relationship that Hindus have with *dargah*s. However, I would like to suggest that the explicit, exclusive, and communal identity of a *dargah* as *Muslim* is a significant and overlooked element of its appeal to non-Muslims and that this element of its appeal is particularly pronounced owing in part to the Hindu tradition's emphasis on the close relationship between familial and religious obligations, particularly for women. Further, the explicit, exclusive, and communal identity of *dargah*s as Islamic is reinforced by another recent development in the culture of *dargah*s: the fact that inexpensive and widely available mass transportation has made it much easier for persons of otherwise limited means to patronize distant *dargah*s. This development allows pilgrims an unprecedented level of opportunity to resolve their problems in relative anonymity, and because—as I hope to demonstrate—the individual's health is conceived of in terms of his or her relationship with his or her family, the anonymous environment of the *dargah* offers the added advantage of allowing problems to be resolved without concern for how the often violent, disturbing, and transgressive healing rituals might be regarded by members of the afflicted pilgrim's family and local community.

Husain Tekri in Context: Islamic Shrines in India

My argument draws upon several years of ethnographic research at the *dargah* of Husain Tekri Sharif in Madhya Pradesh and some of its satellite shrines in Udaipur and Mumbai;[1] participant observation was my

1. I conducted two and a half years of India-based research between 1999 and 2003, with subsequent shorter follow-up visits over the following decade.

primary mode of interaction with Husain Tekri's pilgrims and management.[2] I developed long-term relationships with several female pilgrims in residence at Husain Tekri and supplemented these sources with daily conversations with pilgrims sitting in the courtyards of the *dargah*s and observation of the various rituals of the shrines. Husain Tekri came into existence during the month of Muharram 1304/1886 following reports of a miraculous visit by Husain, a grandson of the prophet Muhammad, whose martyrdom is historically mourned by Muslims during Muharram. In the decades following reports of Husain's miraculous appearance, wealthy donors, mainly members of the Shi'a Muslim Khoja community of Mumbai, funded the construction of shrines in memory of him and other close members of his family, most of whom were also killed at Karbala.[3] The shrines were built with the support of the Sunni rulers of the princely state of Jaora, in which the miracle was understood to have taken place.

Although Husain Tekri is part of the larger category of shrines built in memory of notable Muslim individuals, it is also a unique mixture of several types of Islamic commemorative structures, specifically *dargah*s, *rauza*s, and *imambara*s. Pilgrims to Husain Tekri refer to its shrines as both *dargah*s and *rauza*s. *Rauza* is an Arabic-derived Urdu word meaning "garden," among other things, and it is true that although the courtyards of Husain Tekri's shrines contain no gardens, most of them stand near (or on top of) naturally occurring water sources, the sine qua non of gardens. In the Indian Shi'a tradition, shrines built in honor of Muslim martyrs are often called *rauza*s. The shrines of Husain Tekri are architecturally

2. In referring to Husain Tekri as a *dargah*, I follow the common Indian practice of referring to any shrine built in memory of a notable Islamic figure as a *dargah*; the term, in other words, is used in this generic manner as well as in the more specific sense to refer to a Sufi's tomb. Other specific terms for different types of Islamic memorial structures that are sometimes generically referred to as *dargah*s include *rauza* (discussed in the text), *cilla* (a shrine built to mark a place of Sufi visitation or meditation), and *imambara* (a shrine commonly maintained by Shi'a Muslims containing objects that represent the martyrs of Karbala).

3. The Khoja community in Mumbai is divided into Ismaili, Ithna Ashari, and Sunni components; current Khoja patronage of the shrines is largely Ithna Ashari with some Ismaili.

identical to the types of structures raised over the graves of Sufi teachers, commonly called *dargahs*. However, the interiors of Husain Tekri's shrines do not contain graves, but rather silver miniatures of the far-flung actual tombs of the martyrs in whose memory the shrines are constructed. These miniature tombs, called *zarih,* are surrounded by metal latticework, to which pilgrims cling as they offer their prayers and petitions.[4] *Zarih* are more commonly enshrined in *imambaras*, which are spaces ranging from small cabinets affixed to the wall of a home to the renowned, palatial edifices of the city of Lucknow; *imambaras* of all sizes are uniformly maintained by the Shi'a community in memory of notable martyrs and Shi'a leaders. Husain Tekri is therefore a unique hybrid of several types of Islamic memorial structures, though its hybridity is not unique: all Islamic memorial structures are hybrids in that their culture is shaped by a range of local, regional, and media-driven pan-Islamic influences that reflect their pilgrims' diverse backgrounds.

Healing Practices at *Dargahs*

The two major ritual healing activities common at Husain Tekri are also practiced at *dargahs* containing the graves of revered Muslim figures and at public and private *imambaras*. The first of these activities is the ritual burning of a type of incense known as *loban*. At regular times throughout the day, a smoldering container of *loban* is first offered in front of the *zarih* and then carried by volunteers through lines of waiting pilgrims, who inhale it with the belief that it has therapeutic properties. As the smoke engulfs the crowd, each pilgrim becomes momentarily isolated in a substance understood to be a conduit of divine efficacy. I have described the ritual of *loban* inhalation in detail elsewhere (Bellamy 2006); here I simply emphasize that *loban* by virtue of its physical nature affords pilgrims the

4. According to Platt's Urdu–English dictionary, the Urdu term *zarih,* commonly used to refer to a railing or latticework surrounding a temple or tomb, is "probably a corruption of [the Arabic] zarih" (Platts 2000). In India, the term is also used to refer to models of the tombs of the martyrs of Karbala made of precious metals and jewels. When writing the word *zarih,* native Urdu speakers at Husain Tekri employed a range of spellings, including *jari* and *zari*. For more on the usages of the term *zarih,* see Korom 2003, 68, 278.

1. Women recovering after practicing *haziri*. Photograph by Carla Bellamy.

opportunity to encounter the healing presence of the saints individually and to engage with that healing power in a relatively anonymous context. The second ritual healing activity is known as *haziri* (literally, "presence"), and it can be most basically understood as a process of removing malevolent possessing spirits from pilgrims' bodies. *Haziri* is common at *dargah*s throughout the subcontinent; its most violent form, known at Husain

2. Pilgrims awaiting *loban* outside the *rauza* of Imam Husain. Photograph by Carla Bellamy.

Tekri as *khuli haziri*—literally, "open *haziri*"—involves an interrogation of the possessing malevolent spirit by the martyr or Sufi in whose memory the shrine has been erected. In this interrogation process, the malevolent presence, speaking through the victim's body, initially resists the martyr or Sufi's commands to reveal what sort of magic was performed to place the spirit in the victim's body and by whom the spirit was sent, but once this confession is obtained, the spirit can be removed from the body. To the outside observer, the only perceptible voice is that of the malevolent possessing spirit speaking through the victim's body; the interrogator's voice is audible only to the spirit. Both *haziri* and *loban* are practiced almost exclusively in *dargah*s and *imambaras*.[5] At Husain Tekri, Hindus, Muslims,

5. Shrines replete with images of *dargah*s and Sufi teachers built in the homes of Hindu devotees are also sites of *haziri* and *loban* consumption. Neither the many conversations about *loban* that I had with pilgrims over the course of my fieldwork nor a formal survey

Christians, and Sikhs engage in *haziri* and the consumption of *loban* side by side in the courtyards of its *rauzas*.

Communalism and the Healing Process

Otherness, conceived of in religious or racial terms, is often understood as the source of all that is out of place, debased, and potentially dangerous; many examples of this phenomenon can be found in virtually any cultural context. However, at Husain Tekri the language of religious otherness can also be a positive part of the healing process. Specifically, for some Hindus the appeal of Husain Tekri and similar Muslim saint shrines derives in part from a particularly modern notion of religious identity: here, an Islamic identity that is exclusive and fixed and that denies the shared history of mutual influence that marks all the "major" traditions of the subcontinent. This Hindu attraction to the exclusive, even communal, Islamic identity of a Muslim place is rarely stated explicitly, but, given the ubiquity and psychological weight of communalism, it is necessary to consider what attraction the Islamic identity of Muslim places might hold for those Hindus who patronize them.

Although Muslims and non-Muslims participate in the ritual life of *dargahs*, and there is truth to the argument that *dargahs* are the product of both "Hindu" and "Muslim" influences, it is also true that in contemporary India Muslim saint shrines do have an explicitly Islamic identity—an Islamic identity that in recent years has become increasingly communalist and exclusive in tone. As South Asia grows increasingly communalized as a result of the pressures exerted by Hindutva (Hindu nationalism) and the visions of "true Islam" (freed of Indian "corruption") pedaled by television shows and print media funded in part by

---

about *loban* that I administered among pilgrims at Husain Tekri ever mentioned inhaling *loban* in a Hindu temple setting. Incense is an important component of *puja* (ritual of worship) in Hindu temples, but in its distribution as well as its physicality it is not at all like *loban*. The common association between Islamic traditions and *loban* is also evidenced by a scene in the major Hindi film *Mangal Pandey* (2005) that featured the burning of *loban* during a song exhorting Allah for help ("Al Maddath Maula").

organizations based in Iran and Saudi Arabia, the exclusively Islamic identity of *dargah*s has become more pronounced.[6] In this environment, communalist marking of previously shared sites has become common. Dominique-Sila Khan (2002), for example, has documented the trend toward marking roadside and other minor shrines as Muslim or Hindu, most dramatically in the shift from whitewash to brilliant green or saffron paint, with accompanying banners in similarly lurid tones. The construction of a massive new mosque at Husain Tekri is also testament to this trend: the minarets of the Sunni mosque loom emphatically over the domes of the *rauza*s. Now, as a pilgrim's tonga or rickshaw rolls through the farmland that surrounds Husain Tekri, there is no doubt that he or she is approaching a Muslim place.

Khan regards these changes to *dargah* life as communalist and necessarily exclusionary, and certainly these elements are part of the picture. At Husain Tekri, for example, a habitually cantankerous low-caste Hindu (Teli) lodge owner responded to my questions about Husain Tekri with anger, saying he had nothing to do with "Urdu matters." In everyday speech, "Urdu" is commonly used to refer to anything written in derivations of Persio-Arabic script. This script is itself widely understood to have powerful properties, and anything in which it is written immediately acquires a new level of authority and an Islamic sheen, if not identity.[7] Although this lodge owner's statement may itself seem aggressively communal, after further conversation it became clear to me that he was reacting to the explicit Islamization of Husain Tekri and the seizure of a shrine that had once been as much Teli as "Muslim." As evidence of what he regarded as a hostile, politicized takeover of Husain Tekri, he cited the Urdu and Arabic-inscribed archway that had recently been built over the new main road leading to the *rauza*s; he also claimed that in former times

6. "Reform" of *dargah* culture and "corrupt" Indian Islam more generally existed before these recent media-fueled attempts; see Lelyveld 1978.

7. For a discussion of Arabic and Urdu writing in popular Islamic healing practices, see Flueckiger 2006, in particular chapter 2.

the *rauza*s were simply referred to as the "big *rauza*" and the "little *rauza*," whereas now they are also referred to as the *rauza*s of Imam Husain and Hazrat 'Abbas.

In addressing the question of why Hindus find *dargah*s effective places of healing, if we accept that both the geography and the perception of *dargah*s are increasingly marked by communalism and that *dargah*s are commonly regarded by Muslims and non-Muslims alike as effective places of healing, it is necessary to explore what "health" means to *dargah* pilgrims. At Husain Tekri, I found that pilgrims overwhelmingly measured health and wellness in terms of the ability to successfully contribute to and participate in family life; for women, this definition primarily meant marrying and bearing children, and for men it meant marrying and meeting the family's financial needs. Inability (or unwillingness) to perform these functions owing to physical and mental problems was almost always cited as a major aspect of illness; recovery was similarly measured in terms of successful reintegration into one's extended family.[8] It is of course important not to oversimplify this definition of health: many pilgrims sought to alleviate a tremendous amount of physical suffering and life-threatening illnesses, but the healing process was never understood simply as the alleviation of pain but also encompassed the ways this new freedom allowed pilgrims to contribute to their families' economic and emotional lives. In short, alienation from one's family is the measure of one's illness; reintegration with one's own family and religious community is overwhelmingly the measure of one's recovery.

Certain goddesses and the god Hanuman share with Muslim saints a reputation for healing. However, as Isabelle Nabokov (2000) has argued in the context of healing rituals associated with goddesses, reintegration methods are coercive. As Graham Dwyer (2003) has shown, the method used to remove malevolent possessing spirits at the Balaji temple

8. The tendency to conceive of healing in terms of familial relationships has been documented elsewhere. See Pakaslahti 1998.

in Rajasthan similarly involves a *puja* (ritual of worship) ceremony for Balaji,[9] thus making individual healing contingent upon participation in a central form of Hindu practice. In both cases, individual healing cannot happen without acceding to established authority figures (both gods and ritual specialists) and structures of authority in the Hindu community.

In the context of Muslim saint shrines, the status of the Muslim religious spaces as "other"—when combined with the relatively simple and flexible rituals that are common at many *dargah*s—allows for a great deal of individual control over the pace and nature of the outcome. An outcome arrived at individually rather than coercively is much more likely to result in the successful reintegration of the individual into his or her familial (and therefore religious) community. Individual effort alone is possible only in a place that is understood to be fundamentally other, removed from the pilgrim's familial, social, and religious background. In short, the identity of *dargah*s as Muslim and the relative freedom that non-Muslims in particular enjoy as they participate in *dargah* rituals together offer those seeking healing opportunities and resources that are unavailable in Hindu contexts.

Consider, for example, the following case of a Hindu family that had come to Husain Tekri for the healing of their daughter. They explained that, after repeated unsuccessful attempts to heal their daughter through petitions to various goddesses, they had finally come to Husain Tekri because, they said, there was nothing in their daughter's *kundali* (horoscope) indicating that she was destined to suffer as she had been suffering. They elaborated by saying that there was no explanation for her suffering other than the possibility that "something from the air" had attached itself to her, and for the cure of such problems it was necessary to come to a *dargah*. Many conversations I had with Husain Tekri's pilgrims contained similar statements about "something in the air."

Pret, spirits of deceased individuals, are universally understood to float through the air, which suggests that in blaming the daughter's

9. Balaji is a child form of the Hindu god Hanuman.

problems on "something in the air," the family may have consciously or unconsciously been alluding to the spirits of the Muslim community's dead, who would—by orthodox Hindu definition—be doomed to a life of wandering owing to an "improper" disposal of bodies.[10] On one level, my conversations with Husain Tekri's pilgrims indicated that this attitude is one aspect of non-Muslim perceptions of *dargahs'* power, as is the larger notion of the power of transgression and transgressive behavior. However, there is more going on here than the idea that (ritually impure) Muslim saints must deal with (ritually impure) Muslim spirits. The troubles being experienced by this young woman were inexplicable within the Hindu worldview: a Hindu horoscope is popularly understood to offer an explanation of everything about an individual's life and fate. Thus, in mentioning the daughter's horoscope, the family was acknowledging the limits of their tradition's ability to render the daughter's suffering meaningful. On an existential level, this woman's suffering was inexplicable within the all-encompassing discourse of Hindu astrology and therefore had to be addressed in a context that was clearly "not Hindu." In this case and others, the more communally delineated *dargah* culture is from the Hindu tradition, the more effective it can be in addressing issues that have proved inexplicable within that tradition.

Muslim saint shrines' explicit, exclusive, and even communal Islamic identity has several other levels of appeal, particularly for Hindu women. Specifically, because for most women in South Asia religious life and family life are inextricably linked, if it becomes necessary to solve a family-related problem, seeking help at an explicitly Hindu place may be unappealing, impossible, or ineffectual. That is, if a Hindu woman feels significant estrangement from her family (which is almost universally

10. This Hindu family was under the care of a Shi'a Muslim man named Salim, whom I met during my first visit to Husain Tekri in 2000. Salim often serves as a guide for visiting families from his hometown. It is likely that his presence during the interview made this family particularly disinclined to say anything potentially derogatory about Islamic places such as Husain Tekri. This is not to suggest that the family did not have a deep and positive relationship with Husain Tekri; indeed, the father in the family attributed his success in abandoning the consumption of alcohol to the power of Husain Tekri.

the case among female sufferers of *haziri*), because of the linkage between family and religion she will feel estrangement from Hindu places. In the following excerpts from an interview with a young Hindu woman from Jaipur who often lived at Husain Tekri, the attractiveness of particularly Muslim places of pilgrimage to Hindu women is particularly evident. This woman's explicit evaluation of her situation is mirrored in the stories and actions of many Hindu women I interviewed over my time at Husain Tekri.

The daughter of a *pujari* (ritual specialist) at a Jaipur-based Ganesh temple, Sunila[11] is a thirty-something woman who identified herself as a Brahmin. In a lengthy interview, she described her situation and her ten-year-long relationship with Husain Tekri. Sunila emphasized that Husain Tekri was responsible for her recovery to date. She specifically attributed her continued recovery to an exceptionally grueling regimen of dietary restrictions and physical labor. She was convinced that by eating hulled mung *dal* (a lentil preparation) once a day and sweeping the road that connects the *rauzas*, she was slowly making progress.

To explain the benefit of and need for this regimen, she said that what would have been revealed in her *khuli haziri* was so fearsome that she suffered with *gum haziri* instead. (*Gum haziri*—literally, "hidden *haziri*"—is a term used to describe physical and mental suffering caused by malevolent possessing spirits that cannot be detected by looking at the victim.) She remarked that Maula—a common title used for the male saints of Husain Tekri—had told her that she would never be given *khuli haziri* because the magic that had done on her had been "naked magic" and that if she were to be given *khuli haziri*, she would be given the command to remove all her clothes, which would be unacceptable.

Sunila eventually found that she could not bear the strain of *gum haziri*, and so she told Maula that she needed relief. Sunila explained that Maula responded by giving her a command to sweep the road, and Sunila claimed that as long as she does the work of sweeping the road, she does not suffer physically. She elaborated: "I've still got *gum haziri* going on inside of me, but I don't have pain anymore. If you have *gum haziri*, but

11. Not her real name.

you don't sweep or do some kind of work, then you'll have a lot of pain. Why? Because people who don't do work for Maula ['Ali] are the ones who suffer pain."

It is clear that Sunila also regards *khuli haziri* as a form of labor as effective as the labor involved in sweeping the street. *Haziri* is hard physical labor, and, as such, it necessarily produces results. In the case of *khuli haziri,* the efficacy of the labor derives in part from the corporal punishment that the body of the *haziriwali/a*[12] is forced to bear; in the case of sweeping the road, Sunila claimed that the power of the *pret* dissipates into the garbage that she sweeps. Further substantiating the equivalence of the labor of sweeping and the labor of *khuli haziri,* she maintained that as she sweeps, the spirit that torments her suffers, in part because she performs this harsh physical labor on an empty stomach: "I go along, sweeping on an empty stomach. And when I go on like that, sweeping while I'm hungry, the *pret* is beaten and punished. And his effect on me is removed, and his strength fades."

Sunila also maintained this austerity diet because she found that eating any food that caused her blood to "increase" actually caused her possessing *pret* to thrive by feeding on her blood. She specifically cited a situation two years earlier when she went home to study for an exam related to her career as a schoolteacher. During this time, she took to drinking tea and eating tomatoes, and she accepted papaya from her father. Papaya in particular is widely understood to make blood, and Sunila explained that when she ate this food, the *pret* became stronger because it had blood to drink again, and it was therefore able to torment her with what she described as "sex ki haziri."[13] Many individuals in *haziri* engage in actions that mimic aspects of the physical act of sexual intercourse, so it is possible that Sunila's exceptionally open statements about

12. Literally, "the one with *haziri.*" The two endings indicate the male and female forms of the noun.

13. In the course of her interview, Sunila also explained that the *pret* engaged in *cherchar* (literally, "touch-touching"), which seems to be a somewhat common term for sexual teasing or attacks. For part of our interview, two men sat and listened, which, she later explained, made it difficult for her to explain the exact nature of the torment.

the violating sexual nature of the actions of the *pret* in her body are shared by some who suffer in *khuli haziri*. In any case, Sunila found the combination of reducing her body and performing polluting labor as effective as *khuli haziri* in reducing the hold of the *pret* on her body.[14]

Thus far Sunila's story fits within the broad parameters of the process of *haziri* at Husain Tekri; it is hard labor endured by an individual body. Also typical was Sunila's explanation that the magic done on her had been done by an uncle for the usual reasons—to create unrest in the family so that her father, the eldest brother in the family, would spend all his resources trying to solve the problem and finally have no choice but to turn the temple over to her uncle. In a dramatic and explicit way, Sunila's family life and her religious identity are inextricably linked; thus, when problems erupted in her family, it would have been ineffectual to pursue a solution within the context of Hindu rituals or spaces. When explicitly asked why she did not seek a solution in a temple, Sunila replied: "I've run all the way from the temple [*mandir*] to the mosque [*masjid*]. I was born at a pilgrimage center, in the midst of consecrated temple images of gods [*murti*], the daughter of a *pujari*. I lived in a temple, but because of this suffering I've come from the temple to the mosque. In the very temple where I grew up, my uncle had magic done, and in order to rid myself of this magic I've come all the way to the mosque. And in doing this I've improved, though I'm not completely recovered yet.[15] But I have hope that I will recover completely."[16]

14. Sunila understood her body to have been magically filled with many offending presences, including jinn, *atma*, and different kinds of animals. In the case of animals, the terminology she used to describe their presence was *cauki* (literally, "a sitting place"): "mere upar gai ki [cauki], bhais ki, hathi ki, gadhe ki, kutte ki, kabutar ki, bandar ki, nag ki, chipakli ki" ("cow *cauki* and also the *cauki* of cows, water buffalo, elephants, donkeys, dogs, pigeons, monkeys, snakes, and salamanders").

15. "Aur is men, main saphal hui hun, par puri saphali nahin hui, puri saphalaa mujhe nahin mili." The term *saphal*—literally, "fruitful" or "profitable"—reinforces the notion that it is labor at Husain Tekri that produces results.

16. The hope, optimism, and strength that Sunila expresses here are common among pilgrims at Husain Tekri, and they were a constant source of amazement to me.

Husain Tekri and similar Muslim saint shrines are not mosques; here it seems that Sunila used the terms *mandir* (temple) and *masjid* (mosque) rhetorically to represent two different, exclusive religious communities. As is vividly illustrated in Sunila's case, for Hindu women religious life is dramatically inseparable from family life.[17] If serious problems erupt in a familial context, a young woman may find herself so fundamentally alienated from her own religious tradition that she will feel she has no choice but to seek elsewhere a remedy for the situation. If this is the case, it seems that unless a *dargah*'s management enforces downright aggressive exclusion of Hindus, the more explicit and even communal the Islamic identity of the shrine, the greater its potential appeal to non-Muslim women in particular.[18]

Anonymity, Connectivity, and Modernity

The contemporary communalist politics of the subcontinent and the increasing tendency to conceptualize religious identity as fixed and impermeable have contributed to what is probably a new aspect of the appeal of

17. Although there are too many instances of this phenomenon to mention, a few major examples include: the universal valorization of the long-suffering Sita as an ideal wife and the concept of *stridharm* (literally, women's duty or religion) more generally; Sati as a widely recognized means for a woman to express her devotion to her husband: Rakhi, the immensely popular pan-Hindu celebration of sisters' duty to protect brothers; Karva Chouth, the widely observed pan-Hindu presunrise-to-sunset fast observed by women to ensure their husbands' long life; Sraddha, the annual veneration of deceased ancestors, which is conducted in the home by a hired pandit, but which entails a great deal of food preparation and house cleaning on the wife's part; and, finally, the publication in English of books such as Om Lata Bahadur's *The Book of Hindu Festivals and Ceremonies* (1997). Books like this seek to educate a young generation of diasporic Hindu women of their duty to maintain an authentic and meaningful Hindu culture abroad. In all of these instances, a woman's religious duties are intimately related to her role as a protective and supportive sister, mother, or wife. To be clear, I am not suggesting that "Hinduism" oppresses women; I only note that it would be very difficult for a Hindu woman, apart from becoming a renouncer, to conceive of a Hindu identity that did not entail commitment to family life.

18. For a discussion of the ways that the discourse of family functions in Muslim women's experiences of Husain Tekri as well as further discussion of non-Muslim women's relationship with Muslim places, see Bellamy 2011.

dargahs to non-Muslims. Technology has also helped to reshape the appeal of *dargahs*. If the history of Husain Tekri is any indication, it seems very clear that—until the advent of cheap public mass transit—most Muslim saint shrines were defined largely by local economies and relationships. In recent years, however, the culture of some Muslim saint shrines has become transregional as a result of advances in transportation networks and media. Thus, what was once addressed in local contexts can now be addressed anonymously, far from home. In this way, the culture of Muslim saint shrines has taken a new form: it is now a combination of local, regional, and media-driven pan-Islamic elements.

Anonymity is one important consequence of the tendency of Husain Tekri and similar Muslim saint shrines to attract individuals from distant places who have no preexistent social relationship with them. When this opportunity for anonymity is combined with the fact that the dense network of Muslim saint shrines allows for an endless variety of individually tailored pilgrimages, the result is a place of pilgrimage that allows both male and female pilgrims to address familial and financial concerns without the knowledge of family members, friends, or neighbors. Over the years that I have spent visiting Husain Tekri and related Muslim saint shrines, the existence and value of the anonymity offered by Muslim saint shrines have been repeatedly affirmed. Thus, for example, a Mumbai-based Shi'a family once told me about the nature of the problems that had brought them to Husain Tekri, but when they were approached by a Shi'a woman from Mumbai who is a fairly well-known character at Husain Tekri, they changed their story completely, saying that they had come only for *'ibadat* (worship), and they explicitly denied any familial or financial problems. Clearly, this family had come to Husain Tekri because it gave them the opportunity to work out their various issues in relative anonymity. When that anonymity was threatened, they could convincingly say that they had simply come to Husain Tekri to offer their respects to its saints.

During a visit to a nearby *dargah* in Jaora with some local friends, I witnessed a conversation in which one of my friends asked another local woman if she was visiting the *dargah* because her health was bad or if there were some other problem. This woman made a point of explicitly denying that she had any problems, saying that she had simply come to pay her respects and to spend some time relaxing in the *dargah*'s courtyard. A young Hindu woman who functioned as one of my main informants also explicitly stated that she would not visit her local *dargah* because then all of her problems would be on display for the entire community. Finally, another young Hindu woman, also a major informant, explained that her mother was similarly opposed to her daughter's visiting the Udaipur-based (and recently deceased) Sufi healer Mastan Baba because of what it might do to her daughter's reputation.

In short, because it is culturally acceptable to travel some distance to make a pilgrimage to a Muslim saint shrine, *dargah*s provide individuals with a unique context in which they can deal with serious problems without undue damage to their reputations. At the same time, owing to the existence of Husain Tekri outposts as well as the presumed connection that any Muslim healer or *dargah* has with any other Islamic place, experiences that one has far away from home can remain anchored in one's home; upon return, it is possible to maintain a relationship with Husain Tekri through visiting one of its outposts or any nonmosque Islamic space. Finally, given that successful reintegration into family life is a major characteristic of pilgrims' visions of healing, a relatively anonymous context is essential. In the interest of protecting family reputation, it can always be claimed that a visit to a *dargah* is for devotional reasons rather than for reasons related to physical, financial, or mental problems. Should a longer stay at a distant *dargah* be required, the victim and his or her caretakers can rest assured that the often shocking process of healing will not have an overly negative impact on the rest of his or her life.

Conclusion

I began this discussion by asking why non-Muslims seek healing at *dargahs*. There is no simple or single answer to this question. On the one hand, *dargah*s have deep roots in the subcontinent, and their ritual, narrative, and social lives have been shaped by centuries of contributions from members of all the religious traditions of the subcontinent; in this way, they are not Muslim places, but South Asian places. Perhaps in an earlier time their court-derived culture and ritual life contributed to their universal appeal, attracting a diverse range of petitioners in much the same way that the many royal courts of the subcontinent once did. However, forces ranging from the census to the Indian independence movement to the ahistorical categorizations of "Hindu" and "Muslim" common in schoolbooks throughout the subcontinent have contributed to contemporary notions of South Asian religious identity as fixed and exclusive. When combined with the rise in literacy and, more recently and powerfully, in television, radio, and the Internet—these forces have contributed much to notions of fixed religious identities that fuel communalist rhetoric and acts of violence. When circulated by the modern media, these acts accelerate and further solidify notions of religious identity as exclusive and fixed. This communalization does not and cannot fade from individuals' consciousness, and it has contributed to contemporary Hindu perceptions of *dargah*s as "Muslim" places, but it paradoxically has not caused a marked decrease in Hindu patronage of *dargah*s. Because health is measured in terms of integration with one's family, and because family obligations and religious obligations are strongly linked in the Hindu tradition, feelings of profound alienation from one's family or an inability to serve one's family—a nearly universal complaint of pilgrims to Husain Tekri—cannot be addressed in Hindu contexts. The otherness of Husain Tekri as an explicitly, exclusively Muslim place, the anonymity of *dargah* culture in general, and the relatively unstructured character of the major healing rituals particular to *dargah* culture together offer the privacy and autonomy necessary for discovering a meaningful and therefore effective explanation for a pilgrim's suffering.

Works Cited

Assayag, Jackie. 2004. *Au confluence de deux rivières: Musulmans et Hindous dans le sud de l'Inde*. Paris: Presses de l'École Francaise d'Extrême Orient, 1995. Translated by Latika Sahgal as *At the Confluence of Two Rivers: Muslims and Hindus in South India*. Delhi: Manohar.

Bahadur, Om Lata. 1997. *The Book of Hindu Festivals and Ceremonies.* New Delhi: UBS, 1997.

Bellamy, Carla. 2006. "Smoking Is Good for You: Absence, Presence, and the Ecumenical Appeal of Indian Islamic Healing Centers." *International Journal of Hindu Studies* 10: 207–24.

———. 2011. *The Powerful Ephemeral: Everyday Healing in an Ambiguously Islamic Place*. Berkeley: Univ. of California Press.

Bigelow, Anna. 2004. "Sharing Saints, Shrines, and Stories: Practicing Pluralism in North India." PhD diss., Univ. of California, Santa Barbara.

Burman, J. J. Roy. 2002. *Hindu–Muslim Syncretic Shrines and Communities*. New Delhi: Mittal.

Dwyer, Graham. 2003. *The Divine and the Demonic: Supernatural Affliction and Its Treatment in North India*. New York: Routledge Curzon.

Flueckiger, Joyce Burkhalter. 2006. *In Amma's Healing Room: Islam, Gender, and Religious Identities in South India*. Bloomington: Indiana Univ. Press.

Gottschalk, Peter. 2000. *Beyond Hindu and Muslim*. New York: Oxford Univ. Press.

Jackson, Paul, S.J. 1989. "Perceptions of the *Dargah*s of Patna." In *Muslim Shrines in India: Their Character, History, and Significance*, edited by Christian Troll, 98–111. New Delhi: Oxford Univ. Press.

Kakar, Sudhir. 1982. *Shamans, Mystics, and Doctors: A Psychological Inquiry into India and Its Healing Traditions*. New York: Knopf.

Khan, Dominique-Sila. 2002. "The Graves of History and the Metaphor of the Hidden Pir." In *Culture, Communities, and Change*, edited by Varsha Joshi, 154–72. Jaipur, India: Institute of Rajasthan Studies, Rawat.

Korom, Frank J. 2003. *Hosay Trinidad: Muharram Performances in an Indo-Caribbean Diaspora*. Philadelphia: Univ. of Pennsylvania Press.

Lambek, Michael. 1981. *Human Spirits: A Cultural Account of Trance in Mayotte*. Cambridge: Cambridge Univ. Press.

Lelyveld, David. 1978. *Aligarh's First Generation: Muslim Solidarity in British India*. Princeton, NJ: Princeton Univ. Press.

Mayaram, Shail. 1999. "Spirit Possession: Reframing Discourses of the Self and the Other." In *La possession en Asie du Sud: Parole, corps, territoire* (Possession in South Asia: Speech, Body, Territory), edited by Jackie Assayag and Gilles Tarabout, 101–32. Paris: Editions de l'École des Hautes Études en Sciences Sociales.

Nabokov, Isabelle. 2000. *Religion Against the Self: An Ethnography of Tamil Rituals*. New York: Oxford Univ. Press.

Pakaslahti, Antti. 1998. "Family-Centered Treatment of Mental Health Problems at the Balaji Temple in Rajasthan." In *Changing Patterns of Family and Kinship in South Asia*, edited by Asko Parpola and Sirpa Tenhunen, 129–66. Studia Orientalia no. 84. Ann Arbor, MI: American Oriental Society.

Platts, John T. 2000. *A Dictionary of Urdū, Classical Hindi, and English*. New Delhi: Munshiram Manoharlal.

Stewart, Tony. 2004. *Fabulous Females and Peerless Pirs: Tales of Mad Adventure in Old Bengal*. New York: Oxford Univ. Press.

Van der Veer, Peter. 1992. "Playing or Praying: A Sufi Saint's Day in Surat." *Journal of Asian Studies* 51, no. 3 (August): 545–64.

3

≈

Vavar Swami

A Hindu–Muslim Saint of Kerala

DOMINIQUE-SILA KHAN

THROUGH CAREFUL SCRUTINY of colonial and postcolonial history, one can grasp the complex process by which clear-cut communal identities have gradually emerged in South Asia. Recent research shows how the earlier permeability of religious boundaries tends to be replaced by an increasingly sharp divide between Hindu, Muslim, and Christian communities.[1] The division along regional and caste lines is nowadays often felt to be less important than the sometimes aggressive assertion of religious identities. Hinduism as a single religion is a relatively recent construct that hardly predates the nineteenth century and is largely the result of missionary, Orientalist, and colonial activities (Oddie 2006). Although the legal definition of "Hindu" reflects the difficulties in defining a multifaceted religious phenomenon, it remains one of those taken-for-granted categories that tend to persist and are indiscriminately used, often out of context. And the diversity of Islam has generally been underestimated. The beliefs and practices of its different sects not only diverge but are at times totally opposed to each other. The polarization of Hindu and Muslim communities perceived as two monolithic and hostile blocs is thus a comparatively new phenomenon.

1. An overview of this issue can be found in Khan 2004.

In spite of this polarization, another remarkable fact is the persistence of shared spaces, shared beliefs and practices, and what seems an almost irresistible urge to negotiate or even trespass the newly defined boundaries. In this essay, I have chosen to study the case of Vavar Swami, a sacred figure of Kerala, a southwestern state in India.

During the past two or three decades, Sabarimala—located in the mountainous district of Idukki in Kerala—has grown into one of the largest pilgrimage centers of South India. Each year during the auspicious forty-one-day period known as *mandalam*, numerous devotees originating from various regions of South India flock to the shrine dedicated to the local deity, Ayyappa. At present, their number may well be higher than one hundred thousand. The so-called universal aspect of the tradition has often been stressed; for instance, the fact that people belonging to all castes and creeds may be initiated into the cult and perform the pilgrimage to Sabarimala. All these pilgrims, regardless of their religious affiliation, are referred to as "Ayyappas."

Much has been written about the different aspects of the Sabarimala tradition, a fascinating subject for historians of religions and social anthropologists. But it is primarily Ayyappa himself who has been the focus of these studies. Little or no attention has been paid to another sacred figure who plays a prominent part in the cult—the Muslim saint Vavar, often characteristically referred to as "Vavar Swami," where "Swami" in the South Indian tradition is not only a title for holy men, but also a reference to a male deity. Although Vavar is inevitably mentioned in the legends associated with Ayyappa and has his own shrine at the foot of the temple itself, no attempts have been made to analyze his changing role and position within the living tradition.

Ayyappa and Vavar in Legend and Song

Before I examine the data from my field research, it is necessary to briefly go through the currently available scholarly and hagiographic literature and summarize the legends and narratives that surround Ayyappa and Vavar (Acarya Srimad Hariswami 2002; Kjaerholm 1990; Sekar 1992; Thomas 1973; Vaidyanathan 1978). It must be specified here that Ayyappa has two different "personalities": he is described both as the incarnation of a Brahmanical god (with reference to classical mythology) and as a regional hero. Some folk songs refer exclusively to the former and some to the latter. On the one hand, as a hero, Ayyappa is said to have been the son of a chieftain who ruled over a principality called Pandalam. In his youth, Ayyappa fought the warrior-brigand Udayanan and destroyed his fortress (Sikand 2003, 27–28). On the other hand, in his divine aspect Ayyappa is regarded as an incarnation of Hariharaputra, the son of Shiva and Mohini (the female form of Vishnu), as described in the Sanskrit Brahmanical mythology. According to the local tradition, Shiva and Mohini's son was made to descend to earth to fight the demoness Mahishi.

Now, there is a Malayali legend that establishes a link between these two aspects of Ayyappa: Hariharaputra manifested himself in a forest of Kerala in the form of a child. The rulers of Pandalam, who did not have a son, found the abandoned baby boy and decided to adopt him. If we consider this legend as whole, the first part of Ayyappa's life (his fight with Mahishi) looks like a local Puranic story, whereas the second part (the fight with Udayanan) has all the characteristics of a Malayali heroic ballad.

However, even if both aspects of Ayyappa's personality are made to fit together into a kind of collage, they can easily be distinguished from each other. Vavar characteristically appears only in the stories where Ayyappa is regarded as a local, historical hero. These stories are oral accounts transmitted mainly through folk songs that clearly belong to the Kerala tradition of worshipping and describing the life of heroic warriors. They can be compared to the northern Malayalam ballads sometimes linked to the ritual dance-drama called "Teyyam" or the martial art of Kalarippayattu. By showing how a number of local warriors (too obscure to be mentioned in court chronicles) became in popular imagination symbols of Kerala's regional identity, Philip Zarrilli helps us to understand the value of this type of oral tradition. Before the advent of larger kingdoms in the eighteenth century, Kerala's medieval society was characterized by constant warfare among petty principalities, and disputes were often resolved by duels (1998, 42–55).

There is reason to believe that in this case, as in many other national and regional traditions, real characters were gradually transformed into semidivine heroes or deities. In this way and considering the absence of written documents or inscriptions, the "historical" Vavar who is at the origin of the legend is of less importance than what the "mythical" Vavar has come to mean and symbolize for those who worship him. The same can be said of Ayyappa.

The episode of Ayyappa's legend that is most often cited by priests and devotees and is described in some folk songs relates to his first encounter with Vavar. On Ayyappa's way to the forest, where he had been sent to fetch tiger's milk as a remedy for the queen, the young prince met Vavar and defeated him in a duel. This duel is described in a song referred to as "Vavarankam." Vavar afterward became his friend and faithful lieutenant. According to P. T. Thomas, "Vavar and his men lived in boats and plundered those who came that way on trade, and also those who lived in the coastal regions of the kingdom of Kayamkulam. . . . Since Vavar distributed the major portion of his plundered goods among his followers and the poor people, he had a large number of followers. His activities centered at the ports of Kayamkulam and Karunagapally" (1973, 11).[2]

Accounts taken from the folk songs connected with Vavar portray him as a dangerous pirate.[3] According to K. R. Vaidyanathan, "In those days attacks from the sea by pirates were common. They came under the pretext of trading in salt but once ashore indulged in looting. They were led by a powerful Muslim from Arabia named Vavar who was skilled in military art and well-versed in *mantras*" (1978, 39). The same author writes:

> There are many legends about Vavar and his association with Ayyappa. Some believe he was a Muslim saint from Arab countries who came to India to spread the religion among the people. According to a folk song on Vavar, he was the son of one Alitkutti and Pathumma. He was skilled in the use of arms. He came as a pirate in a ship to loot and plunder. During his encounter with Ayyappa who came mounted on an elephant,

2. The author does not give more details about his activities. Kayamkulam is located in the present Alapuzha (Alleppey) District of Kerala; Karunagapally is near Kollam (Quilon). Both places are part of the backwater network and had once been important from a commercial and strategic viewpoint.

3. Among these folk songs, one should mention "Vavarnakam," portraying the duel between Ayyappa and Vavar, and "Vavar Mahatmiyam."

> Vavar was defeated and subdued by Ayyappa. Ever since, Vavar became a close associate of Ayyappa and helped him in his mountain war against robbers and in defeating the enemies. (116)

Similarly, B. Keralavarma writes, "In those days piracy was common. There was news that an Arab sea-robber Vawar [*sic*] was going to land somewhere near Karunagapally. . . . Vavar's occupation was salt-trade and sea-robbing" (2001, 35).

Although the term *pirate* does evoke a sea robber engaged in illegal and violent activities, one must take into consideration the historical context in order to understand what may be the precise meaning of this word. Piracy, in those times, as is confirmed by various documents from the colonial period, was an integral part of commercial activities, even when peace treaties were concluded. For example, when the Zamorin (the ruler of Calicut) made peace with the Portuguese, the Malabar seamen (the Zamorin's allies) continued to prey upon the shipping and trade of the Portuguese, and the latter responded with similar piratical activities (Kunju 1989, 53–57). All these "unofficial" wars on the sea may have indeed looked like piracy. Ralph Finch, who was in Cochin in 1589, declared that those who worked for the king of Calicut went to sea to "rob and steal." He wrote, "Their chief captain is Cogi Ali [Kunhali] . . . they do much harm on that coast" (quoted in Kunju 1989, 57).

In fact, Vavar may have played, albeit on a much smaller scale, a similar role to that of the Kunhali Marakkars to whom Finch alludes in his writings. Between 1507 and 1600, the Kunhali Marakkars were the Muslim commanders of the Hindu ruler of Calicut in charge of the Zamorin's fleet. Proficient in sea warfare, they were dreaded by the Portuguese: "During the hundred years of war with the Portuguese, this family produced a succession of four remarkable sea captains, whose prowess makes the name of 'Malabar Pirates' resound still in history" (Menon 1999, 115).

Assuming that Vavar had become a "commander" for Ayyappa in the latter's warfare with rival local chieftains, one still has to consider the period during which they lived. Owing to the absence of historical documents, one can rely only on some sacred texts and folk songs, which, as usual, give a much greater antiquity to the tradition than it probably has.

Some claim that Ayyappa had "taken incarnation" eight hundred years ago, whereas others assign him to the eighth century.

Another complication arises from the fact that, as I have explained, the Ayyappa tradition rests on two different, even opposed, types of legends that seem to have been artificially mixed and assembled into a kind of collage. Because this phenomenon is frequently observed with myths and beliefs that originated in different cultures or periods, it tends to give a rather confused picture. On the one hand, Ayyappa is portrayed as an incarnation of the Brahmanical deity Hariharaputra, also known as Dharmasastha, who is the son of Shiva and Vishnu in his Mohini incarnation; on the other hand, he appears as a local hero connected with a much later period of history. The perception varies according to the text referred to. For instance, the *Sreebhutnatha Purana* stresses the former aspect, whereas the folk songs in Malayalam describe the prowess of a young warrior who lived in the Pandala kingdom.

According to various legendary accounts, the Pandala kingdom was ruled by a branch of the celebrated Pandya kings of Madurai. It extended from what was later to be known as Travancore (Malayalam, Thiruvidenkkur) up to Tenkasi in modern Tamil Nadu. At a time when anarchy was prevalent, Ayyappa defeated the dangerous Udayanan, who had built a few fortresses in the region. After his victory, he included in the Pandala kingdom the region stretching from Erumeli to Sabarimala, which are at present the two main centers of the Ayyappa and Vavar cults. In his battles, he was assisted not only by Vavar, but also by Kadutha, a warrior who, quite interestingly, belonged to the once polluting Ezhava (toddy-tapper) caste.[4] This hero is now worshipped along with Ayyappa and Vavar as "Kadutha Swami." Also of interest here is the fact the region of Erumeli was the center of a brisk trade and that many battles were motivated by the desire to control such centers.

4. The Ezhavas, also known as Tiyyas or Chovans, were considered the "purest" of the former untouchable communities of South India. They are not included in the official list of "Scheduled Castes" but are placed in the category "Other Backward Classes." See Iyer [1909] 1981, 277–341.

The absence of written documents should not surprise us. Before the colonial period, very little is known of the checkered history of the numerous kingdoms and principalities of what is now Kerala. Even before the time of Martanda Varma, the king and maker of modern Travancore (Thiruvidenkur) who ruled between 1729 and 1758, much of the country's history remains shrouded in obscurity. The historical background of the Ayyappa tradition is therefore open to conjecture. This does not prevent the legendary accounts from conveying a particular atmosphere that seems to fit roughly into the medieval period prior to the advent of the British, one characterized by frequent warfare between the petty chieftains of the numerous local kingdoms and the importance of commerce. At this time, the pepper trade was of particular commercial significance and frequently associated with the figure of Vavar and other Muslim saints of Kerala.

Vavar Swami: A Hindu Deity?

In the eyes of many Hindu devotees who have preserved the tradition of worshipping Vavar before embarking on the pilgrim's route to Sabarimala, the Muslim warrior-saint surrendered his life to the service of Ayyappa. According to one version of the legend, Vavar even expressed his wish to "join Hinduism" (Thomas 1973, 61–62). His master, however, refused, arguing that all religions were paths to the same goal and that conversion was not necessary. The anachronism—the very idea of converting to one single religion that would be called Hinduism—is of course revealing.[5] If it does not tell us anything about the historical context of the Ayyappa–Vavar episode, it at least conveys the message of "universalism" that is officially proclaimed by the Ayyappa Seva Sangham, the largest organization in charge of the Sabarimala pilgrimage (Jaffrelot 1994; Thomas 1973, 62).[6] In the latter version, Vavar, although important, is only secondary to Ayyappa as his faithful "lieutenant" and disciple.

5. On the issue of conversions, see Robinson and Clarke 2003.

6. Ayyappa Seva Sangham encourages conversions to Hinduism, especially among the former untouchable groups. This issue is an important one that deserves further examination.

This particular perception is in conformity with what I observed in the Hindu context during my field research in Kerala. Vavar appears, together with Kadutha, as a guardian deity. First of all, his most important shrine is located at the foot of the Ayyappa temple at Sabarimala, and devotees are supposed to stop there before climbing the eighteen steps that lead to the sanctum dedicated to the main deity. Yoginder Sikand describes the shrine as follows: "a long structure shaped like a grave built under a tin roof, draped with a green cloth embossed with the Islamic insignia of the crescent and star, and a rusted sword placed across it. Outside, a board in Malayalam and English announced the shrine of 'Vavar Swami'" (2003, 34). The presence here of a Muslim shrine outside a Hindu temple complex is actually far from being an exception. There are numerous examples throughout India (Khan 2003, 21–22, and 2004).

Quite surprisingly, no one seems to know when and where Vavar died, nor is there any mention of his grave. None of the Vavar sacred sites I describe here (including the shrine at Sabarimala, which looks like a grave) is said to contain his mortal remains. In addition to his presence at the foot of the main Ayyappa temple that constitutes the final destination of devotees on the Sabarimala pilgrimage, the saint appears in other contexts as a guardian deity for Ayyappa. Although his Muslim character is affirmed through his installation in sacred structures called *palli*s (the Malayalam word for non-Hindu shrines, applying to Muslim, Christian, and Jewish sacred places), where he is represented aniconically, he is in various ways incorporated smoothly into Hindu contexts. Here I reflect on the meaning of these structures by examining a side shrine and two *palli*s dedicated to Vavar.

The popular belief is that one has first to seek the Muslim saint's permission before embarking on the forest trek to Sabarimala. At Erumeli, just opposite the grand mosque that has been dedicated to him, there is an interesting side shrine to Ayyappa. Erumeli is located in the Kottayam District and is the starting point for the forty-eight mile trek to Sabarimala and a major stop for the pilgrims (if the pilgrim chooses another shorter track, he can now travel by bus from Erumeli up to a village called Pampa). At Erumeli, the small Petta Sree Dharmasasta Temple has been erected at the spot where Ayyappa is believed to have stayed for some time while in Erumeli. On the top of the gate is an image of the god mounted on a tiger. Two side shrines protected by iron gates are dedicated to Vavar and Kadutha Swami. In the side shrine on the left, one can see a green drapery with an embroidered star and crescent hanging under a *yali*-shaped *mandorla* (an ornamental arch crowned by a griffin) and a sword lying on the floor. An inscription reads "Vavaru Swami." In the shrine on the right, the recess contains the same decorative arch, but the drapery is red and has a statue representing a warrior holding a mace and a sword, "Kadutta Swami," as indicated in white letters above the chapel. The shrine's religious affiliation is stressed by the presence of the sacred syllable *Om* inscribed in a Sri Yantra (a sacred geometric diagram) crowned by a conch in the middle part of the gate. The location of both sacred figures makes it clear that Vavar and Kadutha are the guardians of Ayyappa's shrine. In this case, Vavar plays the same role as any village or folk deity (for example, Hanuman and Bhairava for Shiva) whose image has been installed at the entrance of a temple. The word *Swami*, frequently added to Vavar's name, also testifies to the integration of this sacred figure into the Hindu pantheon. However, in this integration one of the main principles of Islam—the ban on image worship—has been respected, and Vavar is represented only by nonanthropomorphic symbols.

Another, much more recent temple to Ayyappa represents an interesting and original case: the Chelumkunnam Kshetram is located in the village Elavally in the Thrissur District. Here, an older shrine was rebuilt by a member of the Ezhava caste, Muthappan, a few years ago and has been left unfinished to this day. The land was donated by the nearby K. Subrahmanian Memorial Ayurveda Hospital, and the funds collected from various devotees. This temple to Ayyappa has been renovated in the traditional Kerala style on the site of the older structure. It is surrounded as usual by a compound wall. Outside the compound, a few smaller subsidiary shrines have been built. Among them are shrines to Karimala Swami and Kochkadutta Swami.[7] Next to them, facing west, is the tiny Vavar

7. Karimala Swamy and Kochkatdutta Swami: the idols of both folk deities are to be found at Karimala, one of the three major mounts to be climbed on the "forest path" that

"mosque" (*Vavar palli*), the most recent of all the structures. Just behind the temple and the Vavar shrine is a kind of semifinished *pandal* (temporary structure used for religious ceremony, weddings, and so on) containing the tomb of Muthappan, the Ezhava who caused the sacred complex to be built. The "correct" orientation of the Vavar shrine, which points to the *qibla* (the direction of Mecca), is curiously stressed by the particular position of Muthappan's tomb; although the tomb is supposed to be a *samadhi* (a Hindu funeral structure), it has the shape of a Muslim grave (*kabr*) and is accordingly oriented north–south, as is the custom in South Asia. In Kerala, however, this orientation seems to be typical for many low-caste communities (Thurston 1975, 144). The grave of Muthappan is venerated along with the other subsidiary shrines, and offerings of fowls and alcohol are regularly made to the Ezhava saint.

Vavar's shrine at Elavally is often referred to as a *palli*. Although the usual Malayalam word for a mosque is *Muslim palli* (to distinguish it from Christian and Jewish *pallis*), the structure at Elavally is not a mosque in the sense that it is not meant for the ritual prayers. Vavar's "mosque" is a kind of memorial shrine. Inside, the usual oil lamp and a green drapery have been installed. Outside, the small square structure is crowned by the star and crescent, and a board reads, "Vavar Swami Kshetram," Temple to Vavar Swami. The use of the word *kshetram*—which apparently cannot refer to a mosque, a Muslim tomb-shrine (Malayalam, *jaram*), or a church—obviously points to the fact that Vavar in this context is being treated like a Hindu deity, as in the previous examples.

However, it is necessary to add that in spite of his integration into the local Hindu pantheon, Vavar's original religious affiliation, far from being denied, is asserted and even stressed. We have seen that he is represented only by symbols (such as the sword). The green color of the drapery as well the star and crescent are evident markers of his religious identity. This phenomenon should be distinguished from the cases where Muslim sacred figures are not only "appropriated," but also "Hinduized" (Khan 2003, 2004).

---

leads from Erumeli to Sabarimala. According to the legend, Karimala was one of the fortresses built by Ayyappa's main enemy, the chieftain named Udayanan.

The presence of a "Vavar Kshetram" within an Ayyappa temple complex, such as the main Vavar *palli* at Sabarimala and the side shrine of Erumeli, is an interesting phenomenon. It should be distinguished from other separate, independent structures dedicated to Vavar, such as the big mosque of Erumeli or a small informal *palli* located at the beginning of the forest path that leads to Sabarimala: "a Muslim 'shrine' for Vavar where a fakir collected offerings of money" (Kjaerholm 1984, 81). These independent structures seem to have a different meaning: they tell us that the Muslim worshippers of Vavar wish to claim the saint as their own, whereas the Hindus tend to transform him, as we have seen, into a guardian-deity. However, based on my observations at numerous Ayyappa temples, it seems that Ayyappa sacred complexes, which comprise a number of subsidiary shrines, do not usually include a Vavar *palli.* In short, the Erumeli side shrine, the Vavar *palli* of Sabarimala, and the Chelumkunnam Kshetram of Elavally may be exceptions.

Another interesting fact: when I asked a Brahmin priest to tell me the exact location of the Chelumkunnam Kshetram, explaining that the temple to Ayyappa also had a shrine to Vavar, he denied the existence of such a place and instead directed me to a mosque that had nothing to do with Vavar. The Brahmin priest obviously meant that a Vavar *palli,* being a Muslim shrine, had nothing to do with a Hindu temple: it was entirely a Muslim affair.

The fact that this temple was founded by low-caste Hindus may have something to do with the presence of a Vavar shrine within the Chelumkunnam complex. In 1997, during the annual festival when the image of Ayyappa was being taken on the back of a temple elephant, the animal went mad and killed two persons. The astrologer interpreted the event as follows: Vavar Swami was angry not to be worshipped in this temple where so many deities had their separate shrines. One might wonder why the same thing did not happen in other Ayyappa temples. It seems that most Ayyappa temples—at least those I visited—were built by high-caste people and had Brahmin priests. Having been built by a low-caste Ezhava devotee, the Chelumkunnam shrine was, so to say, a "low-caste affair." Moreover, Nayars, not Brahmins, conduct the *puja* (worship ritual).[8] Indeed, to illustrate how caste location inflects the style of worship at any shrine, a useful comparison can be made between the temples to the goddess Bhagavati handled by the high-caste groups and those in the hands of the Ezhavas. In the latter, liquor and meat are usually offered to fierce deities. In the former, higher castes engage in ritual performing arts such as the *muttiyettu*—something the lower castes are forbidden to do. Rather, lower castes tend to perform as oracles (*veliccapptus*) and priests in their own shrines.[9] In the Ayyappa shrines, too, one sees dramatic differences in the style of worship offered to a deity in shrines managed by different caste groups.

Let us now consider a different aspect of Vavar's personality as perceived by those who have preserved his tradition.

Vavar: A Muslim Saint?

Although there are no written documents to sustain their claims, about a hundred Mapilla Muslims of Kerala connect themselves with Vavar's lineage. By listening to their narratives, one can gain some insight into what can be referred to as their collective memory. According to Peter Gottschalk, "[N]arratives regarding the past offer a particularly useful tool of examination because by their very nature they often include important

8. Although theoretically classified as Shudras (the fourth ritual category or *varna*) and so supposedly excluded from the Brahmanical initiation that makes them *dvijas* or "twice born," the Nayars, who are divided into various groups for different statuses, are practically treated as Kshatriyas, or noble warriors. However, unlike the Rajputs of North India, they sometimes act as intermediaries between low- and high-caste groups.

9. The famous Bhagavathi Kshetram of Kodungaloor, which is a temple managed by Ezhava priests, has special rituals. See Caldwell 1999, 29–34. Somewhat ironically, the famous Kerala saint and reformer Narayana Guru demonstrated the difference between temples with the same dedication but managed by different caste groups. Brahmins were deeply shocked and objected when he consecrated a Shiva temple at Aruvippuram, about forty kilometers south of Trivandrum: "In a caste-ruled society an *avarna* Hindu, an untouchable, had performed the installation of a deity defying all codes and norms." When questioned by a Brahmin scholar, the guru replied: "This is not a Brahmin Shiva, this is an Ezhava Shiva" (Sivadas and Rao 2002, 25).

ingredients for identity: references to the present community in time and space" (2001, 69). Gottschalk explains that those who communicate these narratives obviously believe that the stories depict actual events of their past. From an academic viewpoint, the analyst may have a different opinion, but it is only by suspending his judgment as to the veracity of the stories that he will be able concentrate on the subtleties of myth. These subtleties allow us to consider the role played by the narratives in a particular society. As Gottschalk explains, group memory plays an essentially social role, allowing scholars to sidestep "the multiple and contentious understandings of *history* and *myth*" (2001, 72, emphasis in original).

However, narratives constituting collective memory are not immutable because they always may be recast to suit the need of the present community or of some of its members (Gottschalk 2001, 72, 79). If we keep this distinction in mind, Vavar's oral tradition may not tell us about "actual" historical events, but it certainly reflects the various and changing concerns of the narrators and their community.

The main representative of the Vavar tradition as transmitted by Muslims is Dr. Abdul Rahman. He claims to be Vavar's direct descendent and is known as "Haji Vavaru Musaliar" (where "Haji" is a title for one who has completed the hajj pilgrimage to Mecca, "Vavaru" obviously connotes his descent from the saint Vavar, and "Musaliar" refers to a religious teacher and elder in Mapilla communities).[10] In March 2004, I went to meet him at his residence, located in a village on the road to Erumeli. Abdul Rahman Musaliar told me that he was the thirteenth descendent of Vavar. As such, he performs certain rituals, particularly during the *mandala* period when the Ayyappa pilgrimage takes place. He is the Muslim priest of the Vavar shrine at Sabarimala and is ritually entitled to place the holy bundle known as *irumudi kettu* on pilgrims' heads, while a Hindu priest ties it. Each year he lends to the shrine Vavar's holy sword inherited from his ancestors.

According to Abdul Rahman, his ancestor was far from being the fierce sea robber depicted in the legends and folk songs associated with

10. Dr. Rahman works as a physician in a local dispensary.

Ayyappa. He was instead a holy man and may even have been a true *thangal* (the Malayalam word for "sayyid," a direct descendent of the Prophet's family). And neither was he subordinate to Ayyappa; the two were friends and worked on an equal footing to establish peace in the troubled area corresponding to the erstwhile Pandala kingdom. Both of them were saints and yogis, and the practice of yoga and meditation had endowed them with special powers, which the naive populace understood as miracles.

Abdul Rahman had traveled extensively in the past and continued to do so. He had visited Hindu pilgrimage centers such as Rameswaram and Tirupati in the South as well as "Kashi"—that is to say, the present Varanasi. But he had also gone to Mecca and Medina as well as to the famous Indian Sufi shrine in Ajmer Sharif, Rajasthan. For him, Vavar was an authentic Sufi and, as such, was concerned with peace and what we today call "communal harmony," hence his association with the Hindu chieftain Ayyappa. The latter, in the *musaliar*'s eyes, was not a divine incarnation, but a saint and a yogi. Regarding himself as the legitimate descendent of Vavar, Haji Abdul Rahman Musaliar pursued the same goal.

Later, on his recommendation, I met his cousin, Haji Abdul Karim Musaliar, at Erumeli, whom Abdul Rahman claimed was more knowledgeable than himself. Abdul Karim, the Erumeli *musaliar,* is the imam of the Vavar *palli,* which was entirely rebuilt in a grand Indo-Persian style about ten years ago. In contrast to the other *palli* shrines described earlier, this one is not a memorial monument, but a "regular" mosque meant for the Muslim ritual prayers. However, the mosque is, in a very atypical fashion, regularly host to intense rituals by entranced Ayyappa devotees. As mentioned previously, Erumeli constitutes an important stop on the Ayyappan pilgrimage. It is the town from which most pilgrims embark directly on their forty-eight mile walk through the forest to the main Ayyappan temple in Sabarimala. It is customary for the pilgrims to stop first at the Vavar mosque in Erumeli when they begin their ritual, ecstatic dance known as *petta thullal.* They break coconuts in a special pit inside the mosque and make offerings of pepper, turmeric, rice, sandal, and incense to Vavar. The performance of rituals by Hindus in a mosque is highly unusual because this sacred space is normally reserved for Muslims and for the performance of Islamic prayers. The same activities would not be unusual in Muslim tomb shrines or relic shrines (*jaram, dargah*), so it is at least possible that, prior to the reconstruction, the Vavar *palli* may have been a *dargah*.

Abdul Karim, like his cousin, asserted that Vavar was an authentic Muslim saint, but not, he corrected, a sayyid. He was a *wali*, "a friend of God" according to the Sufi terminology. Having come from northeastern Persia during the thirteenth century, he was associated with Sheikh Fariduddin, a famous saint who has an important shrine about twenty kilometers from Cochin, at Kanjiramattam. According to the Erumeli *musaliar*, Vavar and Farid were close friends and were also connected to another important Sufi of Kerala, Pir Muhammad, who has his main shrine in present Tamil Nadu.

According to Abdul Karim, Vavar obtained ultimate knowledge at the shrine of Fariduddin at Kanjiramattam (see also Kunju 1989, 195). To this day, many Ayyappa pilgrims come to visit Fariduddin's shrine after returning from Sabarimala. Another intriguing fact is that this shrine's annual festival falls on a fixed date (a rare occurrence), January 14, which is both the last day of the Sabarimala *mandalam* and *makar sankranti*. On this sacred day, according to tradition, one may see from the top of a mountain a supernatural light known as *makar vilakku*, the "light of the Capricorn."[11]

During my visit to the Kanjiramattam shrine, I was told that Shaikh Fariduddin was none other than the celebrated Sufi from northern India who has his tomb at Pakpattan (modern Pakistan) and is also popularly known as "Shakkarganj." According to one of my informants, who claimed to have done research on the oral tradition of Shaikh Fariduddin in Kerala, the saint had come to this part of India in order to bring his message of peace and unity and to "civilize" the local population (Hassankutty 2001).

However, Farid himself probably never came to Kerala, and the *dargahs* dedicated to him in Malabar may have been built by disciples in the

11. *Makar sankranti*, the day when the sun is supposed to enter the zodiac sign of the Capricorn, is celebrated in different ways throughout India.

later sixteenth and seventeenth century. Therefore, if Kanjiramattam was built during that later period, and if Vavar indeed visited the shrine, it would enable us to situate the Ayyappa oral tradition that portrays him as a warrior during that period, which coincides with the Portuguese and Dutch presence in Kerala. However, Abdul Rahman Musaliar's claim to be the thirteenth descendent of the saint would also—rightly or wrongly—point to a much later period (eighteenth or nineteenth century) for Ayyappa. Unless the "actual" events are recent, this discrepancy certainly casts some doubt on the lineage's historical continuity. But we should, as Gottschalk has it, once more "suspend the analyst's judgment . . . and acknowledge the narrator's perspective" (2001, 72). In this way, we can fully perceive the meaning of the different oral traditions that see Vavar as a Muslim saint.

Sanskritizing the Tradition

In order to understand the meaning of Vavar's cult within the Ayyappa tradition, one must consider it in its historical perspective. Although this is far from easy owing to the lack of written documents, it is possible to reconstruct at least a part of it. First of all, it is necessary to stress that the popularity of the Sabarimala pilgrimage is a very recent phenomenon. Before independence, the cult was confined to certain parts of the former states Travancore and Cochin. According to P. T. Thomas, with the extension the Ayyappa Seva Sangham's activities, it spread to other parts of Kerala (1973, 50). Lars Kjaerholm (1984), however, explains how it also became popular in Tamil Nadu in the past four or five decades.

I also suggest that the tradition, apart from the fact that it was a purely local one, was located on the margins of the Brahmanical culture, as indicated by the importance of low-caste and tribal deities and of the Muslim warrior-saint Vavar in the cult. We have also seen that it was an Ezhava who built the "Vavar Kshetram" in the Ayyappa sacred complex of Elavally (the Chelumkunnam Kshetram), and we must remember at this juncture that Kadutha Swami, who plays an important part in the cult, was also an Ezhava warrior. The association of a Muslim sacred figure with a low-caste one is a configuration that I have encountered many times during my field research in North India.

One can also observe that during the past decades, with the increasing popularity of the Sabarimala pilgrimage, the tradition has gradually been Sanskritized. When upper-caste pilgrims joined the cult, its presumably low-caste or "non-Hindu" elements became embarrassing to some of them. Although the tendency toward Sanskritization or Brahmanization of Ayyappa's cult was part of a broader movement (as observed in many other Indian traditions), the boldest initiatives came from various right-wing reformist organizations such as the Vishwa Hindu Parishad (VHP, World Hindu Committee) (Jaffrelot 1996, 196–99). The process may have started in the following way: the authors gave the folk or tribal elements and the popular rituals and customs a highly symbolical, spiritual meaning in conformity with the Brahmanical treatises. An abundant literature in Malayalam, Tamil, and English was published on the subject and made available in various bookstores as well as at the main pilgrimage places. For example, the eighteen steps of the sacred staircase that lead to Ayyappa's sanctum at Sabarimala were said to correspond to different chakras and *nadis* (subtle centers and nerves) of the body according to the philosophy of Hatha Yoga. Similarly, the *irumudi kettu* (the ritual double-knotted bundle worn by the pilgrims) represented the desire to renounce (*tyaga*) the results of one's actions (*karmaphala*) (Acarya Srimad Hariswami 2002, 35, 78–83). These reinterpretations were in part successful owing to the fact that most Malayalis can read—at least in their mother tongue. What we now refer to as Hinduism has shaped itself into a coherent religious tradition by Sanskritizing, which also meant at times "spiritualizing," the folk traditions.

However, although the authors of some of these pamphlets were satisfied with the symbolical and philosophical explanation of "spurious" rituals, such as the ecstatic, semiorgiastic *petta thullal*, others, being activists of the VHP or of similar organizations, wished to ban these rituals altogether. If Vavar was heartily accepted by some as a faithful disciple of Ayyappa, he was firmly rejected by others.

In the latter group, VHP activists did not hesitate to remove from their proposed list of the 108 mantras connected with the Sabarimala tradition the sacred formulas invoking Vavar, such as "Vawaru Swamiye Saranamaiyppa" and "Erumeli Palliyae Saranamaiyappa." Moreover, the same activists explained away the historicity of the Muslim figure of Vavar.

For instance, one of them claims that the cult of Vavar emerged merely from popular imagination and is the result of the distortion of real facts (Acarya Srimad Hariswami 2002, 113–15). Far from being a Muslim hero, he was one of Shiva's assistants, or *bhutaganas*, mentioned under the name "Vaparu" in the Sanskrit treatises on Dharmasasthra. Similarly, Kadutha Swami was not a Ezhava warrior, but another *bhutagana* called "Katusabda." In the same way, this author dismisses a popular theory about the Buddhist origin of the Ayyappa cult, according to P. T. Thomas (Acarya Srimad Hariswami 2002, 26; Thomas 1973, 20–22).

Other less important modifications were made. For example, reformers from the VHP and other similar organizations suggested that the wearing of a black *mundu* (a piece of unstitched cloth tied around the waist) should be rendered obligatory only for those going to Sabarimala for the first time, the "virgin Ayyappas" (*kanni Ayyappa*). Although Ayyappa Seva Sangham, the largest association established to promote Ayyappa's cult and pilgrimage, does not agree with the VHP on other matters related to the cult, it does not say anything against the proposed rule. The VHP made this recommendation because the wearing of black or dark blue garments is generally identified with low-caste and Muslim communities. It similarly told the pilgrims that it was no longer necessary to stop at Vavar's shrine before climbing the eighteen sacred steps.

It is clear that the activists who maintain this view wish to connect the present cult of Ayyappa exclusively with the Hindu Brahmanical tradition, which is why they cling to the texts that deal with Dharmasasthra and tend to neglect the folk songs. They also deny the possibility that Ayyappa's tradition may be rooted in ancient Buddhism, a theory that some associations have adopted for the promotion of Ayyappa's worship—among others, Ayyappa Seva Sangham (Thomas 1973, 20–21). The success of the radical "reformers" of the VHP type, however, is only partial. Popular tradition is not easy to uproot, and the pilgrims find it difficult to give up their old habits.

Conclusion

As I have argued, in the absence of reliable historical documents, collective memory, with its many fluctuations, remains the only source by which we may gain insights into a particular tradition. Narratives and other oral sources associated with a careful survey of the periods of concern can give us some clues about the emergence and evolution of religious phenomenon.

We have seen that in the Ayyappa tradition, Vavar—whenever he is not rejected—is endowed with more than one identity, as when his devotees position him iconographically as a "Hindu" deity as well as a Sufi saint. It is obvious that his integration into Ayyappa's cult as a "Hindu" deity, along with his full acceptance as a Muslim/Sufi saint, permits both Hindus and Muslims and even Christians to worship him without questioning his or their religious affiliations. This is the case at the recently built Vavar "temple" located inside the Chelumkunnam Kshetram of Elavally described earlier. During the annual festival, which takes place on the fourth of the Malayali month of Kumbham, Hindus, Christians, and Muslims flock to the sacred place, where they do not fail to pay obeisance to the Muslim warrior-saint.

In an interesting article about three Christian saints of Kerala, Corinne Dempsey follows Gyanendra Pandey (1993) in warning us that "[d]econtextualized understandings of religion that focus solely on established or projected belief systems and creeds at the expense of less-than-tidy practices forfeit vital complexities and . . . notions of boundaries and identities that are more permeable than rigid" (1999, 175). According to the same authors, such decontextualized, ahistorical constructions with rigid boundaries often generate situations where religious violence is likely to erupt.

Contrary to the artificial constructs of well-intentioned reformers, the Muslim warrior-saint's capacity for negotiating and crossing boundaries symbolizes the religious mind's natural, often unconscious tendency to reject imposed limits and barriers. As a social and collective phenomenon, religion can also be compared to language. Both develop mainly at the level of the unconscious. In the same way as academicians attempt to "control" language through various interventions, reformers try to check, to a certain extent, the organic growth of religion. Both will alternatively reject and integrate a number of elements that have emerged as spontaneous phenomena. In this respect, Vavar Swami's cult has also a highly pragmatic value. Rather than expressing spiritual truths, it stresses the necessity of conviviality. It may also teach us that the permeability of religious boundaries is not entirely a thing of the past.

Works Cited

Acarya Srimad Hariswami. 2002. *The Realities of Ayyappa (a Study)*. Kuttemperoor, India: Yajna Prasadam Pustakakudumnam.

Caldwell, Sarah. 1999. *Oh Terrifying Mother: Sexuality, Violence, and Worship of the Goddess Kali*. New Delhi: Oxford Univ. Press.

Dempsey, Corinne G. 1999. "Lessons in Miracles from Kerala, South India: Stories of Three 'Christian' Saints." *History of Religions* 39, no. 2 (Nov.): 150–76.

Gottschalk, Peter. 2001. *Beyond Hindu and Muslim: Multiple Identity in Narratives from Village India*. New Delhi: Oxford Univ. Press.

Hassankutty, T. A. 2001. *Shaikh Fariduddin jivacharitram*. Kanjiramattom, India: Self-published.

Iyer, Anantha Krishna. [1909] 1981. *The Tribes and Castes of Cochin*. New Delhi: Cosmos.

Jaffrelot, Christophe. 1994. "Les (re)conversions à l'hindouisme (1885–1990): Politisation et diffusion d'une 'invention de la tradition.'" *Archives de Science Sociale des Religions* 87 (July–Sept.): 73–98.

———. 1996. *The Hindu Nationalist Movement in India*. New Delhi: Viking.

Keralavarma, B. 2001. *Swamiyaesaranamayyappa: Lord Ayyappa of Sabarimala, the Legend, History, Pilgrimage, and the Rites*. Kottayam, Kerala: DC Books.

Khan, Dominique-Sila. 2003. *Conversions and Shifting Identities: Ramdev Pir and the Ismailis in Rajasthan*. New Delhi: Manohar.

———. 2004. *Crossing the Threshold: Understanding Religious Identities in South Asia*. London: I. B. Tauris and Institute of Ismaili Studies.

Kjaerholm, Lars. 1984. "Aiyanar, Aiyappan, Continuity, and Change in South Indian Hinduism." *Folk: Dansk Ethnografisk Tidsskrift Kobenhavn* 26: 67–92. At http://www.hindu.dk/1d/ar/Ai-Ai1200.pdf. Accessed July 14, 2011.

———. 1990. "Myth, Pilgrimage, and Fascination in the Aiyappa Cult." In *South Asian Religion and Society*, edited by Asko Parpola and Bent S. Hansen, 121–61. London: Curzon Press.

Kunju, Ibrahim A. P. 1989. *Mapilla Muslims of Kerala: Their History and Culture*. Trivandrum, India: Sandhya.

Menon, Sreedhana A. 1999. *Kerala History and Its Makers*. Madras [Chennai], India: S. Visvanathan.

Oddie, Geoffrey. 2006. *Imagined Hinduism: British Protestant Missionary Constructions of Hinduism, 1793–1900*. New Delhi: Sage.

Pandey, Gyanendra. 1993. "Which of Us Is Hindu?" In *Hindus and Others: The Question of Identity in India Today*, edited by Gyanendra Pandey, 238–73. New Delhi: Viking Press.

Robinson, Rowena, and Sathianathan Clarke, eds. 2003. *Religious Conversions in India: Modes, Motivations, and Meanings*. New Delhi: Oxford Univ. Press.

Sekar, Radhika. 1992. *The Sabarimalai Pilgrimage and Ayyappan Cults*. New Delhi: Motital Banarsidass.

Sikand, Yoginder. 2003. *Sacred Spaces: Exploring Traditions of Shared Faith in India*. New Delhi: Penguin.

Sivadas, Satyabhai, and P. Prabhakara Rao. 2002. *Sree Narayana Guru: The Social Philosopher of Kerala*. Mumbai: Bharatya Vidhya Bhavan.

Thomas, P. T. 1973. *Sabarimalai and Its Sastha*. Bangalore, India: Christian Institute for the Study of Religion and Society.

Thurston, Edgar. 1975. *Ethnographic Notes in Southern India*. Part I. Reprint. New Delhi: Cosmo.

Vaidyanathan, K. R. 1978. *Pilgrimage to Sabari*. Bombay [Mumbai]: Bharatiya Vidya Bhavan.

Zarrilli, Phillip B. 1998. *When the Body Becomes All Eyes: Paradigms, Discourses, and Practices of Power in Kalarippayattu, a South Indian Martial Art*. New Delhi: Oxford Univ. Press.

PART TWO

≈

Porous Boundaries

4

≈

Syncretism and Sin

An Independent Christian Church in Colonial South India

ELIZA F. KENT

ONCE A PEJORATIVE TERM used by missionaries and theologians to refer to the unholy mixture of beliefs and practices from different religious traditions, *syncretism* has of late seen a resurgence in popularity. As Rosalind Shaw and Charles Stewart (1994) argue, syncretism—particularly when redubbed *synergy, hybridity,* or *acculturation*—is now celebrated within some circles as a salutary countermovement to the homogenizing, reifying tendencies of antisyncretic or "fundamentalist" forms of religion. Although religious syncretism is historically more widely encountered than its opposite, it tends to be reviled by those who posit an authentic, pure, core tradition as normative. In South Asia, such "antisyncretist" discourse has a long history. Consider the denunciations of so-called degenerate popular Hinduism by nineteenth-century reformers such as the Arya Samaj and the Brahmo Samaj, who adopted Orientalist versions of the history of religion in India in their renderings of the past. They saw a long downward slide from the glorious days of Vedic purity to the sloppy Puranic mixing and matching of the Kali Yuga. Present-day inheritors of

The author acknowledges, with thanks, permission to quote from the archives of the Church Missionary Society, housed in the Special Collections and Archives of the University of Birmingham.

the nineteenth-century Hindu reform movements, such as the Vishwa Hindu Parishad (World Hindu Committee), similarly worry about the contamination of the purity of the Hindu tradition and the consequent weakening of the Indian nation by various "foreign" forces—notably, Islam, Christianity, and secularism. For their part, nineteenth-century Muslim reformers such as those at the Deoband school in North India also sought to winnow the grain of correct Islamic piety from the chaff of popular saint worship, initiating a "purification" of popular practice that continues to this day.

We are well aware now of the discursive power plays involved in the constitution of such versions of orthodoxy. Awareness of those power dynamics leads many scholars today to celebrate the underdogs who defy elitist constructions of tradition as singular, homogenous, pure, and unsullied. And, indeed, the legacy of imaginative mutual enrichment and tolerance for religious differences evident in multireligious practices throughout South Asia is both impressive and—in these days of seemingly intractable religious conflict—inspiring. One sees, for example, the equalizing force of our shared corporeal fragility at Sufi *dargah*s, saints' tombs, where people from all religious communities come for healing. Surprising varieties of ecumenism can result when the social boundaries between communities are relaxed, as seen in the devotional practices surrounding a Hindu goddess in Manarkad, Kerala, whose festival chariot must be touched by a Christian before it will move (Dempsey 2001, 56). However, close examination of specific synergistic sects reveals that interreligious harmony often comes with its own hegemony. Far from always affirming difference and promoting tolerance, the blurring of religious boundaries can sometimes lead to a heightening of chauvinism and hierarchy.

This essay seeks to explore the sociopolitical dynamics of syncretism by examining the origins of an independent Christian church in nineteenth-century South India whose cosmology and ritual practices exhibit striking combinations of conventional Christian discourse with local non-Christian beliefs and practices. The Yuomayans, a sect founded in 1873 in Mavelikara District (now Kerala), are by no means the only schismatic Protestant sect that arose in India during the British period. English missionary societies' records are filled with tantalizing glimpses of visionaries, prophets, and renegades who troubled the waters for their supervising missionaries when they appropriated the potentially explosive aspects of the Christian message. Although independent African churches have attracted the attention of scholars for decades (see, e.g., Comaroff 1985 and Sundkler 1961), similar movements in India have been largely ignored (for exceptions, see Bayly 1989, 308–12, and Kent 2004, 69–78, 190–96). Yet close investigation of these independent churches yields considerable insight into the sociopolitical dynamics of syncretism in nineteenth-century India.

The syncretic local form of Christianity I examine here was founded by men who had been disciplined by their missionary mentors for straying from the "correct" interpretation of biblical truth. Their response was to develop their own creative form of Christianity that not only incorporated elements from local non-Christian religious traditions but also contained an implicit or explicit critique of their missionary mentors' religion as itself impure, syncretic, and disloyal to "true" and "original" Christianity. I hope to show here that syncretism—both as an accusation leveled by those who speak for the "true" religion and as a variety of religious creativity observable by scholars—is bound up from the beginning in struggles over power and identity. Indeed, *one* of the reasons that syncretism arouses such controversy is that it often exposes past syncretism, thus demonstrating the tenuousness of orthodox constructions of the tradition as pure and unsullied. As I show through the examples here, nineteenth-century Indian converts to Christianity often rediscovered through their own readings of the Bible and church history elements of the tradition that were no longer part of missionaries' active practice of Christianity. Nineteenth-century Indian Christian leaders of independent churches rediscovered and put to new purposes elements of Christianity that had, as it were, gone dormant in British churches, such as glossalalia, messianism, and the purity and pollution laws of the Hebrew Bible. Before I introduce the Yuomayan sect and its charismatic founder, let me define more carefully what I mean by syncretism.

A Defense of *Syncretism*

Syncretism is a notoriously multivalent term used both descriptively and polemically by scholars and theologians of diverse persuasions. Originally coined by the Roman thinker Plutarch (c. 46–127 CE) to describe the strategic banding together of rivals against a common enemy, it began to be associated specifically with religion during the European Renaissance. Erasmus (1469–1536) uses the word in a positive sense to describe how Christian theology had been enriched by its absorption of the wisdom of the Greek classical philosophers, especially Plato and Aristotle. Yet with the breakdown of the Catholic Church's authority as the unrivaled source of religious truth and the resulting proliferation of Protestant sects, the valence of the word *syncretism* switched. By the seventeenth century, it became an accusation leveled against theologians seeking common ground among rival Protestant denominations, whose detractors viewed them as promoting an "entirely unprincipled jumbling together of religions" (Shaw and Stewart 1994, 4). This negative characterization of the process of open religious blending prevailed for a long time, coloring many scholarly studies of movements that blurred the boundaries between religious traditions. For example, in his study of messianic movements in India written shortly after independence, anthropologist Stephen Fuchs glossed the term *syncretism* as "the indiscriminate adoption of various cultural traits of the superior culture by a backward people" (1965, 14). Following the analyses of colonial and postcolonial nativist movements by Kennelm Burridge ([1960] 1970), Bengt Sundkler (1961), Peter Worsley (1968), and others, Fuchs interpreted such borrowing as an attempt on the part of the colonized to locate and tap into the apparently mysterious power of their foreign rulers. But, he writes, "[s]ince these leaders, uneducated as they are, usually fail to understand the true nature of the salient features in the alien culture, and hit on very unessential, though perhaps superficially striking culture traits, their new cult doctrine is hopelessly illogical, contradictory and greatly over-simplified" (1965, 14–15).

Given this checkered history of usage, many scholars advocate abandoning the term *syncretism* altogether because of its association with supposedly clumsy and haphazard efforts to integrate beliefs and practices. In South Asian studies, Tony Stewart and Carl Ernst (2003) have critiqued the concept of syncretism most forcefully. They argue that to the extent that syncretism denotes the amalgamation of beliefs or practices from two or more distinct religious traditions, it is inappropriate to apply it to premodern formations because such a view entails wrongly projecting onto them a distinctly modern notion of "the world's religions" as single, coherent, and discrete formations. Building on this critique, one can add that before the rise of the modern nation-state, what we now confidently call "religion" itself was much more thoroughly bound up with other domains of life, from education and agriculture to the distribution of property and justice (Asad 1993). Stewart and Ernst, however, argue that the term is not just anachronistic; it misleads and distorts even when applied to present-day texts, sects, and movements. The metaphor at the basis of all the newer terms employed to describe syncretism—whether botanical (*hybrid*), chemical (*solution, mixture*), or physical (*amalgam, bricolage*)—suggests that the phenomena in question are impermanent and liable to fall apart when the forces that bring together these intrinsically alien parts subside (2003, 587).

Others have argued that the term should be dropped because it does not really distinguish anything. So-called syncretism, they argue, is simply a ubiquitous and perfectly ordinary aspect of religious change; it is the inevitable result of the transformations, subtle and overt, within religious (or cultural) formations over time as they encounter other formations and take shape in new geographical or historical contexts. As Peter van der Veer writes in an essay on Hindus and Muslims in India, "Syncretism is a term which in comparative religion refers to a process of religious amalgamation, of blending heterogeneous beliefs and practices. As such, it is an aspect of religious interaction over time. This can be seen as such a broad process that indeed every religion is syncretistic, since it constantly draws upon heterogeneous elements to the extent that it is often impossible for historians to unravel what comes from where. One could therefore argue that it is a useless concept" (1994, 208). Although granting that syncretism in this sense is ubiquitous, I want to argue for scholars' retention of the word precisely because so much can be learned about religion's role in the politics of identity formation by looking closely at *how and when syncretism is made visible or invisible*. There are moments when the borrowing that has contributed to the formation of a particular religion is evident and recognized by both adherents and outside scholars (as when some Christians acknowledge that Christianity emerged from Judaism, or Buddhists acknowledge that Buddhism arose from Hinduism), and moments when such borrowing is recognized by scholars or outsiders but is forgotten, not noticed, or possibly even denied by insiders (as when Christians deny scholars' claims about the influence of Mesopotamian cosmogonic myths on the Genesis account of creation, regarding the latter not as an "account" at all, but as the revealed truth about the origins of the world). And there are also instances where the process of amalgamation is so smooth and thorough that, as van der Veer describes, the historical roots of the symbol, belief, or practice in question simply cannot yet be traced by either scholars or adherents (a phenomenon some have sought to distinguish from syncretism as "religious synthesis").

One of the important things that the concept of syncretism reveals is that open religious borrowing in the present often reveals the syncretic nature of earlier layers of religious history, whose importance had been diminished as the tradition's superseded "past." As Shaw and Stewart write, "Syntheses or erasures may become uncontested, reproduced without discursively available intentionality. . . . But if syncretic practices are no longer *consciously* syncretic, should they still be described as such? . . . Even when religious syntheses become part of the taken-for-granted habitus, their composite origins erased from conscious memory, they nevertheless contain the sedimentation of historical experience. As such they may be available for retrieval and rehabilitation at the right historical moment" (1994, 18, emphasis in original). From the historian's point of view, the complex amalgamations of diverse practices and cosmologies that give rise to local traditions do sometimes "fall apart," contrary to Stewart and Ernst's contention, in the sense that different elements are acquired over time and either lose or gain salience depending on the context. This dynamic is particularly evident in the obvious forms of syncretism found in independent Christian churches in India.

Thus, although recognizing that *syncretism* can be a term of reprobation in the power struggles within and between religious communities, I use it in this essay as a heuristic device. By "syncretism," I mean here the mixing and transformation of elements drawn from different religious formations, understood themselves as consisting of practices and beliefs from different sources that develop dynamically over time and across space along a telos-free trajectory. Having noted the dynamic nature of religious traditions, however, we must also recognize their stability. Although the congeries of beliefs and practices that make up a "religion" are dynamic, internally complex, and in conversation with other systems of belief and practice, they are also in a sense frozen at particular moments in time by adherents in configurations that gain recognition by them and by outside observers as relatively coherent and enduring systems.

Syncretism both as an accusation and as a phenomenon observed by scholars cuts right to the core of the politics of identity. The blending or effacing of certain customs, rituals, and beliefs can be a way to assert one's independence from or affiliation with others. Emphasizing or dropping different elements of practice can be a kind of subtle alchemy for transforming the permeability of social boundaries by either hardening them or making them more porous. When the adoption of new practices is used to distance oneself from one's community, it can project a subtle criticism of the latter. But when done in the name of some higher calling, a prophetic vision, or a reinterpretation of scripture, the implicit hostility and aggressiveness involved in the gesture can thereby be denied. The founder of the Yuomayan church, whose early history I examine in the next section, was a master at using innovations in ritual or theology to engineer schisms and alliances within his group and between his followers and others. In my analysis, I seek to illuminate the resemblances between indigenous shamanistic and Brahmanical practices, on the one hand, and some of the more innovative features of Yuomayan religious life, on the other, demonstrating how the group heightened or diminished its differences with other groups by borrowing, rejecting, or modifying aspects of their ritual life. I also argue that the founder's creative syncretism was threatening to the missionary establishment in part because it exposed the syncretic nature of Christianity itself.

Justus Joseph and the Yuomayan Church

The Yuomayan Church, referred to as the "Six Years' Party" in missionary discourse, emerged in the midst of an evangelistic revival that spread throughout Travancore in what is now southwestern Kerala from 1873 to 1875. At this time, Indian Christian evangelists in the village of Manguri

(Mankuzhy) in Mavelikara District sparked a movement that quickly spread to twenty-two congregations in the area. Out of this religious ferment arose a highly original schismatic church that would come to see itself as the culmination not only of all Christian churches, but of all the world's religions.

Two very different types of documents shed light on the early history of this church: the correspondence of Church Missionary Society (CMS) missionaries to and for each other or for Christian audiences in England as well as the letters and writings of the founder and leader of the church, Justus Joseph, written in Malayalam and Yuomaya Bhazha (a new language invented by Justus Joseph). The latter have been translated into English and collected in a thesis by Joseph Chakko Kurundamannil (1978), whose church, the Marthoma, continues to celebrate the legacy of Justus Joseph by including twenty-seven of his hymns in its official hymnal. Kurundamannil came to know about Joseph from lyrics sung by his own Syrian Christian grandmother, who was inspired by Joseph's preaching when she was a teenager; Kurundamannil's mentor, K. N. Daniel, also was baptized by Reverend Joseph (Kurundamannil 1978, 6). Writing from this context, Kurundamannil provides a largely sympathetic portrait of Reverend Joseph, depicting him as a charismatic, if in some ways flawed, pioneer in indigenous church leadership. Indeed, Reverend Joseph was one of the few Indians fully ordained by Protestant missionary societies in the late 1800s, although CMS missionaries' representations of him suggest they came to regret it. These two sets of records, in their very different portrayals of the conflict between Joseph and the CMS, offer insight into how the blending of heterogeneous elements into a new religious configuration contributes to both the creation and the destruction of social boundaries.

According to a tract authored by CMS minister Reverend David Fenn during an evangelistic revival initiated by native evangelists associated with the CMS, a woman in the Manguri congregation had a "remarkable dream" in July 1872 in which "a dark cloud seemed to come down from the sky close to her, resting, she thought, on her neck, and at the time she heard a voice saying to her, 'Except you repent, you will perish.'" One of the evangelists' wives saw a similar vision, and the two women began to speak and pray with others about what they had experienced. Before long, the CMS schoolmaster in the village also was "struck down, his body trembling, and his mind overpowered with a sense of his sins."[1]

Among the chief instruments of the revival were songs composed by Justus Jacob and Justus Matthei, brothers from a Brahmin family of CMS converts settled in Manguri who were originally from Tirunelveli, the center of Indian Christianity in South India. Like Ira Sankey's catchy tunes, Jacob and Matthei's songs spread quickly among the local Christian population. Reverend Fenn observed that the enthusiastic singing appeared to evoke a state of emotional excitement that involved what he called "physical sensations" and a general "clamour caused by several members of the congregation crying out together, so as to drown the voice of him who leads in prayer." Although the missionaries were thrilled to see such clear evidence that their ministry was having an effect on the local population—after all, they had themselves hired the evangelists and supported the revival—they began to worry when it failed to die down as soon as they expected. Fenn concludes his comments about the revival with the observation the congregation seemed "to be pushing extempore prayer rather to an excess" and that the same "physical sensations" recurring day after day to the same people was in his view an "unwholesome" sign that these congregations were lingering too long in the first stage of a new Christian's life.[2]

Two years later a key leader of the revival emerged in the person of Justus Joseph—another brother from this family of Tirunelveli Brahmin converts and an ordained CMS minister. By now, another notable feature of the movement, along with the song-induced ecstatic states, was the open confession of sins in regular services, a practice that shocked the mission's supervisors (Kurundamannil 1978, 58–59). On July 22, 1875, Reverend J. Caley, a relatively new missionary to the field, wrote to the CMS secretary

1. Reverend David Fenn, "The Religious Awakening in Travancore" (short printed tract) [1874?], C I 2/ O95/ 302, Church Missionary Society (CMS) Archives, Univ. of Birmingham Special Collections.

2. Ibid.

in England of his concerns about the propriety of this innovation and the potential for scandal that it harbored: "This confession is a detailed and particular account of all the sins that they can remember themselves to have committed. I need scarcely [mention] that a frank account of the faith has been revealed. Justus Joseph confessed to having committed adultery with his mother-in-law when he was a heathen. Mattai [*sic*] (his brother) confessed to have committed the same sin with his mother-in-law and also with Justus Joseph's wife. But when I do not yet know. Jaco [Jacob] had also committed adultery with Justus Joseph's wife, whether as a heathen or not I do not yet know." These startling confessions grew even more extravagant. Reverend Caley writes, "A man at Chepat confessed to having committed the same with his sister. Two women at Manguri pointed to men in the congregation with whom they had lived in sin. One man confessed to have come under the curse of Deut. XXVII. 21 [a curse upon him who lies with any animal]. In addition to all these, there were others who confessed to drunkenness, stealing, etc. etc."[3] The Justus brothers and their followers attributed this open reckoning of transgressions to a new sense of urgency stimulated by the people's conviction that Jesus's Second Coming was imminent, and they welcomed the sense of cohesion and empowerment that came along with it.

From one point of view, these public confessions can be seen simply as an intensification of Christian piety, brought on by the emotional ferment of the revival with its seven consecutive daily prayer meetings. From another point of view, it may have been that the Holy Spirit was "poured out" on these congregations in a manner that would not be seen in the West until the Asuza Street revivals in Los Angeles in 1906, as Pentecostal scholar Gary McGee (1996) has suggested. I would argue, however, that the emotional intensity of the revival loosened social boundaries, allowing for the freer incorporation of local ritual and cultural elements into the religious lives of these South Indian Christians. Reports of the

3. Papers of Reverend John Barton, Secretary of the Corresponding Committee, "Correspondence Relating to the Irregularities in Rev. Justus Joseph's Pastorate," 1871–76, C I 2/ O40 / 150, Letter No. 2, CMS Archives.

services conducted by the Justus brothers suggest that practices long used among Hindus for inducing trance states were an important element of the church's ritual life. In October 1881, the CMS magazine *Harvest Field* reprinted an article from the *Madras Standard* that, although written in the condescending prose characteristic of colonialist discourse, nonetheless illuminates the ways in which indigenous varieties of shamanistic speech were the model for the group. The author wrote,

> In the course of one of their spirit-stirring hymns—when men, women and children begin dancing about—up jumps one with a loud demoniac scream, and walks rapidly round and round the table always placed in the centre of the shed for public worship. This is not other than the "prophet" and at a particular signal from him, their animating and lively tunes, rendered still more so since the appearance of the prophet on the scene, are hushed all on a sudden, when, with particular gesticulations and violent contortions of the body, he utters some idle gibberish which is eagerly jotted down by the so-called scribe to whom alone is this prophetic language intelligible, and this done, the prophet falls, a sign that the spirit of prophecy had hitherto possessed him has left him, and a dead silence prevails. ("The 'Six Years' Party' in Travancore" 1881, n.p.)

When the prophet returned to consciousness, he had no recollection of what he said, but his words were subsequently interpreted by the principle members of the sect. With its use of music and carefully orchestrated crowd energy to induce ecstatic states, this ritual bears more than a passing resemblance to a variety of practices that are commonplace within popular Hinduism in South India—in particular *kurisolridu* (prophecy) and *samiyadutal* (a variety of possession by benign deities). The introduction of writing to the ritual seems original, but in South Indian ritual the role of *samiyadi* (literally, "god-dancer") and priest are complementary as the priest and authoritative members of the crowd interpret what the *samiyadi* communicates more or less articulately through his words and movements.

When placed in the context of the cultural codes of South Indian religious ritual, the extravagant public confessions that were a signature of the early group's meetings can similarly be seen as resembling local religious rituals. Broadly speaking, spirit possession in India takes two discrete but often complementary forms, which are linguistically and performatively marked as different (Kapadia 2000; Nabokov 1997). Anthropologist Karin Kapadia refers to these forms as "malign" and "benign" possession. *Samiyadutal*, "god-dancing," is a highly valued benign form of spirit possession in which a deity comes to (*vandatu*) an individual, usually after having been deliberately invoked, and communicates to his or her community of worshippers through the *samiyadi*'s speech and gestures. The malign form of spirit possession takes place when a ghost (*pey*) "catches" (*pitikkiratu*) someone unbidden. Treated as an illness, the affliction is diagnosed and cured through exorcism rituals (*peyattam*—literally, "making the ghost dance") that are often conducted by a *samiyadi* channeling the presence of a deity. The drama of an exorcism requires that the *samiyadi* wrest from the possessing spirit a full description of the awful events that led first to its becoming a ghost and then to its relationship with the afflicted individual. Both the precipitating events that led to possession and the relationship between ghost and possessed frequently involve sexual transgressions, whether actual or symbolic (Nabokov 1997). Only after revealing its forbidden and frustrated desires can the ghost be contained and the victim freed, thereby leading to a restoration of moral order. I suggest something similar was at work in the dramatic, often sexually charged, confessions offered by the members and leaders of Justus Joseph's congregation. Whether seen as a form of spirit possession or as a penitentiary ritual, the confession of a monstrous crime (imagined or real) can bring about powerful emotions of relief and integration into one's social group. Though one should not too hastily minimize the differences between them, both exorcism and the public confession of sin culminate, ideally, in a sense of moral order restored. It is impossible to know whether Justus Joseph and his flock actually committed the sexual transgressions to which they confessed, but analyzing these confessions through the cultural categories of Tamil popular Hinduism suggests that in the emotionally charged context of the revival, they drew on local ritual and cultural elements to create a riveting Hindu–Christian form of ritual performance.

Reverend Caley was clearly disturbed by the revelations made in the course of this ritual, but, interestingly, he never doubted their veracity.

Rather, his concern was that although such profound revelations of sin were driven by "real conviction," they could lead to harm by planting wicked thoughts in the minds of those who happened to hear such confessions in church, inspiring others to commit the same sin. It is tempting to hypothesize that beyond Caley's personal embarrassment and professional concern for the church's reputation, he may have also intuited the potentially explosive nature of "bridge-burning" behavior characteristic of new religious movements, in which one's commitment to a sect is heightened through the public transgression of social norms. Such dramatic flouting of convention strengthens one's bonds to those inside the group that values the behavior, while simultaneously weakening or threatening one's social connections to those outside of it. Indeed, in this case, the group coalescing around Justus Joseph and his brothers was about to take steps that would more decisively distinguish them from other CMS church members.

On July 25, 1875, the very day that Reverend Caley confidently wrote to his supervisors in Madras telling them he had brought the crisis under control by persuading Reverend Joseph to limit public confession to a Wesleyan-style "after-meeting," Joseph fired a letter off to the local Malayalam newspaper announcing the end of the world. Based on his numerical analysis of biblical prophecy, Reverend Joseph announced that the Second Coming would occur in five and a half years, by October 1881. This prediction was evidently first announced during one of the ecstatic services led by a fourth key leader in the movement, a Syrian Christian "prophet" named Kudarappallil Thomman. In a letter to the bishop written August 2, 1875, Reverend Joseph reported that during the Easter season, a man, presumably Thomman, stood up in church with "great spiritual power" and cried out loudly for three days straight the following prophecy: "[A] s the 7th day after six days is the Sabbath, so the 7th year after six years is the Sabbath year for Christ's coming." The prophet exhorted his hearers to "search the Scriptures with prayer to get proof proving this Divine Truth."[4] Justus Joseph took it upon himself to do just that. Through care-

4. Barton Papers, C I 2/ O40 / 150, appendix A, CMS Archives.

ful reading of the Bible, he determined first that it was possible for men to know the date and time of Christ's return (against conventional Anglican theology), and then he pieced together clues that pointed to the actual date. Much to his CMS mentors' consternation, he sent notices announcing the coming parousia to people and publications around the world.

Justus Joseph's defiance of missionary authority by claiming for himself and his associates gifts of prophecy and scriptural acumen comes through vividly in his letters to the bishop, CMS missionaries, and various political and religious leaders, including Queen Victoria and Pope Pius IX in Rome. In them, it is clear that his assumption of a greater scriptural authority than that of ecclesiastical leaders was meant to unsettle and perhaps also to offend. Like millennialist prophets in many other times and places, Joseph's annunciation of the world's end was accompanied by criticisms of the established church. His letters are filled with ominous predictions and scarcely veiled threats, such as this letter written on May 26, 1875, to Reverend Caley:

> Last Sunday during the worship service in the church the spirit of Christ revealed some things the gist of which I give below. The glorious advent of the Lord Jesus Christ in the clouds is impending. Ai yoh! The bowels of Jesus tremble seeing his church. The shepherds instead of tending the sheep, feed on their fat. How many of the sheep die of wounds and sickness! . . . Time is ebbing to its end. How could the Lord tolerate the neglect? His anger is ablaze at the false shepherds, the hypocrites. The good Lord has begun the winnowing. Worthless dust though I am, [I] have been called to be his mouth piece. (in Kurundamannil 1978, 57)

Joseph did not reserve judgment for the CMS missionaries alone. The Syrian Christian Church and the Roman Catholic Church also came in for criticism. In a letter addressed to the "Syrian Church," Joseph criticizes it for its ornate liturgical style and use of icons in worship: "Though you are a princess and a queen you are accursed; though you are Rachel the beloved spouse of Israel you are accursed. Lament about your terrible condition. Whom do you serve? The real or the image? Whom do your ministers imitate in their attire and robes? I say, it is Aaron. . . .

What have you built the altars for? For the Supper, a table, not an altar is required" (quoted in Kurundamannil 1978, 66). At stake in these letters, I suggest, is Justus Joseph's efforts to establish firm boundaries between his followers and all other Christians, who are condemned as insincere and corrupt.

But beyond his letters' open defiance of CMS authority and strident criticisms of other Christians, Joseph was also in his ministry generating a subtle synthesis of Christian and Brahmanical religious thought. One of the early names given to the movement was the "Unarvu Sabai" (Nagam Aiya 1906, 132). This name is probably a direct translation of the phrase "revival church" because there were numerous revivals at this time in South India and around the world, which were publicized globally through missionary and Christian publications. But it can also be glossed as "Enlightenment Church" or "Awakening Church" because it draws on the word *unarvu*, which signifies sensation, feeling, or insight. Like the Sanskrit word *bodhi*, *unarvu* can refer to returning to consciousness after falling into a swoon or a deep sleep or by extension to a spiritual or intellectual coming to consciousness. Justus Joseph and his followers believed they were living through a period of anxious waiting for the Second Coming, which required of them the cultivation of a special kind of attentiveness. Such attentiveness would lead eventually to a form of wisdom tempered by humility. As Justus Joseph wrote in a letter to the bishop, which Reverend Caley translated from Malayalam to English,

> He who takes heed, watches and prays, is spiritual, has the mind of Christ and judges all things (1 Cor. II: 15–16). He is not of darkness as others, but of the light, that day will therefore not overtake him as a thief (I Thess. 2: 4); yet, owing to the delay of the bridegroom, slumber even falls on the wise who takes heed, and he sleeps (Matt: XXV:5). When the cry is made he awakes, [yet] on account of the flesh his eyes are heavy and he again sleeps and awakes. Thus he who is spiritual, *until* the final emancipation from the body of death, is in a state of constant strife between flesh and spirit, between light and darkness, between slumber and awakening. To him who is spiritual, the Holy Ghost through the Scripture, gives sufficient wisdom to judge all things; still because on account of the flesh,

> an ignorance which is not able to judge anything also abides in him, he should take heed, watch and pray.[5]

Joseph's clearly articulated sense of the conflict between the spirit and the flesh is certainly consistent with Christian theologies. But I wonder if we can discern here as well a view common to Indic philosophical schools that see the flesh, or rather the senses, as imparting to human nature a kind of "ignorance" and incapacity to exercise good judgment. In order to overcome the entropic drag, as it were, of the senses, one needs to exercise the cognitive faculty of discrimination, or *viveka*, to distinguish between what is ultimately real and eternal and what is false and fleeing. The question has thus always been, for both Christians and yogis, How does one enhance one's ability to access that discriminating wisdom that can judge all things? Reverend Joseph, it seems, advocated a *sadhana* of self-abnegation achieved at least in part through the public confession of monstrous crimes. Reverend Caley writes that Joseph was convinced that "there are numbers who come and go to and from Church yet they know nothing of the power of a new life that is to be had if a man will make a *full surrender* of himself to God."[6] Perhaps Caley's description offers yet another way to understand the strangely exaggerated nature of the confessions given by congregants caught up in the ecstatic, expectant mood that swept through Travancore in the spring and summer of 1875. The confessions may have been part of a spiritual assault on the ego meant to heighten the discriminating powers of attention necessary to discern the Lord's final coming.

The moment when this revivalistic movement finally exceeded the CMS clergy's abilities to contain it came in December 1875, when Caley had to concede that his efforts to guide Joseph's zeal had failed. He officially suspended Joseph from his duties and banned him from entering the churches at Kanneet and Thevalakara. With characteristic resilience, Joseph wrote a letter to the superintending missionary that he could not be fired because he had already quit. He had established his own independent Kanneet Revival Church on October 18, 1875 (in Kurundamannil

5. Barton Papers, C I 2/ O40 / 150, appendix B, CMS Archives.

6. Barton Papers, C I 2/ O40 / 150, Letter No. 3, emphasis in original, CMS Archives.

1978, 77–78). This final act of insubordination led to the CMS's filing suit to regain control over the physical property of the church and the pastorage in Kanneet, a legal battle that Joseph lost. Nonetheless, the members of the Kanneet Revival Church remained active, numbering as many as seven thousand by May 1876. They survived this crisis, along with several disappointing failures of their prophecies. With each failure, the church distinguished itself more and more from other Christian churches in Kerala through unique innovations. At times, the community seemed to seek a position of complete uniqueness in terms of ritual life and community culture, which corresponded to relative economic and social independence. At other times, particularly after the failure of their central prophecy, they seemed to align themselves more with local groups, in part through the incorporation of local elements of Malayali and South Indian Brahmanical culture.

From Revival Church to the Culmination of All Sects

The organization of the Kanneet Revival Church was starkly hierarchical, with Justus Joseph firmly at its head as president. Below him were two chief prophets, Kudarappallil Thomman and Alumootil Eapen, "born again, spirit-led, knowledgeable men" whose "dreams, visions and revelations" were treasured and yet also carefully scrutinized and checked against both scripture and Justus Joseph's revelations. If there were contradictions between them, Joseph did not hesitate to dismiss the validity of his chief prophets' prophecies (in Kurundamannil 1978, 81–82). *Bodhakar*s, at the next level of the hierarchy, were "teachers" equipped with sufficient knowledge of the Bible to allow them to "discern the words of Spirit-filled preachers and interpret them on the basis of the Bible for the illumination of the people . . . [and to] discern the spirits, exorcise the evil spirits, and keep under their control those that prophesy" (quoted in Kurundamannil 1978, 86). Under the *bodhakar*s were the ordinary prophets whose prophecies were checked by *bodhakar*s according to their conformity to scripture and ability to "enlighten" the church (just as the chief prophets' prophecies were held in check by Justus Joseph). The division of labor between prophets and *bodhakar*s, where one person is the human vehicle for a supernatural being and the other interprets the words of the spirit-filled speaker, resembles that found in the benevolent variety of local spirit-possession rituals, in which a ghost or divine being speaks in the voice of a human, whose garbled or cryptic words and gestures then require interpretation by others. Thus, here is possibly another example of church members incorporating local shamanistic practices into their ritual life. One evident departure from either orthodox Protestant or local Hindu practice, however, was the emergence of authoritarian qualities in the Kanneet Revival Church. This began when Justus Joseph arrogated to himself the roles both of unquestionable prophet and chief *bodhakar* who could validate or invalidate any other person's prophecy.

Over time, considerable power and authority became consolidated in the persons of Justus Joseph and his chief prophets and brothers, especially the former. As Kurundamannil writes, "The followers of Justus Joseph were made to believe that Joseph had the full knowledge of the Truth wherein he walked. They held that it pleased the Holy Spirit to reveal to Joseph all the mysteries of heaven and earth, and to make him wise" (1978, 86). As the font of divine wisdom, Joseph was seen practically as a god himself on a par with the divine Holy Trinity. The *Yuomayanithyaksharangel*, a 1901 collection of Justus Joseph's writings, says that, "symbolically, the Holy Spirit was thought to have taken upon himself the name, 'Justus Joseph,' so that any one who believed in that name would be saved" (quoted in Kurundamannil 1978, 87). With this assumption came Joseph's almost complete control over church members' affairs. In letters alternately chiding, threatening, and imperious, Joseph delivered prophecies about virtually all important decisions his followers made, from the management of estates and the investment of money to the arrangement of marriages (Kurundamannil 1978, 102–10). His grip over the church was particularly manifest in the pressure he placed on members to support himself and his brothers financially through tithing and generous gifts. For example, in a letter to a wealthy landlord and church leader, he writes, "On the word of truth I write this to disclose the revelation in regard to your tithes. Seventy five percent of your tithe must be sent to me for the expense of my family. The balance may be given to the local ministers as you please. . . . Next week I will send a boat to collect the rice paddy" (from the *Yuomayanithyaksharangel*, quoted in Kurundamannil 1978, 115). Such demands did not go unchallenged. Joseph's correspondence is also filled with references to acts of resistance on the part of his followers and fellow leaders, especially the chief prophet Alumootil Eapen (Kurundamannil 1978, 110–16).

Even as the movement dealt with internal power struggles, it was faced with an even greater challenge—the failure in 1881 of the central prophecy regarding when the Second Coming was to take place. Hundreds of disillusioned members left the church. But rather than destroying the church altogether, this blow to the central pillar of its cosmology prompted a thorough reconstitution. First, Justus Joseph spiritualized the failure of the prophecy, arguing that Jesus Christ *had* returned, but invisibly. He was now present in the bread and water of the Kanneet Revival Church. To prepare for the full realization of the Second Coming, followers would have to fast and give up eating meat and fish and drinking alcohol. With these changes came many other changes in the church's structure and self-perception. No longer content to regard itself as the most correct Christian church in Kerala, the group around Joseph took a new name, "Yuomayan" (Church of the Eternal Gospel), and regarded itself as something entirely unprecedented—the fulfillment of Christianity and all religions. As Kurundamannil writes, it was now "no more contaminated by any element of the Christian Church; it was completely separate and different" (1978, 122). Joseph revealed for his followers their own unique way of reckoning time, the Yuomayabdam almanac; a new language, Yuomaya Bhazha; and a new name for God, "Ya Ye Yo Yo" (an acronym formed from the first syllables in the Malayali words for Yahweh, Jesus, Joseph, and Johannan—the latter referring to Justus Joseph's son). The community's distinguishing mark was to have no distinguishing marks—they consumed no meat or wine, practiced no circumcision, and did not pierce their ears. The women wore no *thali* (a yellow cord or gold chain necklace worn by South Indian women as a sign of marriage) and abjured jewelry of all sorts (Kurundamannil 1978, 122–24). These changes corresponded to a period of relative prosperity and economic independence for the church as Joseph found success in business building a rice paddy company in collaboration with one of his followers, Evangelist Ghevargese (Kurundamannil 1978, 131–34).

In 1906, twenty-five years after the failure of the group's central prophecy, V. Nagam Aiya wrote in the *Travancore State Manual* that the sect still existed. Its members seem to have dropped the more controversial practice of public confession of sins. Justus Joseph came to be known as "Vidwan Kutti"—a diminutive, affectionate form of "Wise Man" or "Elder," by which he is still known in Kerala to this day. Significantly, they also seemed to have further indigenized their understanding of Christianity by assimilating it with an ascetic form of Brahmanism in continuation of a trend that began around 1885. Nagam Aiya reported that the believers were strict vegetarians and were divided into *gotrams* that practiced exogamous marriage (like Brahmins). The women were supposed to wear colored sari clothes after the fashion of Brahmin women and to eschew ornaments of any kind. By now, the group's services appeared much more toned down, consisting of the usual alternation between readings from the Bible, prayers in the new language and in extempore Malayalam, a sermon, and distribution of consecrated water and bread—the latter not made from wheat, but from rice flour, boiled edible roots, and coconut (Nagam Aiya 1906, 133–34). It seems that as the controversial and radically Christian elements dropped out, the group did not drift back into the fold of other Christian communities in Kerala, as one might expect. Rather, it resolved into an independent Christian church, but one with an aesthetic style shaped strongly by Brahmin culture.

Conclusion

Scholars argue over whether one should distinguish between religious syncretism as a more or less conscious and active process and religious synthesis as the result of this process whose creation has been forgotten or actively denied. In her essay in this volume (chapter 5), Tazim Kassam proposes useful similes for understanding syncretism that offer a nonjudgmental way of recognizing the degree to which religious ideas and practices from one tradition are transformed when people juxtapose or combine them with those from other traditions. Let's think of religious synthesis like a cake, she suggests, and religious syncretism like a salad (138, this volume). Religious synthesis refers to the blending of different elements to such a degree that those elements are entirely transformed in the process; at the end of it, the eggs, sugar, and flour are no longer distinguishable from each other. Religious syncretism, in contrast, refers to instances where people draw on elements of belief and practice in varying combinations in such a way that those elements retain their distinctiveness—as in a salad. They can drop out or be added according to the practitioner's preferences. If one does not like the onions or is allergic to nuts, one can push them to the side. An additional advantage of these similes, in my view, is that they recognize the complex, composite nature of religious traditions in the first place. Our difficulties in defining *syncretism* or in coming up with an adequate word to replace it stem at least in part from our difficulties in defining the boundaries and limits of religious traditions to begin with. I would characterize Justus Joseph's blending of indigenous and Western Christian elements more as religious syncretism than synthesis. He was creating, to employ Kassam's similes, more of a salad than a cake. People such as Kurundamannil's grandmother, for example, who was saved by Justus Joseph at a revival she attended as a child, could take elements of his teaching and leave others. People appreciated Joseph's beautiful hymns, his insistence on the value of the confession of sins, and his cultivation of the correct spiritual attitude necessary for living rightly in anticipation of Jesus' return, but his explicit predictions and prophecies and his autocratic leadership style left a bitter taste in many mouths.

If Justus Joseph's understanding of Christianity has been incorporated selectively into the Marthoma church, he has until recently been treated quite differently by mainstream church historians.[7] As the comments and characterizations of missionaries and Anglican church historians make clear, the millennialist sect founded by Justus Joseph and his brothers has served the annals of the Protestant church in South India mostly as an object lesson in the difficulties of channeling the effervescent energy aroused by religious revivals, where talent and creativity can easily be hijacked by "the adversary," and indigenization can go so far that

7. The important exception to this is the way his story is told by Pentecostal church historians, who tend to celebrate his advocacy of indigenous leadership, antiecclessiastical activism, and charismatic gifts (see McGee 1996).

it challenges the bounds of propriety. Yet one might argue that what was most alarming to the supervising missionaries was the ways in which the movement exposed the syncretism of the early Christian church itself—the "purity" that the Yuomayans sought to recapture in their reforms and innovations. The revival in Travancore in 1873 provided the impetus for reintroducing what we might now call "shamanistic" elements into Christianity. These "shamanistic" elements were surely a part of the Jesus movement of first-century Palestine, with its exorcisms, miracles, and ecstatic speech ("though I speak with the tongues of angels" [1 Corinthians 13:1]), in which the ancient moral codes of the Jews were blended with local religious elements to create a potent mix attractive to Gentiles all over the Mediterranean world (see Hollenbach 1981; Pilch 2002). They were, however, bits of the salad that had long been pushed to the side of the plate, as it were, in "respectable" western European and North American varieties of Christianity.

Syncretism is an inevitable and quite ordinary by-product of the process of cross-cultural communication. This is especially so in the encounter between missionaries and their would-be converts, when people on one side of a cultural and linguistic divide are actively exhorting those on the other to take up a new set of ideas and practices as their own. The uncertainty of the outcome of translating Christianity into a new cultural setting puts a limit on the missionaries' ability to control and even understand the ideas of local Christians. Some Christian churches, notably the Pentecostal Church and the Roman Catholic Church, have come to embrace this feature of cross-cultural evangelism, arguing that such experiments are evidence of the Holy Spirit manifesting itself in a new cultural context. In contrast, the nineteenth-century American and British Protestant missionaries whom I discuss in this essay were positively alarmed by it. Their inability to fully contain or control the process by which local people appropriated Christianity filled them with profound unease. The deepest unease, I would argue, came when new converts recovered and claimed as orthodox certain elements of the Christian tradition that are present in the Bible but were no longer a part of the active religious lives of missionaries or, indeed, of most European and North American Christians.

Works Cited

Asad, Talal. 1993. *Geneaologies of Religion: Discipline and Reasons of Power in Christianity and Islam.* Baltimore: Johns Hopkins Univ. Press.

Bayly, Susan. 1989. *Saints, Goddesses, and Kings: Muslims and Christians in South Indian Society, 1700–1900.* Cambridge: Cambridge Univ. Press.

Burridge, Kenelm. [1960] 1970. *Mambu: A Study of Melanesian Cargo Movements and Their Ideological Background.* New York: Harper and Row.

Comaroff, Jean. 1985. *Body of Power, Spirit of Resistance: The Culture and History of a South African People.* Chicago: Univ. of Chicago Press.

Dempsey, Corinne G. 2001. *Kerala Christian Sainthood: Collisions of Culture and Worldview in South India.* New York: Oxford Univ. Press.

Fuchs, Stephen. 1965. *Rebellious Prophets: A Study of Messianic Movements in Indian Religions.* Bombay [Mumbai]: Asia Publishing House.

Hollenbach, Paul. 1981. "Jesus, Demoniacs, and Public Authorities: A Socio-historical Study." *Journal for the American Academy of Religion* 49, no. 4 (Dec.): 567–88.

Kapadia, Karin. 2000. "Pierced by Love: Tamil Possession, Gender, and Caste." In *Invented Identities: The Interplay of Gender, Religion, and Politics in India,* edited by Julia Leslie and Mary McGee, 181–202. New Delhi: Oxford Univ. Press.

Kent, Eliza F. 2004. *Converting Women: Gender and Protestant Christianity in Colonial South India.* New York: Oxford Univ. Press.

Kurundamannil, Joseph Chakko. 1978. "Yuomayam: A Messianic Movement in Kerala, India." PhD diss., Fuller Theological Seminary.

McGee, Gary B. 1996. "Pentecostal Phenomena and Revivals in India: Implications for Indigenous Church Leadership." *International Bulletin of Missionary Research* 20, no. 3 (July): 112–17.

Nabokov, Isabelle. 1997. "Expel the Lover, Recover the Wife: Symbolic Analysis of a South Indian Exorcism." *Journal of the Royal Anthropological Institute* 3, no. 2 (June): 297–316.

Nagam Aiya, V. 1906. *Travancore State Manual.* Vol. 2. Trivandrum, India: Travancore Government Pres.

Pilch, John J. 2002. "Altered States of Consciousness in the Synoptics." In *The Social Setting of Jesus and the Gospels,* edited by Wolfgang Stegemann, Bruce J. Malina, and Gerd Theissen, 103–16. Minneapolis: Fortress Press.

Shaw, Rosalind, and Charles Stewart. 1994. "Introduction: Problematizing Syncretism." In *Syncretism/Anti-syncretism: The Politics of Religious Synthesis,* edited by Charles Stewart and Rosalind Shaw, 1–26. New York: Routledge.

"The 'Six Years' Party' in Travancore." 1881. *Harvest Field* (Oct.): n.p.

Stewart, Tony K., and Carl W. Ernst. 2003. "Syncretism." *South Asia Folklore: An Encyclopedia*, edited by Peter J. Claus and Margaret Mills, 586–88. New York: Routledge.

Sundkler, Bengt. 1961. *Bantu Prophets in South Africa*. 2nd ed. London: Oxford Univ. Press.

Van der Veer, Peter. 1994. "Syncretism, Multiculturalism, and the Discourse of Tolerance." In *Syncretism/Anti-syncretism: The Politics of Religious Synthesis*, edited by Charles Stewart and Rosalind Shaw, 196–211. New York: Routledge.

Worsley, Peter. 1968. *The Trumpet Shall Sound: A Study of "Cargo" Cults in Melanesia*. New York: Schocken Books.

5

≈

The Living Tradition of Ismaili *Ginans*

Negotiating Cultures in Poetry and Performance

TAZIM R. KASSAM

IN 1908, His Highness Sultan Muhammad Shah, Aga Khan III, the forty-eighth Imam of Ismaili Muslims, won a famous lawsuit that has come to be called the "Haji Bibi case." The case had to do with property that he claimed belonged to him and his community. It hinged on the interpretation of a lengthy *ginan* ("a song full of religious knowledge or wisdom") known as the *Das Avatar,* one of the major *granths* or compilations of *ginans* sung by the Satpanth Khojas, as the Ismaili Muslims were known at that time. The lawsuit ruled that his Khoja followers were not Hindus or Sunni Muslims or Twelver Shi'a Muslims, but Ismaili Shi'a Muslims who believed their living Imam to be His Highness Sir Sultan Muhammad Shah, Aga Khan III, the direct descendent of 'Ali ibn Abi Talib, the cousin and son-in-law of Prophet Muhammad.[1]

I owe my deepest gratitude to my father, whose unique recitation and knowledge of *ginans* are a constant source of inspiration. I thank Zayn Kassam and Corinne Dempsey for their generous and insightful comments. Eliza Kent's compassion, persistence, clarity, careful reading, and suggestions made writing this chapter possible. All errors and defects are mine. My translations of ginans are reprinted with permission of State University of New York Press.

1. *The Khoja Case,* 1866, a paraphrase, typescript, Ismailia Association, Quebec.

In 1957, almost a century and a half later, Aga Khan III's great-grandson, His Highness Prince Karim al-Husayni, Aga Khan IV, acceded to the throne of Imamat as the forty-ninth Imam. Soon after he assumed office, the recitation of the *Das Avatar* was censored and taken out of circulation because, as Dominique-Sila Khan points out, it "was a formula which seems to imply the identification of the Imam with the Supreme God" (2003, 145; see also Khan 1997). At the same time, however, in a *farman* (guidance or decree) given to his followers in Dacca in 1960, Aga Khan IV, recognizing the significance of *ginan*s in the religious life of his Satpanth Ismaili followers, described them as a "wonderful tradition" that must be continued or else an important part of the community's past would be lost (Ginan-e-Sharif n.d., iii–v).

This chapter explores the complex nature of these devotional and didactic hymns that, although still a living tradition, acquired an ambiguous and ambivalent status in the decades after that 1960 *farman* and whose recitation is now strictly regulated if not proscribed in the daily ritual prayers of the Ismaili Muslims. It also looks at the descriptive uses of the term *syncretism* as applied to "mixtures" or "mixed traditions" of religious ideas, specifically the *ginans*.[2] Finally, to appreciate the polyvalent richness of the *ginan*s, it illustrates how my father, who is widely known and admired for his passionate recitation of *ginan*s has negotiated these changes by way of the *ginan* tradition itself. His life has spanned the authority of both Imams—Sultan Muhammad Shah, Aga Khan III, and Shah Karim al-Husayni, Aga Khan IV.[3]

2. In addition to the discussion of the diverse and often divergent usage of this term in this essay, see Kassam 1994; Pye 1972; Roy 1983; Shaw and Charles 1994; and Kent's chapter in this volume.

3. It is important to note that in addition to being a scholar of *ginan*s, as a member of the Ismaili community, I also have direct personal knowledge of the *ginan* tradition, its performance in daily rituals, and the changes to its status this past century. Given the very limited access given to this literature, few non-Ismaili scholars have written on *ginans* (for exceptions, see Daftary 1990 and Ivanow 1948). All the major studies have been authored or coauthored by Ismailis: see Asani 2002; Esmail 2002; Kassam 1995; Kassam and Mallison 2008; Moir and Shackle 1992; Nanji 1978.

I

The British court's ruling in the Haji Bibi case in 1908 was a pivotal moment in the premodern history of the Satpanth Khojas on the Indian subcontinent. Not only did it establish the third Aga Khan's right to the properties in question, but it effectively defined the boundaries of the religious identity of the Satpanth Khojas and validated the status of His Highness the Aga Khan III as their religious leader. The core question of the lawsuit was whether the Satpanth Khojas were Shi'a and, furthermore, whether they were Shi'a Ismailis and, hence, followers of His Highness Sir Sultan Muhammad Shah, Aga Khan III.

Constituting one of the two streams of interpretation of Muhammad's message, the Shi'a shared with the Sunni the belief in the Qur'an as divine revelation and Prophet Muhammad as God's messenger, but they differed from the Sunni regarding the Prophet's rightful successor. The Shi'a held that Muhammad clearly designated 'Ali, his cousin and son-in-law, to guide the nascent Muslim community in all its affairs, be they matters of faith (*din*) or worldly life (*dunya*). Just as Muhammad's authority encompassed both the spiritual and the material welfare of his community, the Shi'a asserted that their Imams, too, were divinely appointed to fulfill that role. The Sunnis disputed the claim that the Prophet had designated a successor and asserted that the Qur'an and memories of Muhammad's example (sunna) were sufficient to guide the community after his death. They also maintained that the leader who would assume political leadership after the Prophet should be determined by election, not succession. The first four caliphs known as Rashidun (Rightly Guided) were not elected, however; they were selected by a council of companions of the Prophet.

The Shi'a hold the first three caliphs thus chosen to be usurpers of 'Ali's claim to the caliphate. Subsequently, with the massacre at Karbala of Husayn, 'Ali's son and Muhammad's grandson, the division between the Sunni and Shi'a was sealed. The political history of Islam is to some extent a record of the conflict within the Muslim *ummah* (community) over claims of religious and political authority. In the century after the massacre of Husayn and his family, the Shi'a, too, had disputes over the previous Imam's true successor and split into different groups. The two main divisions within the Shi'a community—namely, the Ismailis and the Twelvers—took place after the death of the sixth Imam, Ja'far al-Sadiq (d. 765).

The Shi'a constituted a clear political threat to the Sunnis because they claimed that their Imams were the divinely appointed and thus true heirs to Muhammad's authority and leadership. With the help of Sunni theologians who misrepresented Shi'a doctrines and condemned the Shi'a as *mulhids*, heretics, Sunni rulers were able to sanction violence against them. Hence, for most of their history, the Shi'a have been a persecuted minority, so much so that they had to develop a doctrine called *taqiyya* that permitted them to conceal their religious identity when their lives were at risk. One way they did so was by blending in with those around them just as a chameleon matches its skin with the color of its background to protect itself.

The main tenet of Shi'ism was the belief in the necessity of a *hazir* (living) Imam whose primary role was to interpret Muhammad's message and the Qur'an according to the times. It was through the living Imam's interpretation of Islam that God's revelation remained alive and relevant. The Ismailis, in particular, favored an intellectual and symbolic approach to the interpretation of the Qur'an and religious practices, thus allowing for multiple levels of meaning. One of their earliest hermeneutic principles was to make a distinction between the outward or literal form of scripture (*zahir*) and its hidden or esoteric meanings (*batin*). This method of reading texts, or *ta'wil*, sought out the inner, spiritual essence of the Qur'an and of various Islamic rites and precepts. Because the practice of *ta'wil* allowed for a broad canvas of interpretation, it meant that the Shi'a (and the Sufis, who also developed esoteric traditions), were able to absorb ideas that existed in their surroundings more readily and flexibly. In contrast, the Sunnis preferred a method of exegesis (*tafsir*) that stayed very close to the literal, formal, and uniform meaning of the Qur'an.

As a result of their esoteric orientation, the Ismailis developed a system of teaching, or *da'wa* ("calling"—that is, inviting to the faith), that required deliberate study of the religious ideas and practices in the regions where they preached so as to convey their message in terms familiar to those who lived there. Many Sufi *tariqas* (paths), who similarly had a spiritual orientation toward religion, also gave rise to nonnormative or antinomian rituals and syncretic literatures (oral or written) that were influenced by or adapted from the cultures around them.[4]

The latter approach characterized the modus operandi of the Ismaili preachers responsible for the conversion of the Hindu and other Indian ancestors of the Satpanth Khojas. The poetic and musical nature of the *ginans*, their emotional content (*bhava*), and their religious performance formed a continuum in the medieval Indic universe of devotional songs such as *bhajan, shabad, na't,* and *kirtan.* As a result of taking the existing social and cultural situation as essential to their message, the *ginans* reflect a syncretism that can also be viewed as a form of resistance to fixed and dogmatic interpretations of Islam. By making the boundaries of the *ginans* permeable, the *pirs* (preacher-poets) did not just create a path that led from a Hindu or Indic religious worldview to an Islamic one, but the path itself constructed a religious worldview—namely, Satpanth Ismailism. Thus, depending on their esoteric or exoteric orientation, Muslims in any given region varied in their approaches to local cultures. Some drew sharp and clear-cut boundaries ritually and socially in their encounters with non-Muslims, whereas others removed, finessed, or ignored such boundaries.

II

This background regarding Ismaili *ta'wil*, hermeneutics, is crucial to understanding the concept of *Das Avatar* in the *ginans* that identified the long-awaited tenth avatar of the Hindus as the living Imam of the Shi'a Ismailis. Theological and mythopoetic linkages played a crucial role in the teaching methods of the Ismaili *pirs* who spread the *sat panth*, the true path, selectively using symbols, ideas, languages, and practices in the prevalent religious universe. Their poetic compositions achieved such linkages through a deft juxtaposition of words; for instance, the *ginan* "Paratak patrane parakhine pujo" (recognize and serve the manifest one) strings together the words *alakha*, 'Ali, and avatar to create a composite identity for the Ismaili Imam who stands between a transcendent God

4. See, for instance, Richard Eaton's classic work on the spread of Islam in Bengal, *The Rise of Islam and the Bengal Frontier, 1204–1760* (1996).

without worldly attributes (*alakh*) and his manifestation (avatar) who descends to save the righteous from evil and destruction. The Satpanth Khojas revered both their *pir*s and the *ginan*s that they composed as sacred for revealing to them this deeper meaning (*bhed*).

The play on multiple meanings can be seen in the term *ginan* itself, which is derived from the Sanskrit noun *jnana*, "knowledge," or religious insight. *Gyani* in Hindi refers both to one who is well versed in religious scriptures (*shastra*s) and to one who has gained this sacred knowledge directly through spiritual experience. The word *ginan* may also be a double-entendre, a play on the Arabic verb *ganna*, which means "to sing." My definition of *ginan*s as "songs of wisdom" tries to capture both senses of the term, "religious knowledge" and "ritual song." This type of polyglottic linguistic interplay and the resonant and multifaceted meanings it generates was typical of *ta'wil* or esoteric hermeneutics. It is clear from the apt interpolation of Hindu and Muslim terms signifying common religious concepts in the *ginan*s that the *pir*s made a deliberate effort to convey Ismaili teachings through a harmonious blending in with existing religious traditions.

As noted earlier, the Satpanth Khojas sang *ginan*s as a ritual act (*kriya*) for almost eight centuries. The continuity and cogency of this religious song tradition, which was committed to writing around the sixteenth century, were assured by two strongly held beliefs. First, the Ismaili *pir*s were spiritually enlightened holy men whose compositions were inspired by their mystical knowledge, and hence, the *ginan*s were sacred. As expressed in one of Pir Shams's *ginan*s,

> Reciting *ginans*, the guru said this to the endless in number
> He narrated the four scriptures (*veda*) and revealed the four books (*kitab*)
> To all he imparted the true teaching—the path of the religion (*dharma*) of Satpanth
> In many talks the Guru explained that the last scripture (*veda*) was the Qur'an
> . . .
> This is what the Guru Shams said; indeed, this wisdom (*ginan*) reveals the Truth (*sach*).
>
> ("Nara kasamshah" 95:12–18, as given in Kassam 1995, p. 18).

Second, singing *ginans* was a ritual action (karma or *kriya*) parallel in religious merit to chanting the Vedas or reciting the Qur'an, whose very sounds were transformative. To sing *ginan*s or just to hear them being sung was to pray.

III

The *Das Avatar* is attributed to a sixteenth-century figure known as Pir Sadardin (Sadr al-Din), who was credited with converting scores of Hindus to Satpanth. In brief, the *Das Avatar* declares that the tenth avatar or divine manifestation of Lord Vishnu in the Vaishnava system, Kalki, was none other than Swami ("Lord" in Sanskrit) or Shah ("Lord" in Persian), who lived in Daylam *desh*—the principality of Daylam, in Central Asia. It states that this powerful figure, the Nikalanki (literally, "the Unblemished" or "the Immaculate") avatar would rescue all his devotees from the last age of darkness, *kali jug*, and free them from their oppressors and the shackles of *samsara*, the cycle of life, death, and rebirth.

As mentioned earlier, starting around the 1960s, the recitation of the same *ginan* that helped establish the identity of the Satpanth Khojas as Shi'a Ismaili Muslims was discouraged, abbreviated, and finally prohibited in the performance of daily rituals. With it, many older *granth*s and *ginan*s that appeared to be heavily influenced by or rooted in Indian mythology were also discontinued. Further diminishing the status of the *ginans*, the practice of singing an entire *ginan* during daily ritual ceremonies was curtailed in the ensuing decades, so much so that today singers are given only four to five minutes to sing, or they are given a handout with a few verses of the specific *ginan* they are to sing.

Poetic compositions and sacred songs that are an integral part of daily ritual ceremonies play a critical role in the formation and sustenance of a community's self-identity. Reciters memorize their sacred songs and internalize them, so any alterations of the words are easily detected and can cause confusion, conflict, and even anguish. When the changes previously described were first introduced in the newly printed *ginan* books, many members of the community, in particular the elderly who absorbed them as an oral tradition, were distraught and vociferously objected.

Leaders of the community tried to quell their concerns, saying that the directive to alter the wordings had come from the Imam himself.

The Ismailia Association, a religious education board established by Aga Khan III to oversee the community's religious welfare, was responsible for training preachers and teachers, publishing religious literature including *ginans*, and conveying the Imam's *farmans* (decrees). It went through a period of sifting through and editing commonly sung *ginans* and substituting Hindu words with Islamic parallels—for example, replacing "Hari" (an epithet for Vishnu, "Divine Lord") with "'Ali" (the name of the first Shi'a Imam) or by substituting "Mowla" for "Swami."

Be that as it may, these and other changes affecting not only their religious practices but also their socioeconomic and cultural life were part of a realignment of the identity of the Satpanth Khoja Ismailis by their spiritual leader, His Highness Prince Karim Aga Khan IV. Accelerating the process of modernization, economic development, and secular and religious education begun by the previous Imam, His Highness Prince Karim Aga Khan IV initiated significant changes to reposition and firmly situate the identity of his Satpanth Khoja followers within the context of Islamic and Shi'a Ismaili Muslim history. There was never any ambiguity as to the Muslim identity of the Imams or Aga Khan IV. As confirmed by the British court, he, like his predecessor, was a direct lineal descendent of the Prophet and of the first Shi'a Imam, Hazrat 'Ali. To his Satpanth Ismaili followers, he was their *hazir* (living, present) Imam, but, as we shall see, his authority and status were founded upon a much more complex, mythopoetic, and syncretic religious framework and lineage that, because of its Indic worldview, could be used to cast doubt on the authenticity of their "Islamic" identity.

IV

As the Muslim identity of the Satpanth Khoja community became more evident and established under the Aga Khans guidance, leaders of the community worried that the identification of their Imams as avatars in the *ginans* could be exploited and taken literally. Given their history of persecution, Ismailis were particularly sensitive to the accusation by other Muslims that the Shi'a venerate their Imams as incarnations of God.

The notion of avatar in Vaishnavite Hinduism encapsulates the idea that a divine figure such as the god Vishnu assumes a creaturely or human form in times of crisis as a savior figure to vanquish evil and reestablish order and justice. In the *ginans*, the temporary *descent* of Vishnu and other Hindu deities is aligned with the anticipated *arrival* of the Imams to India as historical figures. Rejecting the Ismaili hermeneutic of *ta'wil* as *bid'a* (an innovation or invention), Sunni literalists would not recognize the nuanced way that the *pirs* had appropriated the Hindu concept of avatar by situating and reinterpreting it within the Shi'a concept of Imam and an esoterically Islamic heritage. Satpanth Ismaili leaders feared, and rightly so, that embracing an Indic concept such as avatar would be taken literally by "orthodox" Sunni Muslims, who rejected as "un-Islamic" any local accretions in Islamic practice and texts.

The topic of the Imam's divinity was especially sensitive for Ismailis because they, more so than any other Shi'a or Sufi group, had endured centuries of persecution under Sunni caliphs. The Seljuqs (ca. 1016–307 CE) perceived the Fatimid Ismailis (909–1171 CE) as a political threat, and their grand vizir Nizam al-Mulk (1018–92 CE) had led a military campaign to spread anti-Ismaili propaganda by distorting the Ismailis' esoteric doctrines. Branding them *mulhid* (heretics), a few Sunni caliphs went so far as to say that killing Ismailis was equal to performing a meritorious act. The chronicler Minhaj al-Siraj Juzjani, the principal historian for the Delhi Sultanate, praised the Ghurid ruler Muhammad Ghiyas al-Din (1163–203 CE) for "the slaughter of all heretics" in the province of Multan (whose streets ran in blood) in a region in lower Sindh where Ismaili preachers had been especially active.

The key Shi'a belief that threatened the Sunni caliphs was the concept of *wilayah*, the "friendship" or close proximity of the Imams to both Prophet Muhammad and God, from whence their divinely given power and authority came. The Shi'a were accused of divinizing 'Ali from the time that they declared their allegiance, both political and spiritual, to him—the first Imam, the Prophet's cousin, and the husband of Muhammad's daughter, Fatima. The Shi'a's absolute loyalty to their Imams and faith in the Imams' divinely appointed authority over all Muslims was cast as *kufr*, disbelief, and anti-Islamic—hence punishable by death.

The 1908 ruling by Justice Sir Joseph Arnold that Aga Khan III was the spiritual leader of the Satpanth Ismailis was thus both a blessing and a curse because Arnold decided the case based on the *Das Avatar*'s identification of the Nikalanki avatar with Hazrat 'Ali and by extension all Imams as the awaited tenth avatar. The following verse from the *Das Avatar* exemplifies the way the Imams were identified as avatars (and vice versa) in the *ginan* tradition generally. After describing the first nine avatars, the *granth* declares that the long-awaited savior had arrived (*avatariya*), and he was the Shah—namely, the first Shi'a Imam.

> O the venerable tenth *avatar* has arrived in the form of *Nakalank*
> In the form of Shah Mowla Murtaza Ali whose name we reveal.
> For the sake of truth, O Swamiji, you have taken descent for our good.
> Shah will mount the stallion easily and come riding along
> To rescue the devout, vanquish evil spirits [*asuras*] and demons [*danav*],
> Keeping his promise to save the *jama't* and console the desolate
> He will take in hand Shankara's powerful disc [*chakra*].
>
> (*Das Avatar*, verse 7, in Devraj 1921, 12).

This change in the status of the *Das Avatar* from its use as key evidence that had won the forty-eighth Imam's case to its disavowal a century and a half later reveals the high stakes and political dimensions of *ginan*s and religious texts generally. It also reflects the signal role that contextual factors play in interpretations of any given text, oral or written. In both instances, whether the *Das Avatar* was embraced or being hidden by the Satpanth Ismailis, a process of shifting, dissolving, and redrawing of their religious and communal boundaries was involved. The court took the *Das Avatar* seriously precisely because it was held to be sacrosanct by the Satpanth Ismailis at the time, who considered these songs to contain the essence of the Qur'an and Vedas revealed to them by their *pir*s, spiritually advanced poet-saints. The disavowal of the *Das Avatar* undercut that sacred bond and marked a key moment for the Satpanth Khoja community—namely, a gradual detachment and dissolution of its ethnic, racial, linguistic, and culturally specific identity and ultimately its transformation into a transnational, largely Westernized, and ethnically diverse Shi'a Ismaili Muslim community.

V

Behind these pivotal changes in the latter half of the twentieth century lay the current Imam's attempt to create a viable, pluralist, and transnational Ismaili identity for his followers. As the *hazir* or living Imam, Aga Khan IV's charge was to interpret the faith in the contemporary context.

During the centuries that Satpanth Ismailism was being established on the Indian subcontinent (from the eleventh to the nineteenth centuries), isolated pockets of Shi'a Ismailis from the Persian and Arabic heritage were scattered in other regions, including present-day Syria, Iran, northern Pakistan, Afghanistan, Central Asia, and even parts of China. After the fall of the Soviet Union, many Muslim groups in Central Asia who hitherto had to suppress their religious identities began to surface, and among them were the latter, lesser-known Ismaili communities. They included Ismailis in Tajikistan, Afghanistan, and Ngorno-Badakshan who over the centuries had developed their own ritual practices and literatures. Whereas knowledge among the Satpanth Ismailis in India of these other Ismaili communities was virtually nonexistent even as recently as the 1980s, the Imams had remained quietly in touch with them.

When at the age of twenty-one, the forty-ninth Imam took office in 1957, the world was already in the postatomic age. Rapid changes spurred by nationalism, globalization, mass migrations owing to political uncertainties, economic opportunities, and advances in communications and technology impacted all societies, including his followers. As living Imam, His Highness Prince Karim Aga Khan IV was thus faced with the daunting task of unifying his scattered Ismaili communities. To bring together in a coherent fashion his followers from very different regions, social and cultural backgrounds, levels of education, and disparities in wealth and living standards, he began a program of reshaping their identity and anchoring them squarely within his ancestral lineage of Shi'ism and Islamic revelation.

Since the traditions of the Satpanth Khojas on the Indian subcontinent occupied a predominant position in the Ismaili community's religious rituals, leadership, and wealth, moves made by the Aga Khan IV to bring the scattered Ismailis that were at the margins closer to the center entailed changes that would inevitably diminish the status of the Satpanth tradition expressed in the *ginan*s. The attempt to anchor the Satpanth Khojas and other dispersed followers of the Aga Khan in the Shi'a Ismaili interpretation of Islam and to create an inclusive transnational Ismaili identity essentially marginalized the *ginan*s. This marginalization is clearly reflected in the religious education materials published in the past two decades that have been used to train Ismaili preachers and teachers, which focus primarily on the Arabic and Persian traditions of Ismaili history.

*Ginan*s do not feature in the current religious education curriculum at either the primary or the secondary level. When they are referenced in religious education classes or publications, they are no longer treated as "sacred" texts, but rather as "devotional literature." At the official level in sermons and lectures, the long-cherished belief that these compositions were the inspired works of the *pir*s who initiated their forebears to Satpanth is no longer emphasized, and the mythology, cosmology, and so-called Hindu elements of the *ginan*s have been suppressed. Publications on Ismaili history have produced a public memory of *ginan*s as merely a part of a multicultural mosaic of Ismaili musical and devotional traditions—that is, as a cultural artifact. If narratives of the past reflect contemporary realities and constructions of self-identity, the master narrative that has emerged from the public presentations of Shi'a Ismaili Muslim identity has left out a rich and vital period of its history.

However, judging by the proliferation of *ginan* CDs, there are also signs of a renewed interest arising among the younger generation of Ismailis born in the West who are in search of their origins. The syncretic nature of the *ginan*s in their own cultural matrix offered a language that was rich and polyvalent, paving the way for communication while also drawing lines to delineate a distinctive identity. They simultaneously attracted and excluded various concepts and practices familiar to the *pir*s' audiences. It is not clear whether the multivalence and mythopoesis of the *ginan*s will appeal also in an altered social and historical context. Is their unique syncretic nature still capable of negotiating identities in the contemporary context? More generally, can syncretic traditions such as the *ginan*s that originated in a particular cultural, historical, and geographic milieu still have the potential to be meaningful beyond that milieu? What makes the *ginans* "wonderful," and why must they be continued as ordered by His Highness Prince Karim Aga Khan IV in his 1960 *farman*? These questions are relevant because the *ginans* are still a living tradition and an integral—if attenuated—component in the daily rituals of the global Ismaili *jama't* (community).

VI

We might begin to shed light on such questions by examining the experience of an Ismaili Muslim who belongs to the generation of Satpanth Khoja Ismailis whose lives have spanned the period of two Imams. This figure is my father, a reputed *ginan* singer who was born in Kenya to parents from Kutch, India, and who migrated and settled in Canada in 1973. He belongs to the last generation of Satpanth Khojas from East Africa that most directly experienced the displacement of the *ginans* as the primary, inspirational religious literature that shaped their religious life and identity. This *jama't* witnessed the decline in status of *ginans* from sacred songs composed by spiritually advanced *pirs* to a devotional tradition albeit tainted by its "Hindu" accretions.

Before discussing my father's experience, however, I would like to consider specifically what is meant when *ginans* are identified as a *mixture* of religious practices stemming from the Indo-Persian traditions of Ismailism. What do we mean when we call such traditions as Satpanth Ismailism "mixed"? What types of hermeneutics would help us to appreciate and distinguish between the complex interactions that take place when cultures come into contact? In an effort to theorize on the mixed traditions that emerge when diverse cultures come into contact, I offer three similes that seek to capture aspects of such cultural mixtures as expressed by the term *syncretism*.

Although substantial scholarship documents the specific nature of the innumerable religious groups that populate India, approaches to its major religions (at least in the popular media, but also large in pockets of academe) continue to assume that these religions are static, monolithic entities doomed to be in conflict perpetually, when in fact the religious boundaries that exist between its people illustrate that the relationships and self-identifications of people in India are far more fluid and permeable and closer to the interconnected, relational model represented by the tradition of Satpanth Ismaili Muslims.

Popular images of perpetual and inevitable Hindu–Muslim conflict and violence in South Asia conceal the rich, complex interconnectedness of identities in everyday life. The religious pluralism and multiple affiliations encountered from city streets to village gullies defy simple categorization and pose an intellectual challenge: How does one begin to interpret or explain the relative ease with which religious boundaries are crossed, ignored, emphasized, dissolved, and negotiated on the Indian subcontinent? How does one represent the spaces, junctions, confluences, and thresholds where identities interact and intermingle in creative and mutually enhancing ways?

Many terms have been put into use to reflect on what happens at points of cultural contact and what emerges from those encounters. The challenge is to formulate hermeneutical constructs that resist essentialist discourses that reify the concept of identity. When the term *syncretism* is used to indicate a mixture of identities, there is typically a tacit assumption that the mixed elements originate from uniform, internally consistent, and "pure" and homogenous entities. Yet, historically speaking, every culture has multiple genealogies and geographies, in which case, how does one speak of syncretisms that arise from already syncretic cultures? The concept of identity as a singular, unvaried, pure entity is flawed and romanticized. No matter how isolated a society may have been and for how long, it is heterogeneous at some level. Identity is closer to being a palimpsest of historical encounters, traces of which are inscribed on the many layers of any given culture.

If that is so, is it still useful to use the word *syncretism*, and if so, how? I suggest the term is useful if applied only in a descriptive manner. I offer three similes or models to help categorize the characteristics of cultural or religious "mixtures:" (*a*) cake; (*b*) salad; and (*c*) the figure–ground image of two faces and a vase.

VII

Syncretism comes in different forms. These forms or mixtures come about, purposefully or accidentally, to serve a function for a given time. They are adaptive mixtures of relevance for a certain duration. Some syncretisms "serve" for short periods of time and then lose their meaning or efficacy; others are mixed together in such a way that they become a synthesis and serve to satisfy the religious imagination for longer durations. They can persist or remain stable for centuries, in which case they are no longer recognized as syncretic but as coherent entities. The cake, salad, and figure–ground similes may come in handy to identify how these different elements cohere.

Syncretism, typically defined as the combining of diverse, often unrelated, and at times contradictory beliefs or schools of thought, is a useful term because it points to the fact that the disparate elements do not necessarily fuse into one and disappear, as might occur in a synthesis; rather, they can revert to their independent contexts and meanings. *Das Avatar* is a good example. Outside the Indian environment, the alignment of Shah and Avatar no longer form a coherent and sympathetic pair, and they thus revert to their original context and independent meanings. Other accretions absorbed by the *ginan*s are local enough that their significance has waned over time, especially once the compositions have made their way into other linguistic and religious landscapes.

The exercise of distinguishing between short-lived syncretisms and enduring ones is particularly useful in identifying those shared religious concepts and experiences that underlie more fluid and faded boundaries. The abiding appeal of singing the following verses in another long *granth*, *Anant akhado*, is that they do not require taking up a theological position; rather, they express sentiments such as prayers of forgiveness and yearning for the divine that would resonate with devout and ethical believers of any religious origin.

> O dear lord, pardon us our sins, so full are we of misdoings
> When I behold your countenance [*darshan*] freed am I from all this entanglement.
>
> (Imam Shah n.d., verse 63)

The full impact of the poetic verse is felt only in its performance as an act of devotion and in its original language. There is nothing uniquely "Ismaili" about this prayer; the concept of *darshan*, beholding the divine, is an integral part of Hindu devotional *puja*, worship, but at the same time the term *darshan* is used interchangeably with the Persian word *didar*, which, in the Ismaili context, specifically means to see the Imam in person and receive his blessings.

Another popular *ginan* attributed to Pir Shams, "Aba teri mahobat lagi," conveys the yearning of a devotee who sings longingly for the sight (*didar*) of her divine beloved:

> Alas, I have been struck by love (*mahobat*) for you!
> O my beloved Saheb! My heart has been swept away by love!
> Permit our eyes to meet, O my precious Saheb!
>
> (24:1, as given in Kassam 1995, 205)

As a whole, the *ginan* corpus is not limited to narratives about the tenth avatar and the Imam's arrival. In fact, much of it covers many different topics, such as everyday piety, ethical actions, devotional prayer, and mystical teachings. Theological concepts fade into the background, with the exception of the vision of the "Shah" who has saved countless souls and similarly promises to lead the faithful to salvation. Hence, alongside references to the Imam as the long-awaited avatar, a "Hindu" belief, the same *granth* has the following verse:

> All Hindus and Muslim are souls of the lord [Shah],
> Don't pick out their faults!
> For all souls will come together and meet the Shah,
> The ultimate [Narayan] will take account [of your deeds].
>
> (Imam Shah n.d., verse 177)

The identification, alignment, or parallelism of Ismaili "Shah" and Hindu "Narayana" becomes the rubric for softening or erasing boundaries between Hindu and Muslim, both of whom turn their face toward the divine. The two are held together by their mutual recognition.

VIII

I have previously utilized the image of figure–ground to illustrate how unique elements from different religious currents come together in a long treatise titled *Brahma prakash* (Divine Light), which details the inner path of spiritual enlightenment (Kassam 1995, 231–42). Discrete, selective elements from each spiritual tradition are brought together in such a way that they easily resonate with the concepts of mantra in the spiritual practices found in Hindu sects and Upanishadic and Tantric texts and *dhikr*, the constant repetition of God's names and attributes in Sufism and Islam generally. The *guru-mantra* would appear to a Satpanthi Ismaili Muslim as an obvious reference to their Muslim guru, the living Imam, the Muslim guide who's Word (*shabda* or *nama*) will bring them enlightenment. Spiritually oriented Hindus and Muslims recognize themselves in the *ginan* text, one as the chalice, the other as the two faces, each creating and sustaining the other and bound to the other.

However, one can also employ comparisons to a salad or a cake to signal a different type of syncretism in a cycle of *ginan*s called the *garbi*s by Pir Shams that narrates and reenacts a story of the community's origins (see Kassam 1995, 105–23). The syncretism found in the *garbi*s are more like a salad than a cake because, whereas the individual ingredients that go into making a cake disappear in the process and lose their separate and separable identity, the ingredients in a salad preserve their individuality and can be separated and pulled apart.

The flour in a cake cannot be extracted as flour, but the carrots in the salad can be taken out. The following verse is a good example of a cake. It is carefully crafts cohesion by identifying *nur* (divine light) and *amrita* (divine elixir). Both stand for light, liberation, and transcendence, and juxtaposing them adds new dimensions to their meaning, especially when one recognizes that the word *nur* is also specifically a reference to the Imam's light:

> Blessed the moment when Saheb showers Light upon Light (*nur*)
> When the nectar cup of Immortality (*amrita*) is filled to the brim.
> ("Saheba deakun" 7:3, as given in Kassam 1995, 172)

The simile of the cake is akin to synthesis, a more thorough and stable integration of diverse elements that after a sufficient period of time comes to define a new "pure" and "authentic" form.

The metaphor of a salad allows for the possibility that its individual elements can be removed and new ones added reflecting what Michael

Pye (1972) describes as an uneasy coexistence because they are not fused together. Ironically, because syncretic traditions are less uniform and stable, they are more open-ended. This at times unsettling potential makes them receptive to a plurality of influences. An example of salad syncretism can be seen in the scattered use of terms such as *guru, Shah, pir, Swami, Hari, 'Ali,* and *Saheb.*

Nikos Papastergiadis makes a point about hybridity that serves equally well in pointing to the ambiguity and ambivalence of "salad" syncretism: "the positive feature of hybridity is that it invariably acknowledges that identity is constructed through the negotiation of difference, and that the presence of fissures, gaps and contradictions is not necessarily a sign of failure" (1997, 258). This formulation is just as apt for the *ginans* as a whole. The "uneasy coexistence" of its various Hindu, Muslim, Sufi, Bhakti, and other elements undermines the formation of a permanently fixed, frozen, and reified identity.

At the same time, in the Satpanth context these elements' coexistence is necessary because the repeated juxtaposition of words infuses into each something of the meaning of the other. The term *swami* refers to an ascetic who has joined a monastic order and becomes a revered teacher or guru. In the *ginans*, the monastic connection is dropped, but the sense of a figure possessing experiential wisdom gained through spiritual truths combines with the figure of the Imam or living guide, the Shah or Lord, thus both amplifying the use of "Swami" and making the foreigner Shah familiar. As previously mentioned, in editions of *ginans* published in the past few decades, the name "Hari" has been replaced by "'Ali," and "Mowla" by "Swami." These seemingly small alterations, however, shift the Indic ethos of the *ginans*, extracting them from their embedded position, and to a certain extent even displacing them with "Islamic" concepts of spiritual and ethical guide.

All analogies naturally have their limitations, but the refinement and delineation of such theoretical constructs make them more useful. The syncretisms found in Satpanth Ismailism and expressed in the *ginans* were not a hodgepodge mixture of Hindu and Muslim elements. Rather, they were part of a deliberate process in as much as the *pirs* selectively chose historical and mythic figures, ritual gestures, and moral concepts to provide a hospitable, permeable, and transformative space for Hindu converts and successive generations of Satpanth Khojas to dwell in peace for many centuries.

IX

In contrast to the common dualistic representation of "Islam" and "Hinduism" in the modern era, Satpanth Ismailism is an example of Islamic presence on the Indian subcontinent that has creatively coexisted with other religious currents. Even when the transition from one religious worldview is secured, it gives rise to a new worldview from this mixing together. The movement from faith in the ten avatars of Vishnu to faith in the Shah and, by extension, 'Ali and successive Imams is still meaningful, and the new meaning of "Shah" incorporates Vishnu and his salvific power and actions.

In their daily recitation, even in abbreviated form, the *ginan*s continue to provide a language, quite literally, of words capable of being interpreted anew. This ability is not surprising given the Ismaili hermeneutic of *ta'wil* (symbolic interpretation) described earlier. As we will see in the experience of a particular *ginan* singer, significant portions of the *ginan* corpus can continue to provide a language of negotiation, reconciliation, tolerance, devotion, and spiritual enlightenment. However, the court ruling that Aga Khan III, Sultan Muhammad Shah, had a right to the property used by his followers to assemble for prayer set into motion in the community itself an unsettling process of self-reflection and questioning: Who were the Satpanth Ismailis? Were they Hindu or Muslim? Where did they come from? Why did their rituals conform neither with traditional *puja* in Hinduism nor with regular *salat* in Islam? Would their *pir*s' sacred songs fit into the modern context?

One day I put this question of religious identity to my father: "Are Ismailis Hindu or Muslim? Why do they still recite *ginan*s daily when *ginan*s have a lot of Hindu concepts?" He responded with a rhetorical question: "Who was Pir Shams? Was he a Muslim or a Hindu?" Then he started to recite a few verses from a cycle of *ginan*s called *garbi*s, attributed to the twelfth-century poet Pir Shams, who, according to communal memory, had come to the Satpanth Khojas' forbears from the "West" to guide them to *sat panth*:

> Pir Shams has shown the True Path (*satmarga*) through the *garbi*.
> Those who contemplated the eternal name, they too became immortal.
> Word by word the guru has imparted knowledge and revealed it to all.
> He explained the sacred scriptures (*veda*) and told the ancient tales from memory.
> The guru danced in the *garbi* and then started to recite the Qur'an.
>
> (*Garbi* 10:1–5, as given in Kassam 1995, 338)

He paused for a few seconds and said, "Now listen to another *garbi*:

> Satgur Shams says: O careless ones! How will you cross (the river) to the other shore?
> O Careless ones! You adorn these stones with colorful dyes but this won't buy your creator
> O Careless ones! Why go round and round in circles?
> Grasp the religion of Satpanth.
> O Careless Ones! Discard your idols of stones!
> Free yourselves from past deeds (*karma*) with the truth (*sat*).
>
> (*Garbi* 14:1–4, as given in Kassam 1995, 345)

The specific verses my father sang capture the communal memory regarding the foundation of Satpanth—namely, the narrative of conversion. The Muslim *pir* led his descendents to *sat panth* (the true path), a term that my father used interchangeably with *sirat al-mustaqeem* (straight path), used in the first chapter of the Qur'an, al-Fateha.

Anecdotal as it may be, his response does illustrate that syncretic traditions that originated in a particular historical, cultural, and geographic milieu may still have the potential to be meaningful beyond that context. His Highness Prince Karim Aga Khan IV may have anticipated that in the process of sifting through and setting aside a few *ginan*s and *granth*s that had "served their purpose," his deputies might dismiss the vast repertoire altogether. Describing them as "wonderful" in his 1960 *farman* was a clear directive to prevent this dismissal from occurring.

X

Bearing in mind the centrality of *ginans* in Satpanth Ismailism, let me turn to the view of this living tradition through the narrative lens of my father, who is much admired and loved for his powerful singing. As a devout practitioner, he has played a vital role in the transmission of the culture and teachings of Satpanth Ismailism through the performance of the *ginans* over the course of his journey from East Africa to Canada. Based on his listeners' reactions, it is clear that his singing and daily attendance in Jamat Khana (as Ismailis call their place of assembly for prayers and other social services) has inspired and left an indelible mark on many of them.

My father's name is Huzur Mukhi Rahim Count Kassam Jivraj. He is also known as "Mowla Mowla" (short for "Mowlana 'Ali") owing to his animated greeting. He was conferred the honorific title *huzur mukhi* for having served many decades ago as the conductor of religious ceremonies in a Jamat Khana in Nairobi, Kenya. This role required both he and my mother, Laila, to attend the Jamat Khana twice a day (before dawn and at sunset) to preside over the full ritual prayers and administer to the concerns of any member of the *jama't*. This role involved a daily commitment of about three hours and more on festival days. My father's father was Count Kassam Jivraj, conferred this title by His Highness Sultan Muhammad Shah, Aga Khan III, for rendering exceptional voluntary service to the Imam of the time, to his *jama't*, and to the welfare of all Muslims. On the occasion of his diamond jubilee, the Imam recognized Count Kassam for making the greatest offering during a ceremony that weighed the Aga Khan III in diamonds. In turn, the Imam invested the tributes he received in the form of diamonds from his *jama't* to create the Diamond Jubilee Trust, whose sole mandate was to service the economic needs of his community.

It is important to emphasize that my father's standing as a *ginan* singer does not stem from his being an official in the community. Rather, recognition of him by members of the *jama't* is based on his deep knowledge of *ginans* in both senses of the term—namely, *ginans* as religious ritual and *ginans* as a store of revealed knowledge. Also an entertaining storyteller, he has a store of stories, anecdotes, proverbs, and teachings collected from

3. Huzur Mukhi Rahim Count Kassam Jivraj reciting a *ginan* at Imamat Day celebrations. Photograph by Tazim R. Kassam.

Indian, Islamic, and other sources. This storehouse of happenings, imagined or factual, which he freely embellishes, has deeply influenced his worldview and shaped his identity as an Ismaili Muslim. I offer here a few episodes that reveal how the language, poetry, and music of the *ginan*s govern his speech and behavior. His actions and conversations reveal something about the ways that religious boundaries can still be expertly negotiated and transcended in the *ginan*s.

Huzur Mukhi Rahim Kassam Jivraj was born in Kenya in 1931 when East Africa was still a British colony. His parents were originally from Kutch, India. They traveled to Zanzibar on a dhow when they were very young. After getting married, his parents moved to the thriving port city of Mombasa. The East African coast already had a long history of trade and exchange with Arab Muslims from the Persian Gulf states and with Asian merchants plying their trade from the Far East via the Indian Ocean and the gulf to East Africa and thence to South Africa. By the time my father was born, there were small but thriving settlements of Arabs and Indian merchants and laborers, including Ismailis, Hindus, Sunnis, and Goans, in various towns and cities on the East African coast and inland.

The fifth of eight children, my father is easily identifiable in family photographs as the tallest. In 1954, he married my mother, Laila, and they settled in Bungoma, a tiny little village not far from Lake Victoria. By the time he married at age twenty-three, he had already developed a reputation as a *ginan* singer and as a man of faith because of his regular attendance at Jamat Khana and his performance of various religious ceremonies and social services. In addition to singing *ginan*s, he was known for his unique recitation of the *du'a,* a fixed prayer in Arabic composed of several verses of the Qur'an that every Ismaili is required to offer once in the morning and twice in the evening. His recital of the Ismaili *du'a* was influenced by the melismatic cadences of the Arabic call to prayer and cantillations of the Qur'an that he heard constantly as a child at nearby mosques in the Arab Swahili-speaking sections of Mombasa.

In addition to *ginan*s in Gujarati and Hindi and the Arabic *du'a,* he sang *bhajans, qawwali*s, *shairi*s, *garbi*s, and other different genres of vocal music at *mushaira*s, music/poetry parties, held outside the context of the Jamat Khana. These cultural activities were carried over to Western countries where Satpanth Ismailis had settled, including the United Kingdom and Canada. They were held frequently, at least once or twice a month, in the 1970s when my family moved to Canada. My father hosted many *ginan mushaira*s in which *ginan*s were sung tunefully to accompanying music. Thus, the strongest impression that most of his friends and family as well as members of the *jama't* of his generation have of him is of a passionate *ginan* singer, a fine reciter of the Arabic *du'a,* and a comical singer-storyteller.

XI

The pluralism, poetry, and performance of *ginan*s are vividly illustrated through my father's life history, as I observed in London in 2005. My parents had just arrived from Canada for a wedding. At Heathrow airport,

I met his two long-lost friends, one Hindu, the other Jain, who had also come there to receive him. His friends had arrived in London as refugees in the early 1970s when the dictator Idi Amin expelled all Asians living in Uganda. Whereas these two friends had settled in London, my parents had gone to Canada. Back in Uganda, the three had roomed together at Morogoro Agriculture College. They had not seen each other since their college days almost five decades earlier.

After they exchanged warm greetings at the airport, we piled into one friend's car and drove to my flat. I served tea and biscuits and watched my father. He was leaning forward talking excitedly, happy to be reunited with his friends, Harkhuji and Bhagwanji. He kept on repeating, "Can you believe it? After so many years? It's amazing! It's a miracle!" I had never seen him so overjoyed. Nodding his head vigorously, Bhagwanji remembered my father waking up at 3:00 AM to go to Jamat Khana on his motorbike and the *ginan*s he used to sing for them. Their conversation was in Gujarati and Kutchi, interspersed with English phrases. Bhagwanji spoke Gujarati with my mother, Harkhuji spoke Kutchi with my father, and they all somehow kept switching from one to the other. This polyglotic conversation reminded me of the vocabulary in the *ginan*s: Sindhi, Hindi, Braj Bhasha, and Gujarati, interspersed with Persian and Arabic terms.

My father recalled that they had held music parties and sung *geet*s and *bhajan*s all night. Then he launched into his favorite subject: God (*bhagwan*) was, after all, one and the same in every religion ("bhagwan to ekaj che"). The only difference was the name. One person praises Ram, another Krishna, another Allah, but the main thing was that God (*khuda*) was just one. But people didn't understand. They wanted to fight, which was of no use. Then he sang:

> Listen O *mullah*, Listen O *qazi*
> It is He who gave rise to creation.
>   Indeed, He is Allah (refrain)
> From this very clay, He fashioned the entire world! So how do you tell
>   the Muslim apart from the Hindu?
>   Indeed, He is Allah (refrain).
>
> ("Hama dila khalaq" 36:2–3, as given in Kassam 1995, 232)

My mother joined in the conversation. Her father used to say there is only one religion, and it is a pure heart ("ekaj dharama che, te che sachu dil"). Harkhuji agreed, adding into the mix, "Being good and not hurting even an ant."

Two things—the vocabulary and the topic of the conversation—struck me. A consistent feature in the *ginan*s was the use of a vocabulary that switched from Arabic or Persian to Gujarati and Hindi and Saraiki. In his conversation, my father used the words *bhagwan* and *khuda* interchangeably. There are many verses in the *ginan*s similar to the one just quoted, except these names are replaced with the words *brahmin* or *pandit*. The second observation I made was that even after so many decades had passed, the topic of their first conversation was God and eternal truths. They seemed to be reassured by it. The *ginan*s that my father sang captivated them—yet again. None of them considered their meeting after so long to be sheer luck; rather, each saw it as divine providence. Then they started talking about old friends and acquaintances that had passed away, as a result of which the atmosphere became sad. They fell silent, and my father began to sing in his distinct, powerful voice:

> O Lucky Ones! What did you bring with you into the world?
> What are you going to take back with you?
> O Lucky Ones! You were born naked and naked will you return
> So make a profit of good deeds in your daily dealings and trade.[5]
> ("E Sabhaga," verse 2, as given in *Ginane sharif* 1979, 40)

"Wah Wah!" his friends nodded. "How true." Bhagwanji was a Hindu, Harkhuji a Jain, my father a Muslim. Their affirmation appeared genuine. Singing the *ginan* seemed to remove any anxiety they may have felt from not having met for decades. The verses my father chose to sing expressed a common truth, of which there are many in the *ginan*s. In that moment, the *ginan* had helped facilitate and shape an interaction at the intersection of religious difference.

5. "E sabhaga! nago tu ayo nago to vaesi / kara gina vanaj vepara sabhaga."

Meaningful as the text was, however, it was apparent from their faces and attention that the performance had an even greater impact. My father's spontaneous singing evoked an emotional response. Memories of their past friendship had become vividly present. This performative aspect of the *ginans* is absent in a purely textual analysis of the *ginan*s and thus limits an understanding of its role in drawing them together. If melody reaches into the heart deeper than words alone, then in that brief moment with my father and his friends it felt as though a ritual had taken place. The *ginan* had preserved memories of origins, a time of shared experiences. The poetry was in familiar language, the performance drew them together, and the universal theme helped bridge the time that had separated them.

XII

The appealing performative aspect of *ginan*s can be understood in terms of their belonging to the South Asian environment, such that they evoke nostalgic pleasure through their familiar tunes and melodies in audiences that share the broad cultural inheritance of the Indian subcontinent. But, I wondered, would the impact be the same in the context of Western cultures? Would *ginan*s have the same effect on children who had grown up in London with little familiarity with the languages, poetic form, and styles of singing? An incident that occurred later in my parents' visit suggested that the *ginan*s might still carry on as a living tradition. Such incidents had happened so frequently that I had never paid them much attention until the question struck me.

One night when my father had returned from evening prayers at the Jamat Khana in London, he told me he had gotten a "*ginan waro*"—that is, he had been called on to sing a *ginan*. After prayers were over, a little boy had come running up to him and said, "Bapa, I want to sing *ginan*s just like you!" My father, a tall, rather exuberant man, said he had laughed and replied, "Yes, why not? You can sing just like me!" I had been thinking about how *ginan*s and their tunes were now being transmitted, considering that they were no longer part of the official curriculum taught in the religious education classes. In Kenya, when I was eleven years old, I had to sing *ginan*s by heart, in the right tune and with perfect pronunciation, and then translate them from memory. In the present, individual teachers are left to decide whether to hold separate *ginan* classes, especially considering that they barely have time to cover the official curriculum. When they do make time to teach *ginans*, they often have to learn the tunes from older *ginan* singers such as my father or turn cassette and CD recordings.

I asked my father how common the incident with the little boy was, and he replied that it happened all the time. "They come, youngsters and grown-ups, and they ask me for a tape of my *ginans*. Sometimes they even call me on the phone to learn the tunes." The requests had been made so frequently that he had made master cassette tapes and CDs of his favorite *ginans*, which he copied every time someone requested his *ginans*. "Do they sound like you when they learn the *ginan* from your tape?" I asked him. "Yes," he replied. "The tune and tempo are the same, but the delivery depends on the person's voice and feelings." I asked him if this type of incident happened when he was in a town or city where the *jama't* didn't know him. "All the time," he replied. "After I get a *waro* to sing, everyone asks for a tape or CD. They love how I sing *ginans*, so they want to sing like me." That's how he had learned to sing *ginans*—by listening to his favorite singers. "What about learning from cassettes?" "Why not?" he replied "as long as the tunes and wordings are right."

The story about the little boy in London signaled at least that the music and performance of the *ginans* still have an enchanting effect, assuming some knowledge of the language and cultural background on the listeners' part. However, the renewal and continuity of *ginans* will depend on a reinterpretation of their purpose. Although they no longer have the original purpose intended by the *pirs* who composed them to attract followers, the inspiration, moral teachings, and poetic beauty in the *ginan* tradition are timeless. It is in this context that one might understand why Aga Khan IV referred to the *ginans* as a "devotional tradition" and "wonderful tradition" as opposed to the *sacred* tradition that the Satpanth Ismailis had considered them to be for centuries. In the formation of Satpanth Ismailism, the syncretism of the *ginans* had served the *pirs'* original intention and was therefore efficacious and meaningful for a certain period of time. Presenting the Imam through the concept of avatar and framing the *ginans* as the essence of the Vedas and the Qur'an were apposite and functioned well in a certain context. But if the *ginan*s were to continue as a living tradition, they would have to be culled for religious and ethical norms that are relatively nonspecific to the Indic context.

XIII

As I paid more attention to my father's performance of *ginan*s in Jamat Khanas, at communal religious celebrations, and as he went about his daily chores, it became very clear to me that his primary identity was *ginan* singer. These songs of religious insight provided him with a complex language of poetry, melody, and ritual by which to carry on his daily life not just in spiritual matters, but also in utterly mundane activities. He had a *ginan* verse at the ready for virtually any ordinary situation, including traffic jams. A hundred times I had heard him recite the following verse when people bragged about their achievements or lamented their failures:

> It is I who lets you rise
> It is I who lets you fall
> Nothing is possible without Me.
> If I sent down a seed of My mercy
> A stone would break out in speech.[6]
> ("Sacho dhiyavo," verse 3, as given in *Ginane sharif* 1979, 120)

He also had a treasure trove of Gujarati, Swahili, and even English proverbs, to which he added many quotes from *ginan*s. His favorite one, the gist of which is "Trust only in God," was often used to teach a lesson in self-reliance: "Avara te aash nirash." Loosely translated, this phrase means that to peg one's hopes on anyone but God brings disappointment.

Because *ginan*s are so culturally specific in language and form to the Indian subcontinent, I had assumed that my father would feel displaced in a Western milieu and hampered in his ability to communicate meaningfully with Ismailis born in the West and with a generation that had had no exposure to *ginan*s at home or in the religious education classes.

6. "Eji me karata ne me harata, ane avarate kucha na hoya /
eka tila rahemat me chodun, to pathara bole sohi."

It was striking, therefore, to observe how he finds resources within the *ginan* tradition when faced with such challenges. His profound knowledge, experience, and immersion in *ginan*s give him both moral courage and a fertile vocabulary. Ismailis who seek his advice are drawn to him precisely because his identity is so firmly rooted in his daily religious practice. Rather than being arcane, the *ginan*s have a satisfying familiarity. He exhibits no ambiguity about his religious identity as an Ismaili Muslim even though he is constantly singing *ginan*s peppered with words such as *Swami*, *Gopal*, and *Vishnu* as as well as *'Ali*, *Shah*, and *nur*. When I asked him about this mixing of Hindu–Muslim motifs, in response he sang a *ginan* of Pir Shams:

> Who is Hindu, who is Muslim—God alone knows!
> To me, my mind is my prayer mat, Allah is my judge,
> This body of mine is my mosque.
> ("Hamadila," 36: 6, as given in Kassam 1995, 232)

Such criticism of rigid, formalistic religious divisions that draw lines in the sand are characteristic of many *ginan*s. From Nathpanthis (ascetics) to pandits (priests) and mullahs (scholars), the *pir*s deride their outward piety and extol a more fluid, spiritual faith. For my father, as perhaps for the Satpanth Khojas of prior generations, the emphasis on the authority of the living Imam in the *ginan*s repeated in many different ways is the essence of the *ginan*s. The *ginan*s' basic teaching is that the authority of the Qur'an, Vedas, and previous scriptures are vested in the Imam and that their moral teachings and devotional expression show the path by which that faith is affirmed. Faith in a living Imam is not posited upon a rejection or repudiation of the Vedas and Puranas. To the mind of modern reformers bent on Islamizing Satpanth Ismailism, however, this way of thinking is misguided because it does not excise the "Hindu" material altogether.

My father encountered a reformist one time when we were visiting family in Los Angeles. While we were having dinner, a nephew asked him, "Do we believe in the Prophet? Why do we sing all these *ginan*s? They have too much Hinduism in them." I thought my father would be upset at this challenge. The discomfort around the table was palpable.

Our hosts were clearly embarrassed, knowing as they did my father's reputation as a *ginan* singer.

He remained silent for a minute. Then he looked at my cousin and replied with a rhetorical question: "Do you say your *du'a* every day? In the third part, there is a verse of the Qur'an. It says, 'Obey Allah, obey the Prophet, and obey those with authority amongst you.' Who is the authority?" His nephew replied: "The Imam." "Now, do you know any *ginan*s? Listen to this *ginan*." And in the style of folk singers, he sang:

> Listen! Allah is the Creator of this entire Universe
> This whole world belongs to Him
> Take the name of God who is Everlasting
> Seek the essence, the mystery of this Divine Name
> Listen! Know that Muhammad is the Prophet
> Then you will realize who is the Imam
> A disbeliever gives God partners
> A true believer's heart is the Qur'an
> Seek the essence, the mystery of this Divine Name.
> ("Allah Eka Khasama," verse 1)[7]

His nephew was taken aback and said: "I didn't know the *ginan*s mentioned Allah and the Prophet. Even if they do, *Das Avatar* is not Islamic." If an appreciation of the mythopoetic universe of the *ginans* is lacking, the *pir*s' creativity in mediating two worldviews is likely to go unrecognized and forgotten.

The syncretism that my father saw in the *ginan*s is more of a cake type, the ingredients coming together favorably to create a third identity out of a harmonization of the two. His nephew, however, saw a syncretism that was more like a hodgepodge. He believed that the unwanted elements should be taken out of the *ginan*s or, better still, the *ginan*s removed from daily prayer. If viewed in this light, the instability of syncretism in the *ginans* was headed toward dispersal, even destruction, of the elements

7. As given in an undated typed manuscript in my father's private collection, in my files.

once held together by a shared culture. Such a view may become reality if *ginan*s are not taught and interpreted but remain marginal in religious rituals, sermons, and the religious education curriculum. My cousin represents a generation without the linguistic competence and roots in or direct experience of its South Asian heritage. By virtue of his lack of exposure to the piety in its poetry and performance, his perception of what it means to be "Islamic" is not far from an exoteric, orthodox position.

In contrast, for my father with his store of knowledge and stories, the *ginan*s have provided a language rich enough to navigate through various situations without a loss of identity. Singing *ginan*s is his anchor and guide, and despite the momentous changes in attitude toward the tradition that he has witnessed in his lifetime, he is far more secure in his identity even though he has lived outside the cultural ethos of the *ginan*s for a very long time.

XIV

I once asked my father how he felt about the future of *ginan*s given all the changes that had occurred during his lifetime. He answered, "We have to move with the times. Mowlana Sultan Muhammad Shah [i.e., Aga Khan III, the forty-eighth Imam] used to say repeatedly that if he gives a *farman* [edict] that contradicts his previous one, then it is our duty to listen to the latest guidance because the Imam gives advice according to the times. He is *ibn al-waqt* [son of the times] like the Prophet was *ibn al-waqt*, so the present Imam's word is final." Hence, even though some might have experienced the changes as a loss of tradition and emotional sustenance, the Ismaili *jama't* would generally accept them because, as he explained, "the Imams come for each new generation. He arrives [*avatariya*] to give us all salvation."

The distinction, then, between the concept of avatar as Vishnu's tenth incarnation and the formulation of Nikalanka as the Shah who serves as vice regent of Prophet Muhammad has to do with the Shi'a Imam's perpetual presence within history. As my father explained it, the avatar descends and departs, whereas the Imam must be ever present as the living guide (*hazir* Imam) to interpret the Qur'an. The avatar stands as a placeholder for the concept of *nur*, the Imam's divine light. My father said, "Krishna, Rama, Jesus, Adam—all had *nur*, but God is God," and then he sang a verse from "Bujh Nirinjan," a mystical *ginan* that explains that God is unknowable and ineffable:

> An unfathomable ocean, so vast;
> Whose shores can never be found;
> You may waste a lifetime diving,
> Even so, its bottom can never be found.
> [So deep] that plunging and diving time after time,
> Even *pirs* and prophets cannot reach [the bottom]. . . .
> Do not even refer to the Divine as *Niranjan* (Formless),
> Do not say anything [about it].
> Like a mute dreamer who, remembering his dream constantly,
> Regrets [he cannot tell].
>
> (verse 2, as given in Asani 1991, 121)

The *ginans* of the Satpanth Ismailis construct a bridge both *to* the religious traditions that the *pirs* encountered on the Indian subcontinent as well as *away* from them. They also form a bridge between memories of the past and realities of the present. The attractiveness of the *ginans*—their poetry, melody, mythology, symbolism, and ritualized performance—is closely linked to their familiarity.

The *pirs'* listeners recognized themselves in these songs of wisdom. At the same time, however, the *sat panth* (true path) that the *pirs* taught separated them from that familiarity in crucial ways. The *ginans* taught and expressed a path that progressively led away from the followers' previous loyalties. As seen through the *ginans*, the *pirs* intended for their listeners to swim across the river and settle down under the canopy of a different worldview. What their listeners brought along with them from their past heritage was given a new or double meaning just as the word *waves* in "waves in a river" and "waves good-bye" are not the same. Stepping into the sacred rivers of South Asia, the Ismaili *pirs* of the Satpanth Khojas undertook a difficult journey to a distant shore, where they composed and sang their songs of wisdom in a whole new idiom. The mythopoesis and enduring qualities of the *ginans* bear testimony to the *pirs'* boldness, creativity, and discernment.

Works Cited

Asani, Ali. 1991. *The Bujh Niranjan: An Ismaili Mystical Poem*. Cambridge, MA: Harvard Univ. Press.

———. 2002. *Ecstasy and Enlightenment: The Ismaili Devotional Literature of South Asia*. London: I. B. Taurus.

Daftary, Farhad. 1990. *The Isma'ilis: Their History and Doctrines*. Cambridge: Cambridge Univ. Press.

Devraj, Mukhi Laljibhai. 1921. *Pir Sadardin: Shri Nakalankni Aarti*. Mumbai: Devraj.

Eaton, Richard M. 1996. *The Rise of Islam and the Bengal Frontier, 1204–1760*. Berkeley: Univ. of California Press.

Esmail, Aziz. 2002. *A Scent of Sandalwood: Indo-Ismaili Religious Lyrics (Ginans)*. London: Islamic Publications.

Ginane sharif bhag bijo. 1979. Mumbai: Ismailia Association for India.

Ginan-e-Sharif: Our Wonderful Tradition. English Transliteration of Holy Ginans. n.d. Vol. 1. Vancouver: Shia Imami Ismaili Tariqah and Religious Education Board for Canada.

Imam Shah. n.d. "*Anant akhado ane Anant naa nav chhughaa*: A Translation and Transliteration." Typescript. Private collection (copy on file with author).

Ivanow, Wladimir. 1948. "Satpanth." In *Collectanea* 1:1–54. Leiden: E. J. Brill.

Kassam, Tazim. 1994. "Syncretism on the Model of the Figure-Ground: A Study of Pir Shams' *Brahma Prakash*." In *Hermeneutical Paths to the Sacred Worlds of India*, edited by Katherine K. Young, 231–42. Atlanta: Scholars Press.

———. 1995. *Songs of Wisdom and Circles of Dance: Hymns of the Satpanth Ismaili Muslim Saint, Pir Shams*. New York: State Univ. of New York Press.

Kassam, Tazim, and Françoise Mallison, eds. 2008. *Ginans: Texts and Contexts: Essays on Ismaili Hymns from South Asia in Honour of Zawahir Moir*. New Delhi: Primus Books.

Khan, Dominique-Sila. 1997. "The Coming of Nikalank Avatar: A Messianic Theme in Some Sectarian Traditions of North-Western India." *Journal of Indian Philosophy* 25, no. 4: 401–26.

———. 2003. *Conversion and Shifting Identities: Ramadev Pir and the Ismailis in Rajesthan*. New Delhi: Manohar.

Moir, Zawahir, and Christopher Shackle. 1992. *Ismaili Hymns from South Asia: An Introduction to the Ginans*. London: School of Oriental and African Studies.

Nanji, Azim. 1978. *The Nizārī Ismā'īlī Tradition in the Indo-Pakistan Subcontinent*. New York: Caravan Books.

Papastergiadis, Nikos. 1997. "Tracing Hybridity in Theory." In *Debating Cultural Hybridity: Multicultural Identities and the Politics of Anti-racism*, edited by Pnina Werbner and Tariq Modood, 257–81. London: Zed Press.

Pye, Michael. 1972. *Comparative Religion*. New York: Harper & Row.

Roy, Asim. 1983. *The Islamic Syncretistic Tradition in Bengal*. Princeton, NJ: Princeton Univ. Press.

Shaw, Rosalind, and Charles Stewart. 1994. "Introduction: Problematizing Syncretism." In *Syncretism/Anti-syncretism: The Politics of Religious Synthesis*, edited by Charles Stewart and Rosalind Shaw, 1–26. London: Routledge.

6

≈

Liminal Hindus

Disputed Boundaries and Their Impacts on Sindhi Hindus

STEVEN RAMEY

THE PARTITION OF BRITISH INDIA in 1947 created a political border between the newly independent nations of India and Pakistan that was ostensibly based on the religious identification of the majority in each area (with the exception of Kashmir). In this act of drawing boundaries, political leaders asserted—or surrendered to—a conception that religion provides a central basis for creating a nation. According to this idea, because Hindus belong with other Hindus, and Muslims belong with other Muslims, neither should be placed under the rule of the other when the British left. This conception of nations based on religious difference resulted in the migration of peoples across new international borders in the aftermath of Partition and the subsequent violence that led to the death of more than half a million people. Even though the motives for Partition and the related violence involved significant considerations of land, power, and economics—not just religious difference—these experiences of violence and migration reinforced people's sense of unity

I am grateful to the Sindhi Hindus in Lucknow who shared their experiences with me and to the American Institute of Indian Studies, which provided the fellowship to support my fieldwork there. When interviewees are named within this text, they have been assigned pseudonyms to protect their privacy.

based on religious identification by creating a fear of violence from the other community.

Yet the idea of religious difference that precipitated the creation of a political border is neither unquestioned historically nor accepted universally. On the ground, the limits of this idea are evident in those who refused to migrate. Six decades after Partition, more than a hundred million Muslims reside in India, and a couple of million Hindus and Sikhs remain in Pakistan. On the theoretical level, postmodern and postcolonial scholars have emphasized how the divisions between religions in South Asia developed during particular periods, especially the period of British colonial rule, and have not remained static (see, for example, Freitag 1989 and Pandey 1992). Many groups and individuals contest such government-drawn boundaries and the assumptions regarding religious interactions that accompany them. Moreover, the interactions between individuals and communities whom government definitions associate with competing religions demonstrate the inadequacies of assumptions about unbridgeable difference.

Despite these objections, the power of such government actions influences the experiences of communities and individuals who contest the common assumptions about religious differences in various ways. The recognition of how colonialism influenced contemporary definitions of Hinduism, Sikhism, and Islam as separate religions and the ways people have contested those differences throughout history do not diminish the power of the separate identities in the contemporary situation. Religious identifications, like other identifications (Žižek 1989), are public, social constructions that individuals cannot ascribe to themselves independently of the broader society. Even if the colonizers were responsible for the creation of some of these divisions through a policy of divide and rule, which is a contested assertion in itself, the act of drawing boundaries along religious lines and the related ascription of identities have become a part of the context of South Asia that no one can unilaterally undo. Moreover, the role of the lines dividing religions in the region is quite complex because many different groups, including those who contest the definitions that the governments have accepted, identify and reinforce their own sense of the differences—both in a conscious effort to promote particular interests and in a less conscious maintenance of particular assumptions.

The contemporary power of these acts of boundary drawing as well as their limits become clear in many communities' experiences. In this chapter, I focus on one particular ethnoreligious community whose members identify themselves as Hindus from the region of Sindh. Through a description and analysis of Sindhi Hindu experiences in both Pakistan and India, I analyze the influence of contemporary understandings of religious differences and boundaries as well as the contestations surrounding them, paying particular attention to the ways governments in South Asia employ and validate those boundaries. Whereas the dominant understandings define Sindhi Hindus as a liminal community—straddling the lines dividing Sikhism, Islamic Sufism, and Hinduism—Sindhi Hindus resist those assertions by defining Hinduism quite differently. Nevertheless, like others, they must also adapt to the socially dominant vision of religious differences, which are implicit even in the common terminology that enables communication with non-Sindhis, and enact rituals that blend competing understandings of religious divisions.

Introducing Sindhi Hindus

Sindhi Hindus form a community that both contests the borders established at Partition and adapts to the current configurations of religious differences in South Asia. At the time of Partition, the region of Sindh, with 75 percent of its population identifying as Muslim, became the southeastern province of West Pakistan (now identified simply as Pakistan following the independence of East Pakistan/Bangladesh in 1971).

With Partition's inclusion of their homes in Pakistan, Sindhi Hindus were extremely conflicted about their future. Many of the Sindhi Hindus wanted to stay, particularly considering their business and land assets in Sindh, yet they also worried about their immediate safety in the aftermath of Partition as well as their long-term status in the Muslim-majority nation. Because of Sindhi Hindus' wealth and significance for the functioning of the economy, the government of Pakistan discouraged their emigration, yet some Muslims from Sindh resented their economic power.

As large numbers of Muslim refugees arriving from independent India began to settle in Karachi, the main port and largest city in Sindh, Sindhi Hindus began to depart in greater numbers, creating serious economic disruptions in the region as well as the loss of assets for most Sindhis (Ansari 2005, 53–60; Sipe 1976, 190–91). In part because of restrictions on emigration and the assets that emigrants could carry, some Sindhi Hindus remained in Sindh for more than a decade, slowly liquidating their assets before emigrating, but a significant number of Sindhi Hindus have remained there permanently (Sipe 1976, 194–97).

Emigration created challenges for Sindhi Hindus as they worked to establish lives in other locations. A common tale among Sindhi Hindus in India focuses on the wealth that Sindhi Hindus left behind when they emigrated and how the difficult economic realities of migration compelled the immigrants to sell combs or soap on the streets of Bombay (contemporary Mumbai) to support their families. Over the years, many Sindhi families amassed significant wealth in India and in other countries around the world, although their business success also created resentment among other retail communities whose prices the Sindhis undercut. Emigration also separated these Sindhis from their ancestral homes and from the shrines and religious figures that their ancestors had venerated. Even when Sindhi gurus and spiritual masters themselves migrated to India, they left behind the shrines of their masters. Perhaps more significant, the dispersal of Sindhi Hindus meant that communities from particular areas of Sindh resettled in many parts of India, thus diminishing subregional connections while bringing together Sindhis as a regional community regardless of their ancestral subregion within Sindh. Resettlement in India also disrupted traditional guru–disciple relationships within families. Even when a Sindhi guru migrated to India, some of the families who were devoted to that guru were separated from him or her because they settled in a different part of post-Partition India. Some of those Sindhis who were separated from their family guru naturally became devotees of other Sindhi (and non-Sindhi) gurus who had established centers in the area of these families' new homes, thus further disrupting regional and sectarian networks.

Sindhi Hindus faced another challenge as they established their lives and permanent communities away from Sindh. Although their pre-Partition identification as Hindus had led to their migration from Pakistan, many of the people of India did not recognize Sindhi Hindu practices as being truly Hindu. These questions arose because Sindhi Hindus often incorporate veneration of Guru Nanak and the Guru Granth Sahib, commonly identified as the central text of Sikhism, as well as respect for Sufi Muslim masters. Although most Sindhi Hindus identify all of these elements as Hindu, the broader society in India identifies such practices as diverging from Hinduism, largely because of the religious differences separating Muslims and Hindus, which Partition reinforced, and the claims of Punjabi Sikhs that the Guru Granth Sahib and Nanak are exclusively parts of Sikhism. Therefore, after being forced from their ancestral lands because of the drawing of political borders based on religion, Sindhi Hindus have discovered that the boundaries that governments reinforced have also placed common Sindhi Hindu practices outside of Hinduism.

Sindhi Hindus' practices connect to certain historical claims about Sindh. Various Sindhis emphasize how the Sindhu River (now known as the Indus River) was the site for both an early civilization in South Asia, with its well-known ruins at Mohenjo Daro, and for the composition of some of the Vedic hymns that many Hindus consider to be the foundation of Hinduism. In fact, some Sindhis point out that the Vedas include the name "Sindhu" up to thirty times—using it to refer to a goddess (e.g., Rigveda 1:114) and a river (e.g., Rigveda 10:75) (Malkani 1984, 2).

However, for over a millennium Sindh remained on the periphery of the Hindu world. The region was the first area of South Asia to come under Islamic influence in the eighth century CE and remained largely in control of different Muslim rulers for more than a millennium until the British annexed it in 1843. Many Sindhi Hindus flourished under Muslim rule, becoming important figures in the administration of various rulers and gaining economic dominance in the region. Yet this political history also facilitated significant cultural developments in relation to West Asia that contribute to the questions about their Hindu identification. At times, West Asian forces invaded Sindh directly, as when Persian forces

4. Mosaic depicting Rama, Nanak, and Krishna in a Sindhi Hindu *mandir* (temple) in Lucknow. Photograph by Steven Ramey.

marched through Sindh and defeated the forces of the Mughal Empire in the late 1730s (Alam 1997, 26–30). Along with the political and military influences, significant cultural contacts led to the prominence of Islamic Sufism in the region. Styles of dress, including a traditional hat for Sindhi men, with a flat top and straight sides (similar to a Muslim prayer cap), and a greater acceptance of meat eating than within parts of Hindu society provide examples of West Asian cultural influences on Sindh and Sindhi Hindus.

Another significant influence on the Sindhi region and culture was Punjab, the region to the north of Sindh that is named for five rivers that are tributaries of the Sindhu/Indus. Scholars have identified historical connections between these neighboring regions, with population exchanges in different eras (Cook n.d., 4–9; Levi 2002, 112–19). Sindhis also emphasize the travels of Guru Nanak through Sindh, which separated Punjab from the coast of the Arabian Sea. The Nirmalas and other traveling ascetics related to Nanak's lineage promoted the veneration of the Guru Granth Sahib and Nanak within Sindh (Oberoi [1994] 1997, 128). These elements—as well as the geographical position of Sindh in relation to the Hindu heartland, West Asia, and the Punjab—influenced the development of those ritualized practices that many Sindhi Hindus identify as a distinctive feature of their regional heritage.

Contesting and Accepting Partition

Like the cultural and political influences in Sindhi history, the creation of political borders at Partition has been a major influence on Sindhi Hindus, yet individual responses to the creation of these boundaries have varied considerably. Many Sindhi Hindus have adapted to the exigencies of emigration from Sindh, despite the trials that it created, and some have recognized the ultimate benefit of Partition on the community. One Sindhi in particular who was born after Partition expressed gratitude for the migration, comparing the "backwardness" of Sindhis who remained in Sindh to the positive progress that Sindhi immigrants in India have made. Nevertheless, others continue to contest the creation of those divisions in a variety of ways.

One obvious group that contests the rationale of Partition is made up of those Hindus who remain in Pakistan. According to the Population Census Organization of Pakistan, in 1998 Hindus represented 1.6 percent of the nation's population, which comes to roughly 2.5 million people. Approximately 80 percent of Pakistan's Hindus, close to 2 million individuals, resided in Sindh (Population Census Organization 1998). These Hindus in Sindh have faced some difficult experiences as a minority in Pakistan. The tumultuous political changes in the country and the occasional flare-ups of Hindu–Muslim animosity have reinforced the feelings of exclusion and difference that initially led to the partition of the subcontinent.

However, these Sindhi Hindus remain by choice and are not entirely isolated. Some contacts persist between Sindhi Hindus in India and those who remain in Pakistan, especially through family connections and guru movements. For example, at the time of Partition, one Sindhi Hindu guru, Asuda Ram, and many of his followers remained in their ancestral home, Pano Aqil, Sindh. When Asuda Ram died, his son Chandu Ram became his successor and continued to serve his father's *samadhi* (shrine commemorating the internment of ashes) in Sindh until 1977, when he established an ashram in Lucknow, India. Even from this new ashram, he continues to receive visitors from Sindh and visits his father's *samadhi* occasionally, except when the governments close the border. Similar connections enliven other guru movements in India that have followers in Sindh.

In one twist on the typical Sindhi Hindu tale of Partition, a daughter of a prominent Sindhi retailer in Lucknow, India, returned to Pakistan in the 1950s to marry the son of a prominent Sindhi Hindu family that had remained in Pakistan. Although the couple remained in Pakistan until the husband's death, they sent their sons to study in India, where both sons have settled and married. At her husband's death, the widow moved to India to live with one son. In our conversation, she expressed the trials of her years among the minority in Pakistan and specifically presented herself as a "staunch Hindu."

Whereas these various examples illustrate people defying, either temporarily or permanently, the division of the subcontinent along religious lines by living as a minority across the border, others who emigrated continue to contest Partition ideologically. H. G. Daswani, an Indian civil servant who retired in 2000 and periodically wrote about his Sindhi Hindu heritage, had immigrated to India in 1948 with his parents. He continued to denounce the act of Partition in various articles over the years and in an interview with me fifty-five years after Partition. His argument against Partition involved a range of points, including the lack of a plebiscite, unspecified contradictions to international law, broken promises made by Indian leaders, and loss of the entire province of Sindh (unlike the Partition of Bengal and Punjab). Most significant here, he disputed the notion of difference between Hindus and Muslims in Sindh. In an article published in 1983, he described Partition as the "dismemberment of United India and forcible convertion [*sic*] of sufi-secular [*sic*] Sindh into part of a theocratic State of Pakistan" (Daswani 1983, 5). The phrase *sufi-secular* in his usage combines the South Asian sense of "secular" as not favoring one religion over another as well as a common Sindhi understanding of Sufism as involving a love for the divine in any religion, thus transcending religious distinctions. The difference between Hindus and Muslims in Sindh, he said, was simply their names and their ancestry. In terms of actions, they were basically the same. In our interview, he detailed other similarities between Hindus and Muslims, declaring that "Sindhis are from the same culture. . . . [Our] way of talking, way of reading, way of eating, eating habits are the same. There is no difference between Hindu and Muslim if fanaticism is removed." Therefore, in his view, the entire basis for Partition was faulty because Sindhi Muslims had more in common with Sindhi Hindus than with the Muslim "fanatics," as he called them, who immigrated to Sindh following Partition.

Within Daswani's ideological resistance to the loss of all of Sindh at Partition lies the common fear among Sindhi Hindus that without a homeland they are losing their language and culture. My research suggests that the loss of Sindhi Hindu distinctiveness is not imminent because Sindhi Hindus establish distinctive practices incorporating the Guru Granth Sahib, deities, and Sufi masters in many parts of India and beyond. But this fear is very real among some Sindhi Hindus and parallels the loss of Sindhi language in Sindh owing to the influx of non-Sindhi immigrants and the dominance of Urdu and Punjabi in contemporary Pakistan (Ansari 2005, 147–48).

Although Daswani is not alone, especially within his generation, in denouncing the basis of Partition, the majority of Sindhi Hindus have in essence accepted Partition to some degree and have chosen to move forward in their current situation. One outcome of this acceptance is the growing prominence of Jhule Lal as a symbolic figure for Sindhi Hindus in India. Identifying Jhule Lal as the Sindhi god and an incarnation of Vishnu, many Sindhi Hindus retell how he came out of the Indus River to help Sindhi Hindus. Prior to Partition, veneration of Jhule Lal was most prominent among a subgroup of Sindhi Hindus, but after Partition a Sindhi Hindu leader emphasized Jhule Lal as a unifying symbol to represent their distinctive heritage, and this leader's efforts have been largely successful (Young Sindhi Adults 2006, 10).[1] For example, one Sindhi institution in Chennai, India, has selected Jhule Lal as the most public symbol of their heritage, prominently placing a statue of him overlooking its entranceway.

1. Also, several interviewees who lived in Sindh before and since Partition have anecdotally suggested that Jhule Lal is much more important in the Sindhi diaspora than among Sindhi Hindus in Sindh.

5. Honored lithographs of Jhule Lal (*center*), Satram Das, and Guru Gobind Singh placed before the canopy containing the Guru Granth Sahib in a Sindhi Hindu *mandir* in Lucknow. Photograph by Steven Ramey.

Interestingly, the story of Jhule Lal reflects an assumption of the divisions between religious communities that resembles the assumptions behind Partition. That is, in the story about him Jhule Lal comes out of the Sindhu River in response to the cries of Hindus when a Muslim ruler of Sindh has declared that all Hindus must convert to Islam or be killed. Jhule Lal convinces the ruler to desist from forcing Hindus to convert, and all is well again—even to the point that some Muslims then become followers of Jhule Lal. In other words, despite the commonalities between Sindhi Muslims and Hindus that G. H. Daswani and many other Sindhi Hindus promote, this story emphasizes the existence of differences between Hindus and Muslims in Sindh. The tension, however, is alleviated through the appearance of a Hindu deity who demonstrates the superiority of Hinduism by teaching the Muslims how they should act. Perhaps the popularity of this story relates to its resonance with Sindhi Hindus' traumatic experiences of Partition and its aftermath. It also reflects the ambiguous attitudes among Sindhi Hindus because it rejects, to some extent, the religious differences separating Sindhi Hindus and Sindhi Muslims (the Muslims also became followers of Jhule Lal), yet it also reinforces the generalized boundary separating the communities in India.

As the increasing veneration of Jhule Lal suggests, one consequence of Partition has been the creation of a distinctive and united Sindhi Hindu community. Political activities prior to Partition began emphasizing the distinctiveness of Sindh as Sindhi leaders succeeded in separating Sindh from the larger administrative unit of the Bombay Presidency in 1936. Nevertheless, this political action did not eliminate the distinctive subregional groupings and other divisions among Sindhi Hindus based on occupation (as traders or civil servants), yet the loss of their homeland and the exigencies of migration made the maintenance of these smaller divisions more difficult because Sindhis were separated from their local communities. To maintain their heritage, many Sindhis have abandoned these smaller divisions and focused on the unity of the larger regional community, which Jhule Lal came to symbolize.

Drawing Boundaries Promotes Liminality

Beyond the changes and challenges that the religious boundaries of Partition instigated for Sindhi Hindu experiences, the creation and validation of religious differences have influenced Sindhi Hindus in more subtle ways. Their distinctive practices have complicated their experiences after Partition. Many non-Sindhis in India place Sindhi Hindus in a liminal position, questioning their Hindu identification because these distinctively Sindhi practices diverge from the dominant understanding of the differences between Hinduism and Sikhism. In other words, after feeling forced to leave their homeland because they were Hindu and not Muslim, Sindhi Hindus in India are told that they do not really fit the Hindu majority. This liminality increases Daswani's frustration with Partition because it further supports his argument that the logic of Partition was faulty and that Sindhi Hindus' commonality as Sindhis was greater than the unity of all Hindus. He illustrates non-Sindhis' response to Sindhi Hindus in India and their practices when he writes,

> Often, they [non-Sindhi friends] ask the following questions:—
>
> 1. What is your religion?
> 2. Are you also Hindus?

> 3. How is it that you Sindhis worship Guru Nanak Deo and read Guru Granth Sahib? (n.d., 1)

Daswani is not alone in facing such questions, as other Sindhi Hindus whom I interviewed in India related similar frustrations with a lack of acceptance as Hindus after Partition.

This liminal status of Sindhi Hindus has created a defensiveness among some of them about their Hindu identification. In asserting that venerating the Guru Granth Sahib is a Hindu practice, various Sindhis have argued that all of the Sikh gurus were Hindus and that the concept of a separate Sikh identity did not arise until Gobind Singh instituted the Khalsa. One leader even stated that Nanak's teachings made the concepts of the Vedas accessible to his common followers, and another leader suggested that Nanak was a Hindu reformer, teaching the true meaning of Hinduism in contrast to the empty rituals of some traditional Hindu practices. Other Sindhis have also asserted that because the gurus in Nanak's lineage were Hindus, the Guru Granth Sahib—the majority of which is constituted by the compositions of the first five gurus within Nanak's lineage—is clearly a Hindu text. Other Sindhis have asserted that the Guru Granth Sahib is Hindu because it contains the names of Hindu deities, such as Rama, throughout the text. The inclusion of compositions by Hindu and Muslim figures further supports two Sindhi assertions—that the text is not exclusive to a separate religion but is Hindu and that Hinduism is an inclusive tradition.

In relation to Sufism, the accounts of various Sindhi Hindus I interviewed suggest that many Hindus and Muslims venerated Muslim spiritual masters, some of whom accepted Hindu disciples without requiring them to convert. In at least one case, a Muslim Sufi provided separate dining and housing arrangements for his Hindu disciples and advised two Hindus who wanted to convert to Islam to remain firm in the religion in which God arranged their birth (Gajwani 2000, 41–42). This same Sufi Muslim also visited Hindu temples, serving the yogis there, and practiced yoga and *pranayama* (breath control, typically associated with Hinduism) (Gajwani 2000, 39).

Since migrating to India, Sindhi Hindus have maintained some of this veneration of Sindhi Muslim Sufis, though few have extended their veneration of Sufis to non-Sindhi figures, reinforcing how these practices have a more important connection to regional identification than to religious affiliation. Placing this veneration of Sindhi Muslim Sufis in Hindu terms, many Sindhi Hindus assert that Sufism refers to a deep devotion to the divine that extends beyond the confines of any religion. Two significant gurus within Sindhi Hindu communities—Chandu Ram from Lucknow, India, and J. P. Vaswani from Pune, India—have admonished their followers to be "Sufis," meaning to be in love with the divine (Ramey 2008; Vaswani 2002, 75). A Sindhi guru movement in Chennai similarly identifies its primary site as "Sufi Dar" and continues to venerate Sufi Muslims there alongside Hindu deities, Nanak, the Guru Granth Sahib, and Christian figures, including Jesus. Although Sindhi Hindu descriptions of Sufism often recognize, implicitly or explicitly, the historical relation of Sufism to Islam, they emphasize the extension of the term *Sufi* beyond any one religion. Sindhis frequently identify Dr. Rochal Das, another Sindhi religious teacher-guru, as a Sufi because his master was a Muslim Sufi. Moreover, Rochal Das's son and successor directly asserts that the Hindu monistic philosophy of Vedanta and Sufism represent the same spiritual practice. The only difference is "semantic" (Hari 1982, 15). A third assertion about Sufism comes from a leader of the Sindhi Hindu community in Lucknow who argues that Sufis adopted aspects of Hinduism and thereby learned how to follow Islam properly. Therefore, in this view, Sufism is a Hinduized reform of Islam.

The centrality of Sufism to Sindhi culture is one aspect of Daswani's argument that Sindhi Hindus and Muslims are deeply connected. Although his statements create a false dichotomy between the peaceful Sindhi Muslims and Muslims elsewhere who promoted Partition, the sense of connection between Sindhi Hindus and Sindhi Muslims is significant in terms of religious practices. When non-Sindhis reject the Hindu identification of Sindhi Hindus, such an assertion reinforces the religious connections between Sindhi Hindus and Muslims—via Sufism—meaning that the regional connections among Sindhis are as strong as the religious connections between Sindhi Hindus and non-Sindhi Hindus. As a consequence, the decision to divide the subcontinent based on a particular understanding of religious difference ignored the cultural connections uniting people of particular regions as well as those understandings of religious difference and religious similarity that differed from the assumptions on which the borders of Partition were drawn.

Because of the experiences of Partition, Sindhi Hindus face the challenge of maintaining their distinctiveness as a regional community—a distinct community that itself is fairly new in many respects—while relating to the larger Hindu community. Older generations fear that their children will lose their distinctive heritage through the experience of growing up with non-Sindhi Hindus. Although some second- and third-generation Sindhi immigrants have moved away from their regional identification, Sindhi Hindu communities in many places have put significant resources into creating activities and community organizations that maintain a sense of their Sindhi heritage, which is always being revised. Yet these organizations must negotiate an environment that draws boundaries between religions in ways that place their Sindhi heritage in a liminal position.

Contemporary Drawing of Boundaries

The power of officially declared religious differences does not stop at the creation of an international border or theoretical debates about definitions. Although the advent of an independent, secular state in India after the British left was meant to create a neutral government in relation to religious issues, the secular government has often taken actions that have assigned individuals and contested sites definite religious identifications that overrule their contested identifications. For example, the government identifies particular religions and the boundaries separating them in the census. Defining Sikh and Jain as distinct categories separates those traditions from Hinduism and implicitly rejects other understandings of the connections between those communities that some people in India continue to promote. India's maintenance of separate personal laws for Muslims similarly involves the government in determining who falls under those laws and who does not as well as deciding which interpretations of religious decrees become a part of the personal law. Such issues are clearly visible in the Shah Bano case, in which a divorced Muslim woman in the 1980s sued her exhusband for continued monetary support even though some Muslims understood Islamic law to require maintenance for only three months. After the court ruled in favor of the wife, Prime Minister Rajiv Gandhi promoted a law reversing the court's decision and partially accepting one conservative interpretation of Islamic law. The government also oversees the resources, including land, that have been donated to religious shrines, with different agencies handling shrines identified as Muslim and shrines identified as Hindu. This separation has led to disputes over the identification of sites that attract both Hindus and Muslims, such as the Dattatreya Peetha–Baba Budangiri shrine in Karnataka (Sikand 2003, 64–65). In such situations, the government is in the position of adjudicating religious definitions as it determines which agency should oversee a particular shrine.

The dynamics of religious boundaries are not limited to the perceived lines separating Hindus and Muslims. The governmental recognition of religious differences also relates to disputes within what many people would identify as one religion. Because the act of defining religious identifications necessitates excluding some things from each religion, people who identify with any particular religion often disagree over what is truly a part of that religion. The most notable example of this problem—one that is particularly relevant to the Sindhi Hindus' situation—is the definition of a Sikh. In the early twentieth century, some Sikhs promoted a political movement that asserted that only a particular group of Sikhs were true Sikhs. They further argued that control over Sikh religious sites, known as *gurdwara*s, should reside exclusively with this particular group of Sikhs (Oberoi [1994] 1997). After the colonial government acquiesced in 1925 to part of this movement's agenda and placed *gurdwara*s in Punjab under the control of an elected body of Sikhs, the Shiromani Gurdwara Prabandchak Committee (SGPC), the question became more complicated: Who should have a vote in the election of members to the SGPC? The practices and attributes that a true Sikh shows have remained a matter of dispute among people who identify as Sikh, further complicating the issue of Sikh identity.

This particular issue of the definition of Sikhs closely relates to the experiences of Sindhi Hindus on both sides of the borders created at Partition. With the general Sindhi understanding of Hinduism as including Nanak and the Guru Granth Sahib, the religious institutions of Sindhi Hindus frequently include a Guru Granth Sahib. According to the statements of various Sindhi Hindus and some published accounts, the Guru Granth Sahib was often present in Sindhi Hindu temples in pre-Partition Sindh (Thakur [1959?], 65). Continuing the prominence of the Guru Granth Sahib since emigration, many Sindhi religious institutions, such as the Sindhu Sadan in Chennai, India, place a copy of the Guru Granth Sahib and an image of Nanak alongside *murtis* (statues, literally "bodies") of deities.

The presence of the Guru Granth Sahib in Sindhi Hindu institutions has created some legal difficulties. In Karachi, Sindh, the differences separating Sikhism and Hinduism have been invoked to argue that the Guru Nanak Temple at Arambagh—a Sindhi Hindu institution that houses Hindu deities and the Guru Granth Sahib—should be under Sikh control because the presence of the Guru Granth Sahib makes the institution a *gurdwara*. One individual—arguing that the institution is Sikh—described the Hindus' intentions as a desire to "practice and preach Hinduism from this *gurdwara* on the plea that Guru Nanak and other Gurus were Hindus." He then countered, "But it is a common knowledge that both Hindus and Sikhs are two different religions" (*Eastern News* 2005). His assertion of "common knowledge" is exactly the point that many Sindhi Hindus want to contest and illustrates their concern that the dominant understanding may gain further support from governmental authorities. This dispute has resulted in a lengthy battle in Pakistani courts over control of the institution and the closing of the institution by those courts during that process (*Dawn* 2005; *Eastern News* 2005). Besides appealing to the courts to declare the institution a *gurdwara* under Sikh control, the Sikhs involved in the dispute have also called for a law resembling the Gurdwara Act of 1925 in India to place control of *gurdwaras* throughout Pakistan exclusively in the hands of Sikhs (*Eastern News* 2005). As this example from Sindh suggests, the liminal status of Sindhi Hindus relates to more than mere social pressure to conform to mainstream understandings of religious boundaries. Although I am not aware of other cases involving the use of judicial authority to declare that a Sindhi site with the Guru Granth Sahib should be under Sikh control, Sindhi Hindus in other places have feared this situation.

In Lucknow, India, members of a Sindhi Hindu community installed a Guru Granth Sahib in their community/social service center in 1954 and named that aspect of their center the "Harmandir"—the name of the Golden Temple in Amritsar, Punjab, perhaps the most famous shrine for Sikhs. After two decades of community growth, in 1977 they established a separate institution with a Guru Granth Sahib in its center. For continuity, they maintained the same name for the new institution, the Harmandir. In 1985, however, the community became frightened. Following violence in the Punjab in 1984—including the Indian army attack on Sikh militants who resided in the precincts of the Harmandir in Amritsar, the assassination of Prime Minister Indira Gandhi by her Sikh bodyguards, and the subsequent violence against Sikhs in Delhi and other parts of India—relations between Sikhs and Hindus were severely strained. Rajiv Gandhi, the son of Indira Gandhi who succeeded her as prime minister of India, made an agreement with moderate Sikh leaders in 1985 that included a promise to pass the All-India Gurdwara Legislation. Like the Gurdwara Act of 1925 in Punjab, this bill would have placed historical *gurdwara*s throughout India under the control of the SGPC.

The bill never passed India's Parliament, and its reference to historical *gurdwara*s might have excluded an institution such as the Harmandir. Nevertheless, it created significant concern among Sindhi Hindus in Lucknow that Khalsa Sikhs would attempt to take control of the temple because it contained the Guru Granth Sahib. To counter this possibility, members of the community made a variety of changes to their institution. They changed the name of the institution from "Harmandir" to "Hari Om Mandir." (According to the Harmandir's president, Gobind Wadhwani, the insertion of "Om" "added a Hindu touch.") From that time forward, they also began adding a variety of shrines along the walls, with *murtis* of various Hindu deities, including Jhule Lal, Ganesh, Durga, Radha-Krishna, and Rama, and they placed a copy of the Bhagavad Gita under the central canopy alongside the Guru Granth Sahib. In the courtyard of the

Hari Om Mandir, they added other shrines to Jhule Lal, Shiva, and Hanuman. Over the canopy, they also added a large brass "Om." These various additions to the institution clearly emphasized a Hindu identification that non-Sindhis in Lucknow would recognize, and they were initiated with the hope of preventing Sikh attempts to take control of the temple.

These additions did not, however, displace the Guru Granth Sahib from the center of the institution, even almost two decades later. In 2002, the reading of the Guru Granth Sahib during the Sunday morning *satsang*s at the Hari Om Mandir continued to be the climax of the ritualized event because participants gave much greater attention to this reading than to the discourse that preceded it—which usually focused on the Bhagavad Gita—or to the reading of the enshrined copy of the Bhagavad Gita immediately afterward. When the community performed *arti*, the offering of a burning lamp before a sacred object, the majority of the devotees offered the lamp to the canopy with the Guru Granth Sahib, and few showed any interest in doing so before the *murti*s. Moreover, community members regularly presented cloths to the Guru Granth Sahib as an act of thanksgiving for a particular blessing, such as the birth of a child, but the Bhagavad Gita and the various *murti*s received few, if any, offerings like this. Wadhwani, the former president of the Hari Om Mandir, specifically emphasized this maintenance of full respect for the Guru Granth Sahib to counter implicitly any argument from Sikhs that the community disrespects the Guru Granth Sahib by including *murti*s in the same institution. Perhaps more significant, the maintenance of the Guru Granth Sahib and its continued centrality reflected the depth of devotion that this Sindhi Hindu community felt for the Guru Granth Sahib—even when their fears could easily have encouraged them to remove the Guru Granth Sahib to eliminate any possibility of losing their institution to Sikh control.

In this situation, the fear of governmental and legal attempts to place particular elements under the control of particular religious groups led a community to alter its institution and its ritualized activities. Community members' deep devotion to the Guru Granth Sahib is clear in their refusal to accept Sikh assertions that it is exclusively Sikh. However, that devotion to the Guru Granth Sahib did not exclude, before or after the changes, devotion to Hindu deities and Sufi masters, despite the assumptions within governmental and societal definitions of the boundaries between Hinduism and Sikhism. The changes that they made to the institution were both cosmetic and fitting based on common Sindhi Hindu understandings of Hinduism. In an interesting way, the altered practices at the Hari Om Mandir reflect more fully the combination of practices that make up the common understanding of Sindhi Hindu traditions than the original Harmandir in Lucknow did. This development was further underlined when they installed images of Sindhi gurus, which some identified as Sufis, applying the general Sindhi Hindu understandings of Sufism.

Both the Karachi case and the Lucknow situation illustrate the liminal position of Sindhi Hindus between Hinduism and Sikhism. The power of the legal definition of religious differences, moreover, is clear from the fear it induced. In the Karachi case, the liminality has meant that all Sindhi Hindus were barred from using the institution in question. In Lucknow, the fears led a community of Sindhi Hindus to emphasize Hindu elements of their identity in order to bolster their independent control of the institution that they had created.

Social Impact of Boundaries

The preceding discussions address the direct influence of the government's act of defining religious differences and the fear that the government can enforce particular visions of religious orthodoxy. Partition and the legal decisions about what is a *gurdwara* and who controls it have been powerful forces influencing the actions of and developments among Sindhi Hindus. However, the governmental act of drawing boundaries adds further force to the popular definitions that place Sindhi Hindus and communities like them in a liminal position. When the government legislates a particular designation of religious boundaries, it legitimizes one of a number of contested classifications. With the passage of the Gurdwara Act of 1925 and the political activism that precipitated its passage, the recognition of the separation of Hinduism and Sikhism that predominated in that movement became dominant in South Asia—as seen in the comment by one of the disputants in Karachi about the separation of Sikhism and Hinduism being "common knowledge" (*Eastern News* 2005). Although it may be an overstatement to say that government actions create this legitimacy, those actions clearly contribute to the powerful assumptions implicit in such religious boundaries.

The legitimization of these definitions contributes to other challenges that Sindhi Hindus experience in diaspora. Beyond the frustration of having their identification as Hindus questioned in India, which is evident in Daswani's statements given earlier, living in an environment where government assertions reinforce these dominant conceptualizations of differences has made Sindhi Hindu self-representations difficult. To communicate with others, Sindhi Hindus often follow the mainstream usage of certain terms, yet at other times they switch to common Sindhi Hindu understandings. Whenever Sindhi Hindus use the terms *Hindu* and *Sufi,* they might be referring to Hinduism and Sufism either as most Sindhis define them or as they are understood more broadly in India. Many Sindhi Hindus whom I interviewed switched between these competing understandings.

Gobind Wadhwani, the president of the Lucknow Harmandir during the period when changes were made to the institution, demonstrated this tendency to shift between mainstream conceptualizations and Sindhi definitions as he defended the changes made under his leadership. During a ritualized reading of the Guru Granth Sahib at the Hari Om Mandir, Wadhwani explained that Hinduism comprised a diverse group of elements—including the worship of "idols," the *tulsi* plant, and other parts of nature. A few moments later, he pointed to the canopy containing the Guru Granth Sahib and said, "We Hindus take everything that is good, but the Sikhs are really Hindus." This one sentence demonstrates clearly his shifting between Sindhi understandings and prevailing pan-Indian understandings. "Take" here implies adopting things that are outside the borders, which belong to another. Therefore, his gesture toward the canopy suggested that the Guru Granth Sahib was originally outside of Hinduism. After this statement assuming that Sikhism is a separate religion, he quickly switched back to Sindhi classifications with the assertion "Sikhs are really Hindu." Even the use of "really" in this context demonstrated his experience that many Sikhs and Hindus reject the identification of Sikhs as Hindu. In a more formal interview several weeks later, he similarly stated, "Besides *our own* deities, we pay regards to the Guru Granth Sahib" (emphasis added). The Guru Granth Sahib, therefore, is not their "own" religious text but someone else's—namely, the Sikhs. Wadhwani was not alone in these shifting representations; other leaders at the Hari Om Mandir similarly asserted that the Guru Granth Sahib and Nanak were Hindu, but at other times they described Sikhism as a separate religion according to mainstream definitions. Similar issues complicated Sindhi Hindu discussions of Sufism, as individuals I met described Sufism both as an attitude applicable in any religion and as a religious movement within Islam. The inconsistencies in these representations illustrate the challenges that Sindhi Hindus and others face as they contest definitions of religions that dominate the terminology and modes of expression within the society in which they live.

Within these representations, Sindhi Hindus continue to define religious differences and to use the labels that signify those differences in order to promote their community. Many leaders and community members classify religions in an effort to contest the dominant definitions and place their community clearly within the bounds of Hinduism. They make particular assertions about their community's religious identification and commitment, as seen in Sindhi Hindus' refusal to convert to Islam in the story of Jhule Lal. Moreover, they challenge Sikh assertions that Nanak and the Guru Granth Sahib belong to a separate religion. When Wadhwani asserted that Sikhs are "really Hindus," he was not rejecting the existence of boundaries. He was asserting a different definition of those boundaries that place Sindhi Hindus within the majority community in India. Other Sindhi leaders in Lucknow made similar attempts to redefine the content of each religious label in order to place Sindhi Hindus clearly within the confines of Hinduism. Such efforts reflect a movement away from Daswani's assertions that Sindhi Hindus and Muslims have more in common ethnically than either group has with other Hindus or other Muslims religiously.

Sindhi Hindu assertions of boundaries also serve to affirm the superiority of their community. The story of Jhule Lal reflects a clear division between Hindus and Muslims. In telling the story, many Sindhi Hindus emphasize both the tolerance of Hindu elements—in contrast to the belligerence of the Muslim ruler—and the superiority of Hinduism as the Muslims learn from Jhule Lal and submit to him. Other statements draw distinctions between Sindhi Hindus and the Sikhs. When they contest Sikh assertions that Sikhism is a separate religion, they implicitly suggest that Sikhs misunderstand the teachings of Nanak and other Sikh gurus. Other statements by Wadhwani similarly assert that Sindhi Hindus are "more Sikh than Sikhs themselves," which emphasizes their superior commitment and devotion to the teachings of the gurus in Nanak's lineage. In these ways, religious differences are important for Sindhi Hindus' self-image and assertions of superiority. They simply contest where the boundaries of each religion should be placed.

Creating and Contesting a Liminal Position

Sindhi Hindus' experiences clearly illustrate some of the complexity in the designation of religious differences. Official acts of drawing religious boundaries have had significant consequences for Sindhi Hindus because these understandings have contributed to placing Sindhi Hindus in a liminal position. The creation of new political borders (both physical and metaphorical) defined the Sindhi Hindus as minorities in Muslim-dominated Pakistan and contributed both to their forced diaspora and to challenges to their control over their institutions containing the Guru Granth Sahib. Indian governmental acceptance of certain definitions also reinforced social understandings that labeled the practices of Sindhi Hindus as beyond mainstream Hinduism and complicated Sindhi Hindus' abilities to represent themselves. In these ways, the implications of government definitions of religions, before and after Partition, are quite clear for Sindhi Hindus.

Identifying the power of boundary making in cultural contexts is, of course, nothing new. Postcolonial and postmodern research has emphasized the consequences of religious labels and definitions as they identify the historical nature of the act of drawing religious boundaries—even if communities want to assert a primordial or transhistorical basis for this act. However, Sindhi Hindus' experiences emphasize how these acts of boundary drawing are ongoing, as are their consequences. The designation of religious differences is not limited to the colonizers' divide-and-rule attitudes, nor is it limited to radical groups that want to create some sort of religious oppression. Mainstream Sikhs and Hindus assert particular definitions that exclude Sindhi Hindu institutions such as the Hari Om Mandir, and those exclusions have serious consequences for this contemporary community. Although Sindhi Hindus experience the challenges that these definitions create for their community, they also maintain their own understanding of religious differences. The consequences of historical boundary drawing cannot be undone simply by highlighting the historical context of the creation of divisions. Many groups continue to assert and promote particular understandings of religions in order to further the status of their community in relation to others.

Given the power of the government behind certain understandings of religious boundaries, we see groups such as the Sindhi Hindus having to choose between conforming (in order to attain the benefits of governmental recognition) and opposing the definitions that the government and the broader society promotes. On the one hand, to maintain control over their institution, Sindhi Hindus in Lucknow have chosen to conform partially to society's understanding of Hinduism in that they are not choosing to accept the labeling of their institution as Sikh. On the other hand, they have not conformed completely in that they maintain the Guru Granth Sahib within the institution. Conforming to governmental definitions in one sense reinforces the dominance of those definitions because dissenting voices become fewer when those groups who contest the definitions conform to them publicly. When alternative voices are not heard, the governmental definitions gain a further aura of being the transhistorical, unquestioned state of things.

Sindhi Hindu resistance to these definitions of differences does not appear as a rejection of the act of drawing boundaries itself, but rather as an objection to how the boundaries are drawn. Much like Daswani's frustration with the location of political borders drawn at Partition, many Sindhi Hindus contest the definition of the lines dividing Hinduism, Islamic Sufism, and Sikhism. Rather than rejecting any boundaries, they redefine those boundaries in ways that (*a*) emphasize the status of their community within the Hindu majority and (*b*) argue for their superiority to other groups, in particular Sikhs and "fanatical" Muslims, who—according to many Sindhi Hindus—misunderstand the teachings of their main religious leaders and texts.

We can now see the full range of the dynamics at play in the making of definitions and the drawing of boundaries in this religio-social/political context. Groups such as the Sindhi Hindus who are forced into liminal positions must then negotiate these "boundary" situations—conforming to and contesting them in order to promote their own interests and even struggling to represent themselves without succumbing to the dominant definitions. The combination of governmental boundary drawing, whether intentional or unintentional, and dominant assumptions within a society creates a powerful influence that legitimizes distinct identities and dismisses those who contest those definitions. Groups left in limbo must adapt and struggle to maintain their own identities and the traditions that they consider important.

Works Cited

Alam, Muzaffar. 1997. "The Awadh Regime, the Mughals, and the Countryside." In *Lucknow: Memories of a City*, edited by Violette Graff, 16–31. New Delhi: Oxford Univ. Press.

Ansari, Sarah F. D. 2005. *Life after Partition: Migration, Community, and Strife in Sindh: 1947–1962*. Oxford: Oxford Univ. Press.

Cook, Matthew. n.d. "Of Origins and Migrations: History and Caste among the Lohana in Pre-British Sindh." Manuscript, Department of Anthropology, Columbia Univ.

Daswani, G. H. [pseud.]. 1983. "Sindhis—Past, Present, and Future." *Sindhu*, June 15.

———. n.d. "Sindhis and Religion." Typed manuscript on file with the author.

Dawn. 2005. "Goods Taken Away from Disputed Temple." June 29. At http://www.dawn.com/2005/06/29/local14.htm. Accessed July 13, 2007.

Eastern News. 2005. "Sikh Gurdwara in Hindu Possession." Sept. 15. At http://www.sikhsangat.org/publish/printer_413.shtml. Accessed July 13, 2007.

Freitag, Sandria B. 1989. *Collective Action and Community: Public Arenas and the Emergence of Communalism in North India*. Berkeley: Univ. of California Press.

Gajwani, S. L. 2000. *A Sufi Galaxy: Sufi Qalandar Hazrat Qutab Ali Shah, His Spiritual Successors and Select Disciples—Sufi Saints of the Present Times*. Ulhas Nagar, India: H. M. Damodar.

Hari, R. M. 1982. *Shrimad Bhagwad Gita (Ilim Ludani-Va-Tohid): The Knowledge That Draws Towards Spirituality—the Oneness.* Ulhas Nagar, India: H. M. Damodar.

Levi, Scott C. 2002. *The Indian Diaspora in Central Asia and Its Trade, 1550–1900.* Vol. 3 of Brill's Inner Asian Library, edited by Nicola di Cosmo, Devin DeWeese, and Carolina Humphrey. Leiden: E. J. Brill.

Malkani, K. R. 1984. *The Sindh Story.* New Delhi: Allied.

Oberoi, Harjot. [1994] 1997. *The Construction of Religious Boundaries: Culture, Identity, and Diversity in the Sikh Tradition.* Oxford: Oxford Univ. Press. Reprint. New Delhi: Oxford India Paperbacks.

Pandey, Gyanendra. 1992. *The Construction of Communalism in Colonial North India.* New Delhi: Oxford Univ. Press.

Population Census Organization, Pakistan. 1998. "Population by Region." At http://www.statpak.gov.pk/depts/pco/statistics/statistics.html. Accessed July 23, 2007.

Ramey, Steven. 2008. *Hindu, Sufi, or Sikh: The Contested Practices and Identifications of Sindhi Hindus in India and Beyond.* New York: Palgrave.

Sikand, Yoginder. 2003. *Sacred Spaces: Exploring Traditions of Shared Faith in India.* New Delhi: Penguin India.

Sipe, Keith Raymond. 1976. "Karachi's Refugee Crisis: The Political, Economic, and Social Consequences of Partition-Related Migration." PhD diss., Duke Univ.

Thakur, U. T. [1959?]. *Sindhi Culture.* Sociology Series no. 9. Bombay: Univ. of Bombay.

Vaswani, J. P. 2002. "The Sufi Way to God." *Mira* 60, no. 4 (Feb.): 75–79.

Young Sindhi Adults. 2006. "Jhulelal, the Sindhi God." At http://www.youngsindhiadults.org/Documents/Jhulelal.pdf. Accessed Aug. 18, 2006.

Žižek, Slavoj. 1989. *The Sublime Object of Ideology.* London: Verso.

PART THREE

≈

Firmly Drawn Boundaries

7

≈

Mapping Boundaries

The Science of Knowing Communal Identity in British Cartography

PETER GOTTSCHALK

"EACH HINDU POCKET is becoming more concentrated with its own people, while the story is the same for Muslim-dominated locations," observed a police officer in the state of Gujarat following the 2002 communal violence there. What the press often described as spontaneous riots actually took the shape of pogroms—with members of the state government, led by a Hindu nationalist, supporting the intimidation of, assault on, and expulsion of Muslims. A senior police officer's remarks alluded to the significance of government collusion when he noted, "They hardly failed to lay hands on their targets, thanks to documents like the voters' list." He added, "The mission was accomplished with clinical precision" (quoted in Dev 2002). The murder of nearly two thousand people and the forced emigration of many times more than that seem to be but the latest chapter in the history of interreligious violence in India.

Westerners have long viewed India as a primarily religious place where the depth of spiritual knowledge is surpassed only by the chasm of religious antagonism. Observers have often traced the roots of communal

This chapter includes an extract from my book *Religion, Science, and Empire: Classifying Hinduism and Islam in British India,* reprinted by permission of Oxford University Press, USA.

conflict to Muslim invasions centuries ago. Yet contemporary sources demonstrate that premodern South Asians struggled along Hindu–Muslim lines little more than they did along Hindu–Hindu or Muslim–Muslim lines. Indeed, most South Asians lived under polities in which Muslim sovereigns patronized Hindu temples and Hindu leaders supported Muslim festivals. Because the British controlled most of the subcontinent during these earlier times when a more religiously tolerant (but hardly idyllic) situation apparently turned more lethal, some have blamed them for promoting conflict through a divide-and-rule strategy. Although British rule initiated changes, research demonstrates that communalism resulted less from policy than from how the British *understood* Indians. Clarifying this history is critical not only to better explain the violence that continues in India but also to discern significant problems in modern perceptions of religion and social identity.

Earlier scholarship has built a strong foundation on which to consider the impact of British epistemic projects and their social consequences. Authors such as Ronald Inden, Arjun Appadurai, Bernard S. Cohn, C. A. Bayly, and S. N. Balagangadhara have explored a wide variety of efforts by the British Indian state (that included both Britons and Indians) and private individuals to understand India and its denizens. Some have recognized the centrality of religion to these projects. What perhaps needs greater emphasizing, however, are the ways in which information gathering and knowledge production in British India distinguished religions from one another. That the state did so is clear enough, but what has gathered less attention is *how* it drew distinctions or, in concert with this volume's theme, how they drew lines between Hindus and Muslims, Christians and Buddhists, who often enjoyed far more fluid social interactions than official depictions admitted. The salient difference between British perceptions of religious difference and that of the South Asians who governed before them rests in an effort to bring taxonomic, scientific precision to the definition of each religion and the division of one from another.

The comments about the role of "documents like the voters' lists" and the "clinical precision" of communal targeting reflect three dynamics of the British Raj that, together, have contributed to the perfect communal storms that occasionally rage in India. First was the development of governmental information orders seeking precise data on individuals. Second was the increasing reliance on empirical science for the technique of handling information. Third was the centrality of religion as the principal category by which most Britons knew Indians.

This essay attempts to demonstrate how the ascendant dominance of science intersected with the British fixation on religion to establish and promote a scientific taxonomy of Indian religions. As Indians embraced Western science and its classification systems, they gradually absorbed British categories for not only animals and plants, but also humans and their religions. This categorization contrasted with pre-British information orders that noted groups but rarely defined them. Whereas the Mughals often described those who supported and defied them in caste and religious terms, the British not only described groups but also sought to categorically isolate one group from another by identifying the supposedly unique qualities that defined them. Moreover, the British attempted to identify each individual according to a religious category—presuming that Hindu and Muslim identities were clearly bounded and mutually exclusive.

The development over two centuries of a British information order shaped by science and centered on religion is too complex a story for these few pages. During the British rule in this area, an amazing array of Britons and Indians in service to their empire traversed India—whether officially or not—in efforts to collect information. Land surveyors, itinerant artists, census officials, archaeologists, missionaries, and folklore collectors drew historical monuments, charted village streets, and recorded landholdings (see Gottschalk 2012). In order to discern traces of this information order's historical expansion and describe some of its features, this essay examines Indian and British cartographic depictions of North India. In particular, it explores how three very different mapping projects during a period of 150 years reflect both the changes in the British information order and its perpetual concern for religion. Through these and many other renderings, the British fashioned a *knowable* and *known* India: an object of study and of control quite different from pre-British efforts. Maps of North India—as relics of the British imperial epistemic order—demonstrate how that order did not initiate Hindu–Muslim divergence but rather instantiated it as a central fact in cartography and other forms of British knowledge while permanently reifying religious boundaries.

Scientism

First, we need to consider the term *scientism*, which features prominently in this analysis. This term refers to the hegemonic position of the discourses and practices associated with contemporary Western-originated science as they become authoritative in understandings of the world. Allergic as we properly might be to any additional "ism," *scientism* offers an opportunity to sidestep a difficult issue in addressing South Asia's intellectual history. The term *science* may refer, of course, to any methodical and systematic way of knowing. In this light, many South Asians regard *jyotish*, or astrology, as a science. However, some use the word *science* to connote a specific set of epistemologies defined through mainstream Western-originated standards of empiricism, method, and verifiability. For these people, astrology would not constitute a science, but rather, at best, a "pseudo-science." In light of the significant, historical South Asian explorations in mathematics, astronomy, and other fields, what distinguishes the British imperialists from pre-British South Asians is not the practice of methodical and systematic research, but rather the place of specific forms of knowledge—believed to cohere through a shared empirical methodology—as the preeminent authority for knowing the perceivable world. In other words, *scientism* allows us to recognize the significant place of empirical studies in European and other societies without requiring a judgment of the relative veracity of European and South Asian forms of knowledge.

Scientism can be identified as the unique confluence of a variety of ideal elements, including these four:

1. *Total quantifiability*: the reduction of all significant attributes of objects to a numerical expression.

2. *Progress*: a teleology of improvement that inevitably follows from the efforts of science and characterizes the purported advances of science.

3. *Scientific classification*: the differentiation of objects into entirely discrete, rigidly bounded, and mutually exclusive categories.

4. *Interconnectivity*: a quality that allows the results of one episteme to be incorporated into and/or expressed in any other.

These elements are labeled "ideal" because the ideology from which they arise must be distinguished from the practice of sciences in which they have been imperfectly realized, if not rejected outright. In fact, inconsistencies, discontinuities, and ruptures characterize the everyday practice of scientism's science, as its practitioners often acknowledge. Nevertheless, these elements powerfully inform the rhetoric, self-conception, and popular reception of scientism. Instead of going into detail about each of these qualities, I explore each through the examples that follow. They show how maps of North India reflect both the ascent of scientism and the centrality of religion. These ideal elements, as manifested in the British information order, combined to create a taxonomy of Indian religions confirmed by its apparent scientific—but actually scientistic—method and form.

An historical review of efforts to map North India demonstrates how each of these elements served to create an image of a communally divided India. Three moments in the British Indian representation reflects this creation particularly well: James Rennell's maps of the late eighteenth century; the revenue surveys of the first half of the nineteenth century; and the 1901 and 1931 atlas of *The Imperial Gazetteer of India*.

James Rennell's Maps in the Late Eighteenth Century

The maps created by James Rennell—declared "the father of Indian geography" by Indians and Britons alike—would be seminal in the imagination of both a British India and subsequently an Indian nation. These maps reflected the new interests and aspirations of the English East India Company following its ascent to financial power in Bengal. The maps also demonstrate both the convergence and the divergence of British cartography from South Asian precedents.

By 1764, the East India Company had come to share many of the same concerns for information as the Mughal Empire. Its victory that year at Buxar in Bihar over the Mughal's regional governor not only followed its earlier victory at Plassey in Bengal but also left the company the uncontested military power in Northeast India. By default and in the eyes of the Mughal emperor, this position made the company the recognized revenue collector in that region. Thus, the company now needed as much information as possible on manufactures, trade, and agricultural production. Even more immediately, it required militarily useful knowledge of terrain in order to protect its windfall. These needs culminated, first and foremost, in an effort to map the territory. And, so, only three years after Buxar, the company appointed Major James Rennell as the first surveyor-general of Fort William (Calcutta). Although surveyors had already been dispatched after Plassey, Rennell was charged with the first systematic and comprehensive British survey of Bengal and Bihar (*Guide to the Records* 1980, 185–86).

It would be a mistake to see the British cartographic effort as a total departure from Indian precedents. However, despite certain similarities and continuities, Rennell and many of his colleagues practiced a somewhat different type of placing than did their indigenous counterparts. The changes that the British brought to preexisting mapping systems—some of which they had co-opted—hinted at the impact their scientism would have on divergent indigenous epistemologies. Nevertheless, Rennell drew on Mughal-era information in his effort to create an entirely new construction. In his *Memoir of a Map of Hindoostan*, he explains that, in addition to his own measurements and observations, he relied on the *Ain-i Akbari*, which he considers "a register of the highest authority" (Rennell [1782] 1792, ii–iii).

The *Ain-i Akbari* describes Hindustan district by district, listing each one's subdistricts and quantifying their land area and revenue (see Allami 2001). Its author, Abul Fazl (1551–1602), chief minister of Emperor Akbar, would have gathered these data from an intricate information system that began with the locally based officials—*patwari*s (village accountants) and *qanungo*s (chief registrars)—who periodically measured the fields and maintained the records thereof (Bayly 2000, 22). These data gradually found their way up the system to higher levels of officials, who continually aggregated them into information suitable for their level of responsibility—be it the *mahal* (subdistrict), *sarkar* (district), or *subah* (province). Historian C. A. Bayly has detailed how this empirical information system fit into a much larger structure of surveillance and communication in Indo-Muslim-ruled India (2000, 10–20). Significantly, the British kept the Mughal office of *patwari* in place far longer than they did the Mughal system of land ownership and revenue assessment, tailoring the latter to conform to English practices while largely maintaining existing information-gathering systems. Reflective of their reliance on indigenous systems, the British decision to dismiss all Bihari *qanungo*s in 1793 owing to allegations of fraud had to be recanted twenty years later because of the decision's negative impact on their ability to collect revenue (Robb 1997, 247).

Because early British systems of empirical information gathering about geography and routes bore resemblances to existing indigenous systems such as those upon which Abul Fazl depended, the maps produced by contemporary Britons and South Asians shared certain commonalities. Maps of the world produced by both groups tended to result from state sponsorship, relied on a system of longitude and latitude, and demonstrated the influence of Ptolemy and Arab cartography and astronomy. Both the Mughals and the British also maintained significant archives of route maps and strip maps (Schwartzberg 1992a, 507). Equivalent to today's AAA Trip-Tiks, such maps depicted the path from one destination to another (Gole 1989, 31, 103), though the Mughals did not seem to combine route maps with the use of coordinates (Habib 1980, 95). Rennell relied on similar records made on the march by British military and administrative officials. These commonalities meant that Rennell could readily incorporate Indian sources in the absence of British ones. He ultimately used as many Indian materials as British, though not without double-checking the former and seldom recording the names of their authors (Edney 1997, 84). Despite such parallels, significant differences existed that reflected less on each culture's geographic abilities than on the Britons' remarkable emphasis on quantification and the stature of mapping in their increasingly scientistic culture. These qualities would become most apparent with both the British dependence on the graticule and their insistence on standardization.

For many eighteenth- and nineteenth-century Europeans, mapping represented the epitome of Enlightenment epistemological ideals. Combining the use of measurements, instruments, and inscriptions, geographers sought to determine part of the world's order through direct observation. Early biological taxonomists used maps as a metaphor for their efforts, with, for example, Linnaeus describing his taxonomy as the *mappa naturae*, "the map of nature" (Edney 1997, 17–18, 51). The contemporary inheritance of this attitude is evident in phrases such as "let me map it out for you" and "this book maps our genealogy"—both of which suggest that mapping provides a clear, spatial elucidation. Philosopher of science Donna Haraway has argued that the popular perception of maps as a "kingdom of rationality" implies that they are transparent representations free from bias (1997, 137). In modern Anglophone cultures, therefore, mapping has served as a common metaphor for lucid knowing, comparable to a god's-eye view.

An important component in this supposedly objective representation and a significant departure from preexisting systems was the British use of the graticule—that is, a grid of latitudinal and longitudinal lines on a map. Some South Asian maps noted the longitude and latitude for a few places depicted, which allowed travelers and armies to determine their position relative to particular sites while on the move. However, owing to the difficulties in determining longitude, only some places were so located. All of Rennell's topographical maps, in contrast, imposed a graticule upon the depicted terrain, allocating each site a specific location within this grid and allowing the user to estimate the longitude and latitude of every place located on the map.

The graticule's seemingly strict linearity suggested an objectivity through a purely geometrical determination of position and size, whereas South Asian mapmakers often relied on towns' relative position to one another to situate them. South Asian maps also depicted towns in sizes relative to their significance rather than to their empirically observable size (Gole 1989, 14). This British emphasis on the empirically quantified rendering of places as objects culminated perhaps in the observation made by Colin Mackenzie (who served as surveyor-general at Calcutta after Rennell) that village names should be replaced with their longitude and latitude in order to streamline their administration (Edney 1997, 115). In contrast to the standard British use of the graticule, only a very few of the surviving maps, even world maps, produced in pre-British South Asia made use of it (Schwartzberg 1992b, 392). This distinction demonstrates well the first ideal element of scientism: total quantification.

What is of concern here is not some judgment of the relative worth of British and South Asian maps, but rather the rhetoric of scientistic accomplishment. It might appear that an emphasis on the presence of cartographic features—such as the use of graticule or scale—that we now take as standard in British maps but not in pre-British South Asian ones suggests that the latter lacked something or were less developed. Such a conclusion reflects an assumption that the most accurate mapmaking requires such features. It does not. Take, for instance, the revolutionary map for London's underground train system. It uses neither graticule nor scale, nor does it precisely portray the location of each station in geometrical space, yet a more pragmatic representation of the tube system has yet to be devised since the prototype map appeared in 1933 (Transport for London n.d.).

To restate the point, the degree to which a study such as this appears to be judgmental as it notes a divergence in mapping systems is both a measure of many people's expectations that Western maps are the most accurate and a reflection of the success of European-originated cartography in displacing alternative paradigms. Such a presumption results from the pervasive progressivism that has long accompanied Western discourse on South Asian systems of knowledge—that is, the second ideal element of scientism. Yet despite an enduring effort to place all knowledge systems on a singular track of increasing accuracy and objectivity that culminates in Western-originated science, the history of scientism amply demonstrates the vulnerability of sciences to social, economic, and political vicissitudes. Indeed, as Kapil Raj reminds us, the importance of the imperial context for the development of many European sciences has too often been overlooked (2006, 63). (And so we need to acknowledge that although the contemporary forms of most sciences practiced globally may have originated in the West, many developed partially in the context of non-Western places with the contributions of non-Western labor, wealth, and intellect.)

For instance, the modern history of the European graticule demonstrates how mired in subjectivity it was from the start. The British, French, and Dutch vied with one another to determine the location of the prime meridian: 0° longitude. As a point of national pride, each promoted

Greenwich, Paris, or Amsterdam as the orientation point for this ultimately arbitrary line. Although the final victory of Greenwich must surely have disappointed the French and Dutch, the situation of the prime meridian in Europe—which made Europe the orientation point for this positioning system—served as a harbinger of the globalized Western scientific order that began to unfold in the eighteenth century, in great part owing to the efforts of men such as Rennell.

That the maps created by Rennell's British and Indian successors did not differ from his in orientation, framing, and graticule demonstrates a key component of the European epistemological order—standardization. The great divergence in South Asian mapping methods in the centuries preceding British supremacy reflects a flexibility of technique meant to pragmatically fit each project (Harley 1987, 12). One exception to this pattern may be found in Maratha revenue maps that only occasionally accompanied official survey reports yet demonstrated decades-long continuities (Schwartzberg 1992b, 444).

In its ardent commitment to quantification, European empiricism required standardization to realize the ideals of objectivity and universal comprehensibility. For instance, not only did the effort to establish a system of longitude lead to a European consensus on the prime meridian, but the effort to standardize the measurement of the earth brought about the metric system. Both Jean Picard and Christopher Wren proposed a system using a pendulum to determine one second of length for geodesy, but national pride again prompted an impasse because the length of the pendulum's swing varied between England and France. Neither side would acquiesce. Later, C-A. Prieur du Vernois derived the metric system from a measurement arc taken between Dunkirk and Barcelona. Despite British resistance, most of Europe would accept it. The scientistic drive to quantifiable knowledge makes standardization of measurement—whether through the graticule or the English mile—essential (Robinson 1982, 31–32). In contrast, the areas formerly under Mughal rule had a vast disparity of systems for measuring land. Even the familiar signifier of length, the *kos*, varied in length from place to place (Gole 1989, 14), and British district administrators long sought to grasp the various local standards, which might differ even between two adjoining villages.

This diversity in indigenous measurements reflected a larger plurality within South Asian information orders. Bayly describes the overall Mughal information order as characterized by divergent systems and sources that overlapped one another without any aspiration toward a centralized network. Much of it depended on affective knowledge—information obtained through "participation in communities of belief and marriage, through religious affiliation and association with holy men, seers, astrologers and physicians" (2000, 17, 20–21). Top-down imposition of standardized measures impeded efforts to draw knowledge from local officials and specialists, and the Mughals allowed local practices to proliferate. Mughal geographical systems tended to be oriented around specialized groups who collected data and directed those data to specific individuals instead of to government offices (Bayly 2000, 54–55). Later British systems, in contrast, sought to establish uniform and formal exchanges between offices whose officials constantly changed, rotating through various postings in accordance with British policy. Information, reduced to writing, was disseminated not through interpersonal contact, but through official publications that communicated not only information, but also the state's authority. Overall, therefore, Mughal geographical systems tended to be interpersonal and directed along narrow lines of communication, whereas the British system was impersonal and diffused information more broadly.

However, the latter system was still coalescing in Rennell's day, and geographic information tended to be closely guarded rather than publicly disseminated. The Court of Directors demanded that the surveyor-general's charts go immediately to them in London (James 1949, 1798), and the East India Company effectively cut Rennell off from new survey data upon his retirement (Edney 1997, 202). Although he continued to publish maps on India and promote new publications while at home in England (Markham [1878] 2004, 402), he relied upon his previously collected data because the court had determined the newest information too valuable to share. Nevertheless, Rennell's publication of his maps provided Britons with one of the first widely available cartographic images of India. Perhaps more important, his framing of India would serve to define that space as a singular, bounded place in British and South Asian imaginations. Whereas earlier European maps had tended to place India in a larger Asian continental context or focused specifically on the Mughals' dominions, Rennell's landmark 1782 *Hindoostan* map used a map frame that defined an India reaching from the Indus to Burma and stretching from Kashmir to Cape Comorin, with Ceylon peeking above the southern border. This map would become the viewfinder for British ambitions in the subcontinent (Edney 1997, 15). By situating each town and city as a discreet place in a uniformly measurable space as delineated by a graticule grid and consistent scale, Rennell's maps manifested the quantification element of scientism. This urge to quantification would have important consequences for the understanding of religion in the next century.

More immediately apparent was Rennell's attitudes toward religion, as demonstrated in a nonquantified element of his mapping. An elaborate and, relative to contemporary maps, outsized cartouche fairly dominates the bottom of his seminal 1782 *Hindoostan* map. He describes what it portrays in his *Memoir*: "*Brittannia* [*sic*] receiving into her Protection, the sacred Books of the *Hindoos*, presented by the *Pundits*, or *Learned Brahmins*: in Allusion to the humane Interposition of the British Legislature in Favor of the Natives of Bengal, in the Year 1781" ([1782] 1792, xii). Considering the rapaciousness of East India Company officials at this time, surely Rennell's trust in British humaneness was at least mildly overstated. This notwithstanding, the cartouche interposes a symbol of British rule ("Brittannia") borrowed from Greek antiquity between two Europeans and three Brahmins—intended to represent Indians—who offer books labeled "shaster," meant to depict their "sacred Books." Whereas neither Britannia nor the symbolic English lion behind her nor the two Europeans manifest any expression of religion (beyond the borrowing of Britannia's image from the Roman goddess Minerva), the three Hindus serve as signifiers of Indian religiosity to the British audience. They do so because they are marked as Brahmins and as bearers of the *shastras*, the caste and texts that Britons most immediately identified as Hindu.

Rennell's omission of Muslims in his cartouche—despite his awareness of their significant presence in the subcontinent—may be explained in his characterization of India's history elsewhere in the *Memoir*:

> India has in all ages excited the attention of the curious, in almost every walk of life. Its rare products and manufactures, engaged that of the merchants; while the mild and inoffensive religion of Brama [*sic*], and the manners inculcated by it, attracted the notice of philosophers. . . . It had been happy for the Indians, if they had not attracted the notice of a class of men more inimical to the happiness of mankind: for the softness and effeminacy induced by the climate, and the yielding nature of the soil, which produces most spontaneously, invited the attacks of their more hardy neighbours; and rendered them an easy prey to every foreign invader. Hence we find them successfully conquered by the Persians, Patans, and Moguls: and it is probable, that, like the Chinese, they have seldom had a dynasty of kings, from among their own countrymen. ([1782] 1792, xxi–xxii)

Hence, Rennell classifies the South Asian population as Indian and non-Indian: the first identified by the "religion of Brama" (a common synonym for Hindu religion in this period), and the second by "Mahomedan," according to a later passage (xl). The absence of religious markers among the Europeans suggests that they stand apart from the Hindu Indians and Muslim invaders as free of sectarian prejudice.

Thus, we have what may be an unexpected example of a map communicating information about religion—Indian and British—in a thoroughly nonquantified manner. Nevertheless, the role of maps in Britain as the epitome of the scientistic emphasis on quantification guaranteed that Rennell's work would be granted an authoritative place in the crystallizing British information order. True, the East India Company's anxious monopoly on information blocked popular access to the most up-to-date maps to some degree. But by 1778 the company had distributed six hundred English printings of road maps of Bengal and Bihar based on Rennell's work to Bengal offices and military officials (Gupta 1981, 67). Moreover, the popular demand in Britain for knowledge about India meant that Rennell's work could not be restricted to official circles for long. Indeed, the publisher of Rennell's map of Bengal and Bihar added a paragraph to it congratulating the company for its decision to have it "published to the

World." As noted earlier, Rennell put out a series of popularly available maps upon his return to England. Through the official and commercial distribution of his maps via a publication system unknown in South Asia before the eighteenth century, Rennell thus promoted both a geographic and anthropological portrait of India while simultaneously portraying Britain. By the next century, attention to religious themes would move from the periphery of maps to their center.

Revenue Surveys of the First Half of the Nineteenth Century

The first third of the nineteenth century witnessed the solidification of British rule in Bengal and Bihar as the possibility of invasion by South Asian and European interlopers gradually faded. Administrators in British India thus focused increasingly on the requirements of sustaining their growing empire, and no requirement loomed larger than revenue collection. Although records do not indicate that communal identification played much role in the assessment and collection of land revenue, the maps of individual villages completed as part of various revenue surveys clearly demonstrate both the continuing centrality of religion and the gathering emphasis on strictly delineated boundaries in even the most routine British mapping projects. These surveys also reflect the widening dissemination and public impact of the products of local mapping projects.

British rule required revenue derived from agricultural production. The Permanent Settlement of Cornwallis established proprietary rights for *zamindar*s (landlords) and an expected level of production from each *raiyat* (farmer), depending on the size and quality of the *zamindar*'s land. However, collecting this revenue posed persistent difficulties for the successive district collectors charged with this task. Reports from collectors to the Board of Revenue testify to a litany of problems: falsification of accounts by *patwari*s, the variation in measuring-rod sizes among districts, fraudulent measurements, destroyed records, and outright defiance to providing information by both Indians and resident Britons. Even the landscape seemed set against establishing a permanent record as the inexorable gyrations of the Ganga and other rivers carved away land from one bank and deposited new land on another.

Throughout the first half of the nineteenth century, collectors attempted to make permanent settlements of landholdings—recording them using surveys and maps, yet bedeviled by inconsistencies, inaccuracies, and disputes. In light of this frustratingly inconclusive situation, some East India Company officials proposed a final, all-India survey to settle all land boundaries in order to determine the amount of land under each *raiyat*'s cultivation. This final survey would, they argued, lead to a more efficient and rational administrative and financial situation for the company (Edney 1997, 322). Its intent reveals an overall British urge to scientific classification of discrete, definable objects, as amply demonstrated in the example of one representative district survey. Although the Great Trigonometrical Survey, which occupied a great number of British surveyors for most of the nineteenth century, would be considered the most scientific survey owing to its highly accurate measurements, the revenue surveys revealed how scientism engaged the religious in British India (for accounts of the Great Trigonometrical Survey, see Barrow 2003, Edney 1997, and Keay 2000).

Revenue surveyor Lieutenant W. S. Sherwill supervised a revenue survey between 1844 and 1846 that created large-scale maps of boundaries for all villages in the thirteen *parganas* (divisions) of Bihar's Shahabad District. This was no small task considering that nearly two thousand villages might stand in one *pargana* alone. A *thakbast*, or preliminary survey, undertaken by a nonprofessional Indian staff would sketch a rudimentary outline of each village before the arrival of the European revenue surveyor, who would execute a more complete study. Despite the effort, a later settlement official deemed this boundary survey defective because of its failure to preclude disputes by determining definitively the boundaries of all villages and districts (Hubback 1918, 27)—a judgment that simultaneously demonstrates the contested nature of local boundaries and the British persistence in defining them nevertheless. Expressing confidence in ultimate success, Colonel Thuillier, head of all revenue surveys at midcentury and later surveyor-general, believed that such surveys could establish "the permanent record of the landed tenures" and do "away with the constant necessity for partial measurements" for engineering projects (quoted in Markham 2004, 183).

This conceit derived from the scientistic precept that each entity, to be properly classified and fully understood, could and must be known as a bounded, discrete object. In part, this view relied on the previously described expectation that the ability to know an object required one to positively determine its unique location. This determination could be made most effectively by establishing the position of each neighboring object—hence, in the case of villages, the impulse to establish village borders with certainty. No surviving Indian map from a pre-British revenue survey makes any such attempt to represent village borders. Instead, they tend to demonstrate an emphasis on relative placement rather than absolute location. Indeed, as noted earlier, pre-British indigenous mapmakers seldom provided even longitude and latitude, and if they did so, it was only for a few select locations. Instead, these maps emphasized the general location of villages relative to one another. They most commonly depicted the village in a formalized rectangular form without attempting to portray its actual plan (Schwartzberg 1992b, 444). Indian bureaucracies apparently did not consider such a representation important for their record of revenue information. However, we need again to recognize that any conclusions remain contingent on the paucity of surviving maps.

In British India, the staff of the revenue surveyor dutifully quantified each village's land area and annual revenue. A scale map situated the village relative to surrounding settlements, each named in English and Persian. Within the borders of the most carefully detailed maps, the surveyor Sherwill represented symbolically the four features of each village apparently most important to the company: agricultural resources, roads, settlements, and religious sites. Using discrete symbols for each type of building, these maps attempted to precisely situate mosques, temples, and Sufi shrines. It is notable that even in an operation to map villages for the sake of revenue extraction, company officials marked religious sites. This suggests that just as the presumed physical boundaries of the village defined it as an economic and legal entity, its temples and mosques characterized its social quality. Assuming that Indians primarily identified with and divided along religious communities, Sherwill inscribed the categorical difference between Hindus and Muslims by separately portraying temples, mosques, and shrines—providing a unique symbol for each community's presumably distinct place of worship in his official representation of Shahabad District. His choice to reduce all the public religious buildings in the village to these categories instead of assigning them to a general category such as "place of worship" reflects a British intention to note and reinscribe the same Hindu–Muslim binary evident in Rennell's work seven decades earlier.

Simultaneous with his geographic demarcation of borders in order to definitively distinguish one village from another, Sherwill's religious classifications implied an essential social division. The scientistic paradigm requires the clear definition not only of every object, but also the categories to which each is assigned. Items belong to a category when they share some essential quality common to other members of that category. So, for instance, waterfowl and mammals are distinguishable from one another by qualities that simultaneously define each member and differentiate them from the members of other categories. Objects with qualities held by more than one category confuse the system by challenging its basic supposition of mutually exclusive characterizations. So, for example, the platypus flummoxed early taxonomists because it sports a bill like a waterfowl yet fur like a mammal. We will consider the political consequences of this classificatory system when we return to the consideration of the 1909 atlas in the next section.

These revenue surveys illustrate the tendency of the British to classify Indians first according to religious categories that commonly reflected British expectations rather than Indian self-identifications. Far from the mutually exclusive and antagonistic Hindu and Muslim communities of many British imaginations, actual practices and interactions demonstrated a complexity that belied such easy divisions. British persistence in their views of a bifurcated India strictly separated into primarily religious communities—despite the evidence of many of their own ethnographic surveys—demonstrates the impact of the scientific classification paradigm, the third ideal element of scientism under our consideration.

The revenue survey maps had a significant public impact despite their prosaic nature. British officials foresaw a use for the new maps beyond the esoteric realm of revenue collection. Reflecting on the advantages of the boundary surveys, the Court of Directors in 1854 observed that "the determination of boundaries of Villages and Estates by an enquiry *on the spot* and their delineation on the survey maps" would help defray conflicts over land ownership and perimeters and decrease the resulting court cases.[1] The quality of being "on the spot" had particular significance in the scientistic order with its emphasis on direct, empirical observation. A letter a few years later advised the Board of Revenue that the lieutenant governor hoped local authorities would encourage as wide a distribution of the maps as possible.[2] The practices established by the production and publication of Rennell's maps—empirical observation, map making, and public distribution—continued a quarter-century later, though with an important caveat: in this case, the intended consumers now included Indians, and many were quite young.

At least some schools established by the British worked to educate Indian children in reading government maps, having students trace rivers, indicate towns, and recognize topographical features in their district.[3] In part, this education might have sought to decrease the level of suspicion that often accompanied survey projects. But it would have at least one certain effect. As Benedict Anderson has shown, the confluence of public education, mass publications, and a national imagination commonly culminates in nationalist movements, and India, of course, was no exception. As a prelude to the successful mass involvement in independence

1. Secretary to the Board of Revenue, Lower Provinces, "Extract from a Despatch from the Honorable the Court of Directors No 12 dated the 20th April 1854," found in Letter from the Secretary to the Board of Revenue, Lower Provinces, to the Commissioner of Revenue for the Division of [blank], No. 8, Fort William, June 1, 1855, emphasis added, Patna Commissioner's Records, vol. 238, State Archives of Bihar.

2. Secretary to the Government of Bengal, Letter to the Officiating Secretary to the Board of Revenue, No. 191, Fort William, November 10, 1856, Patna Commissioner's Records, vol. 238, State Archives of Bihar.

3. F. J. Mowah, "Vernacular Education N.W. Princes," 1860, including report from Secretary Council of Education to W. Muir, Secretary to the Government of the Northwest Provinces, no number, Calcutta, June 4, 1853, included in G. Plowden, Officiating Secretary to the Government of India, to C. Beadon, Secretary to the Government of Bengal, No. 749, Nov. 4, 1853, Patna Commissioner's Records, no volume number, State Archives of Bihar.

movements, British imperial maps would serve as the frame within which South Asians could imagine the territorial dimension of a national identity. The 1901 atlas for *The Imperial Gazetteer of India* provided a frame not only for Indian nationalism, but for Pakistani statehood, too.

The Atlas of *The Imperial Gazetteer of India* (1909 and 1931)

Whereas the revenue surveys demonstrated how scientistic mapping perpetuated the sense that Hindus and Muslims represented mutually exclusive communities on the village level, the atlas of *The Imperial Gazetteer of India* reflects how British mapping projected this conclusion on an all-India level. As the result of the state-sponsored mapping of the subcontinent that had begun with Rennell and extended beyond the onerous exertions of the Great Trigonometrical Survey, an authoritative outline of "India" emerged for both the state and the public. Its authority rested on the twin claims of the cartography's state sponsorship and its "scientific" accuracy. But this outline of India served to provide not only an iconic form for the country, but also a screen upon which the British—and increasingly South Asians—would project their conclusions about who resided within those exactly determined borders. For those involved in independence movements, such conclusions were used to answer the question, "Who are we as a nation?" Their responses would borrow heavily from the scientistic information order created by the British, particularly from the quantified data about groups divided into mutually exclusive categories.

As a whole, the twenty-six-volume *Imperial Gazetteer of India* manifests the triumph of scientism in the British information order. Its producers positioned the volume as authoritative in two ways. The first was through its status as a government product. In the preface to the series, the editor—self-conscious of the "official authority that attaches to the work"—assures the reader that almost "the whole of the work has been written by officials under orders of the Indian Government" (*Imperial Gazetteer* 1909, vi–vii). The second claim to authority relies on the specialized fields of knowledge used to confirm local observations. Although the preface notes that the gazetteer draws on materials collected by regional officers, it adds that "special contributions from experts" supplement these materials (vii).

Officials on the ground had the "local experience" related to the "on the spot" qualification discussed earlier, and disciplinary experts provided an authoritatively "scientific" confirmation of these officials' everyday experiences. Since at least the beginning of the Enlightenment, European scientific disciplines had become increasingly specialized in practice, generating authoritative experts as a result.

The gazetteer offers ample testimony to the significance of scientific disciplines. Many of the first volume's chapter names signify not only their subjects, but also the emergent sciences upon whose expertise the British drew: "Geology," "Meteorology," "Botany," "Zoology," and "Ethnology." The rapid crystallization of new academic fields in the nineteenth century was reflected administratively as well. In 1851, the East India Company separated the Geological Survey of India from the geographical work of the Survey of India. The Indian government established the Archaeological Survey in 1861, the Botanical Survey in 1890, and the Zoological Survey in 1916 (*Guide to the Sources* 1992, 146). Innovations in statistical demographics made possible the first all-India census in 1871–72. The government used consecutive censuses as a platform to separately launch the Linguistic Survey (1891) and the Ethnographic Survey (1901).

Despite this epistemological fission and mounting plurality, divergent disciplines remained somewhat interconnected and mutually related. This interconnection lent science the perceived quality of a unified system of knowing. In large part, the first ideal element of scientism, quantifiability, made interconnection possible through a shared mathematical and statistical model. Although government officials would collect nonnumerical data—such as accounts of local practices, beliefs, and narratives—they would often appraise these data merely as complementary to the statistical information most valued by scientism. The Government of India's Home Department explicitly expressed this view when it established an India-wide ethnographic survey in 1900. Its authorizing resolution declared that "an ethnographic survey of India, and a record of the customs of the people is [*sic*] as necessary an incident of good administration as a cadastral survey of the land and a record of the rights of its tenants. *The census provides the necessary statistics: it remains to bring out and interpret the facts which lie behind the statistics.*"[4] The resolution's wording confers confident primacy on statistical information—so confident, in fact, that it takes the census data as the basis from which to explore the ethnographic material already collected in the household surveys *from which the data were abstracted and quantified.*

Cartography offered another important vehicle for interconnectivity by providing a standardized frame identified as "India" within which the results of diverse disciplinary investigations could be projected. This frame resulted from British confidence in their ability to definitively and permanently determine India's boundaries, thus establishing an exactly known space. This approach perhaps finds no clearer an example than in 1909 with the atlas published to accompany *The Imperial Gazetteer of India*. If the twenty-five-volume *Imperial Gazetteer of India* represents one of the most ambitious expressions of the British information order, then its accompanying atlas (reprinted with some alterations) testifies to the culmination of scientism's impact on British (and South Asian) understandings of India.

As one leafs through the atlas, it perfectly conveys these abilities to exactly locate India and know it through the combined efforts of scientific disciplines. The atlas's first plate situates India in the middle of a map of the world. The next represents it in the context of its near neighbors. The succeeding map frames the Indian Empire stretching from Baluchistan to Burma, the Hindu Kush to Cape Cormorin, leaving Ceylon to peep halfway over the map's lower border. The atlas thus gives the impression of a nested set of representations that provide an increasingly exact rendering of India in its precise geographic location, like a predigital Google Earth. Successive maps in the atlas recycle this frame by projecting onto it information about the subcontinent's geography, geology, vegetation, climate, races, languages, religions, and administrative issues deriving from

4. Government of India, extract from the Proceedings of the Government of India in the Home Department (Public), emphasis added, Simla, May 23, 1901, no. 3219/3232, Home Department, Public Nos. 122–33 (Part A), Nov. 1901, National Archives of India.

disciplines emergent during the previous century. A collection of twenty-one provincial maps follows.

By visually expressing the data created by these disciplines within the boundary-defined space labeled "India," the atlas editors facilitated disciplinary specialists' efforts to translate these data into information both available and intelligible to the public. In other words, the form of India—determined by its geographically determined borders and emptied of all content except for its unimpeachable Indianness—served as a medium allowing the translation of abstracted quantifications into visual forms for a consuming public, both Indian and British. The degree to which this Indian essence imbued the map becomes clear when, as form alone, the country's outline attains the status of icon—a powerful symbol of national pride and identity.

The success of this projection as a persuasive representation of India can be readily ascertained in its adoption by early-twentieth-century nationalists. Historian Gyan Prakash has argued that Indian translations of Western science worked ultimately to undermine British hegemony—a fact that is ironic given that the purported superiority of that science succeeded for so long in persuading Indians to submit to that hegemony (1999, 83). Moreover, Prakash demonstrates that these translations simultaneously relied upon and served an imagined nation (118–20). No example better demonstrates this dual role in the context of cartography than the Bharat Mata Mandir in Banaras. Inaugurated in 1936 by Mohandas Gandhi, this temple situates an expansive marble relief map of India as the centrally installed *murti* (devotional image).

Once again, the 1909 atlas illustrates the impact of the categories used to organize the multiple data of these divergent disciplines and the centrality of the category of religion. As the atlas demonstrates, by 1909 linguistic and racial categories served as important organizing principles for imperial attempts to know Indians, and religion remained most central. The British map of India displays the final ideal element of scientism—the interconnectivity of epistemes—not only because it represented the combined result of geographical and cartographical operations, but also because it became a screen upon which the quantified results of other disciplines could be projected. The common use of this map allowed for the comparison and interrelation of data from geology, archaeology, history, linguistics, enthnology, and demographics. The application of the map for the depiction of India's prevailing religions, compiled from census materials and translating demographic statistics into visual form, would sadly foreshadow the most terrible legacy of scientism and religious politics in British India.

Thirty-eight years after the atlas's original publication, the carefully rendered borders of India would be redrawn, much as depicted on one particular plate of the atlas. In order to illustrate the distribution of religions on the subcontinent, the atlas producers turned to the all-India census for data. Although the amount of information collected on each individual increased with each successive census, since its inauguration in 1871 the census had not changed in requiring everyone to declare her or his religion—again demonstrating the primacy of religion in British efforts to know Indians. Because so many respondents declared an identity other than the classifications most used by the government (Hindu, Mahommedan, Sikh, Buddhist, Christian, and Animist), officials forcefully pigeon-holed specific groups into religious categories that they did not claim for themselves. For the atlas, editors ascribed each of these religious communities their own color, with deepening shades to depict where the greatest concentrations of each group lived. Despite the British effort to project the census information onto the cartographically determined frame of India so as to portray a diverse yet united India, less than four decades later they would use census statistics to determine how to divide the subcontinent.

In 1947, following agitation by some Muslims fearful of their place in an independent Hindu-majority India, the British partitioned India into two now independent nations that almost exactly matched the areas colored the darkest red and green in the 1909 atlas. Hundreds of thousands of South Asians died in the resulting violence, overwhelmingly in North India. Although few Britons may have anticipated such an ignoble end to their centuries of rule, their reliance on essentialized, definitively bound, and mutually exclusive categories of religious community had been consistent among them since before Rennell drew the map that served so centrally in British and South Asian imaginations of India.

Websites

The following websites offer images of British-era cartography:

Digital South Asia Library, Univ. of Chicago. At http://dsal.uchicago.edu/maps/index.html.

Perry-Castañeda Library Map Collection, Univ. of Texas at Austin. At http://www.lib.utexas.edu/maps/india.html.

Pritchett, Fran. South Asian Map Links, Columbia Univ. At http://www.columbia.edu/itc/mealac/pritchett/00maplinks/.

Works Cited

Allami, Abul-Fazl. 2001. *A-in-i Akbari*. Vol. 2. Translated by H. S. Jarrett. New Delhi: Low Price.

Barrow, Ian. 2003. *Making History, Drawing Territory: British Mapping in India, c. 1756–1905*. New Delhi: Oxford Univ. Press.

Bayly, C. A. 2000. *Empire and Information: Intelligence Gathering and Social Communication in India, 1780–1870*. Cambridge: Cambridge Univ. Press.

Dev, Nirendra. 2002. "Gujarat Riot Victims Allege 'Ethnic Cleansing.'" Rediff.com, Mar. 12. At http://www.rediff.com/news/2002/mar/12train1.htm. Accessed Feb. 4, 2013.

Edney, Matthew H. 1997. *Mapping an Empire: The Geographical Construction of British India, 1765–1843*. Chicago: Univ. of Chicago Press.

Gole, Susan. 1989. *Indian Maps and Plans: From Earliest Times to the Advent of European Surveys*. New Delhi: Manohar.

Gottschalk, Peter. 2012. *Religion, Science, and Empire: Classifying Hinduism and Islam in British India*. New York: Oxford Univ. Press.

Guide to the Records in the National Archives of India, Part IV. 1980. New Delhi: National Archives.

Guide to the Sources of Asian History: India. 1992. Series 3, vol. 2. New Delhi: National Archives of India.

Gupta, Hira Lal. 1981. *Fort William–India House Correspondence and Other Contemporary Papers Relating Thereto. (Public Series) Vol. VIII: 1777–81*. New Delhi: Government of India.

Habib, Irfan. 1980. "Cartography in Mughal India." *Indian Archives* 28:88–105.

Haraway, Donna. 1997. *Modest_Witness@Second_Millenium: FemaleMan©_Meets_OncoMouse: Feminism and Technoscience.* London: Routledge.

Harley, J. B. 1987. "The Map and the Development of the History of Cartography." In *The History of Cartography,* vol. 1: *Cartography in Prehistoric, Ancient, and Medieval Europe and the Mediterranean,* edited by J. B. Harley and David Woodward, 1–41. Chicago: Univ. of Chicago Press.

Hubback, A. 1918. *Final Report on the Survey and Settlement Operations in the District of Shahabad, 1907–1916.* Patna, India: Superintendent, Government Printing, Bihar and Orissa.

The Imperial Gazetteer of India, vol. 1: *The Indian Empire, Descriptive.* 1909. Oxford: Clarendon Press.

James, Robert. 1949. Secretary to the Court of Directors to the President and Council, Fort William, Jan. 20, 1768. In *Fort William–India House Correspondence and Other Contemporary Papers Relating Thereto. (Public Series),* vol. 5: *1767–1769,* edited by Narendra Krishna Singh, 85. Delhi: Government of India.

Keay, John. 2000. *The Great Arc: The Dramatic Tale of How India Was Mapped and Everest Was Named.* New York: HarperCollins.

Markham, Clements R. [1878] 2004. *A Memoir of the Indian Surveys.* New Delhi: Manohar.

Prakash, Gyan. 1999. *Another Reason: Science and the Imagination of Modern India.* Princeton, NJ: Princeton Univ. Press.

Raj, Kapil. 2006. *Relocating Modern Science: Circulation and the Construction of Scientific Knowledge in South Asia and Europe, Seventeenth to Nineteenth Centuries.* New Delhi: Permanent Black.

Rennell, James. [1782] 1792. *Memoir of a Map of Hindoostan; or the Mogul's Empire: With an Introduction, Illustrative of the Geography and Present Division of That Country: And a Map of the Countries Situated Between the Heads of the Indian Rivers, and the Caspian Sea.* London: W. Bulmer.

Robb, Peter. 1997. *Ancient Rights and Future Comfort: Bihar, the Bengal Tenancy Act of 1885, and British Rule in India.* Richmond, UK: Curzon.

Robinson, Arthur H. 1982. *Early Thematic Mapping in the History of Cartography.* Chicago: Univ. of Chicago Press.

Schwartzberg, Joseph E. 1992a. "Conclusion." In *The History of Cartography,* vol. 2, book 1: *Cartography in the Traditional Islamic and South Asian Societies,* edited by J. B. Harley and David Woodward, 504–9. Chicago: Univ. of Chicago Press.

———. 1992b. "Geographical Mapping." In *The History of Cartography,* vol. 2, book 1: *Cartography in the Traditional Islamic and South Asian Societies,* edited by J. B. Harley and David Woodward, 388–493. Chicago: Univ. of Chicago Press.

Transport for London. n.d. "Design Classics: Introducing Harry Beck . . ." At http://www.tfl.gov.uk/corporate/projectsandschemes/communityandeducation/2443.aspx. Accessed Feb. 4, 2013.

8

≈

In a Single House

Fluid Boundaries in Performed Urdu Poetry

CHRISTOPHER LEE

ALTHOUGH NIGHT HAD COME TO MUGHAL SARAI, a settlement on the outskirts of the North Indian city of Varanasi,[1] the Urdu poetry festival known as a *mushaira* being held there was just getting started. Younger poets and a few older poets known more for their sonorous voices than for the quality of their poetry were reciting their verses in turn on a brightly lit, raised outdoor stage. It would be hours before the big-name poets, who had come from all over India, would perform for the roughly twenty thousand people who had gathered for a long night of poetry.

Riaz Banarsi, a young poet with a pleasing voice, was called to the microphone by the announcer and performed the following *ghazal* to the great approbation of the audience:

> What are you looking at with such surprise?
> It's a riot, of course—what else is new?
>
> Why would you build your house on the beach?
> What's with cursing the ocean now?
>
> There is persistence in intoxicating drugs
> What has happened to this new generation?

1. Varanasi is also commonly known as Banaras; both names are used interchangeably in this essay.

Vexation and pain and love too
What all is in a single heart today?

In a single house: you too and us too
Then what is all this discord between us?

Today Riaz is very melancholy
Dear God, what is this condition?

(Riaz Banarsi)[2]

After performing another *ghazal,* Riaz stepped away from the microphone and moved to join his group of friends among the gathered poets. By the loud praise and cheering from the audience, it was clear that many wanted to hear more from Riaz. The emcee asked the poet to return to the podium and recite some more poetry, which he did, visibly pleased at the honor of being called back for an encore. The *mushaira* continued, one poet after another, some praised by the audience and a few hooted off the stage, until well after the early morning call to prayer.

Mushairas are hugely popular events in North India, particularly among the Muslim community. In Banaras, there are several large ones every year, attracting poets from across India and audiences in the tens of thousands; many smaller gatherings are held with local poets and smaller audiences.[3] Part entertainment, part didactic education, and part living tradition, they are venues for Urdu poets to perform their poetry to eager and participatory audiences, who are quite vocal with both their praise and their criticism.

2. Performed at Mughal Sarai (Banaras) *mushaira,* 1996. All *mushaira* poetry quoted in this chapter comes from tape recordings in the author's collection. Translations of all poetry are the author's unless otherwise noted.

3. This essay is based on in-depth ethnographic research performed since 1993 in Varanasi, Uttar Pradesh, funded at different times by the American Institute of Indian Studies and a Canisius College Summer Development Grant. As a participant-observer, I worked with, lived among, and spent most of my time with my consultants. Early in my research, I apprenticed myself to an *ustad,* a recognized poetry master, studying and eventually performing my sophomoric attempts at Urdu poetry. As such, the research, data, and analyses are grounded in particular Banarsi realities and exigencies. It is my hope and sincere belief, however, that much of this analysis can be generalized to a wider North Indian context.

Poets at contemporary Urdu language *mushairas* use their poetry to do many things: to entertain, to comment upon or interpret current events and history, and to commiserate with the audience on the difficulties of lost or unattainable love. The most important job of the poet at a *mushaira*, however, is to connect with the audience, as Riaz did in the vignette given earlier.

To earn the praise of the audience, the quality of the poetry is important—but there is an important caveat: the poetry of the contemporary *mushaira* is generally very different from what is generally known as classical Urdu poetry. When I was preparing to perform at my first *mushaira* several years after I had started studying poetry, my *ustad*—poetry master—gave me some important advice. "Don't read poetry," he told me. "Read *mushaira*." He explained that pleasing the audiences of the large-scale *mushaira* required different strategies than those used at the small poets-only gatherings I had hitherto attended, which had required poetry of subtlety, technical finesse, and depth of feeling, inspired by the classical model. "Simple, straightforward poetry, read well," is what he recommended; complex poetry that required thoughtful contemplation by the audience was out. Most poets read very different poetry at *mushairas* than they share with other poets or aficionados. What is performed at a *mushaira* is not what most poets would consider great poetry—but neither is it necessarily bad poetry. It is, quite simply, poetry that the poet hopes will capture the interest of the audience and garner praise.

Most studies of Urdu poetry focus on a few elite classical and modernist authors and their work. In this essay, I argue that the popular poetry of the contemporary *mushaira* is particularly important for scholars interested in mapping the fluid boundaries of identity and community in North India. The poet at the contemporary *mushaira* exploits the technical aspects and the built-in ambiguities of Urdu poetry and poetics to express a variety of formations of belonging and community to the predominantly male working-class Muslim audience.[4] These "imagined

4. Women often listen to the heavily amplified *mushairas* from nearby houses and rooftops.

communities" (Anderson 1991) do sometimes focus on religious identity in which Hindus can appear as the cruel, dangerous, and ultimately beloved other. More often, however, they cross religious lines to propose other, inclusive communities in which Hindus stand with Muslims as patriotic Indians, the poor, witnesses to injustice, victims of violence, and, of course, the assembly of lovers. Because of the nature of the most commonly performed style of poetry at *mushaira*s, a community proposed in one couplet quickly disappears—like lines in water—to be replaced with a new one in the next couplet.

Why does a poet such as Riaz get *vah-vah*'s (cheers), but another gets hooted off the stage? Although there are other important reasons, including performance style and the quality of the poetry, I would argue that a key factor in the popularity of some of the poetry being performed at contemporary North Indian *mushaira*s is the poet's ability to create a community to which the audience wants to belong—or sees itself as already belonging. The proposed communities that resonate with the audience get cheered; those that do not are met with silence. Those that are distasteful to the audience are hooted, and sometimes the poet is even chastised by the emcee of the event.

In this essay, I explore the ways that the poetry performed at contemporary Urdu language *mushaira*s can help to understand the shifting and fluid boundaries of real and imagined communities among working-class North Indian Muslims. In order to do so, I must first provide some background on Urdu poetry and poetics, including a discussion of the poetic self and beloved other in Urdu poetry. I then discuss specific examples of the poetic formation of community through Urdu poetry.

Urdu Poetry

> The rays of the morning sun, the breathlessness of an evening of grief
> It is the moon, and somewhere moonlight, the *ghazal*;
> Somewhere it is the beauty of the face of the beloved
> and somewhere her disheveled locks of hair, the *ghazal*.
>
> You can see it is the masterpiece of wisdom
> And the self-obliviousness of a drunkard, the *ghazal*;

It is the intoxication of the eyes of the beautiful
and the purity of the pious, the *ghazal*.

It is also a lament from Sita's lips
And the story of the sorrow-filled heart of Ram
And also the tinkling of the anklets of Radha
and the music-filled flute of Krishna, the *ghazal*.

This is also Akbar, this is Ashgar too
This is Dagh and Firaq and Begum Akhtar too
It is Fana's stylish art and the pain of Jigar
It's adorned with knowledge and art in every way, the *ghazal*.

(Shorish Banarsi)[5]

Urdu poetry holds a privileged place in North Indian Muslim culture and society, but it is not exclusively Muslim in either its references or its practice. There are and have been many non-Muslim poets, and as this poem by Shorish Banarsi illustrates, references to figures of Hindu myth and folklore such as Krishna and Radha, and Sita and Rama, are not at all uncommon, even by Muslim poets. In a recent article, Scott Kugle analyzes an Urdu praise poem for the Prophet Muhammad by poet Sayyed Muhammad Muhsin, which represents well what Kugle calls the "polymorphous sacred in Indo-Muslim imagination" (Kugle 2003, 155). The poem is an imagined pilgrimage to Mecca, which begins in Kashi (Varanasi, the abode of Shiva), moves to Mathura (the city sacred to Krishna), makes liberal reference to Prakrit love poetry, and even juxtaposes "the Muslim God (Allah al-Bari) and the Hindu God (Sri Krishna)," who "through the dazzled eye of love appear to be the same" (168). Urdu poetry is an Indo-Muslim poetics, a site of an historical and cultural union.

The appreciation and practice of Urdu poetry has little to do with religious community, social class, formal education, wealth, or gender. Although many contemporary *mushaira* poets are male Muslims,

5. From the author's collection.

significant numbers of Hindus, Sikhs, and women are also included among them.[6] There is great economic and educational diversity among *mushaira* poets, from university professors, medical doctors, and engineers to small shopkeepers and unemployed silk weavers. The master poet who wrote the poem that heads this section, Shorish Banarsi, is a silk weaver with little schooling who barely earns enough to keep himself and his family above the sustenance level. The audiences are equally diverse; one is as likely to hear Urdu poetry from heroin addicts in a New Delhi bazaar (Dhand 2006) as from the resident of 7 Race Course Road. Former Prime Minister I. K. Gujral once famously said after a meeting at the United Nations, "If only Bill Clinton could speak Urdu, I would have charmed him with a few couplets" (quoted in Baweja 1997, 52). Poetry is part of everyday conversation, used to strengthen an argument or prove a point. The most popular and most commonly performed form of poetry at *mushaira*s is the *ghazal*.

The *Ghazal*

The *ghazal* is the great pride of Urdu poetry and certainly its most famous form. It is traditionally understood to be love poetry: the Kashmiri American poet Agha Shahid Ali defined the word *ghazal* as "[t]he cry of the gazelle when it is cornered in a hunt and knows it will die" (2000, 3). It is said to be derived from the Arabic word *taghazzul*, which means to converse romantically with women. One scholar goes so far as to claim that "[t]he key to understanding the *ghazal* is the realization that it is the poetry of illicit love, of the love of a man for another man's betrothed or another man's wife" (Russell 1992, 35). Certainly this is at least in part true; many *ghazal*s (in particular those heard in Bollywood films) do focus on earthly love. However, many *ghazal*s, including some heard at contemporary *mushaira*s, are far more politically and literarily sophisticated than the syrupy love poetry they are often perceived to be.

6. This research focuses by necessity on men's poetic performances because most of my interviews and interactions during my research in Varanasi have been with male poets. There is a great need for research on South Asian Muslim women's Urdu poetic traditions.

Although the Urdu *ghazal* is derived from Arabic and Persian poetics, it is, owing to its many centuries of development, a wholly South Asian form of poetry. A detailed examination of the technical aspects of the *ghazal* are outside the scope of this essay.[7] However, an understanding of a few formal aspects of the *ghazal* is essential to this discussion: its distich-based nature, the relationship between the poet and his beloved, and what some scholars have called "the *ghazal* universe" (Pritchett 1994, 89).

The *ghazal* consists of four to thirty distiches, or closed couplets, with a rhyme scheme of *aa, ba, ca,* and so on. Within a *ghazal,* the couplets are unified by meter and rhyme rather than by content and can seem disjunctive to those unaccustomed to this approach. For example, in Riaz Banarsi's *ghazal* given at the beginning of this essay, the first and second couplets refer to communal violence and its effects, the third to the social ill of drugs, the fourth to the anguish of love, and so on. A useful illustration is a selection from "*Ghazal* on Half a Line by Adrienne Rich" by the American poet Marilyn Hacker, who successfully carries the distinct couplet-to-couplet nature as well as the rhyme scheme of the *ghazal* into English:

> In a familiar town, she waits for certain letters,
> working out the confusion and the hurt in letters.
>
> Whatever you didn't get—the job, the girl,
> rejections are inevitably curt in letters.
>
> This is a country with a post-office
> where one can still make oneself heard in letters.
>
> (in Ali 2000, 68)[8]

The couplet is the essential unit of a *ghazal;* it is quite common to hear a *ghazal* compared to a pearl necklace, each couplet being an individual pearl. But *ghazal*s, even by master poets, are rarely made up of couplets

7. For more on the technical aspects of the *ghazal,* see Pritchett 1994 as well as Pritchett and Khaliq 1987.

8. Reprinted from *Ravishing Disunities: Real Ghazals in English,* edited by Aga Shahid Ali, copyright © 2000 by Wesleyan University Press, published by Wesleyan University Press. Reprinted with permission of Wesleyan University Press.

of equal worth, and so—as the Urdu scholar Frances Pritchett once put it—the *ghazal* is more like a necklace adorned with a few jewels and some precious and semiprecious stones (personal communication, Feb. 3, 2013). Some particularly powerful, beautiful, or moving couplets may be remembered for life, whereas others are forgotten immediately. I would suggest that it is its couplet-based nature that gives the *ghazal* its power and popularity, certainly in the forum of the contemporary *mushaira*. People almost never quote an entire *ghazal* but will often quote a couplet as a figure of speech, to strengthen an argument, or to make a point.

This aspect of the *ghazal* is particularly useful for the poet in the contemporary *mushaira*. One advantage of couplets is the issue of attention span at an eight- or ten-hour *mushaira*—the audience at a long *mushaira* need not pay attention to a long poem but can take in a couplet at a time or even, if their attention drifts, miss a few without complete loss. Furthermore, the poet can hunt for themes and proposed communities that resonate with the audience and, upon finding one that does, can reorder his couplets within a *ghazal* midperformance to sustain the applause or even (as my own *ustad* suggested to me) to reserve those of a popular theme to read last, for a powerful finish.

The "*Ghazal* Universe"

In order to fully appreciate Urdu poetry, it is necessary also to understand what Frances Pritchett calls the "*ghazal* universe" (1994, 89)—a series of interwoven tropes, metaphors, myths, and folktales drawn from Persian, Arabic, and Indian sources, knowledge of which among the audience is assumed by the poet. One word or phrase immediately conjures up a whole succession of cultural references, and this condensation allows the two relatively short lines of a couplet to carry great power and impact. This process of condensation and expansion makes the Urdu *ghazal* difficult for the nonnative Urdu speaker; it also makes the *ghazal* difficult to carry over into English as poetry: a single couplet may require many paragraphs to explain the identity of a particular character, the significance of a particular action, and so on.

In order to fully explore how contemporary *mushaira* poets exploit the nature of the *ghazal* universe to express, propose, or disseminate a variety of formations of identity and community, a brief clarifying description of the *ghazal* universe is necessary. In this section, I offer some brief highlights, drawing primarily on well-known couplets from the classical tradition that represent the foundation of contemporary Urdu poetic tropes. Most aficionados and certainly poets would know these examples—and many more—by heart. I focus primarily on the nature of the poet and his beloved, not only because this relationship is foundational to Urdu poetry, but also because it is essential to the poetic construction and proposal of community. I argue that poets utilize these aspects of the *ghazal* universe and Urdu grammar to expand the idea of poet-lover (I) to one of community (we).

The role of the poet in the *ghazal* universe is that of the dedicated and suffering lover and his (or her) cruel, indifferent beloved. This relationship sets the tone for much Urdu poetry, particularly in the *ghazal*. As Frances Pritchett describes it, "The *ghazal* universe is founded on the figure of the passionate lover, and mirrors his consciousness. The lover, while longing for his inaccessible (human) beloved or (divine) Beloved, reflects on the world as it appears to him in his altered emotional state. To him its highs are infinite heavens, its lows abysmal depths, its every scene and every moment charged with intense and complex meanings—meanings to which nonlovers, the ordinary 'people of the world,' are blind" (1994, 89–90).

As a "true lover," the poet sacrifices all and abandons his worldly cares in pursuit of an indifferent, uncaring, or capricious beloved. Shamsur Rahman Faruqi points out that in Urdu poetry the role of the poet-lover is to bear suffering, while the beloved's is to cause it (1999, 10). In spite of all this abuse at the hand of the beloved, the poet remains true to his love—indeed, feeding off her indifference. After all, he thinks, she might love him back but is testing him to see if he really loves her. Inspired by his true love, the poet knowingly and uncaringly flouts cultural norms (if only in poetry) and is thus reviled by society (again, only in poetry); children mock him, and others throw stones.[9] In the famous words of the classical poet Momin Khan Momin,

9. This is an important point: most poets, unlike the way they cast themselves in their poetry, did not and still do not flout societal convention, although I have heard unusual behavior explained away with the phrase, "Well, he's a poet!"

With me yesterday in madness there was an army of children where I was
From all four directions came stones to where I was.

The poet will do anything to be near the beloved, and even the lane in which she lives takes on special significance:

What a restful night I passed in her lane!
Right here was a stone pillow, dust was a bed where I was.
(Momin Khan Momin)

The beloved is ever-present in the poet-lover's mind and heart; he worships her, and, as such, she becomes an idol (and the worship of idols by Muslims is, of course, forbidden):

You have spent your whole life in love with idols, Momin
How absurd that at the end of your time you will be a Muslim.
(Momin Khan Momin)

I have dragged you into the Kaaba, Dard
Yet thoughts of idols have still not left your heart.
(Khwaja Mir Dard)

The poet is often given to both self-mockery and self-effacement and wallows in the pain of love. Yet there is a certain pride in his position and behavior. According to Faruqi, "The world of the *ghazal* is one world where the Outsider is the Hero, where non-conformism is the creed, and where prosperity is poverty" (1999, 13). The poet revels in his position as outrageous lover, as nonconformist—he is the "true" lover in a world of false appearances and lust. Self-aggrandizement and braggadocio by the poet is quite common.

Qais and Farhad[10] were not insane like me;
My kind of love was distinct from theirs.
(Mir Taqi Mir)

10. Qais and Farhad are legendary lovers, well known in the *ghazal* universe, whose love drove them to madness.

There are many other poets in the world who are very good
They say that Ghalib's style of speech is something more.
(Asadullah Khan Ghalib)

Of course, the Urdu poet-lover would be nothing without his Other, the beloved. The identity of the beloved of the Urdu *ghazal* has received extensive commentary (among others, see Faruqi 1999, 2005; Pritchett 1979, 1994; Rahman 1990; Russell 1992), in part owing to the convention of using the grammatical masculine form to refer to the beloved. Although the beloved is always *grammatically* fixed in Urdu as masculine, however, the exact identity and gender of the beloved are intentionally opaque.[11] Although there are poems where this has not been the case (see Naim 1979), the use of the masculine form in the contemporary *ghazal* is a poetic convention—that is to say, the beloved may be a man, a woman, the divine, or nearly anything else.

Sometimes the beloved is unambiguously female—her adornments, hair, or physical features are described in ways that eliminate the implicit vagueness. Nevertheless, it is possible to keep gender ambiguous by entirely omitting any verbs or other identifying grammatical structures that eliminate ambiguity. In Sufistic terms, an earthly love is called *ishq-e majazi*, or "metaphorical" love, whereas the love of God is *ishq-e haqiqi*, "real" or "true" love. God as a (potential) beloved is extremely common in the *ghazal*:

Religious school or monastery, the Kaaba or temple of idols,
We all were guests there; You alone were the master of the house.
(Khwaja Mir Dard)

Go to Mecca or end up in a monastery
Where, oh where should a heart in search of You go?
(Mir Taqi Mir)

11. Needless to say, this opacity makes translation more than a little challenging. In the *ghazals* translated here, I have sometimes used "she" where a literal translation should properly have been "he," both because that is how my consultants would read it and because I felt that it is true to the spirit of the original.

In the classical *ghazal*, the beloved is generally a being—woman, man, or God. The modern *ghazal*, however, introduces a fascinating innovation in the concept of the beloved. As Russell points out, the beloved in the "modern" *ghazal* universe may also be an abstract theory or belief. Although not the first, Faiz Ahmed Faiz, an exemplar poet in the modernist tradition, fuses his socialist political beliefs with his poetry and often uses an abstract beloved. In one moving poem, he describes his new allegiance to his former earthly beloved. After describing in traditional terms his old love for her ("The world then was gold, burnished with light— / and only because of you"), he writes:

> All this I thought, all this I'd believed.
> But there were other sorrows, comforts other than love.
> The rich had cast their spell on history.[12]

The new abstract beloved, whether read as socialist revolution or economic justice, retains the necessary requirements for the beloved in the Urdu poetic universe: it is a demanding, out-of-reach ideal and a cause of great suffering and sorrow to the poet. For Faiz, the secret of the *ghazal* is "its continual adjustability to the demands for aesthetic articulation of contemporary experience" (1985, 55).

What is required of the beloved, whether real or abstract, is that He/he/she/it be indifferent, uncaring, distant, and perhaps even unattainable. Just as a flesh-and-blood beloved may slay the poet-lover with a glance imagined as a sword, so may an ideology or even God. Most of the references to the beloved in Urdu poetry are of this ambiguous type:

> I feel as if you/You are near me
> When there is no other around.
>
> (Momin Khan Momin)

12. From Faiz 1991, 5, translated by A. S. Ali. Reprinted from Faiz Ahmed Faiz, *The Rebel's Silhouette.* Copyright © 1991 by Aga Shahid Ali and published by the University of Massachusetts Press.

Bodies were emptied of life
In whatever direction You/you filled your eyes.
(Khwaja Mir Dard)

The particular interpretation of the gender and identity of the beloved is up to the poet and the audience. Urdu scholar and translator Ralph Russell sums it up well: "Who, or what is the beloved of the Urdu *ghazal*? . . . Any person, or any ideal to whom or to which the poet, whether in real life or in fantasy, is prepared to dedicate him or herself, sacrificing everything for its (her, his) sake, and willingly accepting the hostility of conventional society as an inevitable consequence of this love" (1992, 43). This is one of the built-in ambiguities of the contemporary *ghazal* that, as I argue later, is one of its considerable strengths. This ambiguity allows the poet to say the otherwise unsayable and to ward off criticism for mentioning unpopular or controversial topics: a reference to a beautiful woman, if challenged by the conservative, is actually about God; a reference to two people arguing in a single house is simply that—not a metaphor for Hindus and Muslims. Of course, because this ambiguity is widely recognized, such challenges rarely come.

Beyond the lover and beloved, there are far too many metaphors and tropes in the *ghazal* to describe—what Faruqi calls "an exhilaratingly infinite progress of metaphor" (1999, 23). Each metaphor literally makes possible a world of new metaphors, which give life to yet more metaphors through a process called *mazmun afirini*, "theme creation," but which Pritchett dubs "metaphorical-equation creation" (1994, 93). This "extended, proliferating, free-wheeling use of metaphor . . . that generates a constant supply of new images, thoughts, and propositions about the *ghazal* universe" (Pritchett 1994, 93), by which a metaphor or trope expands beyond its original usage, is an important ingredient in the poetry of the contemporary Urdu *mushaira* and as such is worth an extended look.

> To take an altogether fundamental example: the beloved is overpoweringly, cruelly, even fatally beautiful. Therefore "his" beauty slays the lover. It follows that the beloved's beauty is a deadly weapon. This metaphor opens up a number of avenues that have long been richly developed

> and concretized. (1) The beloved's glances are arrows, which lodge in the lover's body, pierce his heart, and so forth. One who shoots arrows must have a bow, so the beloved is an archer, and comments on his archery are in order. (2) The beloved's long curls are nets, in which the lover is hopelessly entrapped. Nets and snares are used by hunters, so the beloved is a hunter and the lover is the helpless prey. Nets and snares are also used by birdcatchers, so the beloved is a birdcatcher and the lover is a bird. As a captive bird, he is kept in a cage, and can comment on the world as it looks from his cage. (3) The beloved's beauty pierces the lover's heart through and through, so it is a sword. Wielding a sword, the beloved is a warrior on the battlefield whose horse wades in the blood of the lover and others whom he has fiercely and triumphantly slain. (4) Alternatively, if the beloved wields a sword, he is an executioner, ready to decapitate condemned men on the scaffold; the lover is thus a condemned man, willingly facing execution. (Pritchett 1994, 93–94)

Faruqi takes this idea even further: he suggests that in reference to the Urdu *ghazal* metaphors be taken in their "literal" sense, such that "metaphors do not represent facts, they are facts" (1999, 23). The metaphorical *as*—for example, the beloved "as" an executioner—becomes the literal *is*—the beloved "is" an executioner. As facts, these metaphors become the foundations upon which further metaphors are built, which lead to more metaphors, and so on.

Of course, what all of this requires on the part of both the poet and the audience is that they must not only know or study thousands of couplets but must stay "current" by attending large and small poetry gatherings and listening to poetry: "This whole universe exists in the consciousness of the *ghazal* knower—who constructs it by reading or hearing verses, and constantly refines it by reading or hearing yet more verses" (Pritchett 1994, 90).

Poetic Formations of Community

How does the Urdu poet make the move from the poetic self to the construction of a poetic community? Through the *ghazal* universe and the expansion of metaphor, as previously discussed, and a twist of Urdu grammar and poetics in favor of ambiguity. In most performed poetry, in particular that which is an appeal for community, Urdu poets use the pronoun *ham*. In Urdu, the standard first-person pronoun (in English, *I*) is of course *men*, but in many regions (including Banaras) and in Urdu poetry in general one may also use the first-person plural *ham* (in English, *we*). In other words, *ham* can mean both "I/me" and "we/us." This aspect of grammar—sometimes called the "royal we" or the T-V distinction (Brown and Gilman 1960)—makes the transformation from poetic self to poetic community possible. For example, in the poem that begins this essay:

> In a single house: you too and us too
> Then what is all this discord between us?

The first line can be read as "In a single house: you too and me too" or "In a single house: you too and us too." In the same way that *you* in English (and Urdu) can refer to either the second-person singular or the plural, *ham* can refer to the first-person singular or plural—and the self of the poet *becomes* the community. In this particular couplet, both the self–community and the beloved other are ambiguous: when the self is individual, the beloved other could be a wife, a brother, or other relative, and the poem reflects upon the inevitable strife in sharing a house. Yet when *ham* is read as the first-person plural, the community becomes (in one reading) Indian Muslims, the "you" or beloved other becomes Hindus, and the single house is, of course, India. The latter was a primary reading when I asked people how they understood this couplet—although many also mentioned the former as a possibility. Another example where a poet utilizes the potential of the individual/communal *ham* is a couplet by Banarsi poet Shad Mashriqi. In this case, "I/we" can be read as the individual poet or the community of Indian Muslims defending itself against allegations of unfaithfulness and disloyalty from the beloved—a common allegation in the *ghazal* universe. The beloved, of course, is recognizable as Hindus to those familiar with the conventions of Urdu poetry—but to others, it is not.

When the country demanded blood, we have given it—
We are the glory of our homeland, not some mutineers.
(Shad Mashriqi)[13]

Poetic Selves and Beloved Others

Countless formations of community, of poetic selves and beloved others are available in the Urdu poetic universe. Although other formations are possible, in this essay I focus primarily on poetically formed communities of Muslims and Hindus, communities together and apart. In these fluid formations that, as mentioned earlier, can change from couplet to couplet within a single *ghazal*, Hindus can appear as the estranged beloved or the terrible destroyer; they can also stand alongside or within a community, indistinguishable from Muslims. Some of the most commonly heard formations of community at *mushaira*s in Banaras—and the most likely to earn cheers from the audience—include Muslim, patriotic Indian, victims of injustice, and the assembly of lovers. In the couplets that follow, I present some of the formations common to the Urdu poetry heard in Banarsi *mushaira*s, using poems wherever possible that, although not uniformly excellent by the criteria of classical Urdu poetry, garnered the audience's endorsement through praise.

I have said that Urdu poetry is often love poetry, and one of the things that brings Hindus and Muslims together is love for both the divine and the human beloved. Poems of this type—in which the community is that of lovers—are common and quite popular at the contemporary *mushaira*. Consider these couplets from Riaz Banarsi's *ghazal* that begins this essay:

Vexation and pain and love too
What all is in a single heart today?

Today Riaz is very melancholy
Dear God, what is this condition?

13. Performed at Rasulpura (Banaras) *mushaira*, 1997.

Why is Riaz melancholy? As Pritchett notes, in the Urdu poetic universe love is generally not a reason for joy. It causes suffering from rejection, from trials, and from separation:

> I accept life-long separation—
> But don't you meet with my rival.
>
> (Hamid Banarsi)[14]

The rival for the beloved's love and attention is a major part of the Urdu poetic universe—he may even be considered an essential third to the dyad of Lover and Beloved. One even finds love and the suffering it entails between the Muslim and Hindu communities, as in this poem in which Muslims speak directly to Hindus as the estranged beloved:

> You haven't given us your whole love
> You don't call us "brother"—you say "Miyan."
>
> (Munavvar Rana)[15]

The term *miyan* literally means "man" or "husband," but in common usage it refers to a male Muslim and implies significantly more relational distance than the more familiar term *brother.*

If love as a theme has a rival for popularity in the poetry of the contemporary *mushaira,* it is the situation of Muslims in India. Several of the couplets from Riaz's *ghazal* fit this type:

> What are you looking at with such surprise?
> It's a riot, of course—what else is new?
>
> Why would you build your house on the beach?
> What's with cursing the ocean now?

Both of these couplets reflect on communal violence and its impact on the Muslim community. Hindus are either absent or are present as the

14. Performed at Rasulpura (Banaras) *mushaira,* 1997.

15. Performed at Mughal Sarai (Banaras) *mushaira,* 2001.

feared destroyer.[16] In the first couplet, a communal riot has become so common that it elicits no surprise; the poet speaks either to an individual or to the community of Muslims. A friend's interpretation of the second couplet (there are, of course, several possible interpretations) is that it refers specifically to Muslims who moved out of their Muslim-majority neighborhoods into new, religiously integrated developments being built around Banaras. Many of these people and their property were then subject to violence during communal riots. Made possible by the expansion of metaphorical equation–creation, communalism and the events surrounding it—in particular the events surrounding the destruction of the Babri Masjid in December 1992—have become a very common theme in Urdu poetry. The following couplet, by the fiery poet Rahat Indori, brought the house down with cheers when it was recited:

> A mosque is destroyed inside me every day
> In this neighborhood, it's December every day.[17]

Yet Muslims are not the only victims singled out because of their religion. In this poem by an unnamed poet, quoted by emcee Habib Hashmi at a Mughal Sarai (Banaras) *mushaira* in 1996, the community is inclusive of Muslims and Sikhs as victims of religious persecution and violence:

> He's a poet, but now he doesn't write "murder site" for a murder site:
> Sometimes he writes Punjab, sometimes he writes Ludhiana.
>
> I have heard that he's lost his mental balance these days
> Where he should write Karbala,[18] he writes Ludhiana.

Muslims "speak" through poetry to other Muslims about things other than communalism; one such theme is religion and religious practice. The following two couplets by Kalim Kanpuri are critical of *some* Muslims:

16. It is important to note that neither I nor the poets nor the audience generally understands this category to represent "all Hindus," just those who take part in communal violence.

17. Performed at Benia Bagh (Banaras) *mushaira*, 1997.

18. Karbala is the site of the massacre of Husain, the grandson of the prophet Muhammad.

Greater than estates is the value of prayer here:
It's a mosque—not the court of some Shah.

Read it with awareness, in a state of love and wisdom,
The Qur'an is a Qur'an—not a newspaper.[19]

"Urdu speakers" are, at least ideally, another potentially integrated, common community in Urdu poetry. At one time, Urdu was spoken across North India as the cultured language of communication—something mentioned by the emcee at every *mushaira* I have attended or heard; often the *mushaira* is called an "assembly of lovers of Urdu," with intentional interreligious implications. In the contemporary milieu, however, Urdu has become increasingly associated only with the Muslim community, and there is considerable worry by Urdu speakers about its future. In previous work (Lee 2000), I outline how the Urdu language, when presented in Urdu poetry, shares a metonymous relationship with the Muslim community. My poetry *ustad* Rashid Banarsi puts it succinctly:

I had understood a lot about the prejudices of this age
Now languages too are Brahmins and Sheikhs? I don't understand.

If there are charges against Urdu as well, that she is an outsider
Then whose homeland is India? I don't understand.

(quoted in Lee 2000, 337)

It is common to hear at *mushairas*, often from the announcer in his sometimes didactic segues between poets, that Hindi and Urdu are sisters.

When I embrace my Mother, my aunt smiles;
When I recite a *ghazal* in Urdu, Hindi smiles.

(Munavvar Rana)[20]

A considerable amount of poetry about Urdu reflects a sense that Urdu will be effaced or absorbed by Hindi. Much has been written about this issue recently (see, e.g., Farouqui 2006); what seems undeniable is that

19. Performed at Mughal Sarai (Banaras) *mushaira*, 2001.

20. Performed at Mughal Sarai (Banaras) *mushaira*, 2001.

many Urdu speakers' children, having attended schools taught in Hindi and English (Urdu-medium schools are not available past the primary level in Varanasi), will not be literate in Urdu the way the previous generation is. Among the more beautiful couplets on this theme is one by Jamil Khairabadi, which was wildly popular with the audience:

> Among my worries, this worry too is included:
> That on my children's lips *sheen* and *qaf* remain.[21]

Sheen and *qaf* are letters whose pronunciation denote differences between Urdu and Hindi speakers.

A poetic community that brings Hindus and Muslims (and many others) together is one of patriots and nationalists. Such formations, where India is the beloved, are quite popular. They can even be found in the religious poems called *na't* with which most *mushairas* begin, as in this example:

> The Prophet's Law has spread and flourished here too—
> Aqil, for this reason, greetings also to Hindustan.
>
> (Aqil Nomani)[22]

Yet although the community implied is Indian, another implication in the poetry is often that Muslims must prove their patriotism and defend or demonstrate their Indianness.

> Wrong-headed people call us "enemies of life"
> We, who also call the earth of this nation Mother.
>
> (Munavvar Rana)[23]

> Perfume fragrances our blood for this reason:
> In our blood is written Hindustan.
>
> (Nadim Nayyar)[24]

21. Performed at Benia Bagh *mushaira* (Banaras), 2003.

22. Performed at Benia Bagh *mushaira* (Banaras), 2002.

23. Performed at Mughal Sarai (Banaras) *mushaira*, 2001.

24. Performed at Mughal Sarai (Banaras) *mushaira*, 2001.

To you, O dust of my homeland, the oath of my ablution with earth:
You tell me what this mark of prostration says.

(Munavvar Rana)[25]

Another popular community formation, particularly at times of communal tension, is one wherein Muslims and Hindus are poetically presented as a single "true" community that has been falsely separated:

Those people whom centuries had joined together
Those relations were partitioned by a moment.

(Dr. Kalim Qaisar)[26]

From where, oh where, can you separate yourself from me?
I am bound to you by a thousand relations.

(Iftikhar Imam)[27]

Finally, Muslims and Hindus are frequently shown in a single community as the victims of political corruption, injustice, drug abuse, and, most recently, globalization:

There is persistence in intoxicating drugs
What has happened to this new generation?

(Riaz Banarsi)[28]

One day, take a look at this fickle Western wind—
It will carry off the holy Ganges water from the God's temple.

(Shorish Banarsi)[29]

If poetry that receives cheers from the audience represents communities to which audience members want to belong or see themselves as already part of, poetry that gets "hooted" often represents the opposite.

25. Performed at Mughal Sarai (Banaras) *mushaira,* 2001.

26. Performed at Mughal Sarai (Banaras) *mushaira,* 2001.

27. Performed at Benia Bagh *mushaira* (Banaras), 1995.

28. Performed at Mughal Sarai (Banaras) *mushaira,* 1996.

29. From the author's collection of Shorish Banarsi's poetry.

Many poets are hooted at *mushairas*, and one reason is the proposal of unpopular community formations.

After reciting a heated, communalist, and even potentially threatening (to Hindus) *ghazal* at a *mushaira*, several couplets of which are reproduced below, an inexperienced poet was not only hooted by the audience but roundly scolded and humiliated by the emcee in his comments following the poet's performance. After a brief lecture on the proper nature of poetry, the announcer criticized the poet by name (which is extremely unusual) and said, "Besides being inflammatory, [his poetry] had nothing. What comes from this stage should be literature [*adab*]."[30]

> There is still life left in the chests of the worshippers of fidelity
> Let the arrows come continuously—there are still bows left.
>
> Tell the communalists of the nation, O Atalji,[31]
> Because of our patience there is still peace.
>
> The world won't be able to lower this flag of Islam
> There is still life left in the hearts of the mujahideen.
>
> The explosions of your bombs have no effect, O Bush—
> Thank God that there is still the Taliban.
>
> Never trade religion for infidelity;
> The story of Hussein still remains.
>
> (Nizam Banarsi)[32]

Communalist poetry, particularly that which even suggests violence, is clearly inappropriate for the *mushaira*.

Not all unpopular couplets are hooted. Many couplets that do not resonate with the audience, for poetic community or other reasons, are

30. *Adab* also means "respect" or "propriety."

31. "Atalji" is a reference to Atal Bihari Vajpayee, the one-time prime minister and leader of the Hindu nationalist Bharatiya Janata Parishad (Indian People's Party) at the time this *mushaira* was held.

32. Performed at the Mughal Sarai (Banaras) *mushaira*, 2001.

just ignored or met with silence, particularly when a poet has previously had a few "hits."

In Banaras, some poets are hooted by an irate audience whose demand for a second or third encore by a particularly popular poet has been refused by the emcee.[33] Along the same lines, audiences may demand that a particular poet perform before his or her preset place on the announcer's list; if this is the case, anyone else who is sent up to the microphone is likely to be "hooted" unless he or she can quickly capture the audience's attention. Bad poetry by established poets may also be hooted (bad poetry by younger, inexperienced poets is generally quietly tolerated), and performing anything other than *ghazal*s or *geet*s (another popular style of poetry) is rarely appreciated. *Nazm*s, extended poems on a single topic, are generally not successful and often meet with the ire of the audience; the one time I heard a poet attempt free verse, he was hooted, and so he quickly returned to a more popular genre.

One genre of poetry, however, seems to be hooted more often than others at the contemporary *mushaira*: the genre called *rivayati*, which I have elsewhere translated (Lee 2001) as "traditional." This is the contemporary poetry of the nightingale and the garden, of aesthetic beauty, which adheres closely to the classical poetic model. To a significant degree, *rivayati* poetry—especially that which gets hooted—is detached from contemporary issues; there are no references to politics, contemporary events, or the like. It closely follows the classical model of lover and beloved, focusing on themes of love and loss. Its beauty often comes from sophisticated word play or theme creation or complex philosophical issues. This is not to say that it is bad poetry; this style of poetry is very popular at small poets-only gatherings. But it is, as my *ustad* said, not *mushaira* poetry. I would argue that, in line with my thesis, the community of aesthetes that such poetry proposes is considered at best out of touch with the contemporary working-class *mushaira* audience.

33. I make specific reference to Banaras here because I have heard from poets that Banarsi *mushaira* audiences are particularly raucous and difficult for poets to please.

Conclusion

Arjun Appadurai reminds us that "[b]etween the landscape of discourses about tradition and the sensibilities and motives of individual actors is a historical discourse that issues not from the depths of the individual psyche or from the hoary mists of tradition but from the specific, historically situated play of public and group opinions about the past. . . . [N]ational and group politics in the contemporary world has to do not with the mechanics of primordial sentiment, but with what I am calling 'the work of the imagination'" (1996, 146).

As I have claimed elsewhere (Lee 2000), the poets who perform in the contemporary Urdu *mushaira* speak of love, longing, and the Indo-Muslim and classical Islamic past but also simultaneously reconstruct that memorialized past into meaningful tropes to better understand the present and imagine new futures for Muslims in North India. Literally and figuratively, it is they who are doing the difficult "work of the imagination." Throughout North India, Urdu poetry is used as a sophisticated and safe way to communicate counterhegemonic alternatives to dominant articulations of history, memory, and ideology, which poets and audience use to make sense of and impart meaning to their lives, experiences, and personal and community histories. It is also a vehicle for the imagining and proposing of new communities and identities.

My claim in this essay is that the poetry performed at contemporary Urdu *mushaira*s can tell us something about the fluid and shifting boundaries of community and identity in North India. Poets creatively utilize various technical and formal aspects of Urdu poetics and grammar to express a variety of formations of community and identity to the largely male working-class Muslim audience, who respond with praise to those formations that resonate and ignore or hoot those that do not.

It should come as no surprise that there is a relationship between current events and the popularity of certain formations of community and identity as represented in the poetry of the contemporary Urdu *mushaira*. I am fortunate to have recordings of *mushaira*s that date back to the late

1980s.[34] Listening to *mushairas* that were held at times of moderate communal tension (*mushairas* are generally cancelled because of curfews at times of high tension), I have noted that there seems to be great audience response to couplets that propose two seemingly disparate communities: the maligned, misunderstood lovers of the nation and exclusive Muslim-only communities. As tensions lower, the frequency of occurrence and the popularity of these communities (again, represented by the cheers of the audience) change. I would suggest that these changes would hold true for other events as well. This topic requires further study and analysis.

At the very same *mushaira* in which Riaz Banarsi performed the poem that began this chapter, the extremely popular poet Sher Jamali was among the last to perform. A couplet he performed to the considerable praise of the audience serves as an apt postscript:

> The nature of the *ghazal* demands the narration of love
> But our society demands something else.[35]

Works Cited

Ali, Agha Shahid. 2000. "Introduction." In *Ravishing Disunities: Real Ghazals in English*, edited by Agha Shahid Ali, 1–14. Hanover, NH: Wesleyan Univ. Press/ Univ. Press of New England

Anderson, Benedict. 1991. *Imagined Communities: Reflections on the Origin and Spread of Nationalism*. Rev. ed. London: Verso.

Appadurai, Arjun. 1996. *Modernity at Large: Cultural Dimensions of Globalization*. Minneapolis: Univ. of Minnesota Press.

Baweja, Harinder. 1997. "Gujral's Diary." *India Today* (Oct. 6): 52–55.

Brown, Roger, and Albert Gilman. 1960. "The Pronouns of Power and Solidarity." *American Anthropologist* 4, no. 6: 24–39.

Dhand, Amar. 2006. "The Practice of Poetry among a Group of Heroin Addicts in India: Naturalistic Peer Learning." *Ethnography in Education* 1, no. 1: 125–41.

34. My own attendance at *mushairas* began in 1993 and was not regular until 1996; I was able to collect older recordings from fans and the companies that organized the amplification.

35. Performed at Mughal Sarai (Banaras) *mushaira*, 1996.

Faiz, Faiz Ahmed. 1985. "The Future of *'Ghazal'* Poetry." *Sonora Review* (Spring): 53–55.

———. 1991. *The Rebel's Silhouette: Selected Poems.* Translated by A. S. Ali. Amherst: Univ. of Massachusetts Press.

Farouqui, Ather, ed. 2006. *Redefining Urdu Politics in India.* New Delhi: Oxford Univ. Press.

Faruqi, Shamsur Rahman. 1999. "Conventions of Love, Love of Conventions: Urdu Love Poetry in the Eighteenth Century." *Annual of Urdu Studies* 14: 3–32.

———. 2005. "The Poet in the Poem or, Veiling the Utterance." In *A Wilderness of Possibilities: Urdu Studies in Transnational Perspective,* edited by Kathryn Hansen, David Lelyveld, and C. M. Naim, 173–91. New York: Oxford Univ. Press.

Kugle, Scott. 2003. "Pilgrim Clouds: The Polymorphous Sacred in Indo-Muslim Imagination." *Alif: Journal of Comparative Poetics* 23: 155–90.

Lee, Christopher. 2000. "'Hit It with a Stick and It Won't Die': Urdu Language, Muslim Identity, and Poetry in Varanasi, India." *Annual of Urdu Studies* 15: 337–51.

———. 2001. "Banaras, Urdu, Poets, Poetry." PhD diss., Syracuse Univ.

Naim, C. M. 1979. "The Theme of Homosexual (Pederastic) Love in Pre-modern Urdu Poetry." In *Studies in the Urdu Ghazal and Prose Fiction,* edited by Muhammad Umar Memon, 120–42. Madison: Univ. of Wisconsin Press.

Pritchett, Frances. 1979. "Convention in Classical Urdu *Ghazal*: The Case of Mir." *Journal of South Asian and Middle Eastern Studies* 3, no. 1: 60–77.

———. 1994. *Nets of Awareness: Urdu Poetry and Its Critics.* Berkeley: Univ. of California Press.

Pritchett, Frances W., and Khaliq Ahmad Khaliq. 1987. *Urdu Meter: A Practical Handbook.* Madison: Univ. of Wisconsin Press.

Rahman, Tariq. 1990. "Boy-Love in Urdu *Ghazal*." *Annual of Urdu Studies* 7: 1–20.

Russell, Ralph. 1992. *The Pursuit of Urdu Literature: A Select History.* London: Zed Books.

9

≈

Fluid Boundaries and the Assertion of Difference in Low-Caste Religious Identity

NANCY M. MARTIN

THE BOUNDARIES OF RELIGIOUS TRADITIONS are being actively contested in India today, though in practice their internal and external structures are fluid and open. Each religion takes a wide array of forms, reflecting the diversity of the communities and adherents who find relevance and meaning within it, and symbols and practices flow readily across what prove to be very permeable and overlapping boundaries between religious traditions. However, religion has been used by the powerful to assert and maintain dominance and in national and regional communal politics, at times fanning the flames of extreme violence. Fundamentalists and politicians today are engaged in ongoing attempts to drain away the fluidity of religious traditions and to build solid walls that both shut down diversity within a given religion and clearly separate and protect one from the other.

And yet religion can be a powerful dimension of the assertion of diverse group identities, particularly among low-caste communities in India who seek to claim an identity different from that imposed on them by the dominant society. Such groups take full advantage of the fluidity of religious traditions to assert creatively their own distinct identities and to critique existing religious and social values, whether through innovative transformation or conversion. Both internal religious diversity and open religious borders are crucial to this process. For the wider multireligious society of India also, this fluidity allows both for an affirmation of difference that is not oppositionally defined and for shared perceptions, values, and dimensions of identity that cross religious boundaries.

Identity, both individual and communal, is negotiated, marked by commonality and difference and shaped through affirmation and rejection. It is not unidimensional, but rather highly contextual and multivalent. And it is established, negotiated, and changed largely through "drawing lines in water," creating a difference that must be maintained. If this assertion of identity is not actively maintained, then others may draw alternate lines and ascribe a permanence to their own lines, defining a given individual or community in their terms—a situation particularly detrimental for low-caste communities and often used to reinforce their inferior status and rationalize their subjugation.

Religion, however, is not merely a tool used by low-caste and oppressed communities to reshape their identities or by communalist politicians to rally support. Religion is a comprehensive expression of the identity of a people, carrying within it alternate views of the nature of the world and society, of individual and community relations, and of the meaning of life. Indeed, anthropologist Karen McCarthy Brown has argued that religion is perhaps best defined as "the most complete and condensed knowledge of a people."[1] This comprehensive aspect of religion can be drawn into the service of communal identity politics as leaders attempt to unify a diverse constituency by positing an overarching common religious identity. But in order to employ religion in this way, the given religion must be reified into a monolithic, unitary tradition, oppositionally defined against other traditions.

Such a fortress mentality goes against the very nature of religions as actually practiced, for as Sathianathan Clarke asserts, they are more like tents than forts: "[A]nalogous to tents, religions are unlikely to be utterly sealed off; the fluidity of their boundaries and substructures are inherent

1. Karen McCarthy Brown, lecture in the course "Methods in Religious Studies," Univ. of California, Berkeley, 1990.

to their very existence. [They] yield themselves to be discretely and deliberately dismantled, relocated, and reassembled. Religions are not finished products; they constantly hand themselves over to their adherents. They are susceptible to continuously being crafted into meaning-giving and meaning-making symbolic dwelling places" (2003, 218). Religions are thus fundamentally multiform. Followers live in vastly different contexts and have diverse experiences and understandings of the world, though they may ostensibly belong to the same religious tradition. As a result, Hinduism, Islam, Christianity, and Buddhism appear in many radically different and overlapping forms among different sets of adherents in various regions of India and the world.[2]

Low-caste adherents as much as any others engage in this dismantling and reassembling activity in a process that includes a transformation in worldview and an assertion of an alternate system of interrelationships and values. An examination of the ways low-caste people in India have shaped alternate religious identities may be helpful as we seek not only to understand more clearly religion's role in identity politics, but also to craft more positive approaches to interreligious relations—namely, approaches that are based neither on antagonism nor on simplistic commonalities, but that take into account the complexities of both identities and religions. Such alternate religious identities arise within the larger historical, social, and political context of interreligious relations and the fluidity and contestation of religious boundaries in India. Therefore, we begin here, focusing particularly on how these trends impact low-caste communities. We then turn to the wider significance of religion and caste relations in the politics of identity in contemporary India before examining the specific religious insights articulated by low-caste communities and the role religions play in their assertion of alternative identities.

For this discussion, I draw on a wide array of examples both within and crossing the boundaries of Hindu, Muslim, Buddhist, and Christian traditions. These examples include interviews carried out in Gujarat and Delhi in 2004 and recordings made of devotional songs sung among

2. For an example of this diversity among Indian Christians, see Robinson 2003.

low-caste communities as well as interviews conducted in Rajasthan between 1993 and 2004. To fully understand religion's place requires that we look beyond the writings and speeches of the leaders and the literary production of the elite within these communities. A particularly rich source of the religious expressions of ordinary members may be found in the devotional songs composed and selected by members of these communities to be sung in religious gatherings held among themselves (particularly when members of dominant communities are not present).

When we do examine these latter forms of self-expression, we find that religion is a site for the articulation not only of a particular identity, but also of values and understandings of the nature of the world. Indeed, my work among low-caste Hindus and Muslims in western Rajasthan leads me to believe that low-caste articulations of religion in India may have more in common with each other than they do with the broader religion to which they belong, be it Hinduism, Buddhism, Christianity, or Islam (Martin 2002, 200–203, 213–14). That commonality is characterized, I would suggest, by (1) an affirmation of particularity and difference emerging out of a given community's lived experience, with religion serving as an essential means of self-expression and resistance, not marked by fixed oppositional definition, but by continual renegotiation with the dominant culture and religion(s); (2) an affirmation of human equality drawing on the universalist elements of the religious tradition or traditions to which they claim allegiance; and (3) a critique of oppression and dominance coupled with an affirmation of social justice, hope, and human dignity. These articulations provide overlapping visions of a world in which the fluid boundaries of religions facilitate the affirmation of distinction and difference but also allow for the sharing of universal principles of dignity, equality, and justice. In so doing, they offer a clear alternative to fundamentalist and communal formations of both religion and identity.

Contesting Religious Boundaries in India

When we turn our attention to religious boundaries that have been asserted particularly between Hindus and Muslims, a multitude of images and voices swirls around us. Some speak of fluid boundaries and shared cultural and religious lives, but others describe violent conflict across those same boundaries, which are portrayed as utterly uncrossable chasms.

The study of devotional Hinduism and Islam in medieval India reveals a world in which the boundaries between Hindu and Muslim were very fluid, with saints such as Kabir and Ramdev having both Hindu and Muslim dimensions of their own identities as well as both Hindu and Muslim followers. Kabir, though identified as a Hindu, was from an untouchable caste of weavers, the Julahas, who had converted en masse to Islam. The Rajput Ramdev, recognized by his followers as an incarnation of Vishnu, was arguably a hidden practitioner of Ismaili Islam (Khan 1997). In this period, Hindus and Muslims alike honored both Hindu bhakti (devotional) saints and Muslim Sufi *pir*s, sang each other's songs of love for God, and visited each other's shrines and temples. In the poems of Kabir recorded in the *Bijak*, we hear him chastising both Hindu and Muslim leaders for arguing over whose religion is superior, telling them in no uncertain terms that they have missed the point entirely and should turn their attention to God (Hess and Singh [1983] 1986). His words suggest lively debate if not competition and conflict between some leaders of these traditions. For Kabir, such conflicts dissolved in the theological and experiential context of the love of God, recognized and affirmed by both Hindus and Muslims of the time. In this fluid milieu, communities and individuals might still maintain their identities as Hindu or Muslim, although their beliefs and practices as either Hindus or Muslims might be very diverse.

Members of low-caste communities today have not been entirely immune to wider, divisive forces that seek to drive a wedge between Hindu and Muslim. However, low-caste Hindu and Muslim musicians in western Rajasthan continue to include the songs of both Hindu and Muslim saints in their repertoires and to use a mixture of Hindu and Muslim imagery within individual songs. The religious milieu in which they live includes a rich weave of Vaishnava, Shaiva, and *nirgun* influences, with Ramanandis and Ramsnehis, Naths and Dasnamis, and followers of the Kabir-panth and the Dadupanth all present. Tantric practices and devotion to hero-deities such as Ramdev, local goddesses, *kuldevi*s, and *satimata*s also enter the mix, as do strands of Sunni, Sufi, Twelver Shi'a,

6. The Shrine of Sufi Saint Mu'inuddin Chishti in Ajmer, visited by Hindus and Muslims alike. © Nancy M. Martin and Joseph Runzo-Inada.

and Ismaili Islam. The content of the devotional songs being sung in this region by Muslim and Hindu singers, both those who are musicians by caste profession and those whose religious calling it is to perform, reflects this rich religious heritage.

These performers sing songs of Kabir but do not choose to sing those songs that confrontationally challenge opposing Hindu and Muslim leaders to give up their disagreements and focus on Ram (a general term of reference for God). Kabir songs recorded in the 1990s instead incorporate Hindu and Muslim images in a positive way (Martin 2000, 405). The saint-poet simultaneously praises Hindu bhaktas and Sufi saints (*pirs*) and speaks of the Lord as "God of all the gods" and "Pir of all the *pirs*." A song performed by a Hindu singer from the Meghwal community (a very low-caste group formerly identified as leatherworkers and weavers) lauds the interior practice of religion, where "there is no Veda, books, shastras, or Gita," over book learning:

> The temple of the body is touched by ecstasy . . .
> The God beyond form lives within
> In the heart, a Muslim teacher [*maulvi*] [resides]
> The mouth [is] a mosque [where]
> Adam is saying his prayers [*namaz*].
> Know the body well—
> What is the inner *maulvi* saying?[3]

People within these communities have a clear identity as Hindu or Muslim and definitive opinions about which saints are Hindu and which Muslim, but how they define these categories remains very fluid, and they willingly cross over into each other's traditions in imagery, devotion, song, and celebration. The categories thus are not exclusionary or oppositional and belie any notion of antagonism between Hindu and Muslim.

The story of interreligious relations in India, however, is not simply one of harmony. Much is at stake, not only in India, but also for our global community. A particularly tragic culmination of the divisive use of religion occurred in Gujarat in 2002 when politically motivated riots rocked the city of Ahmedabad and environs, and Muslims were deliberately targeted in acts of extraordinarily brutal violence that left more than two thousand Muslims dead and tens of thousands displaced (Engineer 2003; Varadarajan 2002).

Two years after these riots, in January 2004, I went to Gujarat and Rajasthan to interview a number of people on the topic of interreligious harmony and conflict.[4] At a relocation camp in Ahmedabad, ironically called "Bombay Hotel" and located between the refuse dump and chemi-

3. This song was sung by Padmaram, a gifted singer from the Meghwal caste, and recorded in 1993 in the studios of the Rajasthan Patrika in Jaipur, Rajasthan, by Padmashri Komal Kothari and myself, with copies housed in the archives of Rupayan Sansthan Folklore Institute in Jodhpur. Here and throughout the essay, all translations are mine.

4. These interviews were done in conjunction with a documentary film project entitled *Patterns for Peace: India as Model for Peace in a Multi-religious Society*, carried out under

cal factories, Muslim women pulled out photographs of their families' burned-out businesses and homes. Their children still had nowhere to go to school and worked instead in the surrounding factories to make possible their families' single meager meal each day—children with shining smiles despite having witnessed unspeakable violence. A woman wept, the tears running down her face as she spoke of her daughter who had been brutally murdered. But others also spoke of Hindu neighbors who had protected them and helped them to escape. Three years later many victims of the violence were still reportedly living in such makeshift communities (Mander 2006).

In Ahmedabad, I also met Cedric Prakash, an Indian Jesuit priest later inducted into the French Legion of Honor in 2006 for his work to advance communal harmony and human rights in India. A poem of the Hindu saint Mirabai adorns his ordination card. He and his Christian, Hindu, and Muslim colleagues at Prashant Centre for Human Rights, Justice, and Peace work tirelessly to counter violence and propaganda and to facilitate peaceful communal relations. He has been beaten terribly and continues to live under constant death threats, but he is adamant in the face of communal violence, working to document and bring atrocities to light and to help the victims, no matter who they are. In words that echo those of Kabir, he speaks of their common humanity in starkly physical terms—there is no one whose blood does not run red.

All too often those victims are members of low-caste communities, whether they are the perpetrators or the attacked (Namishray 2002). Communal riots are most often carried out in urban slums, although in the case of the riots in Ahmedabad Muslim homes and businesses in more wealthy areas were also carefully targeted, including even businesses with silent Muslim partners. Neighbors who have grown up, gone to school, and played together suddenly come to see each other as enemies when outside agitators enter these areas to foment anger and hatred in the name of religion and spread rumors to blame Muslims for alleged or

---

the auspices of the Global Ethics and Religion Forum. The interviews were conducted by Nancy M. Martin and Christopher Baier in 2004, unless otherwise specified.

imagined outrages against Hindus and for the very real deprivations of low-caste communities. Yet it is primarily the families, homes, and livelihoods of both Hindu and Muslim slum dwellers that are destroyed in such riots. These same political forces can as easily turn their propaganda and violence against low-caste and tribal communities, particularly when members of these communities challenge the traditional hierarchies of dominance these forces advocate in the name of Hindu unity.

In Ahmedabad, the riots were used as a justification to drive a deeper wedge between Hindus and Muslims. In their aftermath, Muslims could no longer buy or own property on the west side of the Sabarmati River, the same river that flows past Gandhi's ashram. Subsequent research suggests that this process of ghettoization of Muslims and segregation of the city has continued to grow (Basu and Chaudhury 2007). The horrific violence of the riots was also intended to intimidate those who might dare to counter the vision of the Muslims and Hindus as enemies.

Father Prakash's coworkers, Rafi and Meera Malik, embody an alternate vision of Hindu–Muslim relations in their work and in their lives. This Muslim man and Hindu woman were drawn together by their activism on behalf of formerly untouchable Hindus (who refer to themselves as "Dalits"—"those who have suffered," "the oppressed") and Adivasis (members of tribal communities who fall outside the formal structures of the caste system). They decided to marry after the destruction of the Babri Masjid in Ayodhya by Hindu nationalists in 1992. In the aftermath of the 2002 riots, they organized a livelihood-restoration project and youth camps to bring together Hindu (primarily Dalit) and Muslim youth from the riot-torn parts of the city in order to help them work through their experiences so that they might go back to their communities as emissaries for peace. Meera later began the youth society Hindus United with Muslims (its abbreviation HUM playing on the Hindi word for "we," *hum*) to reach out to the same young people who might be susceptible to joining violent fundamentalist movements and to train them instead to be a force for communal harmony.[5]

5. Rafi Malik, personal interview by Christopher Baier, August 2006.

Others outside of Ahmedabad also spoke in support of more fluid boundaries between religious communities and for intercommunal harmony. For example, inhabitants of the small Gujarati village of Jadar, a two-hour drive from the city, worked together when the riots began elsewhere to ensure that their community was not torn asunder by fear. They spoke directly of their common humanity and shared devotion to God, though some were Hindus and others Shi'a Muslims. In Rajasthan, too, Hindu and Muslim members of a village *panchayat*, governing council, reported that they jointly oversee the festivities at the Hindu Arneshwar Mahadev Shiva Temple, where more than one hundred thousand people come for festivals four times a year. When a Muslim is the head of the *panchayat*, then a Muslim is in charge of this Hindu festival. Hindus and Muslims alike also visit a local shrine of a Sufi saint to honor him and seek his blessings. Though the people of this area are concerned about communal tensions elsewhere, they have known each other for generations, and their lives are entwined through a complex set of social, economic, and personal interrelationships.[6]

Maharaja Gaj Singh of Jodhpur recounted to me his grandfather's words at the time of Partition when he encouraged Muslims to remain in his kingdom, saying that Hindus and Muslims were "like [his] two eyes." In Delhi, Maulana Wahiddudin Khan, an octogenarian scholar of the Qur'an who began his peace work after Gandhi's assassination, called not for a false sense of unity, but for the need to affirm and manage difference. And Dr. Mohini Giri, who has worked for years with widows and street children there, spoke of leading a peace pilgrimage of Hindu women to Lahore and of the overwhelming hospitality that pilgrims received from Pakistani Muslim women when they arrived.

At that time in 2004, there was also what was for me a new refrain coming from multiple sources—an insistence that those who would polarize Hindus and Muslims and foment hatred could only fully do so if they

6. Interviews with members of the village *panchayat* were carried out in January 2004 with the assistance of Indian folklorist Komal Kothari and members of the staff of Rupayan Sansthan Folklore Institute of Jodhpur.

managed to create both a monolithic Hinduism and a monolithic Islam to serve as clear enemies of one another. They would succeed only if they could turn these religions into walled fortresses and convince people that these monolithic religions were the most important dimension of their respective identities. Those who spoke against this trend did so with both deep concern and hope, calling for reason in the face of fanaticism, for sanity in the face of frenzy, for humanity in the face of hatred.[7] Yet the power of hatred and fear should not be underestimated; amidst all these positive voices, there were other voices that I had also not heard previously. For example, a small group of Meghwal singers in Rajasthan reported that Muslims in their village reviled them and called them "Shetan" (Satan).

In the 1990s, strong voices were already speaking out for the need to resist attempts both to shut down religious and cultural diversity and to silence the voices of the people at the margins through the imposition of a monolithic Hinduism, a Hinduism that had no room for traditions considered "folk" or "syncretic." One of these voices of protest was that of the eminent folklorist Komal Kothari. Another was Ashis Nandy, who has observed that this ostensibly "Hindu" agenda of reforming Hinduism has much in common with earlier colonial critiques and nationalist reconstructions of Hinduism in its desire to erase those elements deemed "improper" and thus to "turn Hinduism into a 'proper' religion from an inchoate pagan faith" (2002, 131).

A parallel pressure has also been exerted to define Hindu and Muslim as mutually exclusive categories. The far-reaching nature of this pressure was reflected in the poignant words of Rajasthani professional caste musicians I interviewed in the mid-1990s, who spoke with nostalgia of a more inclusive past.[8] (Members of these castes are traditionally musicians by profession who are attached to other specific patron castes, or *jajmans*, and perform for them on all ritual occasions.) Arjun Singh was an elderly Muslim singer of the Dhadi caste. Though a Muslim, his name

7. Among those who voiced these concerns were activist Madhu Kishwar, scholar Dominique-Sila Khan, and Komal Kothari.

8. These interviews were carried out in 1996 in Jodhpur, Rajasthan.

was ostensibly Hindu, "Arjuna" being the famed hero of the Mahabharata whose battlefield conversation with his charioteer Krishna is recorded in the Bhagavad Gita. Arjun Singh reported that in his generation there were many Muslims like himself as well as Hindus with Muslim names. However, he had given his own son a Muslim name, and this practice had now become the norm. He also reported that although in the past both his Hindu and his Muslim patrons had asked for a mix of songs attributed to Hindu and Muslim saints, his audiences were now more often requesting songs of only the saints of their own religious tradition. Similarly, a Muslim singer of the Langa caste from western Rajasthan reported that a generation back Langas were including the songs of the Hindu saints Mirabai and Kabir in performances for their Sindhi Sepoy patrons, but now these Muslim patrons generally insist on only the songs of Muslim saints. Moreover, in his generation singers knew far fewer songs of Hindu bhakti saints than their forbears did (Martin 2000, 409). The Langas are not formally attached to Hindus as *jajmans*. Nevertheless, they do perform for some Hindu caste groups and thus still find an audience for the songs of Hindu saints. As a result, these songs have not yet been completely lost from their repertoires. But these changes are indicative of a sharpening of boundaries that has reached deep into the nation's social fabric.

Some of these Muslim singers also reported that in the mid-1990s outsiders were coming into their communities and telling them that they were not practicing Islam correctly because they did not, for example, pray five times a day. Pressure was clearly being exerted from the Muslim side to define a "correct" Islam, free from Hindu practices (even as there was pressure on Hindus to practice a "proper" Hinduism). By early 2004, much deeper concern was being articulated that such a move to shut down diversity within Islam, if achieved, would signal the complete victory of the Hindu fundamentalists and would drive such a deep wedge between the people of the two religions that it would make possible the complete demonization of Islam and all Muslims generally.

As it stands, Islam is as multiform in India as Hinduism, overlapping and interweaving with the latter in the lived reality of people's lives. Innumerable examples of these types of religious practices and beliefs, which appear to be more the norm than the exception, can be cited. And even beyond this internal diversity within both Hinduism and Islam, some traditions do not fit easily into either designation. Speaking about India more broadly, Nandy observes:

> Kumar Suresh Singh's survey of Indian communities shows that hundreds of communities in India can be classified as having more than one "religion." (It is doubtful if these believers see themselves as having multiple religious identities; they define their Hinduism or Islam or Christianity in such a way that the symbols of sacredness of another faith acquire specific theological, cultural and familial status.) Thus there are 116 communities that are both Hindu and Christian; at least 35 communities that are both Hindu and Muslim. . . . In all these incidents [these multiple identities are not the result of] recent converts retaining traces of their older faiths [but rather] identities that appear to encompass more than one faith, culturally *and* theologically. (2002, 143–44, emphasis in original)

In Rajasthan, low-caste communities in particular have become affiliated with these types of syncretic religious traditions, which tend to be inclusive and to advocate an egalitarianism that also shuns the exclusivist and exclusionary claims of religious authorities and institutions. The Meghwals are often devotees of Ramdev, whose temple at Ramdevra reflects a clear blending of Hindu and Muslim elements. The Meos of Mewat in eastern Rajasthan also traditionally had highly syncretic, boundary-crossing religious beliefs and practices in which "aspects of heterodox Shaivism, Vaishnava Bhakti, and tantric belief and practice [were] entwined with those derived from Shia and Sunni Islam" (Mayaram 1997, 39). Yet as Dominique-Sila Khan (2003) has reported, efforts are ongoing to expunge Islamic elements and to more thoroughly Hinduize the worship of Ramdev, and Shail Mayaram's (1997) work among the Meos reveals a reverse but similar pressure on this community, who were identified by others and attacked as Muslims at the time of Partition and have felt compelled to embrace a distinctly Muslim identity in the decades since then.

7. Hero-deity Ramdev's *samadhi* (funerary monument, mausoleum), draped in a green cloth with clear Muslim symbols, in his temple at Ramdevra. © Nancy M. Martin and Joseph Runzo-Inada.

Religion and the Politics of Identity

Given this situation in India, how might we make sense of religion's key role in contemporary identity politics? We can readily identify those who might and do use communal violence for political and economic gain, but how are they able to use religion to do this so effectively despite the myriad examples of interreligious harmony and variation in India both in the past and today? And how might we understand the power and place of religion in assertions of identity generally and more specifically among low-caste communities?

Sudhir Kakar (1996) suggests a confluence of factors surrounding individual and communal identity that may illuminate both the specific situation in India and the situations in other contemporary societies. First, with the coming of self-rule in India, a renegotiation of power relations and hierarchy has ensued that heightened the awareness of differences between communities. This awareness was more pronounced than it had been under the "tolerance"—or perhaps more properly "indifference"—of imperial powers, whether Muslim or British in India.

Second, Kakar suggests that elements of communal identity that are already deeply embedded in the construction of self-identity come to the surface of awareness under situations of "identity threat" that call into question sources of self-esteem and understandings of life as meaningful. He identifies the following as threats to identity currently operative in India and elsewhere: "modernization and globalization[,] . . . [f]eelings of loss and helplessness accompany[ing] dislocation and migration from rural areas to the shanty town of urban megalopolises, the disappearance of craft skills which underlay traditional work identities, and humiliation caused by the homogenizing and hegemonizing impact of the modern world which pronounces ancestral cultural ideas and values as outmoded and irrelevant" (1996, 187).

These threats lead to a retrenchment and assertion of group identities, Kakar suggests, as people turn to groups to counter "feelings of loss and helplessness, and to serve as vehicles for the redress of [perceived] injuries to self-esteem" (1996, 187). Under such situations of stress, personal identity becomes deeply entwined with group identity, and threats to group identity are perceived as personal threats. Because religion can add a transcendent or sacred dimension to life's meaning and purpose, threats to religious identity can be perceived as an even greater threat.

In this state of heightened awareness of difference owing to identity threats, self and other may be oppositionally defined. An essential aspect of this process is the projection of what one fears or dislikes in oneself onto another, to the point of demonizing the other and giving a transcendent dimension to one's own sense of group superiority and moral rectitude over the other. Nandy has observed that India's many gods and goddesses and the fluid boundary between the gods and the demons militate against such denial and projection of negative traits (with neither the demons being wholly evil nor the gods wholly good), but attempts to eliminate these aspects of Hinduism reopen the potential for more complete projection (2002, 148). Heightened awareness of group identity fuels the process of projection by highlighting one's relationship to the dominant group or dominant minority group, which then becomes a ready target.

As Peter Gottschalk rightly points out, an underlying assumption in Kakar's analysis is that things were not always thus—that is, more complex identities existed earlier in which religious affiliation was only one dimension of identity, and this allowed for multiple allegiances that could cross the permeable membranes of religious traditions as well as for religious affiliations that did not fit into such mutually exclusive religious categories (2007, 207). This has certainly been the case for low-caste communities in the past, and they have benefitted greatly from this fluidity, though they, too, may be drawn into this mode of projection in the face of overwhelming contemporary identity threats, particularly in urban settings.

Kakar's analysis of the psychosocial dimensions of this process of communal identity formation provides insight into how polarization, hatred, and violence can seemingly be so readily kindled in the name of religion. The solution to this polarization and violence does not lie ultimately in identifying facile commonalities between people, though this is important to counter demonization. Rather, the solution lies in the recognition and maintenance of complex identities and affiliations and in the affirmation of difference, acknowledging not only the distinctiveness of Hindu and Muslim, but also multiple Hinduisms and multiple Islams. According to Kakar, "a multiculturalism, with majority and minority cultures, rather than the emergence of a composite culture" is needed (1996, 196). Muslim activist Maulana Wahiduddin Khan would concur, calling for the management rather than the elimination of difference. The ways low-caste communities have incorporated religious fluidity into their assertions of identity offer possible alternatives for managing such difference in the face of identity threats, ways that are quite different from the agenda advocated by communalist politicians.

Religion and the Assertion of Low-Caste Identity

Low-caste Hindu communities experience all the "identity threats" identified by Kakar and, particularly in urban settings, may follow the course outlined, including identifying Muslims as "other" and participating in communal violence. Yet they have also experienced very real oppression by high-caste Hindus (and in some cases by Christians and Muslims who maintain caste distinctions) and have resisted group identities imposed on them by these dominant communities by asserting their own identities. At the same time, Hindu nationalists have institutionalized practices devaluing these communities and their religious practices. The ninth standard school texts in Gujarat approved in 2002 discuss the issue of minorities in India under the heading "Problems of the Country" and describe scheduled castes and tribes as ignorant, illiterate, and evincing blind faith (a characterization found also in earlier colonial and nationalist discourse, as is anti-Muslim sentiment). If these externally assigned identities are not to be passively accepted, low-caste Hindus must then assert an alternate identity.

These alternate identities are characterized in part by affirming alternate religious affiliations, as in the watershed conversion to Buddhism of members of the Mahar caste (a Dalit community in Maharasthra) under B. R. Ambedkar's leadership in 1956 or the mass conversions to Islam in Tamil Nadu in 1981, or by working creatively within an existing religious framework to transform that tradition, as in the development of new sects such as the Satnampanth. In many studies of such phenomena among low-caste communities, religion has been considered merely a means to increase material well-being and a mode of social advancement and protest. Particularly in the case of conversion from one religion to another, those who have embraced alternate religious positions have often been said to have had no spiritual motivation whatsoever in doing so.[9] Such analysis, however, does not do justice to the religious sensibilities and insights of the people in these communities or to the complexity of motivations and the potentially comprehensive nature of a change in religious worldview.

Not surprisingly, the Buddhism practiced by Ambedkar's followers is not an orthodox Theravada Buddhism, but rather a Buddhism that

9. Sebastian C. H. Kim details examples of such arguments made in the debates around conversion in his book *In Search of Identity: Debates on Conversion in India* (2003), esp. 121–31.

incorporates a much larger measure of social justice into its quest for spiritual enlightenment. It is a Buddhism emphasizing individual ethical autonomy and equality that is marked by practices of *puja* (ritual worship) directed at both Siddartha Gautama and Ambedkar himself, the latter envisioned as a bodhisattva (an enlightened being who compassionately works for the liberation of all beings) with the capacity to respond to devotees' requests (Beltz 2005; Jondhale and Beltz 2004). As Nandy has observed, conversion, as much as other forms of alternate religiosity, is a form of renegotiation with the dominant tradition and not a mere rejection of it and can have multiple motivations and outcomes (2002, 142–43).

Ambedkar's crafting of a new religious identity for himself and his caste fellows occurred over an extended period of some thirty years, and the tradition has continued to evolve. He began by working to reform Hinduism but ultimately rejected it on the grounds that it was irrevocably hierarchical and offered no possibility of equality. His selection of Buddhism came after considerable negotiation rather than simple rejection; in the end, he chose a tradition that was continuous with elements of his identity as "Indian," including its origins and shared notions of karma, rebirth, and so on, but in so doing he also rejected the hierarchy embedded in the dharmic structure of caste. The Buddhism he espoused has distinct parallels with the "engaged Buddhist" movements that arose elsewhere in the decades that followed. The tradition as it has continued to develop also reflects multiple motivations and understandings of what it means to be Buddhist among its members and has integrated forms of religiosity that show both continuity and discontinuity with Buddhist and Hindu traditions. The Mahars have embraced a Buddhism fundamentally characterized by a recognition of the absolute equality of human beings and a call for social justice. And they have asserted an identity that is decidedly "Buddhist" and "not Hindu," but also distinctly "Mahar."

An alternate mode of renegotiation with dominant traditions can be undertaken from within the tradition. The establishment of the Satnampanth by the Chamars (a formerly untouchable caste of leatherworkers) of Chhattisgarh in the 1820s is an example of such renegotiation. This sect rejected the temple worship and rituals that Chamars had traditionally been prohibited from participating in. With time, interactions between members of this sect and members of service castes that had formerly refused to serve Chamars were also forbidden on grounds of purity—the same grounds on which these same castes had formerly excluded the Chamars. By instituting a purification ritual, the Satnami community was effectively transformed into a society of the pure that then guarded itself against the impurity of outsiders. Its traditionally low-caste followers "seized upon the signs of subordination . . . and set them up as symbols of the self-reliance and the superiority of the sect [and in so doing t]hey formalized a clear alternative to the powerful network of relationships with service castes within the village" (Dube and Dube 2003, 232–33, 241). Though not strictly a Chamar sect, the Satnami community limited entry, refusing initiation to people from some castes they considered impure. Once a person was initiated, however, there was no hierarchy within the community, and the sect functioned effectively as its members' new *jati* or caste.

Many other examples of similar types of sectarian religious transformation can be cited, and it must be noted that these forms of subaltern religion, whether asserted through conversion or sectarian formation, also change with time. They, too, are "handed over to their adherents," as Clarke suggests; they are not fixed but undergo constant change as identities are reshaped, symbols and practices refined and retooled, and relationships with other communities renegotiated and developed. However, low-caste communities' active participation in the shaping of religious identities that challenge structures of oppression and move across the permeable boundaries of religious traditions is far more pervasive than the instances of outright conversion to alternative religions or the development of new sects might indicate. The practice of any religion by embodied human beings and by communities always entails interaction with other elements of adherents' identities and experiences. Different communities, including low-caste communities, develop their own understandings of the practice of their religion(s) and of their own identity within that practice. They may choose to assert not a new sectarian or religious identity through conversion, but rather a decidedly "Hindu" or "Muslim" or "Christian" identity, albeit one that they actively shape and create.

Clarke suggests that such subaltern religion is marked not by a simple top-down reception, but by a rejection of the symbolic system of the dominant religion(s) and a resymbolization so that religion making becomes a site of contestation, creativity, and self-assertion. This act of religion making involves heavy borrowing from the existing traditions; it is not a binary opposition to them but rather exists in a complex relationship in which elements of the existing traditions are reconfigured through the particular community's lived experience (1998, 125–30).

An example of this type of complex religion making can be seen among the members of the Paraiyar community in Tamil Nadu. A Dalit caste traditionally known as drummers, they have incorporated this key element of their identity into their own form of Christianity, introducing drumming into their religious practice and the drum symbolically into their understanding of Christ (Clarke 1998). This incorporation and resymbolization are problematic, however, because the drum had been a signifier of their degraded social status, as Corinne Dempsey (2004) points out, and Christian leaders in their community had forbidden its use for this reason. In the dominant Hindu system where death is a source of great impurity, the drum itself is made of cowhide, the production of which requires working with dead animals, and the Paraiyars' services as drummers were particularly associated with funeral services (Clarke 1998, 67–68). Thus, within both the dominant Hindu and received Christian traditions there would have been ample reason to leave this symbol behind. But the Paraiyars are the "people of the drum (*parai*)," and they chose not to discard this identity, but to transform it and to create a distinct Christian identity of their own.

This subaltern type of religion making is characterized by an improvisational and eclectic selection and rejection of elements from the dominant tradition(s) and other dimensions of experience that lead to a kind of "jigsaw-like religious configuration," as Clarke puts it, in which "comprehensiveness and unitary cohesion are sometimes not possible; instead fluidity, temporary relevance and partial enhancement of communal subjectivity are settled for" (1998, 128). He notes also a general lack of an "explicitly combative and radically oppositional" stance in such subaltern religion—for example, an absence of a direct confrontational challenge to the caste system. He suggests instead that resistance takes more subtle and tacit forms, ensuring survival within the context of dominant forces that might react violently against more direct challenges (129). The Paraiyar Christians' redefinition of the religious place of the drum is such an act of resistance. In their reconfiguration, the drum is no longer a mark of impurity and inferiority but rather represents the presence of the divine in the world and becomes a symbol for Christ. In making this claim, they are also asserting a radically different status for their own community as "people of the drum."

Similar composite or syncretic traditions have incorporated Hindu and Muslim practices, symbols, and beliefs in ways that also allow for resistance to upper-caste dominance, including the traditions of the Meos and the Meghwal followers of Ramdev documented by Shail Mayaram (1997) and Dominique-Sila Khan (1997). As Mayaram points out, this internal religious fluidity and the lack of hard and fast boundaries between traditions allow both for constructing distinct identities and for finding common ground between diverse groups and forming alliances to resist upper-caste dominance (1997, 39). Khan and Mayaram have also documented the pressure exerted on these communities to choose oppositional Hindu or Muslim identities in post-Partition and postindependence India—pressure that is perhaps in part motivated by dominant groups' desire to shut down the potential for such alliances.

In addition to the free-wheeling selection and rejection of elements of dominant religious traditions and noncombative yet clear forms of resistance, other shared characteristics can be identified in these low-caste expressions of religion and identity, particularly as they emerge within a given religion. They tend to combine universalist claims to human equality and dignity, critiques of injustice and oppression on religious and human grounds, and the assertion of alternative value systems not based on birth, wealth, or power—all of which easily resonate across the fluid boundaries between religious traditions. These claims, critiques, and values can be expressed in religiously and culturally specific ways based on differing metaphysical assumptions, religious narratives and symbols, and the adherents' contexts and experiences, but in each case they have parallels in other traditions and militate against exclusionary or denigrating behavior or the demonizing of others. Such critiques of oppression and calls for social justice emerge out of the lived experience of both oppression and deep religious practice and belief.

To offer but one example, the Meghwal communities with whom I have worked in Rajasthan express their understanding of devotional Hinduism in part through the songs they sing in the name of saints such as Mirabai and Kabir at their *jagrans*, the all-night singing sessions that are their principle mode of religious gathering.[10] Within these songs, we find a distinctive portrayal of the sixteenth-century Rajput saint Mirabai as a royal woman who renounces her life of privilege for the simple life that many of this community have no choice but to live and who, because of her low-caste Chamar guru Raidas, suffers the same caste oppression to which the Meghwals are subjected. The Kabir of their songs appears not as a critic of religious leaders, either Muslim or Hindu, but rather as a weaver of dignity and resistance (Martin 2000).

Indeed, the songs these Meghwals sing speak not of revolution, but of loving God in the midst of pain and struggle. Theirs is a theology of survival and of dignity and self-respect, which privileges the wisdom and religious authority that are particularly the province of the poor and disenfranchised. Herein we do find a critique of social and religious hierarchies, though expressed indirectly through renunciation and action. For example, in one song the royal Rajput saint Mirabai rejects her royal husband, the *rana* or ruler of Mewar, as well as all that he has to offer her by way of material goods. She embraces instead a life of simplicity and the nonmaterial treasure of devotion and true community. In one such song, she sings:

10. These songs are part of a composite tradition, with any songs that might have been composed by the historical saint inseparable from the songs that have been composed by others in the saint's name across the centuries. The analysis here is based primarily on the repertoire of the singer Padmaram recorded in 1993 but also draws on some songs from other Meghwal singers. For additional examples and analysis of low-caste traditions surrounding these saints, see my essay "Mirabai and Kabir in Rajasthani Folk Traditions: Meghwal and Manganiyar Repertoires" (2000) and Parita Mutka's *Upholding the Common Life: The Community of Mirabai* (1994).

In your country, Rana, there are no devotees.
The people living there are trash, Mewari Rana.
    I do not like your land.
Mine is a higher state—
    I do not like your country.
Though it may be full of goodness—
    I'll sacrifice it, O Ram.
Mine is the highest love—
    I do not like your land.
Kajal and *tika*—
    I abandon them all.
I'll give up braiding my hair,
    as a offering, O Ram.
. . . *Mine is the highest love—*
    I do not like your land.
Necklaces and ornaments, Rana—
    I abandon them all.
I'll give up wearing bangles,
    as an offering, O Ram.
Mine is a higher state—
    I do not like your country . . .
Bai Mira's lord is that gallant one
    who raised up the mountain.
She's your servant, Ram,
    you clever Mountain Bearer.
. . . *Mine is the highest love—*
    I do not like your land.
Meeting the true guru, all is fulfilled,
    in the sacrifice, O Ram.
Meeting my guru, I am complete;
    I do not like your country.[11]

11. This particular version of this song was recorded in 1975 and sung by Meghwal men in the village of Borunda, halfway between Merta and Jodhpur in Marwar. The recording

Mira here refers to God by the generic and inclusive name "Ram" as well as the Krishna-specific appellation "Mountain Bearer," and she willingly gives up all ornamentation, material privilege, and status for the company of other devotees and her wise teacher or guru. For them, she readily sacrifices the lamp-black *kajal* to adorn her eyes and the *tika* for her forehead; she lets loose her braided hair in the manner of a renouncer and discards the bangles and jewelry that mark her status as a privileged married woman (some types of which were also forbidden for low-caste people to wear).

In another song, Mirabai tells the *rana* that she has no use for jewels but wears the beads of sacred basil (*tulsi*) used in prayer, and she rejects his rich food, preferring instead the dry scraps eaten by the poorest of the poor. What he offers are not the things that matter. In rejecting these things, she stands in solidarity with the oppressed and offers a different set of values that are not the purview of the rich and powerful.

If she does not want what the *rana* can give and instead takes refuge in God, then he ultimately has no control over her, though he may even try to kill her. He does try, according to the stories of her life, because she dishonors his family by taking a low-caste guru and not respecting the rules of decorum for a woman of her caste and royal status. But Mirabai does not die and instead dances and sings with ecstatic joy in the temples, alternately said to have bells on her ankles and to be playing a drum or *khartal*s (wooden instruments with jingles, like a tambourine). In a third song, the *rana* asks her to return to the palace, but she responds:

> I will not leave my hut of grass and reeds, Ranaji—
> I have already given up living in a palace.
> *My mind holds fast to songs of love.*

Nor will she accept the camels and brightly colored clothes and rice he offers. It is the love of God alone that is the measure of life's meaning and value.

---

is from the Rupayan Sansthan Folklore Institute collection, recorded under the direction of Padmashri Komal Kothari. For a translation of a similar song, see Mukta 1994, 100–101.

In the Meghwal songs of Kabir, the equality of all before God is affirmed (Martin 2002, 204–12). The bodies of all are crafted by a master artisan and must be kept pure, though when need be God will come as a Dobhi to wash away all stain. In successive songs, God is likened not only to a washerman, but also to a weaver, a potter, and a spinning woman—all traditionally low-caste professions—and devotees are admonished not to waste their precious human birth, so easily frittered away in ceaseless toil and blind searching. Youth, wealth, the love of family and friends—none of these things can bring ultimate security and meaning. The truth is hidden and not in the possession of those who think they know, any more than the true treasure is in the hands of the rich and powerful. Rather, the knowledge people seek and the source of true fulfillment are already within every person's grasp:

> Everyone is calling out "Ruby! Ruby!"
> Yet each has a scarf [*palla*] filled with gems—
> No one unties the knot to see what's inside,
> And so they are like one who has nothing.
> Everyone is crying "Ruby! Ruby!"
> But no one bothers to look.
> Servant Kabir saw and transcended birth and death.[12]

The most valuable jewels are already in the possession of all by virtue of their humanity, and true religious authority is derived from lived experience; knowing and loving God grow within the radical living practice of religion.

Reflection in these songs focuses primarily on the struggle to affirm dignity and to (re)claim one's true identity as beloved of God and to know a loving God while living under inhuman conditions. These reflections are marked by a deep and nuanced sense of joy, hope, and faith—tested and tempered by the fire of suffering. Within this community, the boundaries

12. This song was sung by Padmaram and recorded in 1993 in the studios of the Rajasthan Patrika in Jaipur by Padmashri Komal Kothari and myself, with copies housed in the archives of Rupayan Sansthan Folklore Institute in Jodhpur.

of religious identity as "Hindu" are firmly drawn, and yet there is an imprecision to that identity because members have no singular sectarian affiliation. In the world described in their songs, this "Hindu" identity is inclusive and affirmative rather than exclusionary, and, as noted earlier, diverse Hindu and Muslim imagery is used almost interchangeably. "Those who know" are not limited to one religious label or another, either sectarian or tradition specific.

Highly specific appropriations of the traditions of Mirabai and Kabir also affirm the distinctiveness of a particular low-caste identity, giving it a positive, even heroic valuation. An epic song tradition associated with Mirabai called the *Mira janma patri* (Mira's Birth Story or Mira's Horoscope) depicts her in one scene essentially as a Meghwal weaver woman (Martin 1999; Mukta 1994, 112–14, 233–34). When the *rana* demands that she leave his palace after he discovers that the Chamar Raidas is her guru, she asks to be allowed to live in a hut by the palace walls and to weave the *rana*'s *dhotis* (a man's garment wrapped around the waist). A low point in the story is then marked when he refuses. The tragedy of her situation at that moment resonates with the desperation of those who have suffered under caste oppression and the desolation of women cast out or abandoned. But the *rana*'s rejection is also immediately followed by Mirabai's defiant act of shattering her wedding bangles, and she leaves the palace to pursue an independent life and a higher purpose, offering inspiration and hope in the face of rejection and suffering.

Another Meghwal song describes the vulnerability to sexual exploitation to which low-caste women in particular are subject by retelling the story of Kabir's wife, Loi, who was threatened by a lustful businessman (Martin 2002, 212–13). The businessman agrees to give her the supplies she needs to fulfill Kabir's offer of hospitality to a group of holy men on the condition that she return to sleep with him. When Kabir learns of this bargain, he carries his wife on his shoulders to the merchant's home so that she will not get her feet muddy in the rain. When the merchant asks how she managed to arrive thus in the rain, she tells him. The merchant's lust drains away, and he turns to devotion to God. There is no divine intervention here; instead, Kabir and Loi's integrity and purity of heart change the dynamics of exploitation.

In both cases, these religious stories allow for the expression of suffering under caste and gender oppression, but also for the triumph of spirit. The saints are portrayed as members of the singers' own distinctive communities, sharing their experiences. Here religion serves as an essential and creative means of self-expression and resistance coupled with the affirmation of hope and dignity.

This strategy of low-caste assertion of an alternate religious identity within a given tradition, coupled with the strategies employed in conversion and sectarian formation, suggest that religious boundaries can be drawn without shutting down the internal fluidity of religious traditions or their external openness. They also affirm that religion can be a valuable resource as we seek to deal with the "identity threats" of modernization and globalization and as we seek a more just world in which the equality and dignity of all people is recognized and protected. It is essential that these two dimensions remain connected, and these low-caste religious assertions show us some ways this continued connection might be accomplished. As they make clear, it is precisely the fluidity of internal diversity and external boundaries of religions that provide us with "meaning-giving and meaning-making symbolic dwelling places" (as Clarke describes them), within which people can define themselves as individuals, as members of multiple communities, and as part of a larger humanity in ways that do not depend on demonizing or dominating another.

Works Cited

Basu, Anasuya, and Ray Chaudhury. 2007. "Sabarmati: Creating a New Divide?" *Economic and Political Weekly* (Feb. 24): 697–703.

Beltz, Johannes. 2005. *Mahar, Buddhist, and Dalit: Religious Conversion and Socio-political Emancipation*. New Delhi: Manohar.

Clarke, Sathianathan. 1998. *Dalits and Christianity: Subaltern Religion and Liberation Theology in India*. New Delhi: Oxford Univ. Press.

———. 2003. "Transformations of Caste and Tribe." In *Religious Conversion in India: Modes, Motivations, and Meanings*, edited by Rowena Robinson and Sathianathan Clarke, 217–21. New Delhi: Oxford Univ. Press.

Dempsey, Corinne. 2004. "Dalits and Christianity: Subaltern Religion and Liberation Theology in India" (book review). *Religion* 34, no. 2 (Apr.): 156–58.

Dube, Saurabh, and Ishita Banerjee Dube. 2003. "Spectres of Conversion: Transformations of Caste and Sect in India." In *Religious Conversion in India: Modes, Motivations, and Meanings*, edited by Rowena Robinson and Sathianathan Clarke, 222–54. New Delhi: Oxford Univ. Press.

Engineer, Asghar Ali, ed. 2003. *The Gujarat Carnage*. Delhi: Orient Longman.

Gottschalk, Peter. 2007. "A Categorical Difference: Communal Identity in British Epistemologies." In *Religion and Violence in South Asia: Theory and Practice*, edited by John R. Hinnells and Richard King, 195–210. New York: Routledge.

Hess, Linda, and Shukdev Singh, trans. [1983] 1986. *The Bijak of Kabir*. Delhi: Motilal Banarsidas.

Jondhale, Surendra, and Johannes Beltz, eds. 2004. *Reconstructing the World: B .R. Ambedkar and Buddhism in India*. New Delhi: Oxford Univ. Press.

Kakar, Sudhir. 1996. *The Colors of Violence: Cultural Identities, Religion, and Conflict*. Chicago: Univ. of Chicago Press.

Khan, Dominique-Sila. 1997. *Conversions and Shifting Identities: Ramdev Pir and the Ismailis in Rajasthan*. Delhi: Manohar.

Kim, Sebastian C. H. 2003. *In Search of Identity: Debates on Conversion in India*. New Delhi: Oxford Univ. Press.

Mander, Harsh. 2006. "Inside Gujarat's Relief Colonies: Surviving State Hostility and Denial." *Economic and Political Weekly* (Dec. 23): 5235–39.

Martin, Nancy M. 1999. "*Mira Janma Patri* and Other Tales of Resistance and Appropriation." In *Religion, Ritual, and Royalty*, edited by Rajendra Joshi and N. K. Singhi, 227–61. Jaipur, India: Rawat Press.

———. 2000. "Mirabai and Kabir in Rajasthani Folk Traditions: Meghwal and Manganiyar Repertoires." In *The Banyan Tree: Essays on Early Literature in New Indo-Aryan Languages*, edited by Mariola Offredi, 2:391–418. Delhi: Manohar.

———. 2002. "Homespun Threads of Dignity and Protest: Songs of Kabir in Rural Rajasthan." In *Images of Kabir*, edited by Monika Boehm-Tettelbach, 199–214. Delhi: Manohar.

Mayaram, Shail. 1997. *Resisting Regimes: Myth, Memory, and the Shaping of Muslim Identity*. Delhi: Oxford Univ. Press.

Mukta, Parita. 1994. *Upholding the Common Life: The Community of Mirabai*. Delhi: Oxford Univ. Press.

Namishray, Mohandas. 2002. "The Violence in Gujarat and the Dalits." In *Gujarat: The Making of a Tragedy*, edited by Siddharth Varadarajan, 267–70. Delhi: Penguin Books.

Nandy, Ashis. 2002. *Time Warps: Silent and Evasive Pasts in Indian Politics and Religion*. New Brunswick, NJ: Rutgers Univ. Press.

Robinson, Rowena. 2003. "Fluid Boundaries: Christian 'Communities' in India." In *Communal Identity in India: Its Construction and Articulation in the Twentieth Century*, edited by Bidyut Chakrabarty, 287–305. New Delhi: Oxford Univ. Press.

Varadarajan, Siddharth, ed. 2002. *Gujarat: The Making of a Tragedy*. Delhi: Penguin Books.

PART FOUR

≈

Transcending Boundaries

10

≈

Religious Healing and Ritual Relationships at a Religious Crossroads in South India

JOYCE BURKHALTER FLUECKIGER

THE SMALL GRAVESITE of the Sufi *pir* Sheikh Hussein Qadiri Chishti, originally nestled in a rocky, thorn-bush landscape on the outskirts of Hyderabad, has grown up gradually over the years since the sheikh's death in 1998 into a fully established, enclosed shrine (*dargah*). Its large, light-green dome and numerous mosque minarets mark the skyline of a now rapidly developing, primarily Muslim neighborhood. However, on the sheikh's ninth death anniversary (*sandal*) in the fall of 2007, one-third to one-half of the *sandal* celebration participants crowded into the shrine were Hindu.[1] Most of them were patients/disciples of a healer named

This essay is a substantially revised version of chapter 5 in my book *In Amma's Healing Room: Gender and Vernacular Islam in South India* (Bloomington: Indiana Univ. Press, 2006). I am grateful to Indiana University Press for permission to include it in this volume.

1. Sheikh Hussein's death anniversary was originally on the twenty-seventh day of Ramadan (January 1998). However, in 2006 his son and daughter-in-law, who supervise the *sandal* celebrations, were making a pilgrimage to Mecca on that date, and so, with the "elders'" permission, they moved the *sandal* celebration ahead by one month. In 2007, they told me they were going to keep the date ahead one month so that *sandal* celebrants were freer to participate, not observing the fast of Ramadan and not having to save their monies for Id.

Mustang, who practiced in their neighborhood and whose own *pir*/teacher was Sheikh Hussein.

Mustang was first a young Hindu patient of Sheikh Hussein's wife, Amma, who had set up a professional religious healing practice in a small room attached to their living quarters. At this time, as a Hindu, Mustang was named "Sati." He sat in Amma's healing room regularly, entering into an intimate relationship with Amma and her husband, and eventually became a disciple of Sheikh Hussein. He gradually learned discrete healing practices and later the basics of the entire practice from Amma; during the week he worked as a carpenter, and on Sundays he would help Amma by conducting limited rituals on her behalf. Over the years, Mustang gradually became more and more Islamicized until he was finally circumcised, changed his name from "Sati" to "Mustang," and became a *khalifa* (disciple who has authority to make his own disciples) of Sheikh Hussein.[2] After the elderly sheikh's death, Mustang set up his own healing practice full-time in his home.

Sheikh Hussein, then, is the "grandfather *pir*" of many of the Hindu celebrants who are drawn to his *sandal* through their relationship with Mustang. The sheikh and Amma, buried side by side in the shrine, still exhibit spiritual power (*barkat*) through various kinds of healing miracles experienced by both Muslim and Hindu worshippers coming to the *dargah*. This essay analyzes the cosmology, ritual grammar, and narratives performed in the healing/teaching tradition in which Amma and Sheikh Hussein participated as well as the relationships created therein, which cross boundaries of religious difference and enable religious healing across these boundaries.

Sheikh Hussein is known more commonly as "Abba," literally "Father," or, after his death, "Baba." He was married to an unusual woman who practiced in a traditionally Sufi male role as a professional religious

2. A non-Muslim technically becomes a Muslim when he or she says the creed of faith (*shahada, kalima*) upon becoming a disciple of a *pir*, but in this context the disciple kept his Hindu name until he became circumcised many years after he had formally become a disciple. I analyze this phenomenon as a gradual process of conversion that develops as the disciple–*pir* relationship develops (Flueckiger 2006).

healer who meets the 'public'[3]—meaning she met non-Muslims (Hindus and Christians) and nonfamilial males and charged money for her services. She was called "Amma" or "Ammi" (Mother) by her patients and disciples. Like Mustang, most of Abba's disciples had come to him through Amma, first becoming her patients and then his disciples. Amma and Abba shared and negotiated the traditional *pir* role of healer/teacher; Amma performed her authority primarily in the healing room, and Abba's authority was most visible in contexts outside the healing room, such as at the monthly *sama* (musical assembly) held in Abba's courtyard, at which Abba's key disciples gathered. Although disciples were technically initiated by Abba, rhetorically they gave allegiance to both Amma and Abba. In death, Abba's authority has become paramount, and Amma seems to be honored by those who did not know the couple in life (such as many of the Hindu participants mentioned earlier) primarily as his wife rather than as a spiritual healer in her own right.[4] But this essay focuses on patient–healer relationships and ritual and narrative performances in Amma's healing room while she was still living.[5] Therefore, although Amma died in 2001, I use the ethnographic present tense in my discussion for descriptions of everyday routines.

The Healing Room as a Crossroads

The first time I met Amma in her healing room—in a residential neighborhood for university employees on the campus of Osmania University,

3. All such words in single quotation marks are English words used in what was otherwise Urdu or Telugu conversation or narrative.

4. I open my book *In Amma's Healing Room* with the image of green flags of authority flying at shrines and courtyards in Hyderabad and observe, "I have slowly learned of the male lineages and authorities represented by these flags and have become keenly aware of how easily Amma's narrative . . . could get lost behind lineages of male saints represented by the flags" (2006, 1). It would appear that this loss is already happening for visitors to the grave shrine who did not know Amma in life.

5. The primary fieldwork for this essay was conducted in 1994–95 and for a month at a time each year thereafter until Amma's death in 2001. I have since continued regularly visiting Amma's family in Hyderabad.

Hyderabad, in the winter of 1989, accompanied by two female Hindu colleagues—she asserted, "There are only two castes/*jati* [true distinctions; species—as in Noah and the ark, the pairs of animals go up *jati* by *jati*]: men and women. Muslims, Christians, Hindus—they're all the same." I initially heard this statement as an effort on Amma's part to welcome us "outsiders" into her healing room with a rhetorical exaggeration that sought to emphasize commonality rather than difference. However, when I heard similar statements repeated in numerous other contexts, I came to realize that Amma and her patients *did* actually mean what they said, but that it was context specific—to *this* place, the healing room. As I have sat at Amma's healing table intermittently for almost twenty years, patients have often asked me what it is that I write down in my little notebook. I answer, "I note down whether the patient is Hindu or Muslim, male or female, the presenting problem, and Amma's diagnosis and prescription." Amma often sighs and bemoans repeatedly, "Jo-ice, haven't you learned anything? There is no Hindu or Muslim *here*, at this place."

And so I have imagined Amma's healing room as a crossroads of traditions, where religious traditions intersect and create a mutually shared religious space. The Hindi/Urdu term for crossroads is *caurasta*, which in Indian urban contexts is conceptualized as a center, but only one of many centers in a network of multiple roads with numerous crossings. This kind of healing setting is similarly only one of several crossroads where Hindu and Muslim traditions intersect, share space, or both. Others include certain genres of music, dance, festival participation, language, shrines of saints, and relationships with other living saints or gurus.

In Indian cities and towns, *caurasta*s are meeting places where roads and people come together—in contrast to the American English connotation of the term *crossroads*, which is more often perceived as "roads going out." City, town, and village *caurasta*s are not conceptualized as forlorn or lonely places of personal decision (as in Robert Frost's "The Road Not Taken"); rather, their corners are bustling with tea stalls, bus stands, and movie theaters, filled with crowds and conversation. When someone asks for directions in a traditional Indian town or city, he or she is often given a response beginning with: "Well, go to X *caurasta* [X being marked by some identifiable building such as a hospital, theater, government building, and so on]." Although *caurastas* serve as important identity markers of social space, very few people who pass through them actually live there or even stay there very long: they are public gathering places and social spaces. Furthermore, they are often considered dangerous places because they are not subject to the social and ritual control typical of domestic spaces. It is with these many connotations that Amma's healing room serves as a crossroads, a *caurasta*—a unique social space created by the particular roads that cross through it.

Amma's healing room is a space in which patients of different religious and social identities meet for a common cause, creating a shared identity between them. As Amma emphasizes, at *this* place they are not Hindus or Muslims, but rather patients/human bodies and souls with similar, shared troubles (*pareshani*). But it is not a space where they dwell permanently; it is a crossroads. When they go home and arrange their children's marriages or conduct the death rituals for their parents, it matters very much whether they are Muslim or Hindu. Marriage, death, and image worship are examples of the "end points" of the axes that cross through the healing room, where difference is accentuated.

Amma's spiritual healing takes place not on any one of these axes, but on the shared spiritual plane that encompasses their intersection, a plane on which broad contours of a shared cosmology, narrative repertoire and motifs, and ritual grammar are operative, performed, and continually re-created. Articulations of religious identities and their intersection at such a cultural crossroads seem to be of much more concern to scholars than they are to the participants in the healing room itself. In contrast, Amma's assertion "There are only two castes"—those of gender—*is* actively being articulated and negotiated and is a topic of frequent conversation and debate (see Flueckiger 2006, chap. 4). *Outside* the healing room, however, in other contexts, some Hindus and Muslims may focus on the extended ends of the axes that pass through the crossroads, where distinct religious identities are most clearly articulated; in those contexts, they do not always recognize the crossroads (such as Amma's healing room) as validly representing their respective traditions.

The Healing Practice

Amma's healing practice centers around the written word both in diagnoses and prescription; Amma often says that her healing is solely dependent on the Qur'an, that everything she needs is in the Qur'an. Her diagnoses depend primarily on performing mathematical calculations on the numerical value of the Arabic letters of a patient's name and that of his or her mother. Most prescriptions are also written, consisting of amulets upon which are written verses from the Qur'an, the names of God and of his messengers and agents (*maukil*), or the numerical symbols for these names. In this way, Amma's practice can be identified as "Islamic." Abba once explained to me how these written amulets work: by calling on Allah and his agents to intervene on the patient's behalf: "It's like if I write a letter to you and tell you to come; it's 'urgent'—a telegram. You can't refuse. Like that, there's a mantra. And on [your] name, like if we know the name of your mother. Reading that and reading your name, we make an 'attack.'" The mechanics of this system of diagnoses and prescriptions are the easy part; Amma says that even a parrot can learn this much (although it is not quite so easy for the fieldworker to understand). What are most important and needed for effective healing are the spiritual knowledge and authority with which Amma commands spiritual agents to come to her service: to find a missing child, to close an argumentative neighbor's or relative's mouth, to banish a high fever or possessing spirit, to enable fertility.

I have never seen a patient read what Amma writes on the amulets or ask her for an explanation of the mechanics of her diagnostic/prescriptive system. They come to her not for *what* she practices, but for who she is and *how* she practices; she is particularly known for her unique love for and patience with patients (perceived to be gendered qualities) as well as for her healing successes. The array of different types of amulets and the sheets of paper covered with mathematical diagnostic calculations help to create Amma's authority, and patients are reluctant to leave her table without an amulet (even if the diagnostic calculations reveal their illnesses have not be caused by spiritual forces, the only illnesses against which amulets are effective). The specifics of *how* the amulets work is left for specialists to learn and not for patients to fully understand. Hindu, Muslim, and Christian patients share a very basic worldview that assumes spiritual forces can affect the spiritual, social, and physical body, causing illness, and that such illnesses can be cured only through a spiritual agent, in this case called upon by a charismatic Muslim woman who employs a healing system whose basic ritual grammar is accepted and understood across religious boundaries.

A Shared Ritual Grammar at the Healing Crossroads

The basic grammar and parameters of Amma's healing rituals are not unique to Islamic practice, even if the specifics may not be familiar to her Hindu or Christian patients (or to many Muslims, for that matter). New patients are sometimes confused regarding what to do, at what time of day, and with which paper amulet or ritual ingredient, and so their repeated questions often cause gales of laughter among returning patients and disciples around the healing table. But they *do* understand the power of a particularly powerful healer to call upon spiritual forces to come to her aid through the power of the word. I often heard returning patients explain to new Hindu patients that Amma's amulets are the same as Hindu mantras (oral incantations), although one is written and the other spoken.

Supplementing the prescription of amulets is a prescription called *utara* (literally, "to take off") that Amma orders for forms of what she calls "heavy" evil. Depending on her diagnosis, the prescription is to fill a clay pot with either white or yellow rice, different numbers and colors of flowers, one hundred grams of uncut, uncooked liver, and a nail upon which is impaled a lemon and a black hard seed (used for laundry marking). This filled pot should then be circled three times around the patient's head and three times up and down the patient's body, thereby attracting and absorbing the evil eye away from the patient; the pot should then be carried to and left at some kind of crossroads. The basic ritual itself, of circling an attractive physical object over a person to draw away the evil eye, is one commonly practiced in numerous ritual contexts in South Asia—Hindu, Muslim, Christian. Thus, many elements of Amma's prescriptions are readily accessible and understandable to patients regardless of their religious background. Some upper-caste, vegetarian Hindus may initially recoil from the raw liver ingredient; nevertheless, all those whom I met in the healing room found a way to fill the prescription. (Some Brahmin patients asked their lower-caste servants to purchase the liver, and then the ritual was conducted outside of the house.) From among the many rituals in Amma's healing repertoire, *utara* is the ritual identified most often by some educated South Asian Muslims as "Hindu." One can speculate that this identification is made because the prescription does not involve the written word, specifically that of the Qur'an, and that its ritual grammar is visibly shared with Hindu traditions.

Although ritual grammar may be shared, interpretations of that ritual may differ, in particular the interpretation of the relative hierarchy of spiritual beings being called into service and who it is who actually effects healing. But most patients do not consciously interpret the ritual at all—they have put their faith in a charismatic, successful healer, and they simply follow her prescriptive directions.

An Encompassing Worldview and Cosmology

Spiritual healing is effective across religious traditions, in part, because of a shared, understandable ritual grammar, but perhaps more important in this case because of the encompassing, flexible cosmology in which Amma's patients participate, one that accommodates elements of both Hindu and Muslim worldviews. This encompassing framework accepts the existence of a continuum of power and permeable boundaries between human and nonhuman worlds as well as what *kinds* of beings populate the nonhuman world: deities, ghosts, angels, jinn, saints, and devils (*shaytan*). Amma and Abba as Muslim religious specialists in this multireligious context *are* monotheists, but in a very different way than, for example, my Protestant Christian missionary parents who worked in India for forty years. In Amma and Abba's cosmology, Allah stands alone and is unique as the creator of all things and beings; in this way, the important Muslim concept of the "unity of God," *tawhid*, is affirmed. But after the important affirmation of Allah's distinct quality, Amma and Abba do not deny the existence and power of Hindu deities. They imagine a religious landscape populated by a wide variety of spiritual beings who are not necessarily or inherently good or evil, but simply powerful, many of whom cause illness, and others of whom are agents of healing. Some of these spiritual beings have distinct identities and personalities and can be said to "belong" to one or another religious tradition, although they themselves cross the boundaries of those traditions.

Avatars, Shaktis, Prophets, and Maukils

Because of the fluidity of language usage between Telugu and Urdu in Amma's healing room (she speaks primarily Urdu to her Muslim patients and Telugu to her Hindu patients) and the differences in a range of meanings and usages of some classificatory words, such as *avatar* and *shakti*, what exactly is meant by their usage in a given context can be difficult to discern. For example, when I asked Amma once to tell me about the Hindu goddess festival of Bonalu, which was being celebrated in neighborhoods all over Hyderabad at the time, she immediately responded by acknowledging the goddess's power and then introduced the expansive category of "avatar" (incarnation, specifically the ten incarnations of the Hindu deity Vishnu).

> This [festival] is to remind Hindus in the same way that our *alam* [flags/standards paraded at Muharram, which had just been celebrated] remind us of the suffering of Hussein.[6] Of course, she [the goddess] has *shakti* [spiritual power]. Theirs are *shakti*s [female], and ours are *baba*s [male saints]. [After a long pause she continued.] You know, we, too, have an avatar; ours is the seventh. [I asked who that was]. Muhammad. He's the seventh. You know, there are Ram and Krishna. Who were the others? [I listed a few, but she was less concerned with names and numbers than with the quality of God that the avatar implied.] Yes. Isn't it sweet [*priya*] that God came down in human form?

6. Notice here that Amma is identifying with a Shi'i ritual tradition of Muharram processions, although she herself is not Shi'i and does not personally participate in these processions. Her usage of "our" is broadly inclusive of all Muslims; internal differences are not as marked in this context when she is speaking about the relationship of Hindu and Muslim categories.

In this case, Amma is equating first *shaktis* and *babas* and then prophets and avatars as classes of beings (one might even say *jatis*/species). *Babas* are saints who have accrued spiritual power (*barkat*) and who perform miracles, particularly after their deaths. (Abba himself is now called a *baba* since his death.) They are not deities, and by equating *shaktis* with *babas*, Amma would seem to be acknowledging the spiritual power of the *shaktis* without granting them the status of "goddess" or deity. Similarly, Muslims do *not* call or consider prophets to be deities; but, much like Hindu avatars, prophets are sent by God to teach God's revelation and to correct humans' misbeliefs. A Muslim, on the one hand, may infer that Amma is equating avatars to prophets. A Hindu, on the other hand, may understand Amma's equation of avatar and prophet very differently, assuming she is identifying prophets as gods because Hindus consider Vishnu's avatars to be gods (even if not the deity in his fullest manifestation).[7] Amma is amazed at the compassionate nature of God, that he would show his nature to humans through human form. She does not mean here incarnation in a Christian or Hindu sense—God in human form—but God's love being revealed through humans who are extraordinary, filled with God's love and light: prophets and avatars.

Just as Muhammad is placed in the seemingly infinitely expansive avatar system, Amma and Abba also contextualize the avatars in a specifically Muslim but similarly expansive category of prophets. The Qur'an mentions twenty-five prophets by name. However, Muhammad is reported to have said that there were 124,000 prophets and 315 messengers, creating the possibility of an expandable system of unnamed prophets (Hughes [1885] 1988, 475). In one teaching, Abba described a historical line of prophets in which he included the Hindu deity and avatar of Vishnu, Ram:[8] "Before Muhammad, there were devils and angels

7. For example, when Vishnu comes to earth in the avatar of Ram, he divides himself into four parts to be born as the sons of Dasarath's three wives. Ram is born of two parts, Bharata of one part, and the twins Lakshman and Shatrugna are born from the last quarter of Vishnu.

8. Although this correlation between Muhammad and Vishnu's avatar is not common, Richard Eaton cites a similar cosmology and specific association between the *nabi*

and many other bad things. Ram and Sita ruled for some time. Ibrahim Khali-ullah [Abraham] was born and ruled for some time; many other prophets came. When Ram came, then dharma changed; they became Hindus; they became Reddys; these became their different *jati*s. Only after Muhammad they became Muslims."

In some contexts, especially in the healing room, Amma and Abba emphasize equivalencies between Hindu and Muslim cosmological categories and incorporate Hindu deities into the hierarchy of spiritual powers at Amma's service, but they never blur the distinction between Allah as creator and other powerful beings as created. In one of his teachings, Abba made sure that his disciples understood this distinction. Speaking in Telugu outside the healing room, Abba engaged in conversation with a potential Hindu disciple about the nature of God, arguing that Ram was not God because he had offspring: "Didn't Ram get married? Didn't he have children? We don't call him god. He's called a prophet. We don't call him god [*khuda*]. A prophet means he's a human. Allah sent him to show the right path. Allah sent them [prophets]; he didn't come himself."

On another occasion when we were sitting in the courtyard of a *dargah,* I asked Abba how he understood Hindu deities, whether he thought they had spiritual power (*shakti*). He answered using the nominal rather than adjectival form of *shakti*:

> Surely, they *are shakti*s. But there's a big difference between *shakti* and *bhagwan* [generic term for god]. *Shakti*s give problems to humans; they come on their bodies [i.e., possess them]; they trouble them; they cause them to lose their way. But these saints [such as the one in whose shrine we sat; *buzrugan-e-din*] don't mislead humans like that. If you go to them and ask, they give it. They make you wealthy. They only punish a person if he or she does something wrong. The situation at a temple is that it's a matter of belief. It's like this: a person can even go to a tree and, calling it

---

(prophet) and avatar in Saiyid Sultan's *Nabi-Bamsa* (sixteenth-century Bengal), in which the author classifies "the major deities of the Hindu pantheon, including Brahma, Vishnu, Shiva, Ram, and Krishna, as successive prophets of God, followed in turn by Adam, Noah, Abraham, Moses, Jesus, and Muhammad" (1994, 286).

god, believe in it. It's all a matter of faith [*yakin*]. These are the differences between temples and *dargahs*.

Like avatar (incarnation) and *nabi/pegambar* (prophet), *maukil* (messenger) is another expansive category that may encompass powerful beings from across traditions. Most of the amulets upon which Amma writes call on *maukils*, including the four archangels and various jinn, to carry out her orders—to protect a patient from evil eye, remove fevers, close an antagonist's mouth, and so forth. Hindu deities may also serve as such *maukil*s, including Hanuman, known for his powers to fly through space and cover wide distances and thus a likely messenger. One of Amma's disciples calls upon Hanuman in his ritual practice of *hazrat*, which Amma has given him permission to exercise in her healing room.[9] Hanuman is said to find and call upon the Muslim saint Suleiman Baba, who is then beseeched to reveal the location of lost objects. Amma's disciplined spiritual practice has given her power to order a wide range of *maukil*s to carry out her commands. She told me, "I can make Kali [a Hindu goddess] sit. Kali will come and fold her hands in front of me," at which point one of Amma's Muslim disciples interjected: "Kali, Hanuman, and what's his name—Narsimha Swami [one of Vishnu's avatars]. They all come. They say *namaste* [a greeting] and go away. We call them *maukil*s [messengers], but these people call them *bhagwan* [gods]." Amma added, "We call them *shakti*s." And the disciple continued, "Whoever has *shakti* is called a *maukil*. They call them gods; we don't call them gods. They come when we call them; we have the power to make them work for us. They come to people who are powerful, like Amma. They ask her, 'Why have you called us?' And she asks, 'Why are you giving them trouble?' And she begins to pray, and they leave 'automatically.'"

During lunch break one day, Amma, Abba, and Amma's best friend, a Hindu woman named Munnapa, engaged in a heated discussion about avatars. Munnapa began by saying that Krishna was the greatest of the

9. *Hazrat*, in this context, is a ritual in which the practitioner places a mixture of kohl and oil onto his thumbnail, gazes into the "mirror" of that mixture, and sees the *maukil* or jinn who can find lost objects or sees the "scene" of a family member far away.

avatars, although he, too, changed forms. Amma equated Krishna's changing forms to those of Allah and Muhammad, "Like Allah and Muhammad, like that, Krishna took different avatars." Abba chimed in, saying that the greatest avatar is Shankar (Shiva), "You know, the one who takes the form of the *linga* [an-iconic form of Shiva]; even Ram bowed down before him." But Munnapa repeated again that there was only one avatar, and it was Krishna; the other seven were avatars of him. Another disciple was still stuck on the number of avatars and interrupted him, "But there are eleven, not seven, avatars, and the last is Kalki, the *jalali* avatar [fierce one]." What followed was a free-for-all debate about the correct number of incarnations, seven or eleven of the god, nine or seven of the goddess. Soon everyone seated around the tablecloth spread for lunch began to laugh at the confusion.

Scholars and practitioners of Hinduism are used to hearing a Hindu perspective of an expansive worldview that accommodates the "other"—where boundaries of difference become internal, in which one may find room for religious figures or spiritual agents of other traditions in an expanding pantheon of deities, a flexible system of avatars, and the mantra "there is one truth, and the paths are many." However, a similar inclusivity or encompassment is not commonly associated with Islam. Richard Eaton has identified these kinds of processes as an accretion aspect of conversion, in which people add "new deities or superhuman agencies to their existing cosmological stock, or . . . [identify] new deities or agencies with existing entities in their cosmology" (1985, 113). However, in the passages given earlier, Amma narrativizes and performs just such an encompassing cosmology of powerful beings outside of the context of conversion, a cosmology in which Allah is distinguished as the creator under whom there is an expansive hierarchy of differentiated powerful beings.

Most of the patients who come to Amma's healing table have a much more generalized but nevertheless shared worldview than the one Amma articulates—they share common problems and illnesses, and they acknowledge that these things may be caused by spiritual forces that impinge on the physical world (specifically onto/into the physical body). Patients come to Amma with the assumption and hope that such spiritually caused illnesses can be cured through spiritual healing. They are less concerned about the religious identity of the healer and her agents or the specifics of her diagnostic methods and prescriptions than about her healing successes. As mentioned earlier, none of her patients, Hindu or Muslim, reads or even knows what it is that Amma writes on the amulets, which may be "Islam specific."

The Human World

In the cosmology performed in the healing room, prophets, avatars, jinns, *maukil*s, and gurus lie on a continuum of spiritual power under the creative authority of Allah, and ordinary humans (patients) are situated on the far end of that continuum. Here in the human realm, Amma asserts that any difference other than sexual difference is "man made," socially constructed, not created by God, and hence insignificant on the broad scale of what "matters"—that is, faith and devotion to God:

> You shouldn't doubt Allah, whether you be Hindu or Muslim, or anyone else. Even if someone's a Hindu, but he has *bhakti* [devotion], you shouldn't dismiss him; a Muslim, too, if he has *bhakti*, you shouldn't dismiss him either. One has it and so, too, does the other. One says "Ram Ram" and the other "Rahim Rahim."[10] There's only that much difference, isn't there? One has the call to prayer [*azan*] and the other the [*puja*] bell. There's only that much difference. There's *puja*, and there's *sajda* [one of the physical positions of Muslim prayer, *namaz*]. But there's little difference between them. Allah likes all this play [*khel*]. Look, in the end he liked this [Islam]; and having preferred this play, all this happened. Isn't that right?
>
> . . . In the beginning, there was only Adam-al-salaam. As the number [of people] grew, different trades developed. If you did a *dhobi*'s [washerman's] work, you were a *dhobi*; if you did a *mochi*'s [leatherworker's] work, you were a *mochi*. If you did *puja* [Hindu ritual offering to a deity], you were a *pujari* [temple priest or officiant of *puja*], and if you

10. "Ram" is the name of one of Vishnu's avatars; "Rahim" is one of the names of Allah, meaning "the Merciful One." This saying is very commonly invoked in conversations of interreligious dialogue, equating the two deities as one and the same, with two names.

> read *namaz* [obligatory Muslim prayer], you were a Muslim. This is the way it was. In this way, the children of one father were divided. They became separate.

Here Amma begins by asserting the encompassing inclusivity—and, in this sense, the superiority—of Allah. First and foremost, *he* should not be doubted. But Amma uses "Allah" to refer to the God of Islam, Allah, and as the generic word for god in the same way that the Telugu word *bhagwan* may be used generically. She once chastised an Urdu-speaking disciple for using the term *bhagwan* when speaking Urdu, not because the term was Hindu, but because she perceived it to be Telugu; she told the disciple that if she is speaking Urdu, she should use the word *Allah*. This supreme God, who stands outside/beyond man-made difference can be known in many ways, including through the name "Ram" or "Rahim" (as he may be called in Hindu or Muslim contexts, respectively) and may be worshipped through the Hindu ritual of *puja* (offering flowers, water, and food to the image of a deity) or through the Muslim ritual prayer of *namaz*. The ambiguity of Amma's use of the term *Allah* would seem to be a strategic choice in the context of a Hindu–Muslim audience.

But the primary purpose of Amma's teaching is not theological; rather, it is to critique differences created by humans between one another—that is, *jati* or caste—and to assert the unity of humans born from "one father." In the same discussion, Amma said: "Now I say that the blood is all the same. What are the [true] castes [*jati*]? A man and a woman. *We're* the ones who have divided [humans into] all this caste business [*jat-vat*]—that these are Rajputs, they're Komatis, they're Brahmins, they're this, they're that." This characterization of caste as man made rather than created by God might be interpreted as claiming the superiority of Islam, which does not textually recognize these kinds of caste differences.[11] However, Amma includes "Muslim" as a caste distinction equivalent to *dhobi*, *mochi*, and *pujari* (Brahmin), and hence Muslims are equally implicated in her critique. When Amma ends the teaching

11. In practice, however, there *are* caste-equivalent, often endogamous groups in South Asian Islam.

with the assertion, "What are the true castes? A man and a woman," patients and disciples who are well acquainted with her healing-room rhetoric will fill in the second half of the assertion: "All these are the same: Hindus, Muslims, Christians."

Narrative Motifs and Performance

One of the primary ways in which the shared cosmological plane is created and articulated at the healing crossroads is through Amma and Abba's narrative performances. Although Muslims cannot explicitly participate in worship of the images of Hindu deities, they may and do participate in an expansive imaginative narrative world that crosses easily across religious boundaries, one that includes traditionally "Hindu" narratives. Narrative performances also help to establish Amma and Abba's religious authority.

For example, one of Abba's favorite narratives is that of the founding *pir* of the Qadari lineage, Ghaus-e-pak (also known as Ghaus-e-Azam Dastargir, Gaus-e-Qadr, and Sheikh Abdul Qadir Jilani), to whom Abba traces his own authority and with whom he performatively identifies. The story's two main characters are the two *pir*s Ghaus-e-Pak and one of his contemporaries, Shams Tabriz,[12] both of whom are known for their par-

12. This Shams is likely the same Shams-i Tabriz who was the mystical teacher and beloved friend of the thirteenth-century poet Jalalad-din Rumi, although neither Abba nor Amma ever explicitly made this association; that is, Abba never referred to Rumi. Tazim Kassam has identified three historical figures who are called "Shams," whose hagiographies have often been conflated in oral narrative traditions and who share a hagiographic image as "that of an itinerant, antinomian, and wonder-working *qalandar*: Shams-i Tabriz, the Ismaili Imam, Shams al-Din Muhammad, and the Ismaili preacher Pir Shams" (1995, 76, 82). Although Amma seemed to have little direct contact with the relatively large Ismaili community in Hyderabad, oral traditions move more fluidly than people. The story that follows here is shared by Amma's own Sufi community and the Ismaili tradition of Pir Shams, which Kassam suggests originated in western India. In both, one finds the narrative of Shams raising from the dead a royal child by calling the saint's name, rather than Allah's, the saint being punished by being skinned alive, and then his calling down the sun to cook a piece of raw meat that no one would cook for him because they are disgusted by his looks (1995, 79, 378–79).

ticularly *jalali* (fierce) nature, which this narrative illustrates.[13] The variant given here was performed soon after I had first met Abba, when he was explaining his spiritual lineage to me, tracing it back to the *pir* Ghariban Nawaz (also known as Khwaja Moinuddin Chishti), who is buried in Ajmer (India), then to Ghaus-e-Pak, who is buried in Baghdad:[14]

> ABBA: Ghariban Nawaz's hand is only on India, whereas Ghaus-e-Pak's hand is over the whole world. Wherever you go, you'll see the green flag [the latter's symbol]. It's like this. When people used to take Ghaus's name, their heads would fall off. . . .
>
> There was an important person called Shams-i Tabriz. He used to play with tigers in the jungle. With tigers—in the same way we might play with ten to twelve dogs—he used to play with tigers in the jungle. Do you understand? One day a king had a baby.
>
> AMMA: He couldn't have children; the king's wife couldn't have children. The astrologer had told them that even if they did have children, the children would all die during childbirth itself.
>
> ABBA: The king asked, "Then who will inherit my throne? How can my children be kept alive?" The astrologer told the king, "In the jungle, there lives a *faqir* [Muslim ascetic] who is blind. His name is Shams-i Tabriz. He has the power to bring people back to life."
>
> The queen delivered; she delivered a baby son who died soon after. They hung a curtain and put the child behind it. The king called the army and said, "Go to the jungle and bring back whoever's there [i.e., the *faqir*]." He was playing in the jungle with nine tigers. They surrounded him and caught him. . . .
>
> They took him and went back. They pulled the curtain back. "Bring this child to life." What did the king say? "Bring this child to life." He

13. Abba characterized *pirs* as being either *jalali* (fierce) or *jamali* (cool, easy-going, cheerful). He characterized himself as *jalali*, but usually with a twinkle in his eye. The names of Allah are also characterized as *jalali* or *jamali*; the invocation of his *jalali* names in *zikr* (ritual recitation of names of God) can be dangerous for the novice (Ernst 1997, 97).

14. Ellipses in this narrative indicate interjections made by audience members that have been left out here in the interest of space.

[Shams] responded, "OK. Get up by the order of Allah." But the child didn't get up. Then he said, "Get up by my order." The child shook himself [as if from sleep] and got up.

The king asked, "What is your secret? Why didn't the child get up by the order of Allah, but got up by your order? What is the secret, tell me." [Shams answered,] "What can I say?" "No, no, you have to tell me," [the king insisted]. He called for the executioners and said, "Come and pull off his skin."

The fat, fat executioners came to remove his skin, but it didn't come off; they couldn't get a hold of it. So what did he tell them? "Once, when I was sitting to pee, a drop fell here. Grab my skin from here and pull it off." Then they pulled off his skin, all of it. They pulled it off, and the king ordered him to leave the city.

Covered with flies, filth, and stench, he began to beg from people, but no one gave anything to him. So he went to a butcher; "I'm hungry; give me something," he said. And he [the butcher] gave him a piece of raw meat and told him to have someone else cook it for him. But no one would cook it; no one let him come close because of his bad smell. . . . The poor soul gave him a chunk of meat and said, "Take this chunk of meat and cook it." But whoever saw him told him to move on [no one agreed to cook it].

So he got very angry; being angry, he didn't say anything. . . .

AMMA (interjecting): Then Tabriz said, "I'm going to call *shams* [Arabic for "sun"; called down to cook this hunk of meat]." Saying this, he called the sun. He said, "*Shams*, come down." But just before the sun came, Ghaus-e-Pak came and stood before him. "Don't call it down; don't call it down! If the sun comes down, the whole 'public' will be burned into ashes."

How did he [Shams] respond? "OK, I won't call *shams*. But whenever anyone takes your name, his head separates from his body. You, too, shouldn't use the power of your tongue like that." So he [Ghaus-e-Pak] said, "OK," and went away. Now, raising his [Shams'] hand [towards the sun], the meat was cooked. He ate it and went away, and Ghaus-e-Pak went the other way.

> ABBA: Earlier it was like that: whenever someone took [Ghaus-e-Pak's] name, his head would separate from his body. Shams asked Ghaus-e-Pak to control his *jalali* [fierce nature]; only then he, too, would stop [asking the sun to come down]. So he agreed. When someone is in pain, he says a lot of things; he may say anything [i.e., he may call out the name of the saint Ghaus-e-Pak]. Earlier, in this situation, if you took his name, your head separated from the body.

Why does Abba tell this story? It is, above all, a dramatic story that makes for good performance. But this particular story is chosen from a wide repertoire of possible options; there is a reason it has become a repeated favorite in the context of the healing room. First, it dramatizes/performs rather than discursively declares the spiritual power of saints/*pir*s. And because the narrator, Abba, is himself a *pir* in this same lineage, its performance indirectly confers the authority of the lineage upon Abba, confirming his authority as a *pir*. This is a very different strategy of establishing authority than the performance of *personal* narratives upon which Amma relies to create her public authority. Second, this narrative about the miracles of saints helps to elicit and solidify (unvoiced) assumptions shared among patients about the intercessory power of the *pir* (and indirectly of his wife, the *piranima*) by dramatically exteriorizing this power: the *pir* can cause heads to fall off with the mere mention of his name, play with tigers, raise the dead, and call down the sun. Because Abba is a *pir* in this lineage, he, too, shares in this nature and has access to similar power, albeit diffused (even diluted) from the intensity of that of the *silsila*'s (Sufi order or lineage) founder. And Abba can use this power on behalf of his disciples and Amma's patients.

The narrative also indirectly addresses the controversy debated in some Muslim circles about this very assumption of the possibility of intercessory power by a saint in front of God on behalf of another human. Although this possibility is not theologically problematic for a Hindu, for some Muslims it may begin to approach a breach of a central concept in Islam—*tawhid*, the singularity of God. The fear is that when a saint displays such power, the temptation may be for his disciples not simply to honor him, but to worship him. In the narrative, the *pir* Shams first orders the dead child to rise up from the dead in Allah's name, but nothing happens. Then he says, "Get up by my order," and "the child shook himself and got up." The king notices that the saint's name seems to be more powerful than God's and demands that Shams explain why the child did not get up in Allah's name. Shams refuses to reveal the secret—and I was reminded of Amma's recurrent pronouncement about such secret things: "These are heavy matters." The king himself is presumably not initiated and therefore would be unable to understand the secret even if he were told. Shams's refusal leads to the dramatic unfolding of the rest of the story. This indirect reference to potential controversy (one that I have never heard directly addressed in the healing room) is an example of how Abba often uses narratives to address an issue or question only indirectly, with more multivalency than a direct-discourse answer would be able to do, or the narrative sometimes gives an "answer" that Abba may be reluctant to say directly.

Stories like this one do not sound foreign or strange to the healing-room audience. Even upon first hearing it, both Muslim and Hindu audience members recognize certain of its features, beginning with the physical powers of spiritually powerful humans. But specific narrative motifs are also shared, such as the danger of pollution—in this case of inadvertently leaving unwashed a drop of urine on the skin, the spot of which provides an entry into the otherwise protected boundary of the human body.[15] This is also a narrative-propelling motif in the Mahabharata story of Nal and Damayanti. Although the specifics of purity/pollution rules may vary in particular ritual and narrative examples, the general "grammar" of the power of purity and pollution is shared in many South Asian ritual traditions (including menstrual and postpartum pollution). Similarly, the motif of heads falling off is not unfamiliar to Indian audiences and resonates with Hindu narratives of beheadings

15. This motif is not found in the narrative version reported by Kassam (1995), the omission of which then draws my attention to the motif as having been included for a performative purpose for a particular audience.

and heads being exchanged, such as in the widespread and popular south Indian village myth of Renuka.[16] Because repertoires of narrative motifs and sequences flow across religious boundaries, rarely is a story entirely "new" or experienced as "foreign" at this healing *caurasta*.

Another way in which Amma and Abba employ common South Asian narrative motifs is to localize, expand, and make familiar Qur'anic narratives, such as the one of Maryam, mother of Issa/Jesus. In the context of explaining to a patient that treatments such as her own probably don't exist in the United States, where there are "no poor people," Amma nevertheless asserted that spiritual healing would still be necessary for spiritually caused problems. Her son reminded her that most people in the United States are Christians, but, he continued, "sometimes, even among Christians there are some important [i.e., spiritually powerful] people who pray with folded hands, and there is a cure. But there's a little difference." Amma interrupted him, "No, no, this healing power is available to all humans. If they have devotion, why wouldn't this be the case? Even in our Qur'an there's mention of Maryam and everything that Issa told us. . . . He was a prophet. As many prophets have come and gone on earth, they all have died. But he didn't die. He went up; he became a star and disappeared. So they call him god, but we call him a prophet." Amma went on to narrate the story of Maryam, who became pregnant when the shadow of Jibrail (Gabriel) struck her as she was bathing. Maryam's sister-in-law insisted that Maryam had done "bad things" and that she should be banished to the jungle. There, she gave birth to Issa, with angels in attendance washing the baby with the sacred waters of *zamzam*.

The narrative weaves together both specifically Muslim and Hindu motifs and references as well as shared ones: sacred waters and their healing powers, the shadow of a celestial being compromising a woman's

16. I heard this myth numerous times in oral variants when I was conducting fieldwork around the Gangamma goddess tradition in Tirupati in 1999–2000; textual variants are found in the Mahabharata Bhagavatapurana and Kancippuranam (Shulman 1985, 110–29). For oral versions, also see Elmore 1915, 95.

chastity, and a heroine left stranded in the jungle, where she gives birth with nature and angels as her birth attendants (as in Sita's story in some versions of the Ramayana).

Some narratives performed by Amma and Abba share more than motifs across traditions; they frequently tell or make reference to narrative episodes that are drawn from traditional "Hindu" mythological stories. Consider Abba's mention of the Ramayana (described in the discussions of avatars given earlier) and Amma's accounting from the same epic of the episode of Hanuman flying to a jungle mountain to look for herbs to use to bring the dying Lakshman back to life. When I asked Abba how he understood the elephant-headed deity Ganesh, whose festival was being celebrated at the time with the installation of images at neighborhood crossroads all over the city, including in a clearing right behind Amma's healing room, he did not answer with a theological pronouncement about the deity and his existence or not but simply responded with a story, the story of Ganesh's creation. Like Amma's narrative of Hanuman, he did not preface his telling with an identification of the narrative as "Hindu" or with "this is what Hindus say," but his telling implied that this is simply the way it is.

> Shankar [Shiva] had gone to meditate in the forest. When he was gone, Parvati took dirty bath water [water with which Parvati had already bathed] and formed Ganesh. [Amma: She made a *putla*/doll.] Shankar came back from forest and asked, "Who is this standing outside of Parvati's bath?" [pause] He was born in water, and he's thrown back into water [i.e., at the end of the festival, his clay images are immersed in water]. [Pause; here Abba conflates two narratives, shifting to one of Adipara Shakti, the primordial goddess. None of the gods wanted to have sex with her because, as their creator, she was like their mother.] Parvati wanted to get married, but every man said, "But you're my mother." At last Shankar came. He said he would marry her if she became a little girl [again?], so she became a little girl. . . . Then Shankar went to the forest.

I found the question "How do you understand [*kaise samajhte hain*] a particular Hindu deity?" to be more productive than asking whether

Amma and Abba "believe in" or worship that particular deity. Here, Abba's answer through narrative provides him a space within which to acknowledge the existence of a deity in an imaginative world without declaring that deity to be a god or not. To share a narrative repertoire is not necessarily to imply a shared interpretation of those stories. Abba does not worship Ganesh like a Hindu might before undertaking a new venture, but Ganesh is fully present in his imaginative world.[17]

Narratives performed in the healing room most often emphasize a *shared* worldview and often employ shared motifs or full narratives. However, outside the healing room, performed to groups of disciples only, many of Abba's narratives *distinguish* between Muslim and Hindu worldviews and practices. Abba performed one such narrative during a Friday visitation to the home of one of his disciples, where several Hindu men who wanted to become disciples had also come to meet with Abba. Note that a Hindu–Muslim distinction is performatively dramatized by the code-switching between Urdu and Telugu (the languages spoken by Hyderabadi Muslims and Hindus, respectively, although many Hyderabadis understand both languages). Abba began in Urdu:

> I want to tell you one more thing, but don't be offended. [Switching to Telugu, speaking to the Hindu audience members] Don't take it badly just because a sahib [i.e., a Muslim] is saying this. [Back to Urdu] Don't be offended. I thought of it and am now telling you. But don't get angry.
>
> There was a stone in the jungle. A man brought it home and began to hit and hit it. Hitting it a million times, he made a form [*shakal*] out of it. By hitting it, he made a beautiful image [*murti*], with hands and feet. He made it and kept it in this room; he kept it inside. He decorated it. He broke coconuts in front of it; he brought bananas; he lit incense. He did all this. He came every day at four in the afternoon and offered incense, worship, coconuts, milk, and all those kinds of things [*agarbati-wagarbati*,

17. This particular performance was a much-abbreviated version of the story as it exists in other contexts. Although Hindus and Muslims living side by side may know *of* each other's stories, there may be a limit to how fully they know these stories.

> *puja-wuja, nariyal-wariyal, dudh-wudh*].[18] He brought them to that place and then went home.
>
> One day the Brahmin came at four in the afternoon, and a noise came from inside. [In Telugu] "My god [*devaru*] is coming; my god is coming." [In Urdu] "Who? Who's talking? The stone is talking!" And he was worried, this Brahmin. He was looking here; he was looking there. Where was this noise coming from? He came and put all the *puja* things there.
>
> Then Hanuman said, "You made me, gave me a place to stay, gave me bananas, coconuts, incense, and milk. You've given me everything, and I haven't given you anything. Now tell me, who is god [*bhagwan*]? It's like this: believe in a god from whom you receive something, do you understand? God is one. Allah, the creator [literally "one who gave birth"] is one. Just because you perform this kind of devotion doesn't make him god. Can you call him that? You can't call him that! Why? Because you're born from your mother's womb; god isn't born from any mother's womb.

Notice that although Hanuman and other Hindu deities may inhabit Amma and Abba's imaginative narrative world, their physical manifestation in carved images, worshipped by devotees, is anathema to Amma and Abba. A clear line of distinction between Hindu and Muslim is drawn around both the issues of image worship *and* the unique quality of God as creator. That is, for Muslims, the ultimate distinction between Allah and the Hindu pantheon of deities is that Allah is not created, nor does he have offspring—as do many Hindu deities. The narrative follows these two axes (image worship and the singularity of a creator god) away from the shared world of the crossroads to their outer coordinates, where difference is most

18. Each ingredient here (incense, worship, coconuts, milk) is followed by an echo word that changes only the first consonant of the initial word into a *w* (*wagarbati, wuja, wariyal, wudh*). The use of these kinds of echo words in South Asian languages reduces the formality of the initial word, extends its range to include other objects that fall in the same category as the initial word, and may introduce an ironic tone to the discourse.

strongly articulated.[19] Similarly, although Amma calls upon the goddess Kali or Hanuman to come to her service, she does not worship them.

Returning to the *Dargah*

I return now to the *sandal* celebration of Abba's ninth death anniversary in the fall of 2007 with which this essay opened. The celebrants were visually marked as Hindu and Muslim. The Hindu women wore brightly colored saris, flowers in their hair, and vermilion-powder forehead markings. One newly married young woman was particularly striking in her fancy silk sari, arms covered in gold and glass bangles, and lots of flowers in her hair. In rather stark contrast, all the Muslim women wore black burqas, some of which were decorated with gold or silver embroidery, but most were quite plain.[20] Mustang's wife occupied a rather liminal space between these two marked groups. She became a disciple of Amma and Abba after marriage to Mustang, and after some time she no longer wore the red forehead marking of her Hindu peers.[21] However, she had not taken up the practice

19. On another occasion when Abba, Amma, and I visited a popular *dargah* outside of Hyderabad, I asked them if the kinds of miracles (*karamat*) experienced at *dargah*s were also experienced at temples. Abba's answer was, "No, they don't occur there because they [the gods] are man made." Here again, he was drawing a distinction between the god who is the creator and those that are created, specifically implying that the *murti* (image) of the Hindu deity has no power. But Abba immediately followed this declaration with the qualification that Hindu deities *do* have *shakti* (spiritual) power, but, he continued, "there's a big difference between *shakti* and *bhagwan* [god] . . . *shakti*s give problems to humans . . . they trouble them. . . . And these saints [those of the *dargah*] don't do that."

20. Amma's own female family members now wear scarves across their lower faces so that only their eyes are visible, a style Amma herself never wore. She simply wore a scarf over her head, with her full face showing, along with her burqa cloak. Amma's daughter-in-law, Lateefa, told me that even her youngest daughter, fourteen years old at the time, now wore a burqa, earlier than would have been normal because she was so tall and people assumed she was older than her actual age. Lateefa was concerned that people would wonder about the piety and appropriate behavior of a sheikh's daughter.

21. I remember a Hindu female woman at the ritual upon which she become a disciple asking Amma what she should do about her traditional Hindu forehead marking (*bottu*). In

of wearing a burqa. Most Muslim men wore intricately embroidered skull caps. Many of Abba's close male disciples, including his son Khalid and Mustang, had shoulder-length hair and wore long tunics (*kurtas*); Hindu male celebrants wore pants and shirts and covered their heads (if at all) with a handkerchief. Further, the Hindu female participants did not interact much with Muslim women (including those in Amma's immediate family) and sat in separate groups as we ate in the big hall, within walking distance of the *dargah*, rented for the *sandal* meal.[22] Some of these visually and socially marked differences may have been more exaggerated in the public space of the *dargah* than they would have been in Mustang's or Khalid's domestic healing rooms, which are more intimate both in size and tone, where Muslim veiled women may take off their face coverings, and where the women of Amma's family do not wear a burqa.

But were Amma to analyze these visual differences and spatial social organization, I imagine she might comment on the Hindu celebrants' relationships to Mustang and the appropriate honor that should still be paid to Abba and Abba's *murshid* (teacher) son, or she might express pleasure in the growing numbers of *sandal* celebrants over the years and their experience of Amma and Abba's *barkat*. However, I would *not* expect her to identify the celebrants as Hindu or Muslim, as I have just done; and she might have reminded me, as she did many times in the healing room, that here, too, the celebrants were not Muslim and Hindu, but all humans in relationship with God; Amma and Abba (as grandparent *pir/piranima*), their living *pirs* or gurus; and each other.

We can observe analytically that the ritual grammar at the *dargah*, like in the healing room, crosses Hindu–Muslim boundaries: honoring a guru/*pir* after physical death, believing that he or she continues to exert power at the site of burial/cremation, placing flowers and lighting incense

---

her wisdom and understanding, Amma told her that when she was in the presence of her in-laws, she could wear the forehead marking, but that when she came into the presence of Amma and Abba, she should not wear it.

22. Because I was in the women's section, I was unable to observe if the Hindu and Muslim men ate in separate groups, too.

at the shrine of the spiritual teacher's remains, touching one's head to the gravesite, tying threads at the shrine (or attaching locks) as a sign of a spiritual request and vow. Interestingly, none of the Hindu female celebrants and very few of the men stayed for the late-night *sama*, an Islamically marked musical, devotional assembly of *qawwali* performance.

Missing at the large public gathering at the *dargah*-based *sandal* were verbal interpretations of these ritual acts and narrative performance to create a shared imaginative world among the celebrants. Experientially, I missed Amma and Abba's charisma and authority. Along with these qualities, their teachings and performative rhetoric helped create the unique crossroads of the healing room. The *pir*s of the next generation—Khalid and Mustang—perform more authority than charisma (following the Weberian model of routinized charisma), which was displayed in particular in their roles at Abba's *sandal*.

Conclusion

Issues of religious identities, both self-identification and identification imposed by the "other," have been the focus of heightened scholarly activity over the past two decades, particularly in light of the 1990–92 events surrounding the politicization of the Babri *masjid*/Ram Janmabhoomi site in Ayodhya and the communal violence that followed. Numerous conference panels and publications have analyzed the colonial construction of and reinforcement of Hindu–Muslim boundaries of identity. Scholars such as Cynthia Talbott (1995), Peter Gottschalk (2000), and contributors to an edited volume by David Gilmartin and Bruce Lawrence (2000), among others, consider ways in which South Asians identify themselves beyond Muslim and Hindu.

Other scholars of South Asia have talked about elements of traditions that intersect at what I am calling the *caurasta* in terms of "borrowing," "syncretization," or "hybridization." Tony Stewart and Carl Ernst (2003) have carefully analyzed this language—which is commonly used for describing the interaction of Hindu and Muslim traditions—and find that these traditional scholarly categories are insufficient descriptors of what is experienced on the ground insofar as they tend to "relegate its subjects to a secondary status." Ernst and Stewart observe that "[s]yncretism as both process and description hinges on the assumption that those observed have inappropriately mixed cultural and religious categories that are intrinsically alien to each other." They then proceed to examine metaphors commonly used to describe syncretism and find that these metaphors have "generally negative valuation": borrowing and influence, cultural veneer, alchemy, and hybridization (2003, 586–87).

My task here has been to suggest a model of the crossroads of intersecting and shared cosmologies, narratives, and ritual grammars in order describe the religious landscape of the healing room in such a way as to maintain its integrity without judging it as derivative or secondary. It accounts for both shared worldviews, ritual grammars, and narratives *and* distinct religious identities. Many South Asian Muslims who have heard me talk of this work, in particular those living in the United States, identify many of these phenomenon as "Hindu." But Amma identifies herself as Muslim and maintains that her practices are based on the authority of Allah, his prophet, the Qur'an, and the visions and dreams that she has been given. I want to take this claim seriously—that is, to maintain the integrity of Amma's world, without making it derivative and "not quite Muslim." Although another project may be interested in and able to trace historically various influences back and forth between traditions, here I propose we first understand Amma's own articulation and contextualized use of ritual, narrative, and cosmology shared between Hindus and Muslims at the site of her healing room, where axes of difference intersect and where an expansive, encompassing space is created in which there "is no Hindu or Muslim."

Works Cited

Eaton, Richard. 1985. "Approaches to the Study of Conversion to Islam in India." In *Approaches to Islam in Religious Studies,* edited by Richard C. Martin, 106–23. Tucson: Univ. of Arizona Press.

———. 1994. *The Rise of Islam and the Bengal Frontier, 1204–1760.* New Delhi: Oxford Univ. Press.

Elmore, Wilbur Theodore. 1915. *Dravidian Gods in Modern Hinduism.* Hamilton, NY: published by the author.

Ernst, Carl W. 1997. *The Shambhala Guide to Sufism.* Boston: Shambhala.

Flueckiger, Joyce Burkhalter. 2006. *In Amma's Healing Room: Gender and Vernacular Islam in South India*. Bloomington: Indiana Univ. Press.

Gilmartin, David, and Bruce Lawrence, eds. 2000. *Beyond Turk and Hindu: Rethinking Religious Identities in Isamicate South Asia*. Gainesville: Univ. Press of Florida.

Gottschalk, Peter. 2000. *Beyond Hindu and Muslim: Multiple Identity in Narratives from Village India*. New York: Oxford Univ. Press.

Hughes, Thomas Patrick. [1885] 1988. *Dictionary of Islam*. Calcutta: Rupa & Co.

Kassam, Tazim R. 1995. *Songs of Wisdom and Circles of Dance: Hymns of the Satpanth Isma'ili Muslim Saint, Pir Shams*. Albany: State Univ. of New York Press.

Shulman, David. 1985. *The King and the Clown in South Indian Myth and Poetry*. Princeton, NJ: Princeton Univ. Press.

Stewart, Tony, and Carl W. Ernst. 2003. "Syncretism." In *South Asian Folklore: An Encyclopedia*, edited by Margaret Mills, Peter Claus, and Sarah Diamond, 586–88. New York: Routledge.

Talbott, Cynthia. 1995. "Inscribing the Other, Inscribing the Self: Hindu–Muslim Identities in Pre-colonial India." *Comparative Studies in Society and History* 37, no. 4: 692–722.

11

≈

"Ainn-Bai's *Sarvadharm Yatra*"

A Mix of Experiences

ANN GRODZINS GOLD

I SPENT TWO WEEKS IN RAJASTHAN in the rainy season of 2006 while on a brief trip to gather teaching resources for an undergraduate course titled "India's Religious Worlds." This part of the trip was not a research visit. I called it my "monsoon *yatra*"—*yatra* being a capacious term for all varieties of travel. It was my old friend, research assistant, and frequent coauthor, Bhoju Ram Gujar, who labeled our shared journey "Ainn-Bai's *sarvadharm yatra*" (Ann's all-religions pilgrimage). This designation is decidedly Bhoju Ram's invention, coined in direct response to an outsider-scholar's intervention.[1]

Framing a Road Trip: "Direct!"

During the limited period from July 25 to August 6, I visited numerous Jain, Muslim, and Sikh places of worship, pilgrimage, and healing and

Enormous thanks to Bhoju Ram Gujar, Bali Gujar, and Shiv Lal Mina for sharing this journey with me. My travels were supported by generous funds from a William P. Tolley Distinguished Teaching Professorship at Syracuse University. I am grateful to Alan Babb, John Cort, and Surjit Singh for help before and during my trip; to Daniel Gold and Shail Mayaram for critical readings; and to Tazim Kassam, Eliza Kent, and Dick Pilgrim for editorial pushes toward clarity.

1. Our two-week regional itinerary only touched on Jain, Muslim, Sikh, and Hindu pilgrimage places and thus by no means literally encompassed "all" of India's religions.

went to the famously joint Hindu–Muslim place Ramdevra. I was traveling in the same general region of India, central and western Rajasthan, where I have studied Hindu shrine pilgrimage and miracle stories on and off since the 1980s.[2] I made my 2006 journey in the company of Bhoju and his friend Shiv Lal Mina, who owned and drove the car in which we traveled. Bhoju is a Hindu and a staunch devotee of the Rajasthani hero-god Dev Narayan, considered an avatar of Vishnu. I never conversed deeply with Shiv Lal about his religious life, but his car displayed a goddess image, and Rajasthan's Minas are strongly associated with the worship of local goddesses, or Matajis. Bhoju's wife, Bali Gujar, accompanied us on the longest of our circuits, which took us all the way to Ramdevra and back. With Bali, we also saw the magnificent Jain monuments at Osian and assorted other spots, including the Jain pilgrimage site Nakora Bhairuji in Barmer District; Pushkar, Rajasthan's Hindu sacred center par excellence where we visited a mosque and a Sikh *gurdwara*; and Sarwar, where we plunged into a festival day for a Muslim saint. Like her husband, Bali also has deep faith in Dev Narayan, along with considerable attachment to particular forms of the goddess. The mood for our trip was established early on when we stopped to ask directions of an elderly, traditionally dressed woman who described a route in detail in the local language but concluded her instructions emphatically with the word "*di-rekt*!" Bhoju and Shiv Lal found this woman's incongruous English deliciously comic, and the command "Di-rekt!" became a hilarious theme for our *yatra*—a daring, absurd, and exuberant adventure.

Our "all-religions" journey was certainly mapped on a route no run-of-the-mill Rajasthani pilgrim would have dreamed of taking. Yet my companions experienced this eccentric pilgrims' road with eager curiosity and attitudes wide open to divinity with all its multiple attributes of beauty and potency. At the same time, they did not hesitate to critique human foibles, no matter what their religious orientations. Each day one or two Hindu temples in the vicinity of our charted destinations inserted

2. For samples of my early and more recent writings on aspects of Hindu shrine pilgrimage see A. Gold [1988] 2000, 133–89, and 2008.

themselves into our itinerary as "can't miss" opportunities. I accepted such diversions as an unspoken "equal time" principle to which I willingly surrendered.

Each of us found this journey an opportunity to improve our knowledge of comparative religion. A subtle shifting commentary on this topic—which held intrinsic fascination for all—emerged along the way. I write this account largely from my own perspective without ethnographic pretensions. Now and then I nonetheless attempt to offer insights into my companions' opinions inasmuch as they communicated them to me. Let me, therefore, say a little more about these persons.

Both Bhoju Ram Gujar and Shiv Lal Mina are headmasters of rural government schools. Their solid friendship seems to be grounded in their shared experience as education professionals who come from largely uneducated farming and herding communities. Both are married to women who are totally unschooled; both have raised daughters who are unusually highly educated and career oriented. Although Bhoju was accompanying me in the capacity of salaried research assistant, and I was paying Shiv Lal to drive, the three of us—and, of course, Bali when she was there—behaved as pilgrims first everywhere we went. In other words, we approached and entered each shrine with reverence toward whatever unseen powers' presence or spiritual legacy was signified by these places. I performed required ritual actions far less gracefully and far more self-consciously than did my companions. I was awed by the exquisite care with which they conducted themselves at every one of our stops, always touching their right hand to a step or threshold and then putting it to their foreheads, always prostrating before departure, always discretely depositing coins or notes into the ubiquitous donation boxes.

I was frankly amazed at how easily the customary behaviors that came naturally to Bhoju Ram, Shiv Lal, and Bali—as persons who frequent Hindu shrines—were also perfectly appropriate (with occasional tweakings) at places dedicated to other religions. This adaptability was all the more striking because—with the exception of the famed Ajmer *dargah,* which most rural Rajasthanis who live in the region have visited at least once—none of my companions had previously been to any Muslim shrine, nor had they even once been to a single Jain or Sikh place of worship.[3] Yet they were evidently never out of their religious comfort zones.

When custom demanded an accommodation of dress, such as male head coverings for the Muslim shrines and Sikh *gurdwaras*, Bhoju and Shiv Lal deftly twisted hand towels around their heads without the least embarrassment. This was in direct contrast to my own awkward efforts at wrapping myself appropriately. After enjoying some singing encountered at a Jain temple, the two men spontaneously purchased cassette tapes of Jain hymns to play in the car. I do not believe that this personal ease and openness to diverse religious practices and experiences can be attributed to Bhoju and Shiv Lal's status as educated and upwardly mobile persons, men of the world. Bhoju's wife, Bali, an unschooled village woman, equally had no qualms about entering non-Hindu religious spaces. She wore her village dress with dignity whether among middle-class Jain women in saris or Muslim women in *kamiz-salvar*. In Sarwar, at the site of a Muslim saint's tomb, we encountered very dense crowds. This shrine was connected to the Ajmer *dargah* where, at the time, India's largest annual Muslim pilgrimage fair (*'urs*) was taking place. Unaccustomed as I was to being in the presence of so many bearded men, I found myself inexplicably nervous (something I acknowledge in retrospect with considerable dismay). Bali, by contrast, was not the least disconcerted by the need to plunge into tight crowds of Muslims. She seemed more eager than hesitant to share the experience of power at the tomb of a Sufi saint. She and Bhoju pointed out other Hindus to me, all women it seemed, in the crush nearest the tomb.

Muslims and Jains lived in Ghatiyali, where I had always based my fieldwork, and Bhoju and I had interviewed knowledgeable members of those communities for our oral-history book (Gold and Gujar 2002). However, my research on religion had always previously focused on popular Hinduism, and I had never sought deliberately to observe non-Hindu ritual practices until this particular summer. I learned a great deal on

3. For more on the *dargah* of Mu'inuddin Chishti in Ajmer, see Currie 1989; Olsen 2003; Sanyal 2007; Suvorova 2004.

this brief trip about varieties of religious behavior and ideas among Jains, Muslims, and Sikhs in Rajasthan. We explained at each site that I was gathering materials to use in my classroom in the United States. Our odd party encountered extraordinary cordiality from religious experts as well as from worshipers and shopkeepers. All were exceptionally forthcoming, responding with warmth and generosity to the questions posed by two or three Hindus and an American. Jains have strict rules regarding cameras, and a couple of times I was harshly but justly scolded when I grew confused about where I was and was not allowed to take photographs. I mention such incidents merely because they were the sole and well-warranted exception to the universal welcome that otherwise met our unexpected appearance.

I was in the classroom teaching the course "India's Religious Worlds" just a few weeks after returning from this journey. I used images from our tour throughout the semester. During the second half of the course, I assigned my students Yoginder Sikand's *Sacred Spaces: Exploring Traditions of Shared Faith in India* (2003), a work written in journalistic style but incorporating considerable depth of scholarship on the intertwined religious histories of many shared sacred spaces. In Sikand's observations are ample confirmations of my own experiences. He explicitly aspires not to "romanticize" the sharing of religious traditions or the fluidity of religious boundaries and is a keen observer of abuses and political manipulations of popular religious emotions. It is all the more meaningful that Sikand believes it is genuinely worthwhile to look at shared space as a partial antidote for the poison of communalism (19).

The majority of pilgrimage destinations and places of worship identify themselves distinctly as belonging to a particular religion; some others, such as Ramdevra, are equally self-consciously pluralistic. Contrasts among traditions accordingly may be strategically articulated or blurred. More significant to me were many threads of ritual and meaning linking even the most apparently exclusive sites. In recent years, richly detailed ethnographic writings based on intensive fieldwork have resulted in a number of excellent studies evoking the blended religiosity and characteristic South Asian ambiance pervading popular shrines as well as other contexts throughout India.[4] Although I include reference to some shared spaces, my travelogue's focus is more on shared attributes across traditions.

In this sketchbook account of our idiosyncratic pilgrimage, I attempt to convey my companions' self-conscious articulations of similarities and differences as well as those underlying commonalities that I believe made an amiable journey such as ours not only possible but predictable. In spite of othering discourses current in Rajasthani culture, Bhoju Ram and Shiv Lalji were not apprehensive of making such an exploratory journey. Both had networks among persons of all religions. As teachers, they had Jain and Muslim colleagues; as villagers, they had Jain and Muslim neighbors; as a part-time resident of Jahazpur, Bhoju knew civic-minded persons and businessmen from diverse communities in that highly pluralistic town. He plotted most of our route with the help of suggestions from such acquaintances. Other connections emerged on the road as surprises. For example, at one Sikh *gurdwara* we were warmly welcomed by a man who turned out to have been the previous owner of the auto parts store that Shiv Lal currently runs.

Three sections follow. In the first, I highlight some commonalities and contrasts among pilgrimage traditions that we were able to observe in the course of our journey—including glances at donations, ritual actions, aesthetics, and a hunger for the miraculous. In the second, I look at multiple traditions in a single locality: the growing town of Jahazpur and its environs. In the third, I present three stories we heard on our trip. All are place stories dealing with conflict between Hindu and Muslim powers both human and divine. Such conflicts resolve themselves in a variety of ways in religious narratives. Notably, however, whether Hindu or Muslim appears to prevail (which needless to say depends on who is telling what story in what place), their counterpart remains—subdued,

4. See the chapters by Bellamy and others in this volume. Additional rich ethnographic and historical studies of fluid religious identities in India include Flueckiger 2006; Gottschalk 2000; Khan 1997; Mayaram 1999; Narayanan 2006; Stewart 2000.

distanced, awed, transformed, but in any case vital. In concluding, I characterize our little journey's rewards, as Bhoju joked meaningfully about them on the last night, as incorporating a flavorful if unsettling mixture of experiences.

Swimming across Those Watery Lines: Gestures, Forms, and Desires

Our "all-religions pilgrimage" in truth visited sacred places belonging to just four of India's living traditions: Hindu, Jain, Muslim, and Sikh. Each is, of course, markedly and fatefully distinguished in its histories and theologies, cosmologies and mythologies, scriptures and teachings. Nonetheless, as we went from one to another often in the course of a single day, we experienced a common South Asian religiosity encompassing sensual and aesthetic as well as emotional elements.

On the first half-day of our journey, we drove from the Jaipur bus stand, where Bhoju and Shiv Lal had fetched me, to Ghatiyali, with a stop at the impressive and burgeoning Jain site of Shri Padmaprabhuji near Shivdaspura.[5] At this moment, when we had barely set forth on our adventure, various "othering" discourses predictably came into play. As we surveyed the stunning compound of Shri Padmaprabhuji, my companions muttered that Jains keep their surroundings immaculately clean, but their hearts are dirty—with an implicit but unstated contrast to Hindu spaces and hearts. This dig at Jains notwithstanding, at this juncture Bhoju and Shiv Lal agreed with one another that, of the three unfamiliar religions about which we were hoping to learn, Jainism and Sikhism were *apna*—meaning "one's own." As literate men with government jobs who daily poured over Hindi-language newspapers, they were likely to have absorbed Hindu nationalist rhetoric on the oneness of Hinduism with other religions originating in India. Thus, they anticipated a sense of kinship rather than alienation among Jains and Sikhs. Islam, in contrast, the two men characterized as *ulta*, or "upside down" from their own Hindu

5. Padmaprabhu is said to be the sixth of the twenty-four Jain *tirthankaras*—those enlightened beings and teachers who cause others to cross over the misery of existence.

traditions. For example, they told me, "When we sacrifice goats, we cut the back of the neck from above, but they slit the throat from below; we cut a boy's hair to dedicate him to God, but they cut his penis," and so forth.

Over the course of our brief trip, an ironic situation became increasingly clear to all of us: rural Hindu traditions have far more in common with rural Muslim traditions, and more porous boundaries exist between Hindu and Muslim pilgrimage practices than between Hindu and Jain or Sikh practices. Social class and regional culture may influence commonalities and distinctions more than do religious differences. Rajasthan's Jains are predominantly an urban and middle-class community, and even village Jains are for the most part merchants, not farmers. This identity is at least conceptually rooted in Jain adherence to *ahimsa* (nonviolence) and to Jain identification of agricultural work as a form of violence. Jain pilgrimage centers reflect their community's overall prosperity (only at Jain complexes did I encounter well-advertised ATM machines on temple premises).

Sikh teachings overlap closely with Hindu devotion to a formless deity (*nirgun bhakti*), an important current in rural Rajasthani religion (A. Gold [1988] 2000). My friends commented appreciatively on the peaceful and uplifting atmosphere of *gurdwara*s. However, Rajasthan's Sikhs are identified very clearly as Punjabi. In fact, the names "Sikh" and "Punjabi" are used virtually interchangeably in rural Rajasthan, with the latter far more common. There have been several waves of Sikh migration into the region—one around Partition and another, I was told, in the wake of the green revolution. The latter phenomenon drove up land prices in Punjab so that poorer but ambitious farmers came to Rajasthan in the 1970s in search of cheaper agricultural land. No matter when they arrived, Rajasthan's Sikhs are still strongly associated with their place of origin; moreover, they consciously maintain those links in many ways. We met workmen building new *gurdwara*s in Rajasthan who were brought from Punjab in order to follow traditional construction practices and designs.

Muslim shrines, by contrast, seem to belong entirely to the Rajasthani landscape. Although we did encounter Urdu in a few places, most often attendants of Muslim shrines spoke the common local language. Rather than upside down, Muslim ritual practices seemed to me to present milder shifts, more like harmonic modulations. Muslim shrines feature tombs instead of icons; pilgrims offer roses and sheets rather than marigolds and adornment; they favor greens instead of reds; they sing *qawwalis* instead of *bhajans*. To signify vows, both Muslim and Hindu pilgrims tie strings on pillars, latticework, or trees—although they refer to these strings by different terms. All of these substitutions create different visual and aural experiences, but they do not seem to indicate different religious sensibilities.[6] This is why Hindus attending Muslim shrines are not religiously disoriented.

By stressing similarities, I do not mean to discount profound theological and cosmological differences, of which everyone remains aware, but rather to call attention to a practical religion that may at times choose not to attend to such differences (Flueckiger 2006). Some Muslim saints' shrines have greater numbers of Hindu than Muslim worshipers. Two of the *pir* (saint) shrines we visited seemed to have become Hindu places, with their Muslim roots remaining only in the use of the word *pir*. Others strongly retain an Islamic identity but nonetheless are visited by Hindus in search of help from the Islamic holy persons who are entombed there.[7] To note one difference that is sustained, several Hindus told me with a slight air of grievance that although Hindus readily prostrate themselves at Muslim shrines, Muslims visiting Hindu shrines do not act in reciprocal fashion.

If on the first day of our journey Bhoju and Shiv Lal had articulated a sharp distinction between the three religions that originated in India and the one that did not, Islam, I was happy to record in my notes along the way subtle changes in their attitudes. Near the end of our trip, on August 4, Bhoju surprised me by expressing a grudging but sincere admiration for Islam, as I scribbled approvingly: "Today Bhoju makes a better comparison. He says 'Hindus are *lobhi* [greedy] and *swarth* [selfish] and only go to gods when they need help, but Muslims have *niyam* [good habits],

6. For more on India's Islamic shrines and shrine-visiting traditions, see Suvorova 2004 and Troll 1992.

7. See D. Gold 2005 and Sikand 2003 for similar variations in other regions of India.

much more *niyam* [than Hindus], praying five times a day whether they are in trouble or not.'"[8] This observation evidently resulted more from internal musings than from the actual impressions of our journey, which showed us Muslims seeking aid from saints quite as much as Hindus do from deities.

Quests for help appear to motivate shrine pilgrimage in spite of radical theological variations, and cash flows equally characterize every sacred place. When I sought an image to introduce all of "India's religious worlds" to my class a few weeks after returning from India, the one I chose was the donation box.

No institution can operate without money. My students on the first day of class quickly supplied a series of rationales for religious donations, with which Rajasthanis would readily agree: people give to acknowledge what they owe to divine powers; people give to facilitate good works; people give to show off their virtues in public. Perhaps I had selected something so obvious as to be devoid of South Asian meaning and merely indicative of a crass materiality of necessity—self-evident and universal. However, I would add that these strategically placed boxes index a fourth meaning embedded in the particularities of South Asian ideas about human morality: a push toward selflessness that simultaneously recognizes internal egoistic resistance to generosity. There is a perceived need for religious forces to counter human greed, to lure from our fists, almost magnetically, the coins we may very well be reluctant to give—a need rooted in the importance of lightening and emptying the vessel, the self (A. Gold [1988] 2000). These boxes allow this precisely because they invite anonymous gifts, whereas many other charitable donations, even if grander, serve to enhance a person's reputation and are therefore degraded as acts of selflessness.

The valuation of religious journeys and of rituals performed in sacred sites differs markedly among the four traditions we glimpsed. Some

8. Sikand makes a similar observation when he watches a Muslim pray and thinks about Islamic religiosity as more pure and less chaotic than Hindu forms of worship (2003, 173).

8. Hindu temple donation box. Photograph by Ann Grodzins Gold.

Hindu and Jain texts recommend and elaborate on the practice of visiting sacred places; the Qur'an enjoins only the journey to Mecca. Guru Nanak, the founder of the Sikh religion, explicitly derided the value of traveling to sacred places as superficial. Yet in South Asia, as elsewhere in the Muslim world, the practice of *ziyarat*, or "visiting" saints' tombs, has been vital for centuries, and Sikh places of worship, their *gurdwaras*, are central to their

9. Sikh *gurdwara* donation box. Photograph by Ann Grodzins Gold.

identities.[9] In spite of different attitudes toward sacred space and different evaluations of pilgrimage or visits, South Asian Hindu, Jain, Muslim, and Sikh pilgrims and worshipers do have much in common ritually at the level of popular practice and belief—as I have already demonstrated.

Turning to the foci of reverence within shrines, we find again both fundamental differences and cross-cutting commonalities. Distinctive to Jain shrines are stone images, often beautifully sculpted, of *tirthankaras*—literally "ford makers," as the twenty-four founding Jain teachers are called. These austere meditative figures represent beings who neither crave offerings nor return blessings because they have conquered

9. There exists a Sikh pilgrimage tradition to sites historically important in the lives of the ten gurus (Singh 1995). However, the places we were able to visit were not such sites, but rather *gurdwaras* erected by Sikh immigrants from Punjab and meant to serve the local community.

10. Jain temple donation box. Photograph by Ann Grodzins Gold.

all attachments and are understood to be absent, not present (Babb 1996). They endow Jain temples with a more severe atmosphere, contrasting to that which prevails in Hindu temples. Nonetheless, Hindu deities slip easily into subsidiary niches at Jain places. Bali greeted a silver Ganesh at the magnificent Jain temples in Osian as if she had happily encountered an old friend where she had not expected to see him.

Muslim and Sikh places, committed as they are to formlessness, are less permeable to images. However, they share numerous other elements with Hindu shrines, including offerings of incense, flowers, pilgrims' prostrations, and expectations of miraculous aid. There are multiple variations of food transactions. Sikh *prasad* is prepared at the *gurdwara*; Jains may offer foods ritually, but blessed leavings, or *prasad*, are normally not returned. Hindus adorn their icons; Muslims spread beautiful sheets (*chadar*) upon saints' tombs; at the center of any *gurdwara* is the book, the Adi Granth (or Guru Granth Sahib). And although Sikhism is fundamentally a *nirgun* tradition, holding that the divine is without qualities or form, the Granth is treated in some ways like the icons in Hindu temples—not only as a source of power and grace, but as a living being. Every *gurdwara* has a bed in which the Guru Granth is taken to sleep at night. I jotted in my notebook on July 31, "I liked watching the old woman who went from circumambulating the Adi Granth to the cube-like curtained place where it sleeps. She rubbed her hands up and down—the legs, the legs of the bed of the Guru Granth Sahab."

I was struck by the way what I might call "peripheral aesthetics" merged across traditions, even when central iconographic modes sharply differed. For example, you can hardly find a greater contrast than that between the crowded, bright, and sparkling central shrine of Ramdevji (the Hindu god who is also a Muslim *pir*) and Jain temples featuring austere stone *tirthankara*s in meditative repose. Yet both Ramdevji and several Jain places we visited have adjacent rooms where displays of color paintings in a very similar folk style tell the stories of their respective heroes and heroines or warn against the fruits of bad karma and sin. In other words, kitsch easily moves across fluid lines even when more classical art forms may not. The theme of after-death punishments appears in both Jain and Hindu shrine paintings in spite of the fact that these divergent traditions possess very different notions of the soul and the cosmos.

On the subject of popular artistic representations, I should not fail to mention a Jain genre that is much appreciated by ordinary visitors from all religious backgrounds, although it has received little scholarly attention. This display, referred to as *nasiya*, is found not in the center but on the periphery of almost every Rajasthani Jain temple I visited. A *nasiya* depicts the event in the life of a *tirthankara* called *samavasarana*, when, after attaining enlightenment, he delivers his message to an assembled audience of monks, nuns, kings, and laypeople as well as heavenly beings and animals. I was charmed to see the way that at some sites these scenes creatively incorporated plastic figures, including dinosaurs.[10]

10. The word *nasiya* refers both to a secluded Jain retreat and to a display marking the auspicious moment of enlightenment (thanks to John Cort for clarifying this distinction).

Rajasthan's most spectacular scene of this kind is Ajmer's well-known tourist attraction Soniji Ki Nasiya, built in the late nineteenth century. While gaping at this awesome golden diorama, several stories high, I became aware that I was gazing in the company of large numbers of Muslim tourists. They had come to Ajmer for India's most important Islamic festival, the *'urs,* death anniversary, of the Chishti saint of Ajmer, but included this Jain site as a must-see on their pilgrimage itineraries. We chatted with one man who had traveled many kilometers from India's southern state of Karnataka. He told us that he never misses visiting this Jain place each time he comes to Ajmer for the *'urs.* The wonder of this elaborately peopled Jain cosmology was unobjectionably enchanting to participants in a tradition that for itself eschewed divine image making.

Shared among all four traditions was a sensuous participation in religious life. Bodily gestures of reverence, varying just slightly among traditions, are ubiquitous elements of shrine ritual practice. These gestures involve pilgrims in some combination of washing or bathing, circumambulation, prostration, lighting of incense, uses of food and flowers, musical performances, and other physically and aesthetically potent experiences. Food transactions characterize Hindu, Muslim, and Sikh shrines. Jains generally do not offer or receive *prasad* because their theology rejects the possible transfer of grace. At Nakora Bhairuji, however, *prasad* understood to be Bhairuji's (a subsidiary deity, not a *tirthankara*) is distributed to pilgrims in sealed packets, not to be eaten on the premises, as Hindu *prasad* often is, but rather carried home (see Babb 1996, 95–96). Sikh *gurdwara*s are famed for the *langar,* or pilgrims' kitchen, where all comers receive free food (and from which our party never departed without a full meal or at the very least a rich tea). At several *gurdwara*s, we were told that Hindus and Muslims were welcomed frequently for meals. I had thought the term *langar* unique to Sikh places of worship. However, I discovered at the Muslim shrine of Kapasan the same word inscribed over a door and learned then that the only difference is that at Sikh shrines this feeding is a daily affair, whereas at Muslim shrines it depends on a pilgrim's vow to serve a feast. The Islamic *langar* is thus quite comparable to the Hindu practice of *savamani,* a vowed sharing of food (based on one-and-one-quarter maunds of wheat flour) when a prayer has been answered.

Beyond the donation box with its gross to subtle meanings, perhaps the most powerful commonality among traditions, which in some cases transgresses doctrine, is the hunger for and conviction of miracles. Miracle tales are common currency at Hindu and Muslim shrines. But one of my favorite moments of the pilgrimage took place when we were interviewing the manager of a Jain Center in his businesslike office.

Bhoju asked the manager about vows (*bolari*), and he informed us definitively that such practices were not part of Jain dharma. However, he added in a more confidential tone of voice, even if Mahavir Swami did not grant boons, his "assistants" would do so if requests were made of them. He then launched into an ardent and vivid miracle account, which I summarize here:

> I was doing a job, and I had a lot of pain in my leg, and I was in a lot of difficulty. One day I had a dream, and in that dream I was here [on the temple premises] at the place for hand washing. At this place, I saw ten or fifteen men, but I couldn't recognize their faces. They told me to take the water and massage my leg. So I did this, and suddenly I woke up, and I found myself massaging my leg. Then I came here and took the water and applied it, and since then—for the past three years—I have had no pain at all.

He followed this account with another story, not about himself, but about a poor man who stayed at this place for twenty years and then went into the trucking business and is now a billionaire. He said that Jains "do *bolari* in their minds, never speaking, but their wishes are fulfilled." Over the past twenty-five years, I have recorded countless healing miracle narratives from Hindus eager to testify to these occurrences. I might therefore highlight the difference between a tradition proud of its miracle stories and one that nervously whispers of them, but I would rather stress the thorough similarity in desires for and apprehensions of help from powers beyond the human.

Traversing Traditions in and around Jahazpur

We arrived in the provincial town of Jahazpur on July 27 after stopping in the countryside at an ambiguously identified shrine of what I might call a

Hindu *pir.* Jahazpur's population, according to Bhoju's estimate, is nearly half Muslim. Throughout most of history, civil society in Jahazpur has been well woven, sustaining this diverse community's peaceful pluralism (Varshney 2002). Recent decades witnessed a few disturbances that shook Jahazpur's long-standing harmony but did not succeed in dismantling it. Here we visited Jain and Hindu temples as well as a Muslim saint's tomb.

En route to Jahazpur, we visited a place called "Ramsa Pir." This shrine, in spite of its name's incorporating the Islamic term for a holy person, *pir,* appeared to be thoroughly Hindu. It had icons rather than a tomb, and its affiliated attendants were Gujar and Mina Hindus. Ramsa Pir was for various reasons a fascinating site. Local people told us that it was a fairly recent overlay on a space originally associated with Nath yogis (who themselves have been influenced by both Hindu tantra and Islamic Sufism). The shrine's more recent history involved a Mina shrine priest (*bhopa*), a resident of the nearby village of Khachrol, who became possessed both by the Rajasthani "snake-bite" deity, Tejaji, and by a being called "Ramsa Pir." That is, the *bhav* or "feeling" of these distinct spirits came to him and via his mediation did work in the world for pilgrims' well-being. After this man died, the *bhav* of Ramsa Pir began coming to his daughter.

Although women do get possessed and may even be consulted regarding afflictions, the possession usually happens in their homes. In my decades of research on Rajasthani religion, I have never before encountered a female shrine priest. Moreover, this one—the *bhopa*'s daughter—was quite extraordinary in her relaxed mannerisms, which violated many gender norms. She stood and sat on the shrine, where a woman ordinarily would not go; she smoked; she did not cover her head. This behavior would not have been nearly so striking in a postmenopausal female, but she was very young—early twenties at most. Yet her body language and postures were totally other from those of an ordinary young Rajasthani woman. She told us that although she had been married as a child (still a common practice among some communities in rural Rajasthan), Ramsa Pir "would not let her go." So she gave her husband permission to make a second marriage and returned the jewelry his family had given her. As she put it, such was her *kismat,* fate, and "why should I spoil his life?"

As for the identity of the deity to whose service she had dedicated her young life, she told us, "No one knows whether this is Ramdevji or some other *pir* or just *bhagwan* [God]." But the precise identity is remarkably irrelevant. People come for all kinds of treatments: to exorcise ghosts or to cure snake bites, pain, and madness. Some pilgrims live at the shrine for as long as fifteen days and eat "free of charge" (although they most likely make offerings). To one side of the small space a makeshift pilgrims' shelter had been set up in order to provide shade, using large slabs of stone of the kind typically employed in Rajasthan for roofing. This structure had recently collapsed while pilgrims were cooking. No one was hurt, and the young woman shrine-priest proclaimed this escape from harm to have been a "miracle of *baba*."

Our first morning in Jahazpur town began with a climb to the shrine of Gaji Pir, located on one of the town's surrounding hilltops. The story of Gaji Pir, historically embedded with the specificity of emperors' names and dates, turned out to be of a genre frequently associated with Hindu warrior deities, the trope of the headless horseman (A. Gold [1988] 2000, 46–48; Harlan 2003, 95–100). Gaji Pir's original name was Lal Mohammad, and he joined the army of Salim, who was a son of Emperor Akbar.[11] While he was fighting against the maharana (Hindu ruler of the kingdom of Mewar) in Chittor, he was killed in battle by a sword held in Salim's elephant's trunk (thus, so to speak, by friendly fire). His head fell down in Chittor, but he kept on fighting, without his head, until he reached Jahazpur. Here the townsfolk saw a headless rider. As soon as it entered their thoughts "there is a man who is going along without a head," he fell.[12]

One dignified Muslim elder, a knowledgeable citizen of Jahazpur whose family has been associated with the shrine for generations, gave us considerable additional history having to do with the shrine's coming into possession of both forest and agricultural lands by decrees of various

11. *Gaji* is a variant of *ghazi*, or "a warrior for faith." Anna Suvorova offers a helpful discussion of Islamic warrior saints in South Asia and Hindu veneration of these figures (2004, 155–77).

12. See Harlan 2003, 61, on how the exclamation "Look! He has no head!" serves to subdue a divinely out-of-control warrior.

rulers written on copper plates. He also told us of miracles that happened to him personally. One occurred about fifteen years earlier at the time of Gaji Pir's annual festival, or *'urs.* His niece, who was a little girl of eight or nine, was with him at the hilltop shrine. He told us that she had called to him, "O look, Uncle, hundreds of horse riders are coming, all dressed in white!" And he testified that although he himself could not see the riders, this little girl could see them clearly.

As at many Muslim shrines, there are subsidiary sites with additional tombs near Gaji Pir's shrine. Another story the same man related also had to do with visions of light—in this case a lamp moving from one saint's tomb to another, which both he and his mother saw while protecting their almost ripe crops by sleeping in the fields at night. He reiterated that he had seen such miracles with his own eyes. Then, to cap his praises of Gaji's power, this man informed us that eight or nine of Jahazpur's Hindu families have children named "Piru" who were given to them by this saint. It happened that as we were descending the stairs from Gaji Pir's shrine after our own visit there, we met a Hindu couple of the Soni or goldsmith community who had climbed these stairs regularly for forty years according to a vow they had taken in gratitude for the birth of a son.

There is ample evidence of a deep Jain history for Jahazpur. As the town grows and foundations for new construction are excavated, old Jain images keep emerging. Many of them are extraordinarily beautiful; I saw a number of them lined up in the Jain temple. But another one has ended up elsewhere. Its story is amusing, but also of significance. The *svetambar* and *digambar* sects of Jains in Jahazpur, each of which has its own temple, were apparently engaged in an interminable dispute over which of them rightfully should install this seated *tirthankara.* A local government official grew tired of their argument and ordered that the statue be placed in the Vishnu temple. There it remains, comfortably accommodated, if visually dissonant, just to the side of Lord Vishnu.

In the space of two days, we had gathered some powerful impressions: the Hindu pilgrims climbing to a Muslim shrine whose presiding spirit has an origin story identical to that of many Hindu warrior deities; the Jain *tirthankara* housed respectfully as an honored guest in a Vaishnavite temple; the young, forthright female shrine priest telling us that it genuinely does not matter a bit who Ramsa Pir might be because all that matters is his efficacy.

Narrating Hindu and Muslim Power: Negotiations of Coexistence

Every place has its origin stories as well as its miracle tales. I have selected three favorites gathered on our brief tour that treat elements of inter-community relations. Two of them are chartering tales for Muslim *pirs*' shrines, and both have to do with Muslim–Hindu conflict, although of very different sorts: one between saint and goddess; one between mortal armies. The third tale, of Ramdevji, is merely an episode in the larger epic of this regional hero-god's divinity, and the proofs (*parchya*) by which he displayed it. In all these tales, what I find most striking is the lack of total victory for either side. Stories of contest are inevitably stories of coexistence and accommodation.[13]

The Khalifa and the Devi

The Muslim Chishti saint of Gagaro was commonly called "Shariph Sarkar" or, still more simply, the *khalifa*. The term *khalifa* (in English customary usage, *caliph*) is an honorific reference to a spiritual successor, sometimes used for a disciple providing services. In this case, these services are to the Ajmer Chishti saint. The *khalifa*'s tale was told to us by a Muslim man we met at the shrine. He said that its events took place seven to eight hundred years ago.

> So once upon a time there was a goddess, in Gagaro, who always killed one human being every day; she required a human sacrifice.
>
> So the Chishti saint in Ajmer sent his *khalifa* to Gagaro, instructing him to bring about justice and to deal with this goddess.
>
> At the time that he came, there was a woman with seven sons; six had already been killed by [sacrificed to] the goddess. That day it was the seventh son's turn.

13. Shail Mayaram (2005) makes a similar point, as does Ashis Nandy (2001, 142–45). See also Prasad 2007, 35–44, for alternative Hindu and Muslim miracle narratives about a shared space in a South Indian pilgrimage town.

When the *khalifa* arrived, that mother was cooking special food for her son's last meal, and she was weeping. She did not have enough grain in her house to feed any guests. But the *khalifa* had come to her as a guest, and he said he was hungry.

She said, "I don't have enough. I am picking up grain from the ground."

He said, "Give me what you have!" So she gave him a piece of grain, and by his miraculous power they all were satisfied; they had plenty of food for the son, the *khalifa*, and the woman herself.

Then the saint went to the goddess's place, bringing with him the *pua-puri* [oil-fried, doughnutlike sweets and flat breads] that the mother of the seven sons had made. He went to the very place where the goddess would receive the live sacrifice, and he put the food there. At midnight, while the *khalifa* was meditating, the goddess came and ate the *pua* and *puri*. Then she was about to eat the *khalifa*, but he grabbed her sari, twisted it around his hand, knocked her down, and stepped on her. He pushed her down into the ground, and then she appeared in Indargarh [a fairly distant site where there is a well-known goddess temple]. The people in Indargarh started to offer her goat sacrifices. If they don't give her one goat every year, she will eat one man.

With my romantic yearnings to find nothing but harmony among religions, I was at first dismayed by the implications of the *khalifa* stepping on the *devi*. Was this a celebration of Muslim iconoclasm, of relentless monotheism? Or might it recount a somewhat gentler process of displacement? The *khalifa* does not in fact destroy the goddess; he "deals" with her, taming her hunger—a hunger that had become excessive and dangerous. The ending seems to work out survival for all at the cost of a few goats.[14]

The same man then told us about another miraculous event that happened at this place during the iconoclastic Mughal emperor Aurangzeb's rule. This story is strikingly similar to tales I heard in my earlier

14. For another tale of an Islamic teacher encountering and critiquing goddess worship, see Kassam 1995 on Pir Shams.

peregrinations to Hindu shrines about deities defending their space against Aurangzeb.

> Aurangzeb was going around knocking down tombs [*makbara*]. His practice was to perform three *salam* [deep bows] at a tomb, and if there was no reply, no miracle, he would destroy it.
>
> When he came to this place and did his first *salam*, the *khalifa* was in Mecca. When he did the second *salam*, he was in Ajmer, and when he did the third *salam*, the *khalifa* appeared before him, and so Aurangzeb accepted his power and gave him the whole state of Gagaro.

North Indian Hindu folklore portrays Aurangzeb, the would-be iconoclast, cowed by Hindu miracles. We see here how Muslims adapt this trope to testify to their own saints' powers and perhaps to defy the reformist currents in present-day Islam that critique South Asian Muslims' penchant for shrine visiting and *pir* adulation.

Ramdevji and the Five Pirs

Ramdevji is one of Rajasthan's legendary hero-gods whose stories are told and sung throughout the region. Although popular belief holds that Ramdevji was born into an aristocratic Hindu lineage, and he is given the status of an avatar or incarnation of Vishnu, some scholars such as Dominique-Sila Khan (1997) link his antecedents to Ismaili Muslims' influence in India. Today Ramdevji is also closely associated with untouchable communities; a female untouchable who became his adopted sister plays an important role in his legend and has a prominent place at his shrine.[15] In the summer of 2006, thousands of foot pilgrims carrying brightly striped multicolored pennants were on the road to Ramdevra to attend the annual fair there (even as Muslim foot pilgrims bearing green flags headed for the *'urs* in Ajmer).

Bhoju knew the stories of Ramdevji, but he told me one about the five *pirs* while glancing at a pamphlet, produced in large type and simple

15. For Ramdevji's legend and pilgrimage, see Balzani 2003; Binford 1976; A. Gold [1988] 2000, 148–49; Khan 1997.

Hindi, that we purchased at the shrine. I give my notes from Bhoju's paraphrase to keep an oral flavor and to condense. The undated pamphlet very explicitly frames this episode as taking place in the context of Ramdevji spreading Hindu dharm and Muslims becoming alarmed and calling for their five *pir*s' aid lest "Islamic dharm be destroyed" (Sharma n.d., 58). Bhoju omitted this frame entirely, whether out of distaste or deeming it irrelevant.

> A friend of Ramdevji was bitten by a snake and appeared to have died. His mother and all the neighbors were weeping.
>
> This was when the five *pir*s arrived from Mecca. They met Ramdevji, who was grazing horses on the edge of town. . . .
>
> The five *pir*s did not believe he could be a saint because he was dressed like a king.
>
> They said, "Are you yourself Ramdev Pir?"
>
> He answered, "I don't know if I'm a *pir*, but I'm Ramdev."
>
> "But," they said, "we have come here to discuss religion [*dharm charcha*], and what would someone like you know about religion?"
>
> He answered, "If I am grazing horses, so did Jesus graze sheep and Muhammed had camels." . . .
>
> They all went to the village where Ramdevji's friend had died from snakebite. Ramdevji said to the five *pir*s, "My friend died, so bring him back to life." They were disconcerted and said, "We would have been able to bring him back to life, but we left our stuff in Mecca."
>
> Ramdevji took his friend's hand and said, "Get up! Can't you see some guests have come from Mecca? It is not time for sleep." And he got up!
>
> Then all the weeping people began to shout, "Victory to Ramdevji!"
>
> Even then, the Muslims claimed that this was not much of a miracle: "This is easy to do."
>
> Ramdevji invited them to his castle, saying, "I'll be very happy if you eat at my house."
>
> They answered, "Of course we would eat, but we left our bowls in Mecca, and we can't eat out of any other bowls. Then Ramdevji stretched out his hand and got the bowls from Mecca and set them before the five

11. *Ramdevji and the Five Pirs*, wall painting. The Hindi text reads: "The proof [given] to the Five Pirs from Mecca." Photograph by Ann Grodzins Gold.

> *pirs*. When they saw their bowls, the five *pirs* bowed at Ramdevji's feet. They said, "We are *pirs*, but you are the Great Pir," and they went back to Mecca. From this time people began to call him "Ramdev Pir."

Note that what the story effects is peaceful reconciliation and ultimately syncretism. Ramdev becomes a *pir* for Muslims, as he is today.

Although most of the pilgrims we saw in Ramdevra appeared to be Hindu, the shops around Ramdevji's shrine display Islamic and Hindu offerings together: on sale are green bedspreads as well as garlands of marigolds, along with the beautiful cloth horses unique to Ramdev. We asked one shopkeeper about these diverse offerings, and he firmly assured us that for Ramdevji there were no differences among human beings.

Nau Gaj Baba (Nine Yards Baba)

The Muslim shrine of Nau Gaj Baba is located in the Chittor fort. Chittor was a major seat of Rajput power and is also known as the unhappy

12. Tomb of Nau Gaj Baba (donation box visible at front of tomb). Photograph by Ann Grodzins Gold.

marital home of famed devotional poet and woman saint Mirabai. Today it is one of Rajasthan's important tourist attractions. Although I had visited Chittor several times, I never before found my way to Nau Gaj Baba's tomb until this trip when we were following the leads given us by Bhoju Ram Gujar's Muslim friends.

Here is the foundational story as we heard it at the shrine, told to us by the *khadim* (attendant).

> About seventeen hundred years ago there was a king of Chittor. He had a daughter who was seven yards tall, and so her parents were desperately seeking a tall husband.
>
> They learned that the ruler of Kabul [in Afghanistan] had a son who was nine yards tall. So they sent a marriage proposal from here in Chittor all the way to Kabul.
>
> The groom's party arrived from Kabul with four hundred men and entered Chittor fort. However, just after they arrived, the girl's maternal grandfather found out that her parents were getting her married to a Muslim.

> He objected: "This wedding cannot take place! If it takes place, then we will have to send with her one hundred of our own servant girls—it is not good for our honor [*ijjat*].
>
> [He had no problem with disposing of his freakishly tall granddaughter, but he did not want to send a hundred "normal" Hindu servant girls to Kabul.]
>
> So the grandfather killed his granddaughter. As her blood was flowing, she cursed the fort: "No family can live peacefully here forevermore." Her curse carried the power of a virgin girl's blood, and its force continues today.
>
> Then the tall girl's father, the king, said to the nine-yards-tall bridegroom, "Go back to Kabul, and we'll reimburse your expenses."
>
> But the groom and his men said, "No, now there will be a war! We won't go back."
>
> In the battle, all four hundred men from Kabul were slaughtered, including the nine-yards-tall bridegroom. It was prayer time, *namaz*; and when he sat down to say his prayers, they killed him.

Having come to the close of this doleful tale, the shrine attendant went on to tell us of various miracles that testify to the power of this place. One common miracle relates to the tomb's extraordinary size.[16] If you bring a sheet to offer, you should not measure it, and it will fit just right. You should just purchase any sheet. You must not ask for one that is nine yards or ten yards because then it will always come out short. This taboo on measuring seems symbolic of the failure of a marriage intended to match a tall bride and groom, fatally relying on mere size.

People come here to rid themselves of afflictions caused by the spirits of the dead. Sometimes they drive nails into the tree, thus pinning the ghost soul that is troubling them so it cannot follow them. These pilgrims, the *khadim* assured us, were both Hindu and Muslim. At Nau Gaj Baba's shrine, we encountered a family of *harijan*s (former untouchables) who

16. There is a tradition in Islam, originating in Arabia, of "Tombs of Giant Prophets"; see Wheeler 2006 for "long tombs."

had come with their son, a young man who looked to be in his early twenties. His mother told us that two or three months ago he had fallen down, and it seemed as if he were afflicted by a ghost. They were themselves Hindus but had somehow identified the ghost as a Muslim butcher who had been murdered forty years ago and whose body had been thrown down around the place where the boy became possessed, its soul lingering there. The Muslim shrine attendant demanded one hundred rupees from the *harijan*s. They haggled a while, but eventually the price was paid, and then he did everything the pilgrims needed to their satisfaction, as the mother of the afflicted young man assured Bhoju.

What impressed me about Nau Gaj Baba's tale and place was that out of bad faith and betrayal, out of the murder of the innocent and defenseless, comes a shared conviction of an ultimately benign power. Miraculous power lies at the center of all these shrine stories, bringing blessings into the mortal world. Interestingly, the blessings effected in stories of apparent conflict between Hindu and Muslim traditions in every instance fluidly cross between them. Sikand (2003) has demonstrated that Hindu attendance at shrines to Muslim powerful beings may not necessarily signal communal harmony, but rather the dominant Hindu culture's appropriation of minority sites and even spirits. However, based on my limited experience in Rajasthan, these blurred boundaries or watery lines reflect shared humanity, including experiences of suffering and acute desire for access to divine aid.

Consuming a "Mix"

I returned to Ghatiyali from the long Ramdevra loop of our journey with my purse's side compartments stuffed with *prasad*—grace in the form of sugar candy, but far more than we had been able to consume—from at least a dozen holy places of every variety. Exhausted, I forgot to take these blessed leftovers out to share, as would have been appropriate behavior for a returning pilgrim. The next day I found my bag invaded by ants, which were swarming throughout this uneaten and now inedible *prasad*. This invasion felt a little inauspicious to me: *prasad* as a vehicle of grace is taken seriously, as is the obligation on returning from the road of dharm to share it with those less fortunate than the traveler. It seemed possible in this case that *prasad* from too many powers had removed itself from the possibility of human consumption. What to do? Bali was also momentarily taken aback but quickly advised me to brush the contents of my bag's pockets into the ever-ready vessel of kitchen scraps that was daily fed to the family's milk buffalo. I thought no more about it but like to imagine retrospectively the buffalo herself processing this grace into the rich dairy Bhoju's whole family enjoyed daily.

On the final night of our tour, Bhoju Ram, Shiv Lalji, and I treated ourselves to a meal in a very nice restaurant in Chittor. The English menu advertised a dish called "vegetable *handi*," its name referring to a big round cooking pot. When we asked the waiter what was in this dish, he responded using the English word *mix*. Bhoju, laughing, used this word as an analogy to describe his pilgrimage experience over the past two weeks. "I have become like *handi*," he said, "mix, mix, I am *handi*." For, indeed, we had taken *darshan* everywhere, accepted, consumed, and carried home *prasad* from shrines of every tradition (even the rare Jain *prasad* from Nakora Bhairuji). Bhoju and Shiv Lal had prostrated themselves and taken the dust and blessings of multiple figures of power—sometimes as many as six or seven in one day. Bhoju's humorous comparison of himself to a *handi* made me realize that the incorporation accomplished by these ritualized gestures he had performed so unhesitantly was real, substantial, and slightly unsettling. It was also satisfying and even exhilarating. The three of us were happy that evening. Our "*sarvadharm yatra*" was successful.

Works Cited

Babb, Lawrence A. 1996. *Absent Lord: Ascetics and Kings in a Jain Ritual Culture.* Berkeley: Univ. of California Press.

Balzani, Marzia. 2003. *Modern Indian Kingship: Tradition, Legitimacy, and Power in Rajasthan*. Santa Fe: School of American Research Press.

Binford, Mira R. 1976. "Mixing in the Color of Ram of Ranuja." In *Hinduism: New Essays in the History of Religions*, edited by B. L. Smith, 120–42. Leiden: E. J. Brill.

Currie, P. M. 1989. *The Shrine and Cult of Mu'in al-din Chishti of Ajmer.* New Delhi: Oxford Univ. Press.

Flueckiger, Joyce B. 2006. *In Amma's Healing Room: Gender and Vernacular Islam in South India*. Bloomington: Indiana Univ. Press.

Gold, Ann Grodzins. [1988] 2000. *Fruitful Journeys: The Ways of Rajasthani Pilgrims.* Prospect Heights, IL: Waveland.

———. 2008. "Showing Miracles in Rajasthan: Proof and Grace." In *Miracle as Conundrum in South Asian Religious Traditions*, edited by Corinne Dempsey and Selva Raj, 85–204. Albany: State Univ. of New York Press.

Gold, Ann Grodzins, and Bhoju Ram Gujar. 2002. *In the Time of Trees and Sorrows: Nature, Power, and Memory in Rajasthan.* Chapel Hill, NC: Duke Univ. Press.

Gold, Daniel. 2005. "The Sufi Shrines of Gwalior City: Communal Sensibilities and the Accessible Exotic under Hindu Rule." *Journal of Asian Studies* 64, no. 1: 127–50.

Gottschalk, Peter. 2000. *Beyond Hindu and Muslim: Multiple Identity in Narratives from Village India.* New York: Oxford Univ. Press.

Harlan, Lindsey. 2003. *The Goddesses' Henchmen: Reflections on Gender in Indian Hero Worship.* New York: Oxford Univ. Press.

Kassam, Tazim R. 1995. *Songs of Wisdom and Circles of Dance: Hymns of the Satpanth Isma'ili Muslim Saint, Pir Shams.* Albany: State Univ. of New York Press.

Khan, Dominique-Sila. 1997. *Conversions and Shifting Identities: Ramdev Pir and the Ismailis in Rajasthan.* New Delhi: Manohar.

Mayaram, Shail. 1999. "Spirit Possession: Reframing Discourses of the Self and the Other." In *La possession en Asie du Sud: Parole, corps, territoire* (Possession in South Asia: Speech, Body, Territory), edited by Jackie Assayag and Gilles Tarabout, 101–32. Paris: Collection Purushartha.

———. 2005. "Living Together: Ajmer as a Paradigm for the (South) Asian City." In *Living Together Separately: Cultural India in History and Politics*, edited by Mushirul Hasan and Asim Roy, 145–71. New Delhi: Oxford Univ. Press.

Nandy, Ashis. 2001. *Time Warps: The Insistent Politics of Silent and Evasive Pasts.* New Delhi: Permanent Black.

Narayanan, Vasudha. 2006. "Religious Vows at the Shrine of Shahul Hamid." In *Dealing with Deities: The Ritual Vow in South Asia*, edited by Selva J. Raj and William P. Harman, 65–85. Albany: State Univ. of New York Press.

Olsen, Keri. 2003. "'We All Eat Pickles, Don't We?' Negotiating Identity in the City of Ajmer (India)." PhD diss., Syracuse Univ.

Prasad, Leela. 2007. *Poetics of Conduct: Oral Narrative and Moral Being in a South Indian Town.* New York: Columbia Univ. Press.

Sanyal, Usha. 2007. "Tourists, Pilgrims, and Saints: The Shrine of Mu'in al-Din Chisti of Ajmer." In *Raj Rhapsodies: Tourism, Heritage, and the Seduction of*

History, edited by Carol E. Henderson and Maxine Weisgrau, 183–202. Aldershot, UK: Ashgate.

Sharma, Manohar Lal. n.d. *Shri Ramdev ji ka jivan charitra.* Jaipur, India: Sethi Pustak Bhandar.

Sikand, Yoginder. 2003. *Sacred Spaces: Exploring Traditions of Shared Faith in India.* New Delhi: Penguin Books India.

Singh, Gurmukh. 1995. *Historical Sikh Shrines.* Amritsar, India: Singh Brothers.

Stewart, Tony K. 2000. "Alternate Structures of Authority: Satya Pir on the Frontiers of Bengal." In *Beyond Turk and Hindu: Rethinking Religious Identities in Islamicate South Asia*, edited by David Gilmartin and Bruce B. Lawrence, 21–54. Gainesville: Univ. Press of Florida.

Suvorova, Anna. 2004. *Muslim Saints of South Asia: The Eleventh to Fifteenth Centuries.* New York: Routledge Curzon.

Troll, C. W., ed. 1992. *Muslim Shrines in India.* New Delhi: Oxford Univ. Press.

Varshney, Ashutosh. 2002. *Ethnic Conflict and Civic Life: Hindus and Muslims in India.* New Haven, CT: Yale Univ. Press.

Wheeler, Brannon. 2006. *Mecca and Eden: Ritual, Relics, and Territory in Islam.* Chicago: Univ. of Chicago Press.

12

≈

From Liminal to Social in the Modern Age

Transcendent Sacrality and Social Service in the Aghor Tradition

JISHNU SHANKAR

THE THEME OF OUR VOLUME, drawing lines in water, conjures up a metaphor that is especially conducive to looking at changes that have taken place in the Aghor tradition of cremation-ground ascetics—especially with reference to followers of Aghoreshwar Mahaprabhu Baba Bhagwan Ram, otherwise known as Baba Bhagwan Ram, who established a society dedicated to social service, Shri Sarveshwari Samooh, thus giving to the Aghor tradition a prominent and clearer social face.[1] Given the

1. A note on spelling: The noun and adjective forms *A/aghor, A/aghora, A/aughar, A/audhar, A/aghori* and *A/avadhut* are used for members of the Aghor tradition. The word *aghor* is a noun in that it derives from the name of the fifth face of Shiva, the Aghor face. It forms a compound noun with the word *tradition*: *Aghor tradition*. It is used as an adjective to qualify distinctions of tradition (*parampara*), philosophy (*darshan*), as in *Aghor philosophy*, or ascetic practices (*sadhana*), as in *Aghor sadhana*. Followers of the Aghor tradition, typically monks (*sadhus*), are referred to as *aughar* or *aughar sadhu* in Bihar, Uttar Pradesh, and Madhya Pradesh states of India and as *aghori* more commonly in Bengal. However, the term *aughar* can be easily turned into an adjective by making it *aghori*, which is then sometimes used as a nominal adjective in northern India. *Aghora* is an English variant of the word *aghor*, deriving from the Sanskrit nomenclature of the term, and can be used as a noun. *Audhar*

hoary age of the Aghor tradition, I think it was a heroic act on Baba Bhagwan Ram's part to turn itinerant mendicants roaming in wildernesses and cremation grounds into a community of socially responsible individuals, an act that, although initiated in his lifetime, will be carried through by his disciples. This puts a curious challenge before his followers. Giving a social face to the tradition has also meant creating a social personality for the institution that is markedly different from the erstwhile image of the *aughar* ascetic prevalent in the popular conception. Although on the one hand it makes the Aghor tradition accessible to society, on the other hand it puts followers of the tradition on the defensive when asked to explain the so-called reformist trend that is so different from the transgressive practices *aughar*s are well known for. They have to face the curious dilemma of how to maintain their social persona and continue their social work while either defending or negating the very same practices that are said to accord special powers to them and make them especially suitable for social work. As a respected social community, they become similar to other such groups where the pressure to conform to the acceptable social norm may lead them either to deny or at least to fudge the very social conception that qualifies them as "Aghor." My essay does not focus much on the transformation that Baba Bhagwan Ram introduced to perceptions of Aghor in society, for that has been done in several earlier works (Barrett 2002; Chaturvedi 1973; Gupta 1993; Ag. Ram 1991; Shri Sarveshwari Samooh 1981, 1982, 1984). Rather, my interest is in the nature of change at specific points in Baba's own life where he seems to have consciously drawn a line for transformative effect on the Aghor tradition.

Aghor is widely regarded as belonging to the Shaiva-Shakta tradition. In the Rigveda (10.85.44), God Rudra is described as terrifying and fierce,

---

is a less common variant of *aughar* and is used mostly as an adjective, as in "Baba Audhardani." *Avadhut* is the term given to accomplished ascetic practitioners who have achieved enlightenment following the Aghor path. I use the word *Aghor* to qualify ascetic practices and philosophy. To denote an ascetic of this path, I prefer to use the term *aughar* because it is the prevalent term in the region of Varanasi city (also known as Benaras/Banaras or Kashi).

but also benevolent and compassionate.[2] His auspicious form, united inseparably from his feminine power, called Shivaa, is described in the Rudradhyaya chapter of Yajur Veda (Taittiriya Samhita, 4.5.1.1).[3] In this text, this feminine power is described as "Aghoraa." According to followers of the tradition, this illustration implies that Rudra is Shivaa, and Shivaa is *aghora*, a Sanskrit word that is currently given as *aughar* (Chaturvedi 1973, 5). The association of *aughar*s with various Shaiva schools is discussed very well by Roxanne Gupta (1993) and David Lorenzen (1972). Although the discussions of the *aughar*s' links with other Shaiva–Shakta schools are fascinating, the exact links between them are mostly conjectural. Literature published by the Shri Sarveshwari Samooh society treats the modern-day Aghor tradition as a synthesis not only of the Shaiva and Shakta schools, but also more broadly of the Shaiva, Shakta, and Vaishnava schools, as I point out shortly. Given certain striking similarities between the *sadhana*s (ascetic practices) of *aughar*s and the Buddhist monks (Chaudhary 1985; Horner 1971; Rao 1964), scholars also conjecture about historical exchanges between the two traditions (Davidson 2002; Mishra 2001).

Before going further, I should describe Baba Bhagwan Ram's place and the lineage he belongs to within the Aghor tradition. He was initiated into the Aghor tradition by Baba Rajeshwar Ram, an ascetic of imposing stature, who was himself the tenth guru in the lineage started by Baba Kinaram sometime in the middle of the seventeenth century.

Baba Kinaram's History

Baba Kinaram was born in the Ramgarh village near Banaras in approximately 1601 CE. He was first initiated into the Vaishnava tradition by Saint Shivaram of the Ramanuj sect at Karo village in Gazipur. His life story is full of miraculous incidents where he acted on behalf of the poor, the oppressed, and women without worrying about consequences. These

2. The Rigveda (10.85.44) states: "Aghorchakshur patighnyedhi shivaa pashubhyah sumanaah suvarchaah," "Not evil-eyed, no slayer of thy husband, bring weal to cattle, radiant, gentlehearted" (translation from Griffith 1897, 506).

3. "Yaa te rudra shivaa tanuurghoraa paapkaashini": "That body of thine, O Rudra, which is kindly, Not dread, with auspicious look" (translation from Keith 1914, 195).

incidents include the stories of his freeing a poor boy from the clutches of the *zamindar* (landlord) for nonpayment of taxes, interceding on behalf of *faqir*s (mendicants) and saints imprisoned by the Mughal ruler of Junagadh, and bringing back to life a corpse floating in the Ganges River at the behest of Baba Kaluram at Kashi. One belief is that Baba Kaluram initiated him at Krin-Kund with the Aghor mantra, and another belief is that he was already initiated into the Aghor tradition by Guru Dattatreya at Girnar. From that time on, Baba Kinaram began to live at Krin-Kund. There are many other stories in which Baba Kinaram intercedes on behalf of women (Gupta 1993; U. Singh 1999), and the theme of Kinaram as the protector of fallen women persists in Banaras (Varanasi), where he has been looked upon as the patron saint of prostitutes. Even as recently as the 1950s, the prostitutes and dancing girls of Banaras used to make offerings at the Sthal (literally "place," the sect's seat of authority and main ashram) twice a year (Chaturvedi 1973, 79).

Although many people associate *aughar*s with social transgression, it bears note that *aughar* saints have often fostered important ties with more orthodox forms of Hinduism such as Vaishnavism. When Baba Kinaram was an adolescent, his first guru was a Vaishnava saint. In addition, Baba Kinaram established four Vaishnava monasteries as well as four Aghor monasteries. This is important to note because with the more recent changes in the social persona of the Shri Sarveshwari Samooh organization, the *aughar* sect has been characterized as reformist. Yet as I show later, the synthesis of Vaishnava and Aghor elements visible in the life of the *aghor* lineage founder, Baba Kinaram, also occurs in Baba Bhagwan Ram's life, whose first mentor in his childhood was also a Vaishnava saint. Moreover, Baba Bhagwan Ram himself conducted several Vishnu *yajña*s (sacrificial ceremonies) during his lifetime.

The undercurrent of helping the needy out of personal compassion runs continuously through Baba Kinaram's life stories. This trend culminates in later gurus in their support for mass uplift, as can be seen in Baba Bhagwan Ram's life story. It is because of Baba Bhagwan Ram's life and work that today we have not one but two different views of the Aghor tradition. It is as if Baba Bhagwan Ram, in the ocean of the Aghor tradition, drew a line in the water, wherein his initiative is very much in keeping with the history of the Aghor tradition and yet somehow different even as it continues the tradition. Let us look briefly at the context where this line has been drawn.

The traditional and widely prevalent view of the Aghor tradition is that of the cremation-ground-dwelling *aughar* ascetics with their transgressive practices. Whether it be from the Sanskrit dramas such as Bhavabhuti's *Malati-Madhava* (S. Shastri 1998) and Krishnamishra's *Prabodha Chandrodaya* (Briggs 1982, 226; R. Shastri 1977), the colonial administrators, or even the popular worldview (E. Balfour 1885; H. Balfour 1897; Crooke 1895; Eliade 1958; Parry 1985; H. Wilson [1862] 1976), this view has relegated *aughar*s to the marginal reaches of the Hindu religious universe. As expressed in the writings of colonial administrators and early scholars, it represents Victorian and Brahmanical conservative biases. However, it may be also in keeping with the intentions of the *aughar* ascetics themselves, who define themselves as walking embodiments of Shiva (Shri Sarveshwari Samooh 1984, 10). Like Shiva, the quintessential ascetic in Hindu thought, ideally they inhabit cremation grounds, wander freely clad in scanty clothes or in the ashes of the cremation ground; are prone to use intoxicants in meditation; do not subscribe to the distinctions of or discriminate between pure and impure, high and low, Brahmin or Shudra, love or hate; possess nothing except what the cremation ground provides for them; and live a life of absolute freedom. Being a part of a culture of "cremation-ground asceticism," they are not attracted to society, nor, by extension, are they interested in the views held by society toward them.

The other view, seen through the life of Baba Kinaram and promulgated institutionally through the life and work of Baba Bhagwan Ram, is that of an *aughar* ascetic who has through his or her practices living on the cremation grounds acquired the ability to accept all that is considered impure and defiled by society and transform it into something that is wholesome and socially good. The notion of transgressive *aughar* ascetics who, precisely because of their transgressions, have the power to handle elements that other ascetics cannot is very much a part of Hindu society's understanding of them. This understanding is most starkly evident in the city of Banaras, where a popular legend of Neelakantha Shiva (Dhal 2000, 74–78) portrays him as drinking poison so that the gods and demons could rest at peace.[4] Such social recognition of the powers of the *aughar*s to intercede on behalf of humans—their ability to take upon themselves that which is regarded as most vile and polluting socially—presents to us the second image of the *aughar*s.

In this view, they appear not as fearsome, transgressive ascetics of the cremation ground, but in fact as accessible ascetics living in ashrams working for the social good, transforming the socially polluting to the socially purifying and the socially sick to the socially healthy. This view is well recognized in the holy city of Banaras and has some international acclaim, too.[5]

Liminality

One may wonder why, if *aughar*s have powers that are socially beneficial by virtue of their transgressive practices, the portrayal of them has often been negative. For certainly, from an emic point of view, *aughar*s regard some of the best-known personalities in Indian history as having been *aughar* ascetics, even though their popular portrayal may not reflect the practice of Aghor *sadhana*. Yagyanarayan Chaturvedi's *Aughar Bhagwan Ram* lists Vishwamitra, Vamadeva, and Vashishth from the Ramayana as well as Vikramaditya, Aghoracharya (700 CE), Bhairavacharya (Kavi 1964), and Abhinavagupta as practitioners of the Aghor *sadhana* (1973,

4. According to the *amritamanthan* (churning the ocean to obtain ambrosia) story in Hindu mythology, when the demons and deities churned the ocean, fourteen jewels surfaced. One of them was a poison variously named "Halahala" or "Kalakut," which scared both the demons and the deities. The poisonous fumes threatened to devastate the world, so Shiva drank the poison. The poison was so deadly that his throat became blue, which is why Shiva is also known as "Neelakantha," the "Blue-Throated One."

5. The *Guinness Book of World Records* listed the society's achievements in December 15, 1998, under the title "Most Leprosy Patients Treated": "The Awadhoot Bhagwan Ram Kusht Sewa Ashram Hospital at Parao, India, has treated more leprosy patients than any other hospital. The total number of registered patients since 1961 has been 99,045 with full Leprosy and 147,503 with partial Leprosy—all of whom were fully cured. The hospital was established in 1961 and receives no government funding—it runs entirely from public donations and gifts. Patients are treated free of charge using Ayurvedic herbal medicines and the Fakiri system, a method invented by the Indian religious saints" (Guinness 1998).

13–16). Also, practices relating to the dead, though awe inspiring, are not exclusive to *aughar*s from a global perspective. They are universal enough to be found fairly commonly in many other parts of the world. Anthropological literature mentions the Yanomami as grinding the bones of their dead and eating them to honor their dead (Woznicki 1998). During travels in Italy, I have seen several churches that display skulls in a glass box in open view, and friends have informed me that churches in Poland contain the remains of the saints to whom each particular church is dedicated. Celtic lore certainly describes sacrifices and dead bodies (Matthews 2002).

It appears that the almost formulaic negative portrayal of *aughar*s stems from their historical and social liminality. *Aughar*s can be called historically liminal because it is difficult to trace the exact historical links of the Aghor tradition to any specific personality or movement in Indian history, their oldest referent being the Aghor face of God Shiva himself. This historical liminality, their small numbers, and the lack of any organization to represent them make them easily confusable with other cremation-ground-based practitioners (Chaturvedi 1973, 16). *Aughar*s can be regarded as socially liminal because by definition in the Indian milieu the cremation ground is a liminal place, and those who dwell there, be they dead or alive, belong neither to the social world nor, because of their still existing physical forms, to the spirit world. At best, they exist at the liminal margins of the social structure, prone to easy misinterpretation. This misinterpretation is doubly accentuated by the aggressively renunciate nature of the *aughar* ascetics themselves, who have cared little about how others view them. Their ideal goal, to be one with the deity of their desire, drives them to be impervious to all social criticism and praise. Their practices predispose them to accept all that is considered socially discarded, to have a totally nondualistic view of the world, and not to adhere to the caste system. Such a philosophy puts them at the other pole from a strict Brahmanical view of caste and social structure.

It is not out of place here to mention that transgressive behavior has its own social merit when socially accepted and takes place in defined spheres of activity. A soldier's violent actions on the battlefield are not transgressive because they are socially approved and, even more so, expected. However, the same kind of behavior outside of the battlefield—say, in the domestic sphere—is not only transgressive, but antisocial. There clearly exist two different structures of behavior. One is the domestic, socially ordained structure of behavior and practice common to our daily lives, and the other is the structure of behavior and practice to which ascetics of the cremation ground adhere. As long as these two structures of behaviors and practices remain separate, they can coexist in juxtaposition to each other, albeit with some tension, and the smaller of the two tends to be marginalized as liminal. It is when the two come together that we have either fodder for awe-inspiring stories and legends or for both criticism and defense of the liminal practices. This coming together is very much a part of ascetic necessity. Jonathan Parry has pointed out the contradiction that exists among ascetics of South Asia, that although they need to renounce the world to follow their spiritual goal, they must nevertheless seek alms from householders for subsistence. This contradiction is resolved in the *aughar*'s lifestyle because "[h]is loincloth is a shroud, his fuel the charred wood of the pyres, his food human refuse. By scavenging from the dead (who have no further use for what he takes), the Aghori escapes the clutches of the living, and in theory at least realizes the ascetic ideal of complete autonomy" (1985, 67). Parry's line of thinking is corroborated when we read that Baba Bhagwan Ram used to say, "Aughar aur ghar ke hote hain" (*Aughar*s belong to a different house) (Shri Sarveshwari Samooh 1981, 23).[6] What does "aur ghar" (the other/different house) mean in his statement? I think it refers not only to Aghor practices, but also to a whole different value system. In contrast to the value system of the "normal," household-based, domestic society, the Aghor value system is a totally renunciate philosophy that will go to any transgressive extent to achieve its goal—the deity of one's desire. The two systems, though juxtaposed, are mutually exclusive. One relates to renunciation and the *intense desire* to achieve a favorite deity—even if it is through the crema-

6. Shri Sarveshwari Samooh published a trilogy of books outlining Baba Bhagwan Ram's statements on Aghor philosophy from 1981 to 1984: *Aghoreshwar smriti vacanamrita* (The Nectar of Aghoreshwar's Remembered Words, 1981); *Aghor guru guh* (Mysteries of the Aghor Master, 1982); and *Aghoreshwar samvedanasheel* (Aghoreshwar Compassionate, 1984).

13. Sarkar Baba (Baba Bhagwan Ram) at the Sonoma Ashram in California, 1990. Photograph by Ari Marcopoulos. Courtesy of Baba Harihar Ram Ji, Shri Sarveshwari Samooh Sonoma Ashram Foundation.

tion ground; the other conforms to living a normal life, even if it portends a life of endless bondage, either to senses or to social customs.

During his lifetime, Baba Bhagwan Ram sought in diverse ways to break down or mitigate this dichotomy. For one, he always differentiated between "Aghor *panth*" (the Aghor path) and "Aghor *pad*" (the Aghor state or position) in such a way as to open the tradition to participation by lay followers. "Aghor *panth*" can refer to the transgressive practices of the Aghor tradition—something that followers of other traditions can adopt. But "*Aghor pad*" refers to the Aghor state—a state of being involving nonduality and nonhate toward everything in the world, a state that one can achieve without necessarily going through transgressive practices. He says to his disciples, for example,

> A person's clothes, appearance and hard asceticism indicate his desire to be praised by society, his desire that society should call him good. I think we are "devotees of God in the form of *Prana* (life force, life breath), and we are very close to him." To be recognized in this way is a matter of pride for human beings. By smearing ashes on his body, carrying a wooden staff, wearing a loincloth of jute, is the young ascetic really searching for his *Prana* in this way? Is he trying to look for God or to recognize his own soul? No, looking for praise, respect and recognition are his goal. This is false-knowledge. Praise, respect, and recognition make a place in your heart very easily but when they begin to leave, it really wrenches your heart out. (Shri Sarveshwari Samooh 1982, 18)[7]

Baba Bhagwan Ram's unique contribution is that not only has he transformed what are called transgressive practices into practices within the socially accepted structure of the ashram, but he has also enabled the two different structures to coexist harmoniously, each supporting the other constructively. Parry, however, has raised doubts about the broader social implications of the *aughar* doctrine by wondering whether it applies to the society as a whole or only to the *aughar* ascetic: "The doctrine that

7. Translations of non-English material are mine unless otherwise indicated.

the essence of all things is the same may clearly be taken to imply a radical devaluation of the caste hierarchy, since from this point of view there is no fundamental difference between the Untouchable and the Brahmin. What is less obvious, however, is whether this teaching is one which relates only . . . to the ascetic (caste is irrelevant for *him* but not for the world at large), or whether the Aghori's devaluation of the social order is to be interpreted as a message for *all* men" (1985, 68). Baba Bhagwan Ram's daily behavior as well as the policies and programs he instituted at his ashram point toward his effort to translate this *aughar* doctrine into something that can be practiced by *all*, not just by the ascetic. The power of the erstwhile transgressive ascetics and the radically egalitarian worldview they affirm now become available for social use, and the domestic or lay participants now feel empowered to go beyond the limitations of their daily social lives by participating in something that had formerly been set apart as dangerous.

Baba Bhagwan Ram and Shri Sarveshwari Samooh

In this section, I look at the lines Baba Bhagwan Ram drew to provide a platform to create a community out of solitary *aughar*s. I begin with the efforts he made right from the days of his own solitary *sadhana*, much like the departure of a hero on a transformative quest not only to attain his own enlightenment, but also to transform the tradition that enabled him to do so. The moment of enlightenment fulfilled Baba Bhagwan Ram's spiritual quest, but as a successful hero he returned to society instead of merely enjoying spiritual bliss in solitude, and in sharing the fruits of his powers he created a community that would transform the way people thought of the Aghor tradition.

Baba Bhagwan Ram was born on Sunday, September 12, 1937, to Babu Baijnath Singh and his wife, Lakhraji Devi, in the village of Gundi near Arrah railway station in Bihar. At age five, he lost his father, and at age seven he left his home and began to wander and live in the groves around the village. He was initiated in the Vaishnava tradition by the village holy man and teacher. His spiritual thirst ultimately took him to Banaras, where he was initiated into the Aghor tradition at Baba Kinaram's Sthal, Krin-Kund, by the then tenth guru of the tradition, Baba Rajeshwar Ram. After a number of powerful experiences at the monastery, Baba Bhagwan Ram began to wander in the city of Banaras and alongside the river Ganges with its many villages and cremation grounds, especially in Chandauli District. I suspect it was in these days of his wanderings that an acute social consciousness took hold of him, and he realized the potential that the Aghor tradition had for social work. I believe it was in this period itself that he began to draw lines in the water of the Aghor tradition as he realized what needed to be changed in the tradition to turn it into an efficacious social institution. Once he returned to society after gaining "enlightenment," he put into practice what he had realized during his wanderings. Let us look at some instances of how he drew these lines.

Baba's period of *sadhana* had already begun when during the course of his wanderings he visited his home village. Here we read of one of the first instances of his drawing a line that made him relinquish social ties and cross over into the realm of the transgressive. Baba Bhagwan Ram made a determined effort to leave behind his earlier conditioning and succeeded by entering his village wrapped in shroud cloth, carrying the dead body of a dog, and holding a bottle of alcohol. Most of the people decided that day that he was no longer fit to be reinstated in the family (Chaturvedi 1973, 160).

In this incident, Baba Bhagwan Ram clearly violated a number of social norms, thereby severing himself from family life and locating himself within the extrasocial world of the *aughar* ascetics. Drawing this boundary between the ordinary and the extraordinary was essential to fulfilling his quest free of family ties and social supervision. Then came the day when his *sadhana* would bear fruit. One day as he was wandering on the bank of the river Ganges at the Mahraura cremation ground, he attained enlightenment. Describing that experience, Baba Bhagwan Ram said he saw his life force arise in front of his eyes within eight concentric, colored circles. After that, he gained many supernatural powers, such as healing, invisibility, wish fulfillment, and the bestowing of grace (Shri Sarveshwari Samooh 1981, 57).

In 1953, after performing a Vishnu-*yajña* at the request of devotees from the villages of Hariharpur and Tajpur near Banaras, Baba Bhagwan Ram established his first ashram there and called it "Adi Ashram

14. Baba Bhagwan Ram's ashram, circa 1967. Photographer unknown.

Hariharpur." Stories of Baba's severe ascetic penance began to circulate in Banaras and surrounding areas. Those in his company would experience miracles as if they were natural, everyday events in life. As Baba's popularity grew, devotees began to flock for his *darshan* (sacred glimpse). This is where I think Baba Bhagwan Ram drew another line—this time not to distinguish his way of life from that of ordinary people, but to effect change within the Aghor tradition. With so many people coming to consult with him at all hours of day and night, Baba had to choose whether he wanted to live a free and unfettered life full of spiritual bliss, as enlightened *aughar* saints had done before his time, or to share the riches of his enlightenment with those who came seeking his company. He chose the option of social responsibility, making a fundamental change to the *aughars*' austere renunciate practice—and thus renouncing renunciation.

Baba's own guru, Baba Rajeshwar Ram, wanted him to take charge of the Kinaram Sthal, an icon of *aghor* asceticism, but Baba Bhagwan Ram did not think that was the best course of action for him to follow. Instead, on September 21, 1961, he laid the foundation of Shri Sarveshwari Samooh in the holy city of Banaras, an organization with a mandate to fight social evils such as leprosy, dowry, and illiteracy. Leprosy is still a dreaded disease in India, and at that time even the government of India did not have adequate facilities to treat it. It is not just a physical disease, but also a social disease where the patient's entire family is stigmatized as being punished for their sins; as a result, many families oust members afflicted with leprosy from the house, leaving them to fend for themselves on the streets. Given the Aghor practice of nondiscrimination and treating even the most disfigured, downtrodden, and persecuted as equals, Baba had no difficulty stepping in to make his own those who had been rejected by their own families. He started an ashram and a leprosy hospital, Avadhut Bhagwan Ram Kusht Sewa Ashram (Avadhut Bhagwan Ram Leprosy Service Ashram), at Parao, Varanasi.

It is important to look at Baba's denial of the seat of Kinaram Sthal and his desire to establish a whole new seat that would, in some senses, rival the *sthal*. We can presume with some certainty that Baba, once enlightened, had a good idea of what he wanted to do with the rest of his life. He did not want to be encumbered by the weight of the seat of a tradition that was so old and established it could not be changed easily. Also, it would have been disrespectful to the history and traditions of the *sthal* as well as to his own guru, who was alive at that time, to begin altering the age-old practices that *aughar*s had become synonymous with. But for Baba to come back to society for social service, it was essential that the outer manifestations of an *aughar*'s life be brought into closer conformity with the structures of "normal" social behavior, leading to practices that could not be contained within the older structure. Although Baba always had a great respect for the Kinaram Sthal's principles, being so old and established, the *sthal* was fairly well concretized in form and tradition and in people's minds. In effect, then, when Baba drew the line and started a new seat of Aghor—one that had links with the old tradition yet was new in its form and spirit—it was the beginning of a new form of Aghor culture, rooted in hard ascetic practices but blossoming within society. Metaphysically, it amounted to Shiva acting as Vishnu, the nurturer in the Hindu pantheon.

Many years later, in 1978, after consulting with his guru Baba Rajeshwar Ram, Baba Bhagwan Ram had an eight-year-old boy—Siddhartha

Gautam Ram—installed as the future successor to Baba Rajeshwar Ram (Parry 1982, 103). Baba Rajeshwar Ram relinquished his mortal frame within four months of signing the succession papers, relieved that the new successor would have Baba Bhagwan Ram's guidance.

The society that Baba Bhagwan Ram founded served the leprosy patients but also sought to inculcate a better social consciousness in the larger society. The organization's aims were simple but powerful when practiced in daily life by its lay members: to consider the whole of humanity as one's family; to have respect toward women; to encourage little boys and girls toward progress in their lives; never to behave in a cruel manner toward children; to donate a little once a year to the organization; to conduct life-passage rites according to the methods observed in the ashram without placing strictures on family members to do the same; to help members of the society in need; to pursue one's respective business honestly; and to meditate daily to the best of one's ability on the mantra given by the ashram.

Shri Sarveshwari Samooh progressed rapidly under Baba's direction, soon becoming a refuge for hundreds of thousands to get leprosy treatment free of cost. People began to donate resources and land to the ashram. Maharaja Vijaybhushan Singh Ju Dev of Jashpur in Madhya Pradesh state donated three villages from his estate in September 1959, where Baba then established several ashrams (B. Singh 1992, 22–23). The facilities of the hospital, which produced *ayurvedic* (traditional) medicine within the ashram precincts, slowly began to improve. Enough agricultural land was donated to the ashram to cultivate fields and become self-sufficient.

Changes to the Aghor Tradition

Baba has often been described as a saint who departed from the beaten path. That is true in more ways than one, but most significantly through his effort to make what was a liminal tradition into a socially responsible and established one. It is true that Baba Kinaram before him had also helped people through his magical powers, and had established a number of monasteries. But the form of help that Baba has given to Aghor, a coherent social organization through the establishment of Shri Sarveshwari Samooh, is unique in the history of the Aghor tradition. Baba joined

Aghor to society in such a manner that common people can understand what Aghor stands for, and they can also participate in its practices rather than regard it as an inaccessible, transgressive, cremation-ground-based tradition.

Baba brought about these changes in the following way:

1. He moved Aghor tradition from the cremation ground into the ashram system.

2. He discouraged his followers and *sadhak*s (monks, spiritual practitioners) from performing miracles in society.

3. Through Sarveshwari Samooh, he inspired people to work toward the benefit of society.

4. Through festivals such as Navaratri (the nine-day worship of Mother Goddess, celebrated twice a year at six-month intervals) and Gurupurnima (the Hindu festival of veneration of the guru), he empowered the people to participate in Aghor practices and presented to them a very simple way of worshipping the *shakti* (Verma 2004, 71).

Baba's emphasis on social service is evident even in his conversations with his ascetic and renunciate disciples—not just his householder devotees. He spoke to his disciple Yogini Meghmala in the following way: "If your use of the cremation ground benefits the nation and society, then continue to do so. Otherwise the ashrams where I have stayed for long periods and performed many penances, the places whose very soil I have breathed life in, reside in those and guide the path of your guru-brothers. . . . If you have an interest in such places, you should do so" (Shri Sarveshwari Samooh 1984, 94). This quotation provides a telling contrast between the necessity of a cremation-ground-based lifestyle and the *sadhana* of service that an ashram-based lifestyle entails. And yet how necessary, then, is practice in the cremation ground? Most tantric texts would extol it as an ideal place for attaining esoteric magical powers. Baba Bhagwan Ram, however, interpreted it as a sacred but unifying place where all distinctions of caste, class, status, wealth, gender, and ego are subsumed into the nondiscriminating fire of the pyre. An experience of such immutable transformation of human life and body generates detachment from normal worldly pursuits as well as a realization of the fallacy of discriminating between humans on the basis of social, economic, political, or gender traits. He then transposed the states of mind generated by the cremation-ground experience to social life, pointing out that all human beings burn in the pyre of their own desires and that an *aughar* who transcends his own pyre by burning up his desires becomes a true *aughar* in several senses of the term. The *aughar* can then remain unmoved by the transient events of life yet serve all without discriminating on the basis of physical form, wealth, caste, class, or gender (Shri Sarveshwari Samooh 1982). In essence, Baba Bhagwan Ram raised the fundamental question, Why spiritual pursuit? Should it be just a personal route to divinity, or should it be a service-oriented route to becoming divine in the perception of those who are served?

Baba Bhagwan Ram did not deny the efficacy of the cremation ground as an ideal place for *sadhana* or the necessity of a focused spiritual pursuit, but elements of the Aghor lifestyle clearly did not merit retention in the new social context of the ashram. In fact, one might say that Baba changed the old ways of *sadhana* in the ashram context because those ways were becoming another kind of conditioning—indeed, a form of addiction—for those disciples who regarded transgressive behavior as a goal in itself. For instance, Baba prohibited the use of intoxicants, including alcohol, in the ashram. He could see very well that Aghor life had components that were designed to break the conditioning of an ascetic's former life, liberating his mind from fetters of social enculturation. However, these very same components, outside of the cremation ground, within the boundary walls of the ashram, could produce a conditioning that bordered on indulgence. This is the third line Baba drew to change the Aghor tradition with respect to a practice that had become synonymous with the Aghor way of life—a change that his own guru, Baba Rajeshwar Ram, was not very happy with.

Bindeshwari Bhaiya, who used to be the *ayurvedic* doctor in Baba's leprosy hospital, narrated a story of how Baba actually beat him with the pipe of his hookah one evening in 1974 when he caught him drinking within the ashram precincts (Ak. Ram 2003, 130–34). That incident led to the prohibition of all intoxicants within the ashram and for all his devotees. Baba then sent Bindeshwari Bhaiya with *prasad* (sanctified food) from his ashram to Kinaram Sthal, knowing full well that his guru would give

Bindeshwari Bhaiya alcohol as part of the meal. With Bindeshwari Bhaiya's refusal of the alcohol, Baba would be able to convey the change, the line he had drawn, to his guru, at once changing an old way of life and establishing a new one. As expected, when Baba Rajeshwar Ram found out about this prohibition, his reaction was, "[D]oes an *aughar* ever give up alcohol?" He then bought a bottle of alcohol, came to Baba Bhagwan Ram's ashram at Parao, Varanasi, and created a scene. Bindeshwari Bhaiya described it thus:

> When he (Baba Rajeshwar Ram) came to Parao, Baba [Bhagwan Ram] was sitting on his chair. On seeing the old abbot's *ricksha*, Sarkar Baba (an honorific way to address Baba Bhagwan Ram) went inside his room. The old abbot entered his gate and then his foyer, clicking his wooden sandals loudly on the floor. He followed Baba into the room where he had gone. I followed the old abbot in. When I entered Baba's room, Baba was standing in a corner with bowed head, looking straight at the old abbot. The old abbot was looking over Baba very carefully up and down. Then the old abbot turned and came out. He kicked the two flower-pots kept outside. They both broke into a hundred pieces! . . . At night, while massaging his feet, I said to Baba, "The old abbot put me in a fix. He said, I will beat you if you don't drink."
>
> Baba began to laugh when he heard this. He said, "Let it be. No one is going to drink in my ashram from today." (Ak. Ram 2003, 130–34)

Baba evidently changed the old ways in opposition to his own guru's wishes not because he hated alcohol, but because he wanted to break the conditioning of alcohol and other substances normally used in *sadhana*. These substances, in the ashram context, were antithetical. He could see that people experienced a certain thrill in coming to him and in *behaving* as they thought he would have behaved during his *sadhana*, but doing so set a socially negative example for the young people associated with the ashram—it promoted self-indulgence and alcoholism more than service and self-control. Not only did Baba stop the use of alcohol for everyone in the ashram, but he accepted that policy for himself, too. However, this change clearly meant departing from the "old ways"—it was an act of transgression against the transgressive practices of the Aghor tradition itself that did not go unnoticed by his own guru. Their silent confrontation in his room displays that Baba remained respectful yet defiant, and his own guru made it clear through his actions that this change was not to his liking. Had Baba been at the *sthal* at this point, he would have found it much harder to succeed in his endeavors. But at his own ashram, his new vision of Aghor was accepted. However—and this is where the metaphor of drawing a line in water truly becomes stark—not only did Baba start a new stream of Aghor from the old river, but in fact he also tried to give this older tradition a more coherent form by publishing both books that he authored as well as old *sthal* documents that he had "rescued" and edited. Given the hands-off attitude that his own guru had toward all things material as well as the unhindered participation of those associated with the *sthal* in its activities, Baba took the initiative to modernize the *sthal* with electrical fixtures and light bulbs—actions that, again, displeased his guru, though later in his life he accepted them in his own "hands-off" way.

Regarding the *sadhana* of monks and lay devotees in his ashram, Baba Bhagwan Ram used to say, "There are many different kinds of *sadhanas*. All *sadhanas* are practicable, but not all *sadhanas* are practicable by everyone." According to him, Aghor *sadhana* in a social context entails—on the part of the Aghor *sadhak* or practitioner—being true to the promises made to the guru. These promises require, first, that one eschew wealth, fame, power, and position.

Having observed very closely during his *sadhana* days the facts of everyday social life that made people miserable, and in keeping with his vision of helping those who came to him without elaborate sermons, Baba advised his disciples to observe the following simple restrictions in their daily lives: not to hurt anyone; not to gamble or steal; to avoid drunken behavior, alcohol, and other drugs; not to lie or give false testimony; to live with a greed-free heart; to remain steadfast to their duty; not to give in to feelings of retaliation even when insulted; to keep free from association with greedy and dishonest people; to remain grateful to those who benefit them; and to observe celibacy except with one's own wife in daily life. As the reader may perceive, if a lay disciple followed these instructions, in his life he would observe ascetic practices and gain equanimity while cultivating empathy for other human beings. For his monk disciples who had progressed on the spiritual path and had attained magical powers, Baba's instructions involved even more self-sacrifice:

> The pure vision that has risen in you will be beneficial. You become the deity of well being for every living being. As need be, you become water, you become air, you become the earth, you become the sky, you become the light, you become the fire. Whenever, wherever you see living beings suffering from a lack of something, you become that thing, and present yourself to them. . . . Young ascetic, *aughar*-Aghoreshwars perform these actions regularly in a mysterious manner. It is nothing to wonder at, hey! Now you will have to do this too. You will understand. (Shri Sarveshwari Samooh 1982, 24)

Baba recognized that his disciples had the power to make things happen, but he shrewdly mitigated their human propensity for egotism born of power as well as the temptation to display magical power for social prestige into something that is sublime.

It was not as if he was opposed to the more esoteric Aghor practices; it was just that he felt they had their rightful place elsewhere. It is for this reason that one can see among Baba's disciples not only *sadhana*s that deal with personal character and social service, but many other kinds of more "typical" Aghor practices also. An episode from *Aghoreshwar Samvedansheel* (Shri Sarveshwari Samooh 1984, 98–99) illustrates the practice of *ashtang* (eight-limbed) *sadhana* whereby the practitioner can separate all his body parts like so many appendages without any loss of blood and then become whole in an instant. Another *sadhana* described in fascinating detail in *Aghor Guru Guh* (Shri Sarveshwari Samooh 1982, 25–29) demonstrates how Baba trained two of his disciples, Sambhav and Darshi, as well as a devoted householder named Gohan in esoteric practices of the cremation ground where they could experience the unity of their life force with that of their guru—all this without the slightest trace of egotism and while being asked to use their powers for social benefit.

Not only did Baba try to prevent the misuse of spiritual accomplishments (*siddhis*) for display of powers, but he brought *shakti-puja* into the ashram—defining it in a unique way. Baba addressed all women older than a certain age as "Mother." This is nothing unusual in the saint traditions of

India. But he described all married men as worshippers of *shakti*. Instead of worshipping what he described as cartoonlike pictures of Goddess Durga wielding various kinds of weaponry, he reinterpreted Durga as the *shakti* residing within the *durg* (fortress) of the home and the family, toward whom all men need to have empathy and appreciation. This could happen only when they had control over their senses, when they were not drunk with masculine ego or alcohol, and when they had cultivated the right attitude toward women. He felt strong enough about this issue that he set up a special forum within Shri Sarveshwari Samooh for women to voice their ideas and concerns. As Verma Ji, a devotee of Baba, writes: "He wanted women to express their experiences. They should express their views on widow remarriage, exclusion of women on auspicious occasions, dowry, and so on, and that they should oppose these social evils. He wanted them to relinquish the feeling of shyness and fear of public speaking, and to express their views openly and bring their talents to light" (Verma 2004, 155). Baba's forum was not, however, simply a discussion forum. He himself instituted the system of dowryless weddings in the ashram, where weddings would be performed with the consent of both the bride and the groom, without dowry or excessive ceremony, and the whole simple ritual would be over within an hour—in marked contrast to the expense, pomp, and show of the normal Indian wedding.

Other works of social service that Baba initiated in the ashram include education for both boys and girls, hospital and eye camps, and disaster relief. We have just to examine the websites of three different Aghor ashrams run by Baba's disciples to see the reinterpretation and repositioning of Aghor in the social realm. There were no websites during Baba's own lifetime, but now Baba Kinaram's *sthal*, the Shri Sarveshwari Samooh ashram at Parao, and the ashram at Sonoma, California, have very active websites. Yet they are as plain as any other social website, without the iconic markings of the Aghor tradition.[8] What we find on them are histories of

8. Baba Kinaram Sthal: http://www.aghorpeeth.org/Index.aspx; Shri Sarveshwari Samooh ashram at Parao: http://aghoryaan.org; ashram at Sonoma, California: http://www.sonomaashram.org/.

the Aghor tradition, Baba Kinaram, and Baba Bhagwan Ram as well as the activities of social service run by them, but without the transgressive motifs that have so characterized Aghor.

The data presented in this section can be summarized as constituting two essential elements. On the one hand is the generation of spiritual power through avoidance of self-indulgence of any kind, whether sensory as in the case of normal householders or spiritual as in the case of monks and mendicants. On the other is the use of powers gained by spiritual practice for social benefit via self-control for the normal householder and through self-sacrifice for the monks and mendicants. These two essential elements are not entirely separate, either. For a steadfast householder devotee, self-control and adherence to his guru's words can generate enough equanimity and fearlessness to lead him to the cremation ground for further explorations. For the steadfast monk who gains powers in the cremation ground, the ultimate test of his spirituality is in their application within the social realm for the benefit of others. This is where the line drawn in water becomes especially clear in its imaginary existence.

Baba Bhagwan Ram created an institution where esoteric practices take place outside of the ashram in the wilderness or cremation grounds, but their application happens within the realm of the ashram for helping those who need succor. The life of a monk disciple initiated by him is no longer confined to the cremation ground, although for certain kinds of specialized practices he may have to visit it on occasion. And so now there is a link between the cremation ground and the ashram. By training his disciples in esoteric Aghor practices, and by renovating the Kinaram Sthal and publishing its literature, Baba reinforced the age-old tradition and ensured its continuity. At the same time, within the bounds of his own ashram and for his devotees and disciples, he created an atmosphere of social service and human harmony that, following the Aghor principle of nondiscrimination, allows householders and monks to mingle in an exchange of amity that benefits both. The monks attain *siddhi*s (spiritual powers) but cannot use them for display or personal gain. The householders attain spiritual company and knowledge without having to leave their families or normal daily lives. Baba Bhagwan Ram has given not just an alternative view of Aghor to the world, but an alternative way of conducting penance to those seekers who have yet to become adept at the life of a cremation ground. Even if they become adept at it, their accomplishments can only be recognized if tested in the fire of social service. Society and spirit, divided intellectually, become one whole again in this practice of holistic nondiscrimination.

If we look at Baba Bhagwan Ram's initiative from a wider perspective, we can see that the ethos of "service" is not new to Hindu religious groups. Indeed, as William Pinch points out, "many Indian monks were respected as able healers, and service (*seva*) remains a central ideal of most Indian religious traditions" (1996, 3–4). This ethos of service is echoed among at least some of the householder Nath yogis of Rajasthan, where ritually warding off hail and pestilence is a sought-after skill, and in Khakhar's description of Kanphata yogis' charity work in the Kachh region of Gujarat, especially during droughts and famines (Gold and Gold 1984, 117; Khakhar 1878, 52). Similarly, to serve "*jiva* as Shiva" was a motto that Swami Vivekananda learned from his guru Swami Ramakrishna Paramahansa and put into practice at Belur Math with the philosophy of "karma yoga," a philosophy that animates the Ramakrishna Mission's practices even today (Ramakrishna Mission 2006–2009).

What is noteworthy with these examples and perhaps significant to Baba Bhagwan Ram's contribution is that these examples do not reflect an effort to change an existing tradition into something new according to the needs of the times. The service performed by the Nath yogis in my example appears to take place within the existing structures of the tradition, and the Ramakrishna Mission's practices can be seen as a new institution started by a charismatic leader, not an attempt to change an already existing one. Further research on the philosophies and practices of modern-day spiritual leaders in India can throw more light on the tenet of service and the many ways in which it takes expression to give us a better picture of *seva* in the Hindu religious landscape.

In summation, one might well ask, Can the changes such as the ones Baba Bhagwan Ram initiated work within an old structure? Or does it necessarily involve restructuring the old in a fundamental way? This restructuring is evident in India in two of the very popular stories of the subcontinent—that of the Buddha, who embarked on a quest for finding a solution to sorrow and ended with the promulgation of a new religious order, and that of Rama, who went into the forest to obey his father and did not just triumph over the demon king Ravana, but also united the Indian subcontinent through a series of alliances. Baba Bhagwan Ram returned from his spiritual quest to modify both the tradition to which he belonged and the society that makes the larger frame for the spiritual tradition. He institutionalized the individualized compassion we have witnessed in the stories of Baba Kinaram. Unlike Buddha, though, Baba did not live to be eighty years old. He relinquished his mortal frame at the age of fifty-five, leaving behind a legacy to his disciples where they coexist in two domains simultaneously: as a part of the larger tradition of *aughar*s who are detached from their senses and society and as new social workers who have a mandate to serve the society through all their senses. Depending on point of view, the waters flow divided by the imaginary line or not.

Works Cited

Balfour, Edward. 1885. "Aghora." In *Cyclopaedia of India*, 1:42. London: Bernard Quaritch.

Balfour, Henry. 1897. "Life History of an Aghori Fakir." *Journal of the Anthropological Institute* 26: 340–57.

Barrett, Ron. 2002. "Aghor Medicine: Pollution, Power, and Healing in Banaras, Northern India." PhD diss., Emory Univ.

Briggs, George Weston. 1982. *Gorakhnath and the Kanphata Yogis*. New Delhi: Motilal Banarsidas.

Chaturvedi, Yagyanarayan. 1973. *Aughar Bhagwan Ram*. Varanasi, India: Shri Sarveshwari Samooh. Mu'inuddin Chishti

Chaudhary, Suryanarayana, trans. 1985. *Buddhacarita of Asvaghosa*. New Delhi: Motilal Banarasidas.

Crooke, William. 1895. "Aghori, Aghorpanthi, Aughar." In *Tribes and Castes of the Northwest Frontier*, 1:26. Calcutta: Office of the Superintendent of Government Printing, India.

Davidson, Ronald M. 2002. *Indian Esoteric Buddhism*. New York: Columbia Univ. Press.

Dhal, Dr. U. N., trans. 2000. *Siva Purana (Uttarakhanda)*. New Delhi: Nag.

Eliade, Mircea. 1958. *Yoga: Immortality and Freedom*. Princeton, NJ: Princeton Univ. Press.

Gold, Daniel, and Ann Grodzins Gold. 1984. "The Fate of the Householder Nath." *History of Religions* 24: 113–32.

Griffith, Ralph T. H. 1897. *The Hymns of the Rigveda.* Vol. 2. 2nd ed. Benares, India: E.J. Lazarus.

Guinness Book of World Records. 1998. "Most Leprosy Patients Treated." At http://guinnessworldrecords.com. Accessed Mar. 2005.

Gupta, Roxanne Poormon. 1993. "The Politics of Heterodoxy and the Kina Rami Ascetics of Banaras." PhD diss., Syracuse Univ.

Horner, I. A., trans. 1971. *The Book of the Discipline (Vinaya-Pitaka).* Vol. 4 (Mahavagga). London: Luzac & Company.

Kavi, Sankara, trans. 1964. *Harsa Charita of Banabhatta.* Hindi translation by Pt. Jagannatha Pathaka. Varanasi, India: Chowkhama Vidyabhawan.

Keith, Arthur Berriedale. 1914. *The Veda of the Black Yajus School.* Harvard Oriental Series. Cambridge, MA: Harvard Univ. At http://www.sacred-texts.com/hin/yv/. Accessed Mar. 2005.

Khakhar, D. P. 1878. "History of the Kanphatas of Kachh." *Indian Antiquary* 7: 47–53.

Lorenzen, David N. 1972. *Kapalikas & Kalamukhas.* New Delhi: Thomson Press (India).

Matthews, John, ed. 2002. *Secrets of the Druids.* New York: Black Dog & Leventhal.

Mishra, Saroj Kumar. 2001. *Aghor Mat: Siddhant aur sadhana.* Varanasi, India: Aghor Shodh Samsthan Aur Granthalaya, Aghor Parishad Trust, Avadhoot Bhagwan Ram Kusht Sewa Ashram.

Parry, Jonathan P. 1982. "Sacrificial Death and the Necrophagous Ascetics." In *Death and the Regeneration of Life*, edited by Maurice Bloch and Jonathan Parry, 74–110. Cambridge: Cambridge Univ. Press.

———. 1985. "Aghori Ascetics of Benares." In *Indian Religion*, edited by Richard Burghart and Audrey Cantlie, 51–78. New York: St. Martin's Press.

Pinch, William R. 1996. *Peasants and Monks in British India.* Berkeley: Univ. of California Press.

Ram, Aghoreshwar Bhagwan. 1991. *Aghor Vachan Shastra.* Varanasi, India: Shri Sarveshwari Samooh.

Ram, Akinchan. 2003. *Bhagwanramleelaamrit.* Raigarh, India: Aghor Guru Peeth Trust.

Ramakrishna Mission. 2006–2009. "Ramakrishna Math and Ramakrishna Mission." At http://www.belurmath.org/Ideology.htm. Accessed Nov. 26, 2010.

Rao, K. B. Ramakrishna. 1964. "The Buddhacarita and the Samkhya of Arada Kalama." *Adyar Library Bulletin* 28: 231–41.

Shastri, Pt. Ramanatha Tripathi, trans. 1977. *Prabodhachandrodaya of Sri Krishna Mishra Yati*. Varanasi, India: Chaukhambha Amarabharati Prakashan.

Shastri, Sri Shesharaja Sharma, trans. 1998. *Malatimadhava of Mahakavi Bhavabhuti*. Varanasi, India: Chowkhambha Sanskrit Series.

Shri Sarveshwari Samooh. 1981. *Aghoreshwar smriti vachanamrit*. Varanasi, India: Shri Sarveshwari Samooh.

———. 1982. *Aghor guru guh*. Varanasi, India: Shri Sarveshwari Samooh.

———. 1984. *Aghoreshwar samvedansheel*. Varanasi, India: Shri Sarveshwari Samooh.

Singh, Bala Sharan. 1992. *Aghoreshwar Kaa Saannidhya: Mere Sansmaran*. Varanasi, India: Shri Sarveshwari Samooh Sansthan Devashanam.

Singh, Udayabhan, trans. 1999. *Aghoracharya Baba Kinaram Ji*. Varanasi, India: Aghoracharya Baba Kinaram Aghor Shodh Evam Sewa Sansthan, Krin Kund.

Verma, Krishna Kumar. 2004. *Aughar Sant aur Aghor Parampara*. Banora, India: Aghor Guru Peeth.

Wilson, H. H. [1862] 1976. *Religions of the Hindus*. Vol. 1. New Delhi: Asian Publication Services.

Woznicki, Andrew N. 1998. "Endocannibalism of the Yanomami." *Summit Times* 6, nos. 18–19. At http://users.rcn.com/salski/No18-19Folder/Endocannibal ism.htm. Accessed Aug. 2006.

13

≈

Indian Arrival Day

Shifting Boundaries in the Celebration of a National Holiday in Trinidad

LINDSEY HARLAN

IN TRINIDAD, Hindus, Muslims, and Christians with Indian ancestry celebrate Indian Arrival Day, a national holiday commemorating the arrival of the first group of indentured servants from India on May 30, 1845. In public venues, including schools, places of worship, and community centers, people tell the story of arrival and reflect on the ancestral lines that have led from an India of the past to the present-day nation of Trinidad and Tobago.

This essay explores ways in which commemorations of Indian Arrival Day have not only distinguished Indo-Trinidadians from others in this cosmopolitan nation but also utilized the trope of arrival as a metonym that relates the experience of Indian arrival to the broader project of nation building.[1] In various discourses, Indian arrival refers to the first

For generous guidance throughout my research in Trinidad, I am grateful to Brinsley Samaroo. I am also indebted to Funso Aiyejina, Kusha Haraksingh, Aisha Khan, Sherry Ann Singh, Sais Bagnola, Kumar Mahabir, Stephen Harris, Paula Richman, and Rick Asher. For help on my larger research project, I am deeply thankful for the help provided by many others, who will be acknowledged in future publications.

1. Most people of Indian descent live on the island of Trinidad and are typically referred to as "Indo-Trinidadians" or "East Indians." Viranjini Munasinghe notes that "East Indian" is more common than "Indo-Trinidadian" in popular parlance and that it connotes

Indian arrival, more broadly to the first and subsequent arrivals of Indian indentured laborers, and finally to the continuation of "arriving," in the sense of succeeding, by contemporary Indo-Trinidadians who enjoy relative prosperity. Indo-Trinidadians and others have strategically deployed this multivalent trope of arrival as a metonym linking the Indian presence to the citizenry. Identification of the arrival of Indians with the formation of the citizenry has been both useful and troublesome according to the agenda of those making it. In political rhetoric, arrival has frequently served as a cipher for Indian integration, one that indexes nation and nationalism while preserving a distinctive and undiluted Indian ethnic identity. The distinction of Indianness has been linked to a secondary or underling metonymic relation in which the separate religions of Hinduism and Islam (or emblems of them) have operated individually to express the distinctiveness of shared ethnicity—-one common not only to Indo-Trinidadian Muslims and Hindus, but also to Christians. Prominent among the contexts for this expression is the celebration of Indian Arrival Day. In the discourse of many Afro-Trinidadians and others who are not of Indian descent, however, arrival of people from many places in India who together forged an ethnic identity has often served as a cipher for mixing or dilution that accords with a hegemonic ideology promoting cultural blending or fusion.[2]

What follows considers the twofold notion of arrival as something that has (1) served to associate linkage of Indian (Hindu and Muslim) arrival with arrivals of others and (2) bonded together many religiously diverse Indo-Trinidadians as a distinct ethnic community, one resisting

---

marginalization. She also treats various valences of alternate terms for Afro-Trinidadians (2001b, 30 n. 3). The hyphenated term should not be understood to distinguish Trinidad from Tobago, but to refer to (the far less frequently used name) "Trinbagonians." Although indentured servants were recruited from various places in South Asia, the majority came from what are now Bihar and Uttar Pradesh; the major "reconstruction" or reimagining of community draws heavily from traditions of this region. See Samaroo 2004, 45.

2. For analysis of blending and distinctiveness or purity, see Munasinghe 2002 and 2006. On cultural tropes, see also Khan 2004 and Munasinghe 2001a. Compare these works with Bauman 2004 and Thomas 2006.

blending or fusion with other ethnic groups. Because this essay appears in a volume constituted primarily of essays on India and presumably will be read by those sharing a common interest in and familiarity with India, it begins by providing relevant historical context. It then turns to its twofold agenda by focusing first on the controversial, initial recognition of Indian Arrival Day as a national holiday and by considering key arguments in the strenuous debates about the appropriateness of celebrating the arrival of Indians rather than the arrival of all peoples in the nation. Next, it examines the shifting inclusivity and exclusivity of representations of identity and community made in the context of celebrating Indian Arrival Day. These representations demonstrate that not only those opposed to making Indian Arrival Day a national holiday but also some who support it have selectively but powerfully identified the arrival of religiously diverse Indians as a metonym for cohesion and so the constitution of the ethnically and religiously diverse citizenry. By way of conclusion, it compares this multiply constructed Indo-Trinidadian metonym with a hegemonic Afro-Trinidadian or Creole metonym expressing an encompassing but much contested national identity.[3]

Brief Orientation: Colonization and Immigration

Situated off the coast of Venezuela, reaping rich oil revenues, and sharing myriad doubly diasporic ties with Canada and the United States, Trinidad was given its name, "Trinity," by Christopher Columbus, who claimed the territory for Spain in 1498. The British captured Trinidad from the Spanish at the beginning of the eighteenth century and shortly afterward began to

3. Munasinghe argues that marked ethnic groups, especially Indo-Trinidadians, are included in the state as citizens but excluded from "the symbolic space of the nation" and its "*control* over the state." She speaks of the "tenuous if mythical congruence between nation and state" that is "reproduced through hegemonic processes whereby a privileged race and class seek to establish a metonymic relation to the nation" (2001b, 1, emphasis in original). "Creole" here is used in its broadest context to refer to people of European ancestry, African ancestry, and a combination of the two (Yelvington 1993, 21n5). For insightful analysis of the term's multivalence and its treatment in scholarship, see Munasinghe 2006. For more on mixing in the construction of ethnicity in identity politics, see Khan 1993.

settle and import slaves. Various European powers, including the French and Dutch, laid claims to the islands of Trinidad and Tobago, but the British prevailed and joined the islands to make a single Crown colony late in the nineteenth century.

Citizens with Indian heritage represent about half of the population of this nation (now about 1.3 million) and live on Trinidad rather than on the relatively sparsely settled island of Tobago. Most of the non-Indian population traces its origins to Africa, from which many ancestors arrived as slaves. The importation of indentured servants from India began after slaves were emancipated in 1834. Most indentured Indians worked as agricultural laborers and were distributed most heavily in the sugar-producing areas, mostly in the central part of the island, which is dominated by the Caroni Plain.[4]

Despite the degrading, disease-ridden, and painful conditions under which Indians served their terms of indenture, since 1995 Indians have celebrated Indian Arrival Day as the beginning of their presence. Because peoples of African descent had since 1985 celebrated Emancipation Day as a national holiday commemorating the liberation of slaves from their life-long condition of enforced servitude,[5] members of the Indian community were eager to have a holiday recognize their ancestry as well, but their efforts met resistance from those who did not necessarily understand the arrival of Indians as an appropriate counterpart to the liberation of slaves. Although the emancipation of slaves was clearly a cause for celebration, the arrival of replacement laborers (who, like slaves, suffered many indignities, including severe limitations on their freedom)

4. The importation of indentured servants continued until 1917 and brought over less than 150,000 laborers. See Samaroo 1987.

5. Recognition of Indian Arrival Day was followed by recognition of Spiritual Baptist Liberation Shouter Day in 1996. Prior to the passage of Indian Arrival Day, there was recognition of Eid and Divali, both in 1969. When arrival was recognized, Whit Monday, celebrating Pentecost, was dropped. See the fascinating Opinion of the High Court of Justice of Trinidad and Tobago, *Sanatan Dharma Maha Sabha of Trinidad and Tobago et. al. v. Attorney General,* which was rendered by Judge P. Jamadar, December 26, 2006. Emancipation Day replaced Discovery Day, celebrating Columbus.

did not strike everyone as an occasion meriting commemoration by a national holiday.

The Dilemma: Arrival Day or Indian Arrival Day?

Indo-Trinidadians began to lobby for a holiday to celebrate Indian arrival well before Trinidad gained independence from the British in 1962. A push for recognition began in 1945, along with planning for a grand centenary celebration to be held in Skinner Park. The holiday was not given official status, however, until just prior to the sesquicentennial of Indian arrival in 1995.[6] This was an election year in which the Afro-Trinidadian-dominated People's National Movement Party (PNM) led by Prime Minister Patrick Manning would lose to a coalition government led by Basdeo Panday, who became the first Trinidadian prime minister of Indian descent.[7]

Speaking in 1995 in support of the motion to celebrate Indian arrival with a national holiday, Trevor Sudama, an Indo-Trinidadian member of Parliament, argued alongside many others that the PNM government should create the national holiday because it would act "to sensitise other ethnic groups to the diverse inputs and contributions . . . in the historical evolution" of Trinidad and Tobago and so "contribute to fostering greater inter-ethnic respect, tolerance and understanding." It would thus have "a wider historical significance for the whole national community" (quoted in Jayaram 2003, 131).[8]

Sudama's image of a day celebrating Indian arrival did not depict Indian arrival as standing for the arrival of all citizens, but it came ever so close: it suggested that celebrating Indian arrival would contribute to cohesion among the citizenry. Official appreciation of Indian arrival would create interethnic respect and serve as a sort of national social glue. Given

6. Among the prominent groups that agitated for recognition were the Indian Revival and Reform Association, the Hindu Seva Sangh, the Divine Life Society, and the politically powerful Sanatan Dharma Maha Sabha. See Ramlakhan 1998 and 2004.

7. In 2010, the country elected another prime minister with Indian ancestry, its first female head of state: Kamla Persad-Bissessar.

8. Jayaram excerpts a pamphlet that Sudama issued about the proceedings (2003, 140n4).

that many Indo-Trinidadians, feeling marginalized by a history of Afro-Trinidadian hegemony, equated "national" with "Creole," many Indo-Trinidadians believed that granting recognition to Indian arrival would foster national cohesion. Not just an expedient excuse for recognition, the claim of potential national cohesion seemed plausible to many Indo-Trinidadians because their recognition would make them feel included within the nation, reduce the resentment caused by the exclusive celebration of Emancipation Day, and so foster patriotism. Opponents, however, argued that the holiday would fossilize, if not foment, ethnic splintering.

The PNM-controlled government ultimately passed a motion with hopes of satisfying proponents agitating for recognition of Indian arrival, but it stipulated that although the annual holiday would be celebrated on May 30, the day of Indian arrival, it would be known not as "Indian Arrival Day," but as "Arrival Day." This compromise rejected a much disparaged previous proposal that would have replaced the celebration of Indian arrival with a commemoration of the date on which indentureship was abolished in 1920 (Ramlakhan 2004, 195). Although Indo-Trinidadians were pleased that Arrival Day would be celebrated on the date of arrival and thus signal their long-standing Indian presence, they were unhappy about the name's glaring elision. It rendered the holiday plastic and pliable, for it could now be shaped to fit the experience of people from various communities and so expand the advocated arrival commemoration to encompass those citizens not tracing their origins to India. It seemed that not only the shape of the name but the shape of the body of celebrants had, theoretically at least, shifted so as to be identifiable with everyone coming whenever from wherever, though the timing of the celebration, May 30, would also suggest that the holiday's primary valence connected Indians with their predecessors in 1845.

The elision deeply offended many Indians. They argued that because the national celebration was to occur on May 30, it should be named to indicate the significance of the date. If the timing of the holiday made the significance obvious, then why not mark the holiday as "Indian"? As Basdeo Panday objected in the *Trinidad Guardian*, "They could call it what they want; we all know it as the Indian Arrival Day. Why not call it just that? Why are you ashamed of the word Indian?" (quoted in Jayaram 2003, 132).

Moreover, calling the holiday "Arrival Day" rather than "Indian Arrival Day" defeated one of the proponents' goals: providing recognition that would parallel or complement the recognition of Emancipation Day, which had become a national holiday during the sesquicentennial year marking passage of the Emancipation Bill by Parliament. The sesquicentennial of Indian arrival, Indian proponents argued, should likewise usher in an annual holiday, one that would mark the contribution of the Indian presence to the nation on a similar anniversary. Indo-Trinidadians were unmoved by opponents' argument that Emancipation Day was not called "African," so there was no cause to complain about the dropping of "Indian."

Indo-Trinidadians who were concerned about the new holiday's name believed that it would tend to cause the Indian presence to merge with and even be diminished by the constellation of arrivals in a multiethnic crowd. The others in this crowd would include not only those descended from African slaves, but those whose forebears were Chinese laborers, Syrian merchants, and Europeans—the latter even including those implicated in one way or another in promoting and profiting from slavery and indentureship. They asked, should the arrival of any and all really be construed as analogous to and encompassing of the arrival of Indians who served as indentured laborers during British rule?

The replacement of the name "Arrival Day" with "Indian Arrival Day" following the elections and the installation of Panday as prime minister did not, of course, put an end to conflict over Indian arrival as a cause for celebration. Even many Indo-Trinidadians who had pushed for a national holiday continued to press the point that although Indian arrival should be publicly celebrated by Indo-Trinidadians, arrival had not been a joyous occasion for poor Indian indentured servants, many of whom had been duped by recruiters with embellished descriptions of indentured life that bore little resemblance to the harsh conditions under which they actually were to live.[9] These conditions led many, including academics, to

9. On this duping, including the representation of Trinidad as "Chini-dad" or "Sugar Land," see Samaroo 1987, 26–28. Samaroo notes that because of the misrepresentations,

characterize indentured labor as a form of slavery or an institution highly comparable to slavery, even though they supported Indian Arrival Day celebrations.[10]

The representation of indenture as slavery identified, to a greater or lesser extent, the experiences of African and Indian laborers. If Indian Arrival Day commemorated Indian slavery, then, it would certainly seem, Indian slavery, whose inception was the reason for recognition of an Arrival Day, served in this context as a metonym for all enforced servitude in Trinidad. Hence, those Indo-Trinidadians who accepted the representation of indenture as slavery but who had rejected the initial (generic) "Arrival Day" holiday could be seen as replacing one Arrival Day's metonymic structure (the arrival of one group indexing the arrivals of all) for another closely associated but more restrictive one (the slavery of one group—Indians—standing on that day, paradoxically and uncomfortably, for the slavery of all). In the context of *Indian* Arrival Day, however, the arrival of Indian "slaves" marks clearly the particular ancestors worthy of commemoration on that day as *Indians* whose (temporarily imposed) slave labor was to be distinguished from and to be substituted for that enslavement whose termination was celebrated by Emancipation Day.

Metonyms aside, not all Indo-Trinidadians have accepted the characterization of indentured servants as slaves. In fact, many have vehemently objected to it. Stressing the sacrifice of ancestors who *chose* to come from India, they tend to stress the voluntary nature of their forebears' decision to leave home. This willingness to give up freedom is the preeminent cause for celebration: the sacrifice enabled future generations gradually to enjoy upward mobility and to make important contributions of voluntary

---

recruiters, like captors in Africa, were engaged in kidnapping (25). Among the promises made by recruiters were high wages and easy work—for example, "sifting sugar" (Klass 1961, 9). Kusha Haraksingh says that in the "later years of the indenture system, when returning migrants had exposed the emptiness of the promises which had been held out, the recruiters were often able to approach the villages only at their peril" (2002, 3).

10. For an example of scholarship representing indenture as slavery, see Tinker 1993. On the potential irony of participation in Indian Arrival Day events by academics writing about indentureship as slavery, see Lokaisingh-Meighoo 2001.

and valuable labor to the benefit of this new homeland.[11] Moreover, as Viranjini Munasinghe has noted, despite many academicians' emphasis on the colonial exploitation of Indians who were deprived of freedom, many Indo-Trinidadians see their ancestors' lack of shackles as demonstrating not only self-determination, but also superiority over those who were forced to come to Trinidad (2001a, 279). The impact of this choice is amplified by many indentured servants' later choices to stay in Trinidad after their indentureship was over and to settle on Crown land offered them in exchange for surrendering passage home. Only about one in five Indian immigrants went back to India after serving out the terms of their contract in Trinidad (Vertovec 1992, 73). Needless to say, the claim of superiority is rebuttable. African slaves were not offered a choice (whether to arrive or leave, given impoverishment), and their descendents hardly see their lack of choice as indexing inferiority. Moreover, even if liberated slaves lacked funding to make a real choice between staying or leaving this place that had come to be their home, the acquisition of the ability to make choices as autonomous human beings is (as the holiday's name would suggest) what is celebrated on Emancipation Day.

Much more can be said about the complex semiotics of commemoration, choice, and agency in the context of Indian arrival. One might, for example, protest that the dichotomy of choice/no choice is patently simplistic. Many Indians came to Trinidad to escape hunger, poverty, political persecution, and other desperate circumstances that left those who signed up with little choice (Klass 1961, 10). One might also speak, however, of the frequent imaging of these immigrants as "adventurers" and "pioneers," blazing a trail to a brighter future.[12] Furthermore, one

11. For example, speaking on Indian Arrival Day in 2008, Basdeo Panday, serving as the opposition leader, said that indentured laborers had "made sacrifices and endured hardships so that future generations would have a better life" (quoted in *Indo-Asian News Service* 2008). See also David Dabydeen's preface to the volume *India in the Caribbean*, which commemorates the 150th anniversary of Indians in the Caribbean (Dabydeen 1987, 9).

12. Timothy Roodal, mayor of San Fernando, used both terms in his welcome speech during the 1945 celebration at Skinner Park. See Ramlakhan 2004, 186, citing Kirpalani, Sinanan, and Seukeran 1945, 70; and *Trinidad and Tobago News Blog* 2007.

might mention representations of agency that liken indentured laborers to entrepreneurs, whose investments in their own labor, then in land, led to prosperity.[13] And one might point to the ubiquitous popular comparison of immigrants to Lord Rama, who voluntarily struck out for the wilderness and brought dharma to a distant land. Such discussions, however, would occasion undue digression from our focus here on Indian Arrival Day.[14]

Thus, let us turn to other factors effecting the shifting communal boundary designated by Indian Arrival Day in contemporary culture. To do so, it is helpful to inspect some popular sources that image and comment upon Indian Arrival. Focusing on their representations of various holidays, including Indian Arrival Day, will enable us to see clearly how they demonstrate demarcation, cohesion, and identification while rendering the religiously diverse Indian community one that indexes the nation.

Commemoration and Religious Divisions That Model Ethnic Cohesion

We begin by looking at *The History of the Indentured Labourers*, a double issue of the popular Chhote Bachche series of comic/coloring books. Volume 1 is "a special issue commemorating Indian Arrival Day" and has on its cover a picture of the *Fatel Rozak* (also spelled *Fatel Razak*), the boat that brought the very first indentured Indian laborers.

Volume 2, which is clearly intended for older children, tells the story of Indian labor in Trinidad, then moves on to detail material culture, illustrated by various representations such as Indian culinary implements, musical instruments, and items of clothing. Starting with this educational

13. Finance Minister Christine Sahadeo imaged Indian indentureship as "entrepreneurship" and praised Indian laborers' "industry, thrift, sacrifice, and creativity," which led them to influence all of the country's economic sectors ("NCIC's Indian Arrival Day 2007 Celebrations" n.d.).

14. Choice, however, is also delimited in representations that emphasize not Rama's decision to leave, but rather the exile that his father's decision to honor his promise enacts. In the *Trinidad Guardian*, Ravi Ji describes Rama as providing "a popular reference for jahajis to manage indenture which they, too, saw as a banvaas—exile" (2006).

15. Cover of the comic/coloring book *The History of the Indentured Labourers*, Chhote Bachche series, issue no. 6, vol. 1 (2002), special issue commemorating Indian Arrival Day. Designed by Ashoka Publications Ltd., Trinidad, West Indies. Courtesy of Sandra Maharajh-Shah.

booklet is useful because the pedagogy, intended to instruct the next generation, makes the messages it conveys particularly vivid.

The first volume narrates the story of arrival via to-be-colored pictures with captions. Page 1 provides a depiction of Indians initially arriving together on the *Fatel Rozak*. It explains that they worked in the cane fields, then it immediately sorts Indians into three communities: Hindus, who "celebrated Diwali and Shiv Ratri"; Muslims, "who celebrated Eid Ul Fitr and Hosay"; and Christians, who "celebrated Christmas."[15] It then reasserts homogeneous cultural identity through shared Indian material culture, including items of clothing, jewelry, fruits, vegetables, sweets, household utensils, and musical instruments. Finally, it identifies the Indian presence as being synonymous with the territorial whole. With no delimiting antecedent, the last page explains that they (Indians) "settled in villages throughout Trinidad." Thus, the distinctiveness of Indian religious identities, indexed by holidays, is both asserted and dispersed, and the arrival of Indians on Trinidadian soil transmutes from a point on the periphery to dispersion throughout the island.[16]

Let us sort out the implications of these representations by first considering the assertion of religious division but at the same time cultural/ethnic unity among the arriving Indians and then analyzing the representation of Indians as spreading throughout the land. The coloring book characterizes religious divisions as constituted by divergent practices—more specifically, the differing observances (or cultural performances) of calendrical rituals identified with Muslims, Hindus, and Christians. The text mentions two holidays for Muslims, two more for Hindus, and one for Christians.

The rituals practiced on these holidays are examined here to demonstrate how religious adherents and others utilize them to construct differences and demonstrate solidarity among Indians after arrival. Here I focus in particular on Divali and Hosay because they are occasions providing for ethnic identification across the religious boundaries they construct and so differ from the Christian holiday of Christmas, which is widely celebrated by Afro-Trinidadians. At the same time, Divali and Hosay have often been enlisted to index the entire religious praxis and so the identity of Indo-Trinidadian Hindus or Muslims. In this vein, the writer Earl Lovelace observed

15. About 90 percent of those arriving were Hindus. Almost all the rest were Muslims. The early converts were converted by the Canadian Presbyterian Mission. Both "Diwali" and "Divali" are common spellings in Trinidad. I typically use "Divali," which accords with the majority of quotations and citations used in this essay.

16. On dispersal and success, see Mung 2004.

that Indian laborers "were tied to their culture because in this new land where they were strangers, it gave them a sense of being" and that religious observances such as Hosay and Divali gave the Indians "a hold on self." (1988, 340, quoted in Munasinghe 2002, 683). The two holidays sum up in a powerful way the religions that so profoundly informed identity and helped Indian laborers manage dislocation in a new land where they felt like and were treated as a group of strangers. The holidays, then and now, have operated as ciphers of religions that in turn, as Aisha Khan has pointed out, have operated as emblems of culture (2004, 14).

The coloring book's selection of two holidays for Muslims suggests a subtext of simultaneously sorting and joining Shi'is (Shi'ites) and Sunnis. Like Sunnis (including Afro-Trinidadians), Shi'is celebrate Eid (or Id), which marks the end of Ramadan fasting. Shi'i observance of Hosay, however, commemorates the split between Sunnis and Shi'is. Occurring during Muharram, a month sacred for both sects and so uniting observances temporally, it recalls the slaying of the martyr Hussein in the Battle of Karbala. Originating in Iran, the ritual of commemoration was brought to Trinidad by Indo-Trinidadians for whom Indian praxis was the foremost measure of authenticity.[17]

Although the Shi'is constitute a minority of the Indo-Trinidadian community, the festival has frequently served to represent Islamic and Indo-Trinidadian culture as well as national integration. This is especially clear in the context of Indian Arrival Day, for many reasons. One is that Hosay developed during the first decades of Indian indentureship as the most prominent expression not only of Muslim faith, but also of Indian cultural cohesion. Historian J. C. Jha states that "from the 1850s, this festival became the annual demonstration of Indian national feeling" (1974, 5). Although "national feeling" may have begun as feelings of loyalty to the country to which so many Indians hoped to return, it transmuted to nationalism in the context of anticolonialism. Before examining this expression of nationalism, however, let us focus on Hosay's prominence as cultural performance.

17. On Hosay in the context of Iran, India, and Trinidad, see Korom 2003.

Hosay, both in the eyes of Muslims who participated in it during the indentureship period and in the eyes of other Indian contemporaries, many of whom participated as observers and facilitators, was a powerful metaphor for Indian culture. According to historian Kelvin Singh (1998), Hosay was the most prominent Indian festival celebrated during the earliest years of the Indian presence in Trinidad. The celebration by Shi'is was, as many religious performances are, not only expressive but didactic: it represented for Muslims and to others the presence of Islam in Trinidad. The festival, with its highly visible and audible processions, demonstrated presence of, and articulated messages about, the importance of devotion that resonated both with Muslims and with Africans and Hindus, some of whom joined in Hosay activities. Colonial masters also heard the message of self-assertion in the festivities and became concerned enough by its creation of solidarity among Indians and its joining together of Indians and Africans that they imposed severe restrictions on Hosay observance.

The consequences of these restrictions bring us to another reason for Hosay's prominence in Indian Arrival Day celebrations: the infamous Hosay massacre, which brought to a tragic end the rioting that erupted in 1884 as a response to the much reviled restrictions. Fearful that the defiance demonstrated a threat to their divide-and-rule strategy, the British responded with force.[18] They fired into the crowd, killed almost two dozen participants, and injured more than a hundred others. The Hosay rioting/massacre, in which victims were assailed for commemorating martyrdom, has come to be a symbol of indentured Indians and their sacrificial suffering. Because this suffering is one of the main reasons that proponents of Indian Arrival Day sought recognition, it is not surprising that Hosay remains an important symbol on three levels: of Islam as an Indian religion, of the Indian community as co-celebrants and sufferers across religious boundaries, and of the nation in its recognition of the sac-

18. This successful strategy was also used to separate Indians from Africans and encouraged enmity between the two by fostering the "stereotypes of the uncivilised African and the heathen East Indian." On this and challenges to this strategy, see Samaroo 1974.

rifices and contributions of its diverse citizenry through the commemoration of Indian Arrival Day.

A good example of Hosay's ability to function as a metonym operative in three registers is found in the Indo-Caribbean Cultural Council's *Indian Arrival Day* magazine from 2004. The issue's opening editorial begins with a statement associating arrival, Arrival Day, and the massacre. It says that the Indian Arrival Day of 2004 not only "commemorate[s] the 159th anniversary of the arrival of Indians to Trinidad and Tobago" but also "marks the 120th anniversary of the Hosay Riots of 1884" (Mahabir 2004, n.p.). The editorial characterizes the rioting with its aftermath as "perhaps the bloodiest event of British rule in colonial Trinidad." Thus, it stands as the culmination of violence wrought by the British in the history of all colonials under their rule. Bringing the reader to the present day, the article also compares the violence perpetrated by the colonial government that day to the kidnapping of Ashmead Baksh in 2004. The juxtaposition certainly seems to imply that the PNM government, which regained power in 2002, bore some responsibility for the fate of this Indo-Trinidadian and others, thus linking the past with current grievances.

A similar linkage of politics then and now is made in another of the magazine's articles. Written by Devant Maharaj, who has served as the chief executive officer of the Hindu radio station belonging to the Sanatan Dharma Maha Sabha (Great Assembly of Eternal Dharma) and then as transport minister, it speaks of the contemporary relevance of the massacre but then observes that the festival illustrates Muslim–Hindu cooperation in that both celebrated the festival together and perished together. Titled "The Need for a Jahaji Massacre Memorial" the article (D. Maharaj 2004) refers to the event to be memorialized by the inclusive term *jahaji,* which designates travelers on the same boat and so links the destinies of Hindus and Muslims. *Jahaji* is typically paired with *bhai,* "brother," and so constructs these fellow Indians and their families as fictive kin.[19]

Devant Maharaj (2004), Sat Maharaj (secretary-general of the Sanatan Dharma Maha Sabha) (2004), and historian Kelvin Singh (1998) contend

19. For recent reflection on such relationships, see Ramsarran 2008, 179.

that had not the participation of laborers in the Hosay celebration been discouraged by the massacre in the 1884, Hosay might now have rivaled Carnival, the major Afro-Trinidadian cultural performance. The distinction of Indians from other (African) participants suggested by this comparison, however, is seldom projected backward in discourses on early Hosay performances in the context of the massacre. In a 2004 article on Indian Arrival Day in the *Trinidad Guardian,* Sat Maharaj emphasizes that the massacre was aimed at Muslims as well as at Hindus, who "were also killed in that colonial disregard for the humanity of Indians" in their Trinidad *janam bhoomi* (homeland). In this context, Hosay opposes Indians to the British and so positions them alongside Africans. Having united Hindus and Muslims as celebrants, Sat Maharaj's article represents the festival as "multiethnic and so a symbol of all oppressed by the British.[20] Thus, Hosay shifts to another register, and it represents and ultimately encompasses everyone who was anticolonial or who is now patriotic in the contemporary independent state. In short, the representation of this holiday indexing Muslim presence is blurred by significant Hindu participation, just as it is in the context of the massacre, most of the victims of which were Hindu. The conceptualization of this holiday as a manifestation of ethnic presence is itself blurred when the Hosay massacre is associated with national unity of all patriotic, anti-British Trinidadians.[21]

In its shifting contextual polysemy, Hosay resembles Divali, to which Sat Maharaj, having discussed the Hosay riots, turns his focus as he represents its relevance to Indian Arrival Day. Characterizing Indian Arrival Day as "an abundant display of Indian culture," he says that its celebration, like Divali's lamps, will "light up Trinidad and Tobago," the homeland (*janam bhoomi*) (2004). Thus, the commemorations of Indian history and culture, including not just Hosay, but also Divali, the festival of lights, will enlighten the whole of Trinidad and Tobago.

20. He breaks down the "multiethnic festival" into its composite religious groups.

21. See "Make May Indian History Month" (2004) by Ravi Ji, who organized a procession to the massacre site for the last day of Pitri Paksha. On the massacre, see Mahabir 2004.

The celebration of Divali, the second holiday named in the children's coloring book with which this section began, is without a doubt the largest demonstration of Hinduism and Indian presence on Trinidad today. A national holiday granted recognition in 1966 after prolonged lobbying, Divali has visual displays that take two major forms. One is the decoration of the path or driveway to each home with *deya*s (oil lamps), which invite the presence of Lakshmi, a goddess of good fortune. In Trinidad, these lamps are also positioned on bamboo, which is split into sections and bent backward to form a sort of inverted bamboo candelabra. The second form involves the light and noise of fireworks, including "bursting bamboo," which functions roughly like a firecracker. These rituals manifest the Hindu presence to Hindus, other Indians, and other others, including Trinidadians but also increasingly tourists.

The major destination during Divali season is Divali Nagar, or Divali Town, now held on the grounds of the National Council of Indian Culture, where there is also an annual celebration of Indian Arrival Day. Some estimates put recent attendance at this Divali site at about one hundred thousand. Begun two decades ago at one of Trinidad's main shopping malls, this communal celebration of Divali quickly outgrew its premises and was removed to the fifteen-acre Divali Nagar plot, managed by the National Council of Indian Culture, which also organizes the Indian Arrival Day function. For both holidays, major leaders, including politicians from both the PNM and United National Congress, speak on the significance of these holidays for the nation. Outside the main attendance hall, there are many booths, some displaying literature published by local temple associations and others selling various products, especially food in an outdoor "food court." The central hall itself hosts diverse performances, including Ram Lila, the folk reenactment of Lord Ram's life.

As with Indian Arrival Day, the celebration of Divali is commemorated with magazines containing articles on Divali ritual and Hinduism, as well as Divali greetings that identify the holiday not only with Hindu culture, but also with Indo-Trinidadian culture and the nation. As in the case of Hosay, Divali is frequently described as the Indo-Trinidadian rival to Carnival. An example is to be found in the 2004 issue of the Divali series published by the Indo-Caribbean Cultural Council. In its email announcement of the magazine's publication, the council represented Divali as "the second largest open-air national festival after Carnival in multi-ethnic Trinidad and Tobago." It then provided a description of Divali practice, including the lighting of oil lamps on bamboo and "free cultural performances by actors, models, drummers, dancers, musicians and singers."[22]

The Divali magazine variously articulates the sacrality of the festival, as do the discourses of many pandits (priests) in the congregational gatherings of Hindus in temples during the Sundays preceding the holiday. They explain, for example, that the holiday celebrates the return of Lord Rama and Sita to their kingdom after Sita's rescue from the demon king, Ravana, and they commemorate the initial appearance of the goddess Lakshmi, who was churned from the Milk Ocean. Thus, like *Indian Arrival Day* magazine, including the issue focused on Hosay, the articles in the Divali magazine—written by scholars, religious leaders, and politicians—are in one way or another didactic. And like many speeches and much of the literature available at the Divali Nagar, the issues explicate Hinduism and the Indian culture it expresses to Hindus and others. As the announcement explains, the celebrations include non-Hindus (including Muslims and Christians) but also non-Indo-Trinidadians, who "actively join in the celebration by lighting deyas, wearing saris, and partaking in eating traditional foods and sweets." In this context, as in the context of Divali celebrations in so many other diasporas, Divali is both a religious observance and a metonym for culture, which must be taught, whether through cultural performances or lectures or articles (Harlan 2003, 2004).

The 2004 issue of the Divali magazine has fashion as its annual theme. Fashion, we are told, conveys authentic culture. The online announcement of the issue says that the issue "carries articles on, and photographs of, local designs of clothes, jewelry and accessories that have become an

22. The source of emails announcing new issues of the Divali magazine is Kumar Mahabir. The announcement and table of contents of the 2004 issue is found at http://icctrinidad.wordpress.com/2004/10/28/divali-2004-trinidad-festival-magazine-2004-divali-festival-souvenir-magazine-2004-trinidad-and-tobago-caribbean-theme-caribbean-indian-fashion/, accessed Jan. 22, 2011.

undiluted and unbroken tradition from India to the Caribbean for over 150 years" and that although there have been cultural fusions of Indian and Caribbean traditions in other contexts, "fashion remains one cultural expression which consumers insist must be authentic in style, and direct from India." Thus, on Divali, Indian authenticity is enacted, as it is in many Divali fashion shows in other diasporic contexts, by wearing Indian clothing conveying identity. The same is true when the context is fashion worn in pageants. The announced issue contains two articles, "Miss India Heritage Trinidad Beauty Pageant: Proud to Be Part of This Culture" and "Miss Indian Arrival World Beauty Pageant: Preparing for the World Beauty Pageant in 2005."[23]

Divali has served on other occasions as an opportunity to teach about how to live in a multicultural society, reflected in a statement by Indo-Trinidadian historian Brinsley Samaroo in 1970, a tumultuous year in which there was a coup attempt by members of the Jamaat al Muslimeen group, composed overwhelmingly of Afro-Trinidadian Muslims. In this statement, contained in a small pamphlet entitled *Divali: 1970* (Samaroo 1970), Samaroo speaks of the insidious colonial legacy that both Afro-Trinidadians and Indo-Trinidadians have inherited with its "European sense of values." He warns that searching for roots to replace these values is fine, but these roots must be "relevant to the new society" being created. As to Divali, he says, attempts to link it simply with an "Indian separateness" are to be avoided and that "celebration must be seen as part of our national heritage." He then encourages Indo-Trinidadians to encourage those who are not of Indian descent to participate by learning about Indian heritage, which could help prevent "further division in an already fragmented society."[24] A history professor who also served as a member of Parliament

23. See the announcement at http://icctrinidad.wordpress.com/2004/10/28/divali-2004-trinidad-festival-magazine-2004-divali-festival-souvenir-magazine-2004-trinidad-and-tobago-caribbean-theme-caribbean-indian-fashion/, accessed Jan. 22, 2011.

24. The pamphlet containing Samaroo's remarks was produced by the University of the West Indies. On political splintering despite solidarity in the aftermath of independence, see Brereton 1981, 236–40.

and in other leadership roles, Samaroo serves here as teacher and enactor of a nationalist and anticolonial civil agenda at a critical moment in the project of nation building. As his comments suggest, Divali, public performances of which typically include cultural events and speeches, has often been didactic in ways that enable an identification of holiday, religion, ethnic community, and nation.

Having witnessed how Divali has been utilized to stand for a religion, ethic community, and nation, let us look at least quickly at the Chhote Bachche coloring book's mention of the other Hindu holiday, Shiv Ratri, and the Christian holiday Christmas. A much less prominent holiday than Divali, Shiv Ratri would seem to stand here as synecdoche for the whole Hindu calendar, of which Divali is the foremost representation. Its inclusion in the text also provides indication of the theological diversity of Trinidadian Hinduism: most temples include large images of a variety of Hindu deities. The different theological contexts, however, should not be thought necessarily to designate separate sects because all these deities are typically worshipped in temples and homes together with other popular Hindu deities.[25] In short, the inclusion of Shiv Ratri here provides an indication of the larger liturgical and so religious context that Divali represents.

As to Christmas as an emblem of Christianity, the coloring book's oblique reference to the conversion of Hindus and Muslims to Christianity is given comparatively short shrift here, which is necessary because the agenda is to examine metonyms for the Indian presence in the context of Indian Arrival Day. Although many Christians of Indian origin participate in Arrival Day and other key religious holidays, including Divali, as holidays emblematic of Indian culture, neither Christianity nor Christmas serves easily as a metonym for Indian culture. Moreover, the conversion of many Indians by Presbyterian missionaries during the colonial period (often as a condition for offering education to children who would otherwise be denied) and more recently by evangelical missionaries has been

25. This is not to say that there are no sectarian differences. Most center on the question of what is and is not "Sanatanist" or orthodox.

a subject of criticism even by those who have continued to observe and cherish the Christian traditions of their converted ancestors.[26]

Given the grievances against Christian colonizers and missionaries, and given that Christianity is the religion of most Afro-Trinidadians, most Indo-Trinidadians, including those who are Christian, continue to understand Hinduism and Islam as "root traditions" that enable a unity through heritage. Christian conversion signals a departure from root traditions, even though many non-Christian Indo-Trinidadians enjoy certain aspects of Christmas and may even use Christmas decorations.[27]

In this connection, it should be stressed that the celebration of various religious holidays by Indo-Trinidadians often invites participation by people not identifying themselves with the religion to which each holiday belongs. One reason is the frequent intermarriage between Indo-Trinidadians belonging to different religions. Another is a tendency to invite neighbors and friends to participate in such celebrations.[28] Despite the diversity of participants, Indo-Trinidadians tend to identify or classify people in terms of the ritual actions performed primarily by believers. Difference is frequently constructed via perceptions of the variant religious praxis of believers rather than beliefs. Aisha Khan argues that conceptualizing difference according to religious praxis has facilitated a sense of sameness or unity among Indo-Trinidadians. This homogeneity has been expressed in unifying statements such as "everyone believes in God" (2004, 155). The relegation of difference to praxis rather than to

26. The High Court addresses the painful legacy of this conversion in the 2006 case *Sanatan Dharma Maha Sabha of Trinidad and Tobago et al. v. Attorney General.*

27. The first day I was in Trinidad in 2001, a taxi driver, ruminating on religion in Trinidad after learning that I was a religion professor, expressed a phrase I have heard many times since then: "Everybody loves Christmas." I am not claiming that this is true, but rather that many people express it as a truism.

28. A 2004 editorial in the *Trinidad Guardian* observed that Trinidad is "the only country in the world where you will get an invitation to attend a Hindu Ramayana in a Muslim home where Christians and Hindus have been invited to share in the breaking of the Ramadan fast" (Mathur 2004).

faith has a facilitated solidarity perhaps unimaginable in India at the present time.

Working against this perspective, which hovers somewhere between embedded cultural assumption and ideological conviction, is the recognition that both root religions have made progress toward defining themselves over against other religions. The tendency to establish sharper boundaries reflects a refocusing from religious actions to religious doctrines. Khan refers to a sort of hardening of religious identities in the context of various impetuses, including influences from Hindu and Muslim organizations promoting definition and orthodoxy (2004, 151, 227). Mass communication and travel between the Caribbean and South Asia (including visits to Trinidad by South Asian religious teachers and pilgrimages by Trinidadians back to South Asia to find relatives, visit sacred sites, learn from religious teachers, and shop for Indian goods) have provided exposure that has both demonstrated variation and advocated cohesion based on one or another unified vision of Hinduism or Islam.

This hardening of boundaries of which Khan speaks has also been a reaction to inroads made by evangelical missionaries, who have appealed to youths disenchanted with "traditional" religion of their elders. To counteract the appeal, Hindus established organizations to encourage greater involvement by young people (Narayan and Shrivastava 2001, 180–86; Vertovec 2000, 63–86). Finally, self-definition and reinforcement of boundaries may be a reaction to what many faithful Hindus and Muslims have seen as the corrosive and corrupting effects of an alluring neocolonialist modernity evident in American- and European-owned businesses on Trinidadian soil, in American television and radio programming, and in the periodic visits home to Trinidad by expatriates or citizens with working visas in the United States and elsewhere.

These pressures have spread concern that Hinduism or Islam should be not only more unified, but also more "authentic" in a way conforming to practice and interpretation in South Asia. An example that comes to mind is the often heard appeal to reduce the "Carnivalesque" atmosphere of the Hosay celebration. Mir Jafar Abdullah, known as the "Nizam of Lucknow," reinforced this message in the inaugural lecture at a conference in

2008 on Hosay at the University of the West Indies.[29] He also gave various media interviews and made appearances at Indian radio stations. In these venues, he spoke of the importance of purging overly celebratory elements of Hosay processions and of emphasizing the solemnity that characterizes processions in Lucknow. Thus, conformity to a practice promulgated elsewhere requires a change not only of practice, but also of attitude.

A widely recognized example from the Hindu context is some Trinidadian Hindus' condemnation of much of the ritual (especially possession and animal sacrifice) performed in Kali temples. Keith McNeal's scholarship has detailed the general tendency among Hindus to exclude Kali worshippers, who are seen as holding on to antiquated Tamil (Madrasi) practice that does not accord with the dominant religious ideas and ethos of contemporary middle-class Trinidad or India. Despite characterization of their religion as déclassé or degraded, Kali devotees have become increasingly organized, and some have begun to emphasize Tamil identity and promote the study of Tamil language. Such activities tend to challenge the hegemonic Hindu identity/ethnicity promulgated by Sanatanist organizations, which frequently advocate teaching Hindi in temples and schools.[30]

Although the impetus toward hardening or standardization in recent decades has been much observed, it should be recognized that one can detect periods of ebb and flow in the pressure to impose visions of authenticity and to codify orthodoxy. For example, after the end of the indentureship period, when Hindus moved from plantation barracks into villages, they partially reinscribed various Hindu conventions that had been partially or even largely abandoned, including caste.[31] Although this inscription was partial and for the most part short-lived, it contributed to

29. The international conference was entitled "Hosay/Muharram and Cultural Space," University of the West Indies, St. Augustine, Trinidad, March 7–8, 2008.

30. On Kali worship, see McNeal 2003. I base most of my comments on Kali on my discussions with practitioners and observation of rituals at Trinidadian Kali temples.

31. The division between Hindus and Muslims grew as Indians began to settle on land after indentureship, but, says Bridget Brereton, it was "never anything as troubled as in India" (1993, 51). Here she is speaking of the nineteenth century, but the same observation has been made of the subsequent century. See also Haraksingh 1988.

the emergence of a distinctive class of Brahmin pundits (van der Veer and Vertovec 1991). In addition, during the first half of the twentieth century a revival of interest in authenticity spun out from admiration for nationalist politics in India. Trinidad saw a flurry of political activity by a variety of social reform groups, including the Sanatan Dharma Maha Sabha and Arya Samaj. This period also witnessed the founding of Hindu and Muslim schools, which were able to focus on the project of recovering roots. This project's legacy continues today in various forms, including the encouragement of children and grandchildren to learn from their elders about their religious and cultural heritage from India.

Although Hindus and Muslims have so often envisioned and represented themselves as inheritors of a common Indian culture, their notions of Indianness have not been tied to any Indian map or time period. Thus, the Indian roots that are celebrated on Indian Arrival Day refer to an India that is not a political entity—for example, a nation now vying with Pakistan for control of Kashmir—but rather to an amorphous, shifting, and atemporal (or preindependence) India with fluid imaginative boundaries, allowing for positive identification with India as a font of culture without geographic fixity. Muslim graduate students with whom I spoke on Indian Arrival Day were eager to have me know that although most Muslims have looked to Pakistan as a resource for contemporary culture as well as for religious education and guidance, they have no problem with celebrating the India from which their indentured ancestors arrived and brought their religion and culture to the land that is now Trinidad and Tobago.

As the coloring book makes so clear, from the beginning Muslims were separate, and yet this separateness, a value that they share with Hindus (and even with those people whose ancestors came over in the same boat but then converted or produced descendents who converted to Christianity), has been used (by Muslims and others) to image an Indianness that encompasses all those coming from India to Trinidad, beginning with that first voyage.

At this point, let us return to the coloring book's final assertion: the Indian immigrants settled "throughout Trinidad." This statement is a stark representation of dispersal that identifies Indo-Trinidadians with the whole of Trinidadian territory. This depiction refutes the widely shared perception of Indians as congregating or belonging together in specific areas, in particular the agricultural regions of central and southern Trinidad. Although many Indians did ultimately settle on lands in these areas, over the years they also spread out from there and engaged in many nonagricultural pursuits. Thus, despite their oft-expressed reverence for Dharti Mata (Mother Earth) and their "affective rurality" (which has augmented their appreciation of land and its produce), Indo-Trinidadians have defied the trope of country folk by occupying all geographic and occupational sectors that would be beneficial for them and, it is frequently argued, for the nation.[32] As Emmanuel Ma Mung (2004) has noted, diasporic peoples have often vaunted dispersion throughout territory as an index of success, one that complements (even as it displaces) the previous density strategy that uses proximity and clustering to promote solidarity and achieve prosperity.[33]

Thus, the story of arrival on the Trinidadian shore by Indians, who are religiously heterogeneous but largely homogeneous in their construction of Indianness, has become a powerful narrative, one in which the Indian presence suffuses and becomes synonymous with the whole of Trinidadian topography. The result is an imaging of inextricable presence that permeates, if also romanticizes, the landscape of Trinidad. One sees this permeation with particular clarity when the geographic features of Trinidad and Tobago are likened in religious services and popular discourse to Indian topographic features such as the Ganges (in Trinidad, the Caroni or Marianne rivers) and the Himalayas (in Trinidad, the lush northern ridges covered by pine and rain forests), as they have been, for example, in a recent invention of ritual tradition by the energetic activist, Ravi Ji.

32. On "rurality" and Indo-Trinidadian identity, see Khan 1997 and 2004, 68–75. Some of the produce is from plants that migrated with Indians and that have been particularly valued because of their origin.

33. This notion of dispersion conflicts with and augments the identification of Indianness and Caroni, which is so often expressed as the locative center of Indian population, now so widely dispersed (Ravi Ji, personal communication, Mar. 2008). See the classic collected volume *From Calcutta to Caroni* (LaGuerre 1974).

This pandit, who is widely known for innovative ritual, organized a reverential *pradakshina*, or circumambulation, of Trinidad, timed to coincide with a conference on the Indian presence in the Caribbean at the University of the West Indies.[34] He conceptualized the circumambulation as beginning in the center and then encompassing the periphery. Thus, he arranged for volunteers to begin their *pradakshina* at the Divine Life Society, which has a central location on the island (personal interview, March 11, 2008). Although the media gave little advance publicity to the run, it attracted many participants and so ultimately drew significant media attention. Because of its success, the *pradakshina* was repeated a decade later to coincide with the centennial of Vivekananda's coming to America for the World's Parliament of Religions in 1893. Ravi Ji described this visit as a "watershed event" in which a Hindu Indian addressed the world (personal interview, March 11, 2008).

This time the *pradakshina* began and ended at the headquarters of the National Council of Indian Culture—that is to say, the site of the Divali Nagar and of a prominent annual celebration of Indian Arrival Day. Participants planted *jhandi*s, flags, every eighth of a mile to mark their progress around the island and so demarcated a sacred periphery. Although Hindu homes are frequently identifiable because of *jhandi*s (representing Hindu deities) in their yards, this planting of *jhandi*s should not be taken to suggest religious exclusivity for two reasons. One is the inclusive agenda with which Ravi Ji is frequently associated, and the other is the way in which Hinduism has been deployed as a metonym for the Indian presence, the subject of the conference that inspired the initial *pradakshina*.[35] In short, the twice-performed ritual demon-

34. This conference was one of three conferences on Indo-Caribbean history at the University of the West Indies in St. Augustine. See Dabydeen 1987, 11, and Selvon 1987, the opening address to the 1979 conference.

35. Ravi Ji has been criticized for not drawing a clear division between Hindu and other devotional traditions in various contexts, particularly by the Sanatan Dharma Maha Sabha, which, for example, has bemoaned the Phagwa (Holi) celebrations he organized on the grounds of the National Council of Indian Culture. At these celebrations, young people perform *pichakaree* songs in English, which lambaste various targets, as calypsos do. The Maha

strates geographically the success of members of the Indian community in identifying themselves with Trinidadian territory as citizens while resisting cultural dilution.

Conclusion: Continued Contestation

Having examined the debates and contending representations that led to the creation and continued celebration of Indian Arrival Day, and having seen the important ways in which Muslim and Hindu holidays have represented Indo-Trinidadian presence, I should note that the meanings conveyed by the variously positioned observers of this national holiday continue to be multiple, debatable, and fluid. Although the date, name, and official status of the national holiday have been fixed for more than a decade, it continues to occasion contestation and reinterpretation. In this respect, the holiday is hardly unique. All national holidays are to some extent continually reconstrued by citizens in the light of those citizens' diversely constructed national histories, social affiliations, and personal agendas. These holidays continue to be potential or actual times of negotiation and resentment even as they convey nationality and nationalism. As Michael Geisler has observed, "[N]ational symbols turn out to be tricky cultural macros, for they preserve within the architectural structure of their historical reference not only the[ir] . . . 'victorious' definition but also, just beneath the surface, the fossilized debates, discourses, and contestations that have crystallized around them over decades or, in some cases, centuries" (2005, xxxi).

As a national symbol, Indian Arrival Day is still a new holiday, one that clearly continues to reveal contestation. Although some continue to argue that recognizing only Indian Arrival is discriminatory because it privileges the arrival of Indians, others still voice their conviction that Indian Arrival Day identifies the separate Indian community with the nation and so, through cultural preservation, encompasses the diverse whole. This conviction was expressed vividly in a 2004 celebration of

Sabha promotes Chowtal singing in Hindi on Phagwa. When I attended the *pichakaree* function on the grounds of the Divali Nagar in 2006, one of the subjects was the Hosay massacre.

Indian Arrival Day at a school in the southern part of Trinidad. The extensive program included a Miss India Arrival Day pageant, during which semifinalists modeled Indian fashions.[36] The participants, who came from diverse religious and ethnic backgrounds, wore elegant imported clothes and adopted well-known Indian posing conventions (such as the stylized, one-arm-extended display of sari borders). These students literally modeled an Indianness that identified Indian heritage with the diverse nation observing a national holiday. This identification was made even clearer when the judges crowned a student of African descent "Miss Indian Arrival Day." In the pageant, as in so many of the performances taking place throughout the nation, Indian Arrival Day occasioned a performance of pedagogy in which Indian culture was associated with the whole. Far from indicating a mission accomplished, the performance represents an ongoing endeavor to promote the recognition of Indian arrival as a phenomenon of importance to all.

Thus, although debates about Indian Arrival Day have communicated intercultural tensions, performances and other representations by Indo-Trinidadians have often portrayed the holiday as an occasion for promoting a felicitous solidarity. For example, in 2008 veteran politician and economist Winston Dookeran said, "The Indian Arrival Day is an opportunity for a new reflection and a new thinking and a new vision for all the peoples of Trinidad and Tobago." His statement thus links Indo-Trinidadians to others in its enjoinder for everyone to rethink a situation that is less than optimal, as he makes clear when he goes on to encourage people to "develop another formidable legacy beyond the crushing burden of oppression and inequality, and eke out a common humanity" (quoted in *Indo-Asian News Service* 2008). Dookeran identifies the challenge of enlisting the bitter legacy of discrimination to help bring about a common humanity. It is not surprising, then, that the descendents of Indians who left Trinidad and immigrated to distant shores in many other nations, including Canada and the United States, have followed suit and

36. Multiethnic participation in fashion shows is not unusual. See the photograph by Steve McPhie, in *The Express*, on May 29, 2004.

celebrate their own versions of Indian Arrival Day with rituals that construct commonality of heritage and define cultural space that fits within and is identifiable with their nations.

Works Cited

Bauman, Martin. 2004. "Becoming a Colour of the Rainbow: The Social Integration of Indian Hindus in Trinidad, Analysed along a Phase Model of Diaspora." In *South Asians in the Diaspora: Histories and Religious Traditions*, edited by Knut A. Jacobsen and P. Pratap Kumar, 77–96. Leiden: Brill.

Brereton, Bridget. 1981. *A History of Modern Trinidad, 1783–1962*. London: Heinimann.

———. 1993. "Social Organisation and Class, Racial, and Cultural Conflict in Nineteenth Century Trinidad." In *Trinidad Ethnicity*, edited by Kevin Yelvington, 33–55. Knoxville: Univ. of Tennessee Press.

Dabydeen, David. 1987. "Preface." In *India in the Caribbean*, edited by David Dabydeen and Brinsley Samaroo, 9–12. London: Hansib.

Geisler, Michael E. 2005. "What Are National Symbols—and What Do They Do to Us?" In *National Symbols, Fractured Identities: Contending the National Narrative*, edited by Michael E. Geisler, xxi–xlii. Middlebury, VT: Middlebury College Press.

Haraksingh, Kusha. 1988. "Structure, Process, and Indian Culture in Trinidad." In *After the Crossing: Immigrants and Minorities in Caribbean Creole Society*, edited by Howard Johnson, 113–43. London: Frank Cass.

———. 2002. "Hindu Legal Thought in Trinidad." Paper presented at the conference "The Hindu Presence in Trinidad and Tobago," Oct. 25–27, Univ. of the West Indies, St. Augustine, Trinidad.

Harlan, Lindsey. 2003. "Reversing the Gaze in America: Parody in Divali Performance at Connecticut College." In *South Asians in Diaspora: Histories and Religious Traditions*, edited by Knut Jacobsen and P. Kuman, 161–79. Leiden: Brill.

———. 2004. "Divali." In *The Encyclopedia of Religious Rites, Rituals, and Festivals*, edited by Frank A. Salamone. New York: Routledge.

The History of the Indentured Labourers (comic/coloring book). 2002. Chhote Bachche series, issue no. 6, 2 vols., produced by Sandra Maharajh-Shah. Longdenville, Trinidad: Ashoka.

Indo-Asian News Service. 2008. "Indian Diaspora Faces Discrimination Even after 163 Years." May 31. Available at Lexis/Nexis.

Jayaram, N. 2003. "The Politics of 'Cultural Renaissance' among Indo-Trinidadians." In *Culture and Economy in the Indian Diaspora*, edited by Bhikhu Parekh, Gurharpal Singh, and Steven Vertovec, 123–41. London: Routledge.

Jha, J. C. 1974. "The Indian Heritage in Trinidad." In *From Calcutta to Caroni: The East Indians of Trinidad*, edited by John Gaffar La Guerre, 1–24. Port of Spain, Trinidad: Longman Caribbean.

Khan, Aisha. 1993. "What Is 'a Spanish'? Ambiguity and 'Mixed' Ethnicity in Trinidad." In *Trinidad Ethnicity*, edited by Kevin Yelvington, 180–207. Knoxville: Univ. of Tennessee Press.

———. 1997. "Rurality and 'Racial' Landscapes in Trinidad." In *Knowing Your Place: Rural Identity and Cultural Hierarchy*, edited by Barbara Ching and Gerald Creed, 39–64. New York: Routledge.

———. 2004. *Callaloo Nation: Metaphors of Race and Religious Identity among South Asians in Trinidad*. Durham, NC: Duke Univ. Press.

Kirpalani, Murli, Mitra Sinanan, and Lionel Seukeran. 1945. *Indian Centenary Review: One Hundred Years of Progress, 1845–1945*. Port of Spain, Trinidad: Indian Centenary Review Committee.

Klass, Morton. 1961. *East Indians in Trinidad: A Study of Cultural Persistence*. New York: Columbia Univ. Press.

Korom, Frank. 2003. *Hosay Trinidad: Muharram Performances in an Indo-Caribbean Diaspora*. Philadelphia. Univ. of Pennsylvania Press.

La Guerre, John Gaffar, ed. 1974. *From Calcutta to Caroni: The East Indians of Trinidad*. Port of Spain, Trinidad: Longman Caribbean.

Lokaisingh-Meighoo, Sean. 2001. "The Diasporic Mo(ve)ment." In *Nation Dance: Religion, Identity, and Cultural Difference in the Caribbean*, edited by Patrick Taylor, 171–92. Bloomington: Univ. of Indiana Press.

Lovelace, Earl. 1988. "The On-Going Value of Our Indigenous Traditions." In *The Independence Experience, 1962–1987*, edited by Selwyn Ryan, 335–44. St. Augustine, Trinidad: Institute of Social and Economic Research, Univ. of the West Indies.

Mahabir, Kumar, ed. 2004. "The 1884 Massacre of Indians." *Indian Arrival Day* (Indo-Caribbean Cultural Council) 5, no. 1 (May–June): unpaginated.

Maharaj, Devant. 2004. "The Need for a Jahaji Massacre Memorial." *Indian Arrival Day* (Indo-Caribbean Cultural Council) 5, no. 1 (May–June): unpaginated.

Maharaj, Sat. 2004. "Commemorating Indian Martyrdom." *Trinidad Guardian*, May 26.

Mathur, Ira. 2004. "Something's Rotting in T & T." *Trinidad Guardian*, Nov. 14.

McNeal, Keith. 2003. "Doing the Mother's Caribbean Work: On Shakti and Society in Contemporary Trinidad." In *Encountering Kali: In the Margins, at the Center, in the West*, edited by Rachel Fell McDermott and Jeffry K. Kripal, 223–48. Berkeley: Univ. of California Press.

McPhie, Steve. 2004. "Ministry of Agriculture's Indian Arrival Day Fashion Show" (photograph). *The Express*, May 29.

Munasinghe, Viranjini. 2001a. *Callalou or Tossed Salad: East Indians and the Cultural Politics of Identity in Trinidad*. Ithaca, NY: Cornell Univ. Press.

———. 2001b. "Redefining the Nation: The East Indian Struggle for Inclusion in Trinidad." *Journal of Asian American Studies* 4, no. 1 (Feb.): 1–34.

———. 2002. "Nationalism in Hybrid Spaces: The Production of Impurity out of Purity." *American Ethnologist* 29, no. 3 (Aug.): 663–92.

———. 2006. "Theorizing World Culture Through the New World: East Indians and Creolization." *American Ethnologist* 33, no. 4 (Nov.): 549–62.

Mung, Emmanuel Ma. 2004. "Dispersal as a Resource." *Diaspora* 13, nos. 2–3: 211–25.

Narayan, R., and Ashok Shrivastava. 2001. "Diasporic Hindus of the Caribbean with Special Reference to Trinidad." In *Hindu Diaspora: Global Perspectives*, edited by T. S. Rukmani, 165–90. New Delhi: Munshiram Manoharlal.

"NCIC's Indian Arrival Day 2007 Celebrations." n.d. At http://www.triniview.com/special_events/070607.html. Accessed June 7, 2011.

Ramlakhan, Rajnie. 1998. "The Origin of Indian Arrival Day." *Sunday Express* (Indian Arrival Day special), May 28.

———. 2004. "The Recognizing of a People: Indian Arrival Day." In *The Construction of an Indo-Caribbean Diaspora*, edited by Brinsley Samaroo and Ann Marie Bissessar, 182–98. St. Augustine, Trinidad: Univ. of the West Indies School of Continuing Education.

Ramsarran, Parbatti. 2008. "The Indentured Contract and Its Impact on Labor Relationship and Community Reconstruction in British Guiana." *International Journal of Criminology and Social Theory* 1, no. 2 (Dec.): 177–88.

Ravi Ji. 2004. "Make May Indian History Month." *Indian Arrival Day* (Indo-Caribbean Cultural Council) 5, no. 1 (May–June): 34.

———. 2006. "Journey Through the Landscape." *Trinidad Guardian*, Apr. 12, 2006.

Samaroo, Brinsley. 1970. *Divali: 1970* (pamphlet). St. Augustine, Trinidad: Univ. of the West Indies.

———. 1974. "Politics and Afro-Indian Relations." In *From Calcutta to Caroni: The East Indians of Trinidad*, edited by John Gaffar La Guerre, 84–97. Port of Spain, Trinidad: Longman Caribbean.

———. 1987. "Two Abolitions: African Slavery and East Indian Indentureship." In *India in the Caribbean*, edited by David Dabydeen and Brinsley Samaroo, 25–41. London: Hansib.

———. 2004. "Reconstructing the Identity: Hindu Organization in Trinidad during Their First Century." In *The Construction of an Indo-Caribbean Diaspora*, edited by Brinsley Samaroo and Ann Marie Bissessar, 44–73. St. Augustine, Trinidad: Univ. of the West Indies School of Continuing Education.

Selvon, Sam. 1987. "Three into One Can't Go—East Indian, Trinidadian, Westindian." In *India in the Caribbean*, edited by David Dabydeen and Brinsley Samaroo, 13–24. London: Hansib.

Singh, Kelvin. 1998. *Bloodstained Tombs: The Muharram Massacre, 1884*. London: Macmillan.

Thomas, Deborah. A. 2006. "New Savage Slots, Response to Viranjini Munasinghe's 'Theorizing World Culture Through the New World: East Indians and Creolization.'" *American Ethnologist* 33, no. 4 (Nov.): 573–75.

Tinker, Hugh. 1993. *A New System of Slavery: The Export of Indian Labour Overseas: 1830–1920*. 2nd ed. London: Hansib.

Trinidad and Tobago News Blog. 2007. "Indian Arrival Day in Trinidad and Tobago." May 25. At http://www.trinidadandtobagonews.com/blog/?p=254. Accessed Feb. 3, 2013.

Van der Veer, Peter, and Steven Vertovec. 1991. "Brahminism Abroad: On Caribbean Hinduism as an Ethnic Religion." *Ethnology* 30: 149–66.

Vertovec, Steven. 1992. *Hindu Trinidad: Religion, Ethnicity, and Socio-economic Change*. London: Macmillan.

———. 2000. *The Hindu Diaspora: Comparative Patterns*. London: Routledge.

Yelvington, Kevin. 1993. "Introduction: Trinidad Ethnicity." In *Trinidad Ethnicity*, edited by Kevin Yelvington, 1–32. Knoxville: Univ. of Tennessee Press.

Contributors

≈

Index

≈

Contributors

Carla Bellamy is assistant professor in the Department of Sociology and Anthropology at Baruch College, City University of New York. She is the author of *The Powerful Ephemeral: Everyday Healing in an Ambiguously Islamic Place* (2011) and of several articles and essays on religious practice in contemporary India. In 2007, she received the Elisabeth Schüssler Fiorenza New Scholar Award for her article "Person in Place: Possession and Power at an Indian Islamic Saint Shrine," published in the *Journal for Feminist Studies in Religion.*

Joyce Burkhalter Flueckiger is professor of religion at Emory University. Her books include *In Amma's Healing Room: Gender and Vernacular Islam in South India* (2006) and *Gender and Genre in the Folklore of Middle India* (1996).

Ann Grodzins Gold is professor of anthropology and religion at Syracuse University. She has done extensive fieldwork in Rajasthan's Banas Basin. Her books include *In the Time of Trees and Sorrows: Nature, Power, and Memory in Rajasthan* (coauthored with Bhoju Ram Gujar, 2002) and *Fruitful Journeys: The Ways of Rajasthani Pilgrims* (1988, reissued 2000).

Daniel Gold is professor of Asian studies at Cornell University. He is the author of numerous articles and reviews, and his most recent book is *Aesthetics and Analysis in Writing on Religion: Modern Fascinations* (2003).

Peter Gottschalk is associate professor of religion at Wesleyan University. He has done extensive field work in Bihar and is the author of *Beyond Hindu and Muslim: Multiple Identity in Narratives from Village India* (2000) and *Religion, Science, and Empire: Classifying Hinduism and Islam in British India* (2012).

Lindsey Harlan is professor of religious studies at Connecticut College. Her books include *The Goddesses' Henchmen: Reflections on Gender in Indian Hero Worship* (2003) and *Religion and Rajput Women* (1992).

Tazim R. Kassam is associate professor of religion at Syracuse University. The author of *Songs of Wisdom and Circles of Dance: Hymns of the Satpanth Isma'ili Muslim Saint, Pir Shams* (1995) as well as of numerous articles and reviews, she has also been the editor of the regular feature "Spotlight on Teaching" for *Religious Studies News*.

Eliza F. Kent is associate professor of religion at Colgate University. She is the author of *Converting Women: Gender and Protestant Christianity in Colonial South India* (2004) and *Sacred Groves, Local Gods: Religion and Environmentalism in South India* (2013).

Dominique-Sila Khan holds doctorates in literature and anthropology from the Sorbonne University in Paris. She is currently working as an independent researcher in Jaipur, associated with the Institute of Rajasthan Studies. She is the author of *Crossing the Threshold: Understanding Religious Identities in South Asia* (2004).

Christopher Lee is associate professor of religious studies at Canisius College. He has done extensive fieldwork in Banaras (Varanasi), India, and most recently in Jeddah, Saudi Arabia. He is completing a book tentatively entitled "Banaras, Urdu, Poetry, Poets" on Muslim weaver poets in the Hindu pilgrimage city of Banaras.

Nancy M. Martin is associate professor of religious studies at Chapman University. The editor of numerous books on ethics in world religions, she is also the author of a forthcoming book on the sixteenth-century saint Mirabai. Her current projects include a documentary film on interreligious harmony and violence in India and a study of oral traditions of Mirabai and Kabir among low-caste communities in Rajasthan tentatively titled "The Renunciant Rani and the Weaver of Protest."

Steven Ramey is assistant professor of religious studies at the University of Alabama. He has done extensive fieldwork on Sindhi Hindus in India and the southeastern United States. He is the author of numerous articles and reviews and of the book *Hindu, Sufi, or Sikh: Contested Practices and Identifications of Sindhi Hindus in India and Beyond* (2008).

Jishnu Shankar is senior lecturer in Asian studies at the University of Texas at Austin. In addition to many publications on Hindi language pedagogy, he has written on the Aghor tradition, including *The Book of Aghor Wisdom* (2007).

≈

Index

Italic page numbers denote illustrations.